Understanding English

Understanding English

BY PAUL ROBERTS

SAN JOSE STATE COLLEGE

HARPER & ROW, PUBLISHERS
NEW YORK, EVANSTON, AND LONDON

UNDERSTANDING ENGLISH

Copyright © 1958, by Paul Roberts

Printed in the United States of America

H-N

Library of Congress catalog card number: 58-5110

To Donald H. Alden

Contents

Preface

In the company of others appearing in the last year or two, this book is an attempt to relate the complicated data of linguistic science to the equally complicated purposes of the course in English for college freshmen. It tries to do more than that: the intent is to give practical advice on matters of concern to the freshman English course, whether these are touchable by the rigorous procedures of linguistic science or not, and many of them are not. But throughout the book the point of view is single, and it is that of linguistic science. The assumptions and the findings of modern experts on language study have nowhere been knowingly ignored or set aside.

In the years since World War II, the linguistic scientist has been probably the most important impingement on the teaching of English—whether as a foreign or as a native language —and certainly the most controversial. To some he is a wizard bearing methods which will enable the most hopeless freshman to learn French in six weeks and to write English like Addison's by the end of the term; to others he is a goon madly bent on the destruction of literacy everywhere.

Cool blood finds the truth well toward the middle. Linguistics is certainly respectable, certainly a science. It is somewhat less stable and controllable than physics or chemistry, but a good deal more so than psychology or sociology. The linguist is steadily finding out more about language, and since language is what English teachers teach, the relationship of linguistic science to the English course is immediate and important. The teacher of English cannot reasonably ignore linguistic science any more than the teacher of astronomy can reasonably ignore physics.

However, it should be remembered—and isn't always—that linguistics is the science of language, not the science of teaching language. When it happens that the linguist is also a teacher of English, he will necessarily have views on the teaching of English; but strictly speaking these views cannot be part of the science. The science can provide, and insist on, certain basic principles and much relevant data, but it cannot, as science, say anything at all about the uses to which these principles and data are to be put or the methods by which they are to be purveyed. These are matters of art and ethics and as such are in the province of the teacher. What the teacher cannot justifiably do is use principles and data denied by the science. The teacher of music can teach music however he pleases and for whatever ends he chooses, but he cannot alter the laws of harmonics.

What are the principles guaranteed and insisted on by linguistic science? The aim of this book is to explain and illustrate them insofar as they are relevant to the needs of the freshman student in a writing class, but a few may be underlined here. Linguistic science would hold the following points to be unassailable: that writing, being a symbolization, is secondary to speech, though not necessarily less important; that correctness in speech or writing is relative to time, place, and circumstance, though certainly not unimportant; that change is a normal and necessary characteristic of language, though not necessarily of writing; that there is no such thing as universal grammar—a structural system in terms of which any language can be explained and analyzed—but that each language has its own peculiar structure; that any normal child of 5 or 6 is a perfect speaker of his language in the sense that he can manage its sounds and syntax automatically.

From such principles each teacher of English will form his own views on how English should be taught. My own are that it is possible to build on this base an English course that is interesting, useful, and intellectually respectable—qualities which I, at least, was not very successful in attaining while teaching English with traditional materials and on traditional assumptions. Certainly I should not wish to make extravagant claims. The student who studies this book will not, as a natural consequence, write like an angel. Learning to write is hard, and progress depends on matters largely beyond the control of the classroom. But I should hope that the student would get from the book a better understanding of his language, a better understanding of writing, a better understanding of himself in the community of writers. I should hope that he would find it interesting.

The chapters on sound and syntax present, in a much compressed form, the kind of analysis given in my secondary school text *Patterns of English* (Harcourt, Brace: 1956). This in turn leans heavily on two books: *The Structure of English* by Charles C. Fries (Harcourt, Brace: 1952), and *An Outline of English Structure* by George Trager and Henry Lee Smith (Studies in Linguistics, Occasional Papers, 3: 1951). My work might be described as a blend of Fries syntax and Trager-Smith phonology, though I have made a number of modifications and extensions of my own, particularly in syntax. In general, wherever I ran out of science I have not hesitated to play such hunches as occurred to me.

A book like this one, which proposes sharp departures from usual procedures, has a special obligation to make itself clear to teacher as well as student. Matters which are elementary and obvious to some readers will be new and difficult to others, who will therefore want thorough explanation. I have tried not to let thoroughness degenerate too often into discursiveness and repetition, but in the circumstances it did not always seem wise to avoid even such vices as these.

As a further aid to the teacher unfamiliar with linguistic theory, I should like to mention here some of the books which I have found especially useful. This will serve also as a further acknowledgment of my own indebtedness.

THE PLACE OF LINGUISTIC SCIENCE:

Carroll, John B., *The Study of Language*. Cambridge: Harvard University Press, 1955. 289 pp.

This is perhaps the best book for general orientation. Carroll gives something of the history of linguistic science, explains its relationship to such other disciplines as psychology, anthropology, and sociology, and appraises its practical accomplishments and possibilities. Among other things he discusses the implications of linguistic science for the teaching of English.

POPULAR DISCUSSIONS:

Hall, Robert A., *Leave Your Language Alone!* Ithaca: Linguistica, 1950. 254 pp.

Sapir, Edward, *Language; an Introduction to the Study of Speech*. New York: Harcourt, Brace, 1921. 258 pp.

The length of the list reflects the scarcity of good popularizations in this field. (Bad ones abound.) Sapir's book is informative and useful, despite its age. Hall gives, somewhat aggressively, the view of language problems generally held by American linguists.

GENERAL WORKS:

Bloomfield, Leonard, *Language*. New York: Holt, 1933. 564 pp.

Gray, Louis H., *Foundations of Language*. New York: Macmillan, 1939. 530 pp.

Jespersen, Otto, *Language: Its Nature, Development and Origin*. London: Allen and Unwin, 1922. 448 pp.

Bloomfield was the leading figure in American linguistics in its formative years, and his book is a focal point in the study. It presents what was known at the time of its publication and points out many lines of development which have been profitably followed since. It is not easy reading. Jespersen has played a similar role in European linguistics. In recent years he has been largely ignored by American linguists, which is less than his due. His books are informative, gracefully written, and stimulating. Gray's book is concerned principally with historical and comparative linguistics. It gives a full discussion of the languages of the world and their relationships.

DESCRIPTIVE METHODS:

Bloch, Bernard, and George L. Trager, *Outline of Linguistic Analysis*. Baltimore: Linguistic Society of America, 1942. 82 pp.

Gleason, H. A., *An Introduction to Descriptive Linguistics*. New York: Holt, 1955. 389 pp.

Harris, Zellig S., *Methods in Structural Linguistics*. Chicago: University of Chicago Press, 1951. 384 pp.

Pike, Kenneth L., *Phonemics: A Technique for Reducing Languages to Writing*. Ann Arbor: University of Michigan Press, 1947. 254 pp.

Though all of these are best undertaken with a teacher, the serious student with some general preparation will find them possible and profitable. Gleason's book is the text now most used for introductory courses in colleges and universities. It is accompanied by a very useful workbook. The Bloch and Trager *Outline* has also been much used in such courses; its brevity makes it difficult for the student who undertakes it without help. Pike's book provides a good understanding of practical problems in phonemic analysis. Harris gives a full discussion of the theory of linguistic description; the book is intended for the advanced student.

AMERICAN ENGLISH:

Krapp, George Philip, *The English Language in America*. New York: Century, 1925. 2 vols.

Lloyd, Donald J., and Harry Warfel, *American English in its Cultural Setting*. New York: Knopf, 1956. 553 pp.

Mencken, H. L., *The American Language*. New York: Knopf, 1936. 769 pp. (*Supplement I*, 1945, 740 pp.; *Supplement II*, 1948, 890 pp.)

Pyles, Thomas, *Words and Ways of American English*. New York: Random House, 1952. 310 pp.

Mencken's well-known work reflects the personal biases of the author, but it provides vast quantities of useful information about English in America, and it is very entertaining. The Krapp volumes cover some of the same ground in a more self-contained way. The scope of the Lloyd-Warfel book is about that of *Understanding English,* but it is addressed to a wider audience. It also presents a combination of Fries syntax and Trager-Smith phonology. Pyles gives a brief and readable account of some of the things that have happened to English in America.

PHONOLOGY OF AMERICAN ENGLISH:

Pike, Kenneth L., *The Intonation of American English*. Ann Arbor: University of Michigan Press, 1946. 200 pp.

Trager, George L., and Henry Lee Smith, *An Outline of English Structure*. Norman, Oklahoma: Battenburg Press, 1951. (Studies in Linguistics, Occasional Papers, 3. 92 pp.)

Pike's is a pioneer work in a field only recently investigated. The phonology in the Trager-Smith *Outline* has won very general acceptance by American linguists in the years since its publication. It is addressed to specialists and is not easy for the reader without preparation.

GRAMMAR:

Fries, Charles C., *The Structure of English*. New York: Harcourt, Brace, 1952. 304 pp.

Jespersen, Otto, *The Philosophy of Grammar*. New York: Holt, 1925.

Roberts, Paul, *Patterns of English*. New York: Harcourt, Brace, 1956. 314 pp.

Roberts, Paul, *Understanding Grammar*. New York: Harper, 1954. 550 pp.

Whitehall, Harold, *Structural Essentials of English*. New York: Harcourt, Brace, 1956. 154 pp.

The Fries book was a major step toward our understanding of the English sentence. It is frequently criticized by linguists for its comparative neglect of intonation and its occasional reliance on meaning in analysis. But these criticisms should not be allowed to obscure the very great significance of the book. It is addressed to the general reader, but even so it requires careful reading, since it is often misunderstood and misquoted. The Whitehall book, which follows Smith-Trager closely and Fries at a much greater distance, presents a useful and stimulating analysis of sentence structure, but it is too early to estimate its general effect. Jespersen's *Philosophy*, like the other Jespersen volume mentioned above, is not at all in tune with the work of American linguists, but it is a thoughtful and interesting inquiry into age-old problems of grammatical analysis. *Patterns of English*, a high-school book, describes English grammar as it is described here, but at much greater length. *Understanding Grammar* is a critical examination of the traditional system.

USAGE AND CORRECTNESS:

Fries, Charles C., *American English Grammar*. New York: Appleton-Century, 1940. 314 pp.

Leonard, Sterling A., *The Doctrine of Correctness in English Usage, 1700–1800*. Madison: University of Wisconsin, 1929. 361 pp.

Leonard, Sterling A., *Current English Usage*. Chicago: National Council of Teachers of English, 1932. (English Monographs, 1.) 232 pp.

The problem of what constitutes correctness in language is a concern of nearly all the books mentioned in this bibliography, but particularly of the three named above. Fries' work is based

xvi PREFACE

on letters in the files of a government agency in Washington. It describes usage in relation to the educational levels of the writers. Leonard was among the most effective of those educators who, in the thirties, attacked the notion of absolute correctness and established the idea of "levels of usage." His work has had considerable influence on textbooks produced in the last two decades.

AMERICAN DIALECTS:

Atwood, Elmer Bagby, *A Survey of Verb Forms in the Eastern United States.* Ann Arbor: University of Michigan Press, 1953. 53 pp.

Kurath, Hans, *Handbook of the Linguistic Geography of New England.* Providence: Brown University Press, 1939. 238 pp.

Kurath, Hans, *A Word Geography of the Eastern United States.* Ann Arbor: University of Michigan Press, 1949. 88 pp.

The great survey of American dialects is still in progress. This is the *Linguistic Atlas of the United States,* which is moving to completion as fast as the availability of money and trained personnel permits. When it is finished it will provide a thorough scientific record of the speech habits in the different parts of our country. The works mentioned above, developed from *Atlas* materials, provide a good introduction to dialect study.

LANGUAGE AND CULTURE:

Boas, Franz, *Race, Language, and Culture.* New York: Macmillan, 1940. 647 pp.

Whorf, Benjamin Lee, *Language, Thought, and Reality: Selected Writings of Benjamin L. Whorf.* Edited by John B. Carroll. New York: Wiley, 1956. 278 pp.

The close connection between anthropology and linguistics is seen in the number of scholars who have been linguists by virtue of being anthropologists, or vice versa. Boas is one of the most famous of these. Some of the chapters in this book exhibit the relationship between the disciplines. The Whorf thesis, which suggests that a person's view of the universe is firmly controlled by the language he speaks, is one of the most exciting ideas of recent years. Its degree of validity is still being debated by linguists, anthropologists, and philosophers.

HISTORY OF ENGLISH:

Baugh, Albert C., *A History of the English Language.* New York and London: Appleton-Century, 1935. 509 pp.

Numerous good histories of the English language are available; Baugh's, a careful and thorough presentation, continues to be received as a standard work.

LINGUISTICS AND PSYCHOLOGY:

Miller, George A., *Language and Communication.* New York: McGraw-Hill, 1951. 298 pp.

The connections between linguistics and psychology arouse increasing interest among scholars, some of whom now speak of their field of study as *psycholinguistics.* Miller discusses the work that had been done up to the time of publication. Much of it has obvious bearing on the problems of teaching English.

I should like to express my thanks to Professor Francis Lee Utley of Ohio State University for a close and careful reading of the manuscript, which resulted in the elimination of many faults. In the course of the preparation of the book, I learned a great deal from conversation with Fulbright colleagues: in Cairo, Professor George Faust of the University of Kentucky; in Rome, Professor Frederick B. Agard of Cornell University. I am grateful to them. Much of what I know about the application of linguistic science to the teaching of English I have learned from Professor Donald J. Lloyd of Wayne University, to whom I am indebted also for many years of steady and friendly encouragement.

P. R.

October, 1957

Understanding English

1
Something to Begin With

1. The Fact of the Matter

One trouble commonly faced by students in a course in writing is the fact that they do not enjoy writing. Indeed, not to put too fine a point on it, they hate writing. But this feeling does not in any way make them different from the rest of humanity. Everybody hates to write—practically everybody —and perhaps no one hates it more than the person who does it constantly as part of his job. Ask any newspaper man or advertising man or author what he thinks about writing, and you will learn that he does not consider it an unadulterated pleasure.

The writer of this book, in the course of a long and sedentary existence, has put a good many millions of words through the typewriter and still does not find a blank piece of paper any cause for bursting into joyous song. You will find that you can think of any number of reasons to put off making a blank piece of paper less blank. You can go and get a cup of coffee or lug in a more comfortable chair or adjust the window shade or take a little nap or sharpen a pencil or go for a brisk walk. These activities, you will explain to yourself, are absolutely necessary to produce the proper frame of mind, to get you in the mood. But they never do get you in the mood.

Eventually, however, when you've had your walk and drunk your coffee and become too ashamed to put the thing off any longer, you sit down and start putting words on paper, and now you're past the worst of it. The writing itself is never as bad as the thinking about it. Indeed, you may find that it now and then develops odd pleasures. You write what strikes you as a fine phrase, and you say to yourself, "My that's a fine phrase. Who would have thought that I could write so fine a phrase as that?" There is much satisfaction in describing something accurately or narrating something humorously or explaining an idea clearly—or just in thinking one has done so, whether anyone else agrees or not. The time may come when you reflect, "This is an extraordinarily splendid piece of writing. It is selfish of me to keep this to myself instead of sharing it with others." When you reach this stage, you'll begin to know what trouble is.

But in truth the question of whether one hates or likes writing or hates and likes it at the same time is interesting but not very important. Like it or not, most of us have to do a lot of it. It is sometimes said that the modern world runs on oil or on coal or on wheels. It could just as well be said that it runs on paper. We Americans especially spend an enormous amount of time putting words on paper. Millions of acres of forests are cut down to provide us with paper to write on. To be sure, most of this writing is something less than immortal. Generally, as soon as we write it, someone files it or burns it or wraps fish in it. Nevertheless, the writing is done, and our material success is likely to bear a close relation to how efficiently we can do it. Unless one is a philosopher and can be content to live humbly, hauling and carrying, he will do well to learn how to write.

2. Fluency

Good writing is a complex of many features, of which two stand out as obvious and important: fluency and correctness. These qualities sometimes contend against one another; the more fluent writing is, the less correct it may be, and vice versa.

If your writing at present has neither of these virtues, the one to strive for first is fluency, which we can define as simply the ability to get your ideas on paper in a reasonable length of time. It is common for students to hand in a five-hundred-word theme with some such remark as, "I hope this is good; I spent nine hours on it." Spending nine hours on a five-hundred-word paper is nothing to brag about. It indicates that something is badly wrong with your writing. You should be able to turn out five hundred words in an hour and polish them to boot. Sometimes, of course, it will take longer; you may have to look up some facts or you may get off badly and have to scrap the whole thing and begin over. But ordinarily, no. Nine hours is too long. Two hours is too long.

In any writing class the students will vary considerably in fluency. One student may be able to skate along indefinitely, filling page after page with something or other. (Whether it's any good or not is a different question.) Another may find that an hour's deep thought and pencil chewing produces only a couple of dozen words, many of them misspelled. The first student we can call lucky: he already knows how to write and now needs only to learn to write well. The second has a harder task, but he needn't despair. Something can be done about it.

If you're a twenty-words-an-hour writer, you most likely face a problem in psychology rather than in language. Probably—assuming that English is your native speech—you're as fluent a talker as the next person. When you talk to your friends you are able to have your say, to relate what is in your mind—perhaps, indeed, at greater length than your friends could wish. In doing so, you are using much the same materials which are used in writing—sentence structures, phrases, words. In speaking, you select these features quickly, almost automatically, in response to the situation or to what someone else has said or to what is in your mind. It's possible to develop some such quickness in the writing process too, and that is what fluency is.

Partly—and obviously—it comes from practice. If you have written very little in your lifetime, it is no wonder if you write slowly. You'd speak slowly too if your speaking were limited to a couple of hundred words every three months. But if you could write an hour every day and keep with it, you would find yourself in a month's time writing much faster, and much better too. Thoughts and sentences would come more quickly and with less effort until eventually your problem might be to keep your writing from becoming *too* glib and automatic.

Physical conditions play a large part in writing. It's not so much a matter of being comfortable as it is of getting used to a routine. If you become accustomed to writing in a particular room, it may be hard to write in another. If you form the habit of smoking while you write, you will soon find it virtually impossible to write without smoking. What you write with quickly associates itself with your whole writing process. If you're used to a pencil, it is hard at first to write with a pen. A writer accustomed to composing on a typewriter will often become tongue-tied (or pen-tied) if he must write in longhand. You therefore make it easier for yourself if you can do your writing each day in pretty much the same environment.

For some students the problem is a deeper one and is not to

be solved merely by conscientious practice or by making or breaking routine habits. Some students have what it has been conventional to call a psychological block against writing. Confronted by a white piece of paper, they are taken by a paralysis that freezes their fingers and empties their minds. Such maladies may be rooted in family problems or in earlier school experiences. Perhaps writing has been nothing but a long succession of dismal failures, to which one is reluctant to add. Perhaps the student has an overwhelming fear of being incorrect. Experience may have taught him that anything he commits to paper has a better than even chance of producing a cluster of red marks in the margin, and so his mind and hand may refuse to commit anything to paper.

If you happen to be in such a dilemma, the first thing to do is to break the jam. You must get used to the pen passing across the paper and making words on it. At this stage you needn't worry about whether the words are spelled correctly or not. Don't worry about correctness at all. Just write, as long and as much and as often as you can until writing becomes muscularly and psychologically routine and easy.

Sometimes it is pleasant to forget not only correctness but all matters of form and coherence. You just let your mind wander, and you write down the thoughts that pass through it. This is what is called "stream of consciousness" writing. You just sit in your chair and your mind flutters along as you scribble or punch the keys with the flies buzzing around what a place for flies as big as my dear girl if you don't stop making that racket how do you expect me to wonder where Agnes put the fly spray and really it was rather humiliating because there I was with Betty and Hal and he had promised to come at six-thirty sharp which just goes to show that you can never depend on—

The object of this sort of thing is not to produce literature but simply to loosen up the mind and muscles and to make the words flow. Your instructor may not give you any such assignment, but if your problem is pen paralysis, you'll do yourself a favor by undertaking it on your own initiative. Give it half an hour a day, or fifteen minutes, and decide that for that period your only duty is to keep the pen moving along the paper. For that time forget all about correctness and form. Write about yourself or the room you're in or school or people you know or anything at all. Just keep writing. You'll be surprised at what a few weeks of this will do toward making the thing come easier.

Do whatever you like with what you've written. Burn it or stack it up with your souvenirs or haul it around with you and force your friends to read it.

3. Grades

We'll suppose that you have either attained fluency or are in the process of attaining it, and we'll consider the writing that you hand in to your teacher to be criticized and graded. Grading a theme in an English class is a more complex matter than grading, say, an examination in mathematics or history. It is well for the student to understand something of the complexity.

A grade on an English composition may be an evaluation of the student's performance on all of the following points: organization, development, paragraphing, interest, coherence, effectiveness, smoothness, style, maturity, sentence structure, punctuation, spelling, diction, logic, and miscellaneous mechanical matters. Some of these are matters of fact and some are not. It is a fact that a word is spelled correctly or is not; no argument about spelling need last longer than it takes to reach a dictionary. But the question of whether writing is dull or interesting is a matter of opinion, and the instructor's

CORRECTION MARKS

Here is a list of symbols commonly used by teachers in correcting papers. Section references are given for those difficulties discussed or alluded to in this text.

x   Correct the obvious error.

sp   Correct the spelling error. (65)

uc   Use a capital (upper case) letter.

lc   Use a small (lower case) letter.

p   Correct the error in punctuation. (157–173)

agr   Make the subject and verb agree in form. (101)

dm   Avoid the dangling modifier. (167–168)

mm   Make the modification clear. (127–130)

ref   Make the reference of the pronoun clear. (128)

|| Correct the faulty parallel structure. (132, 135)

coh   Improve the coherence. (254)

¶   Start a new paragraph.

no ¶   Don't start a new paragraph.

cl   Avoid the cliché. (213–214, 245)

d   Improve the choice of words (diction). (242, 244, 246–248)

w   Eliminate unnecessary words. (243–244)

k   Improve the awkward construction.

ᕉ   Delete

opinion is the only one that counts. The student cannot judge his own writing. He sees it by itself and has nothing against which to measure it. A teacher sees it against thousands of other student compositions and actually has very little difficulty in deciding whether it is, in comparison, good or bad or average.

Grading practices vary considerably from school to school and from teacher to teacher. Some instructors will assign each composition just one grade, as "C plus" or "A minus" or "D." Others will give a double grade: "C/B," "A—/D," etc. In the double-grade system, the grade above the line stands for what can be summed up as content: logic, coherence, style, interest, power, etc. The grade below the line stands for mechanical matters: spelling, punctuation, sentence structure, and so on.

Both systems have virtues and drawbacks. The double grade is rather more informative. It allows the teacher to indicate, perhaps, that although the paper is wretchedly spelled and chaotically punctuated, it has a good deal of sparkle and interest. On the other hand, the double grade is to some extent an artificiality, since it is very difficult to separate content and form. A student may have various noble thoughts to communicate, but if his sentence structure is bad, the noble thoughts may not get through to the reader.

One instructor who used the double-grade system explained his grading process in a way which may be illuminating. He would say, "When I begin reading a paper, I assume that the grade below the line will be A. Then any mistakes in spelling, punctuation, etc., cause me to revise the evaluation downward. But I assume that the grade above the line will be C— i.e., average. Then, as I read, I revise this grade upward or downward, according to whether I find the paper interesting, informative, and mature, or dull, empty, and childish."

It is sometimes hard to understand how a paper with no mistakes can get a low grade. But clearly it is not enough to write papers with nothing bad about them. We need also to work in a positive virtue or two.

4. What to Write About

The subject matter of the composition is not usually the student's problem. Commonly the instructor assigns topics, and the student writes about what he's told to write about. But choice of subject obviously affects the product, and a few words about subject matter may be useful here.

Students are often prone to blame their failures on the topic assigned. Whatever the topic, some will not like it and will feel aggrieved at having to write on it. They could have done brilliantly, they will explain, if only the instructor had chosen a subject more suited to their personalities. It is of course true that some topics are easier than others and some easier for some people than for others. But learning to write is not just a matter of learning to write what is easy. It is a matter of learning how to write whatever we have to write, and the sensible procedure is to pass lightly over the easy forms and practice on the hard ones.

Probably the easiest kind of writing is simple narrative, the relation of a sequence of actions. A familiar topic for children is "What I Did on My Summer Vacation." No doubt you encountered that one several times in your salad days. A difficult kind of writing is literary criticism—an analysis of a poem, for example, or a short story. In the freshman English course, writing is likely to be largely expository—that is, designed to explain an idea or point of view or process. In general, you can expect college assignments to lean to the difficult topics rather than the easy ones.

Students often argue that they should be asked to write only on topics in which they are interested. Again one can obviously do one's best on such topics, and for that reason they are no full test of one's ability. A good writer should be able to spin along on subjects of which he knows little and in which he has no interest whatsoever.

One teacher used to assign as composition topics just whatever entered his mind as he made the assignment. He would come into the classroom and say, "Good morning, ladies and gentlemen. Will you please write me a paper on piccolos." (Sometimes it would be washing machines or fish or Boy Scouts.) If anyone objected that he knew nothing at all about piccolos, the instructor would say that this was all the better. It gave more scope to the imagination.

5. Putting a Paper Together

Such things as planning a paper and developing it and correcting and revising it will be considered at some length in later chapters. Here we can just note a few obvious points in the interest of getting started.

Planning a composition involves no very deep mysteries. You just decide, before you begin to write, what in general you are going to say about the topic and in what order. You would not set out to build a house by grabbing some boards and starting to whack them together; you would first make a plan. Neither would you sail into a composition without some advance planning. This may range from simply assembling a few ideas in your head to working out an elaborate outline. But planning of some sort there ought to be.

The first thing to decide is your specific approach to the subject. This is particularly a problem when the assigned topic is very general. Suppose you are told to write a five-hundred-word paper on "Boy Scouts." Obviously there are hundreds of

things to be said about Boy Scouts, and you can't say them all
in five hundred words, so you pick out some single feature
and concentrate on that. This may very well be reflected in
the title you choose for the paper:

The Boy Scout Law
Does Scouting Reach the Right Boys?
How the Boy Scout Movement Is Supported
Training Leaders for Scout Camps
Why I Dislike Boy Scouts

And so on. There are hundreds of possibilities. The chief
thing to avoid is trying to cover too much territory. For example, it would not be sensible to write on "The History of the
Boy Scout Movement in America." Five hundred words won't
hold it.

When you've narrowed down the topic, you then decide
what you're going to say about it. This will be more or less
indicated by the nature of your theme. If you are writing on
"Why I Dislike Boy Scouts," you will presumably list three or
four or five reasons for disliking them and then decide the
order in which you will discuss each reason. Most likely you
will take them up in the order of climax; that is, you begin
with the least important or most trivial reason and work up to
the most weighty. Or if the topic is "How the Boy Scout
Movement Is Supported," your main points will be the sources
of support, and again you will decide the order in which to
take them.

A topic like "Does Scouting Reach the Right Boys?" suggests a different kind of arrangement. Probably you intend to
answer the question: "Yes, it does" or "No, it doesn't." And
probably you also intend to persuade your reader that your
answer is right and the other answer wrong. Such a paper is
likely to have this general form:

FIRST THIRD OR QUARTER OF PAPER:
"Some people say that such-and-such is true. They argue that.
. . ." [Now you give the opposing arguments.]

LAST TWO-THIRDS OR THREE-QUARTERS:
"But these people really don't know what they are talking about."
[Now you give the evidence or arguments for your side, arranging
them in whatever order seems most effective, most likely the order
of climax.]

More can be said about the organization of compositions,
and we shall return to the subject in Chapter 28. Meanwhile
common sense will take you a long way. The important thing
is to have some kind of plan before you begin writing; don't
just dive in hoping for the best.

6. Correctness

It is difficult to say anything about correctness in writing
that is both simple and true. Correctness is a complicated business. Perhaps it is true to say this: that it is better not to worry
about correctness at all than to pursue it unintelligently, with
no understanding of what it is.

The first thing to understand is that we can find a sharp
line between right and wrong only in a few aspects of writing.
The most obvious of these is spelling. In the present century
the overwhelming majority of English words are spelled correctly in only one way; all other ways are wrong. It can be
shown that many wrong spellings are better than the right
ones, since they show the sounds of the word more clearly.
But this is beside the point. Most words are now universally
acceptable in one spelling and in one spelling only.

Even where two alternate spellings exist, it will usually be
true that only one will be correct for a given piece of writing.
For instance, the spellings *through* and *thru* are both in general use; but the receiver of one's writing (teacher, school

paper, magazine editor, employer) may insist on only one or the other, and that one will then be the right one.

The first obvious remedy for spelling trouble is the use of a dictionary. Dictionaries and their use will occupy us at length in Chapter 26. Here we need only observe that every college student should own one and that it should be adequate to the various demands which college work may make of it, the correction of spelling being only one of these. Adequate college dictionaries include *The American College Dictionary, Webster's New Collegiate Dictionary,* and *Webster's New World Dictionary.*

Bad spellers are sometimes urged to look up in the dictionary every word that they are not sure of. This is good advice provided that the writer is not doubtful about too many words. If you have to look up half the words in your paper, you have a problem that the most industrious thumbing of the dictionary can't solve, and you will have to get at it in some other way.

Slow writers should avoid becoming slower by stopping every three or four words to look into a dictionary. This tends to break the flow and make one forget the last half of the sentence he was about to create. A writer whose problem is lack of fluency should push right along through the first draft without worrying too much about spelling and then use the dictionary while correcting or copying the paper.

But obviously everyone should use the dictionary to check the spelling of new words, words he is not accustomed to writing, or especially complicated words. If you write a paper about a rhinoceros without verifying the spelling, you are either a very brave writer or a very lazy one or both.

Beyond spelling and some few other mechanical matters, correctness becomes less tangible. Seldom can one decide whether a sentence is correctly constructed or correctly punctuated by looking into a reference book. There are really only two ways to achieve correctness in writing. One is by reading a great deal of good writing, or at least acceptable writing. Through such reading one may build up a feeling for sentence structures, an awareness of English patterns and the conventions of their punctuation. A person who learns in this way may be able to write perfectly good sentences without being able to explain the difference between a prepositional phrase and a bag of oranges.

The other avenue to a command of writing is through an explicit study of language structures. This is in part the purpose of this book. We proceed not by learning definitions or diagramming sentences but by examining the signals through which users of the language express their meanings. We begin with speech structures, and then we see how these structures are symbolized in writing. This leads to an understanding of such matters as sentences, participles, appositives, modifiers, and their normal behavior.

If you have some particular, frequently recurring difficulty, it would be no more than sensible to use the index and forge ahead by yourself. If, for example, you commonly write fragments, you might go to the chapters on sentences and their punctuation and try to figure out what your trouble is.

7. Some Mechanical Matters

Instructors have various likes and dislikes in different points of form, and yours will no doubt give you instructions on how to fold your papers, whether to write on every line or every other line, what information to put on the outside of the paper, and the like. Some practices, however, are almost universally observed.

First of all, never write an English composition in pencil. Never. All English teachers expect to go blind eventually, but

most of us try to postpone this unhappy event by refusing to
read papers written in pencil. Even if your teacher will read
pencil-written papers, you can be sure that the sight of one
won't make the writer appear any more lovable, and it would
be idiotic to give yourself a needless handicap. All class papers
should be written in ink. If you don't own a pen, buy one, and
be sure that it is loaded and in your pocket or purse before
you set off in the morning.

Most instructors permit papers done at home to be written
either in ink or on the typewriter. Whichever the medium,
the writer should be at pains to achieve legibility. A teacher
may try to overlook bad handwriting or sloppy typing, but
will not often succeed. It is hard to be impressed by the style
and message of a paper that has been one long handwriting
puzzle from beginning to end.

Remember that it is possible to produce an illegible typescript, and take care not to. Don't let your ribbon advance into
old age, don't type with dirty keys, and don't hand in pages
sprinkled with typographical errors. If you own a typewriter
but can't use it very well, take a course in typing and meanwhile do your English papers in longhand.

Whether you write on the typewriter or in longhand, be
sure to leave ample margins. An inch all around is ample unless your instructor wants more. If there is no margin, the
instructor has no space in which to comment on what a splendid piece of writing you've turned in. It is usual practice to
write on one side of the paper only.

The guiding principle is to make things as easy as possible
for the reader, whether the reader is an English instructor, an
editor, or a possible employer. This is an elementary and obvious precaution, and it pays off. If the paper is clean and
legible and handsome, the reader may overlook shortcomings
in other matters.

SUGGESTIONS

1. Select one of the following general subjects, and from it work out five titles specific enough for a short paper: advertising, baseball, campus politics, the study of foreign languages, presidential elections, traffic problems, Christmas shopping, boarding houses, relatives, cats.

2. Take one of your titles and indicate briefly how it might be organized. What points would it cover and in what order?

3. Write the paper.

4. Write a paper on piccolos. (Music majors shouldn't do this one; music majors should write a paper on fish.)

5. Write a "stream of consciousness" passage fifteen minutes long. Just keep your pen moving for fifteen minutes and see what comes out.

2

Something About Language

8. The Basic Material

The subject of this book is the material we use when we write: the English language. The kind of writing we do depends on our course of study or job or field of interest. We may write letters or scientific reports or speeches or stories or literary criticism or analyses or explanations or publicity notices or historical papers or minutes of a meeting or any of a hundred other things. All of these special kinds of writing have their special problems and trade tricks, and all can be specially studied. But obviously they cannot all be studied in a general course in English. Here we concentrate on the one thing common to all of them—the basic material, the English language.

We assume that the more understanding we have of English, the better we shall be able to make it do what we want it to do. Understanding English, or any language, is not easy. Language problems are very complicated and unlike any other problems we meet. They are also, for everybody, unavoidable problems. We all live in language all our lives long, and our success and happiness are likely to depend not a little on how well we cope with language difficulties.

If the problems of language are complicated, they are also

17

interesting. They are interesting not only—indeed, not particularly—to students but to everyone who uses language. You will yourself have noticed how often ordinary conversations turn to matters of language—to someone's accent, for example, or to the meanings of words or to affectations in speech and the like. In fact, it is not uncommon to find people of little education discussing matters which also absorb serious students of language: the meaning of meaning, the reasons for change in language, relationships between languages, and so on. Language is interesting to all of us, because it is the one thing that we all share and all use.

9. What Language Is

Before going further, let us try to define the term *language*. Let us agree to use *language* to mean "the system of speech sounds by which human beings communicate with one another." This is not the only possible definition, nor the only correct one. The term is used in many other senses. It is customary, for example, to speak of "the language of bees," "the language of flowers," "the language of the eyes," and these imply other and quite different definitions of language. We shall find it convenient, however, to exclude these other meanings.

Notice that the definition specifies *speech sounds*. This means that writing, gestures, Morse code, and other such communication systems are excluded. The exclusion does not imply that these systems are unimportant. Indeed, we shall ultimately be more interested here in writing than in speech. But it is most important not to get speech and writing mixed up. We shall try to guard against this by using *language* to refer to speech sounds only. When we want to refer to writing, we shall simply call it writing.

Notice also that our definition restricts *language* to the communication system of human beings. We may suppose that lower forms of life have communication systems also. The bees and the ants communicate, and moose calls to moose and perhaps mouse whispers to mouse. All these goings-on we ignore, confining the word *language* to the speech communication of people.

A question less easily brushed off is whether some animals cannot be taught human speech. Parrots repeat what seem to be human sounds, and some apes can learn both words and meanings. Chimpanzees are particularly bright in this respect, and some have acquired a considerable vocabulary. You pronounce the word *cup,* and the chimp ambles off and gets a cup and brings it to you and actually says the word *cup* when he hands it over. Is this not a case of an animal using human language? Well, no, not really, for there is one thing the chimp can't do. He can't learn the system.

Suppose we had an exceedingly brainy ape, and suppose that we succeeded in teaching him these five sentences:

> The cup is here.
> The bread is here.
> The table is here.
> I see the cup.
> I see the bread.

A human being, having learned these five sentences, could easily produce a sixth: "I see the table." But this is the step the ape cannot take. He can learn random utterances and their meanings, but he never learns the system, so he can never use the materials of the language to create new utterances. Until the apes become smart enough to do this, human beings will have a monopoly on language and can continue to mismanage the world as they please.

10. What We Know About Language

Many things about language are a mystery, and many will always remain so. But some things we know.

First, we know that all human beings have a language of some sort. There is no race of men anywhere on earth so backward that it has no language, no set of speech sounds by which the people communicate with one another. Furthermore, in historical times there has never been a race of men without a language.

Second, there is no such thing as a primitive language. There are many people whose cultures are undeveloped, who are, as we say, uncivilized, but the languages they speak are not primitive. In all known languages we can see complexities that must have been tens of thousands of years in developing.

This has not always been well understood; indeed, the direct contrary has often been stated. Popular notions of the language of the American Indian will illustrate. Many people have supposed that the Indians communicated in a very primitive system of noises. They said "Ugh" and they said "How" and they uttered a few miscellaneous grunts, and otherwise they communicated by waving their arms at one another. But study has proved this to be nonsense. There are, or were, hundreds of American Indian languages, and all of them turn out to be very complicated, very elaborate, and very old. They are certainly different from the languages most of us are familiar with, but they are no more primitive than English or Greek.

A third thing we know about language is that all languages are perfectly adequate. That is, each one is a perfect means of expressing the culture of the people who speak the language. A corollary is that languages are not really comparable, in the sense that we can ask, "Which is the better language—French or Navajo?" French is an excellent language for expressing French culture, but it would be a very poor language for expressing the culture of a Navajo Indian. The best language for the latter purpose is Navajo.

Finally, we know that language changes. It is natural and normal for language to change; the only languages which do not change are the dead ones. This is easy to perceive if we look backward in time. The English of 1600 would be nearly unintelligible if we heard it today, the English of 1300 would be completely so, and the English of 900 would be entirely strange and foreign.

What is not so easy to accept is that the change is still going on and will go on in the future. Remember that when we say *language* we mean speech. English writing may change considerably in the next few centuries, or it may not. But the English language will change certainly, and we can suppose that if recordings of our present speech are played a thousand years from now, the listeners will not be able to understand them without special study.

The fact of language change is more easily stated than explained. Each generation learns its language from the preceding generation, but it never learns it perfectly. The child tries to imitate the speech sounds of its parents—tries very hard usually—but it never quite succeeds. Small differences persist, and these, accumulating over centuries, add up to big differences. The interesting thing, however, is not that children fail to produce an exact imitation, but that they all fail in about the same way. If a *p* sound becomes more like a *b* sound or an *ah* sound more like an *ai* sound, it becomes so not for random speakers in a new generation but for all speakers. Language does not change sporadically and chaotically but steadily and uniformly in clearly marked directions. But we do not yet know just why this is so, and we cannot predict very well precisely what changes will take place in the future.

Change goes on in all aspects of language. Grammatical features change as do speech sounds, and changes in vocabulary are sometimes very extensive and may occur very rapidly. The vocabulary is the least stable part of any language.

11. What We Don't Know About Language

Several questions frequently asked about language are unanswerable and may always remain so. First of all, we do not know how language began. Men have wondered for a long time, and many theories have been proposed. It has been suggested that people learned to speak by imitating the sounds of nature or by making noises while doing heavy labor or by singing and then attaching meaning to the sounds they sang. Other more metaphysical theories have been advanced. But all this is speculation only. The plain fact is that there is no evidence through which we can study the origin of language, and there never will be any. If we could find some language just being born, we could get clues to the mystery, but this we cannot find because, as has been said, all men on earth already have languages and all their languages are already old and fully developed. We can guess all we like about how language originated, but we shall never know.

Neither shall we ever know when it originated. Writing began about six thousand years ago, but all we know about the beginning of language is that it must have been long before that. Fifty thousand, eighty thousand, a hundred and fifty thousand years ago—pick any number you like. Anthropologists have studied the bone structure of Neanderthal man, who wandered in the forests of Europe some seventy thousand years ago; but all they can tell us is that there is nothing in the bone structure which would have prevented Neanderthal man from talking, if he knew how.

Finally, we do not know where language developed. The exact spot isn't of much moment. It wouldn't matter much now whether the great event took place on the steppes of Asia or on the banks of the Congo. But it would be interesting to know whether language began at one place and then spread over the earth or whether it was developed independently in several places. For if language developed among one group of men and spread from them to all the others, then it would be true that all the present languages of the world are related. They would all have a common ancestor.

But this also we can apparently never know. When we examine the present languages of the world, we can see relationships between some of them but not all. It can be shown, for example, that English and Greek are related. Different as they now are, they go back to a common ancestor. They were at one time the same language. It can also be shown that Finnish and Hungarian are related and were once the same language. But this cannot be shown of English and Finnish. So far as we can see, English and Finnish are not related. If they do have a common ancestor, it lies so far back in time that we can see nothing of the development.

12. Languages of the World

One of the striking things about languages is the great number of them. In our usual existence we Americans only occasionally come into contact with languages other than our own and are perhaps aware of only a few dozen. But actually there are thousands of different languages, mutually unintelligible, spoken in different parts of the world.

Equally surprising is the large number of language families. A language family is a group of languages related to one another, going back to a common ancestor, but not related to any other languages. The language family to which English belongs—Indo-European—has dozens of members, including such different languages as English, Persian, Spanish, and Russian; but Indo-European is only one of several hundred language families. We shall not need to catalogue all of these languages or language families here, but it may be of interest to know some of the names. They range from very important families like our own (important in the number of people who speak them and in their political power) to very minor ones, spoken now by only a handful of people and doomed to die out soon.

One important language family is Sino-Tibetan. This includes Tibetan, Burmese, Siamese, and most of the languages of China. It is thus spoken by hundreds of millions of people. Another is Semitic, to which belong Arabic and Hebrew. Arabic is itself really a collection of languages, like Iraqi Arabic, Syrian Arabic, Egyptian Arabic, and so on. Another language family is Altaic, of whose members the best known is Turkish. The Turks came into the Middle East from Asia, and other languages related to Turkish are Mongol and Manchu.

Most of the languages spoken in Europe today are Indo-European; that is, they are related to our own language. But there are a few exceptions. One is Basque, which is spoken by half a million people in the Pyrenees Mountains. No one has ever been able to find in it any relationship to any known language. It is thought to be a remnant of Iberian, the language in Spain before the coming of the Romans.

Another non-Indo-European language family of Europe is Finno-Ugrian, spoken by several peoples of eastern Europe. The best known are the Finns, the Lapps, and the Hungarians. Finnish and Hungarians are therefore relatives but not close ones, being as different, perhaps, as English and Greek.

These are just a few of hundreds of language families still

in existence. There are over a hundred language families among the American Indians alone. Not different languages, mind you, language *families*. Some of these have familiar names: Navajo, Algonquian, Paiute, Hopi. Most are less well known. In Africa, in Asia, in the islands of the Pacific, a great many other language families are to be found—all complicated and very old.

One effect of the shrinking of the modern world, the spread of western civilization and efficient methods of communication, is to reduce the number of different languages. American Indian languages, for example, are dying out all the time. Linguists have discovered languages that were spoken by only three or four people, all of advanced age. When they died, the language died with them. If the time should come when no Indian children learned the language of their ancestors, but learned instead English or Spanish or French or Portuguese, then there would be no more Indian languages.

It is not beyond possibility that all languages but one will eventually die out. It could happen, in the course of millenia, that some one language—English, Russian, Chinese, Arabic, depending on political developments—would drive out all the others and become the universal language, everybody's native tongue. But even this unhappy event would not mean the end of language change, which nothing in the world can halt. The universal language, whichever it was, would go on developing. If then communications should again weaken or break down, new dialects would develop, the dialects would eventually become mutually unintelligible—i.e., would become different languages—and perhaps in time the differences would be so great that no relationship between the languages could be seen.

None of this, however, will be observed by anybody now alive.

13. Indo-European

The most important of language families is the one to which English belongs—Indo-European. This is most important because it is spoken by the most people and by peoples with the most advanced civilizations. This language family has not always been widespread; some 4500 years ago it was the tongue of what must have been a rather small group of nomads. For a number of reasons, none of them linguistic, the language of this people has spread all over Europe and the Americas and across much of Asia.

This group of languages is called Indo-European because it is spoken chiefly by peoples of India and Europe. All the languages of Europe are Indo-European with the exception of Basque, Finnish, Lappish, and Hungarian. In addition, the family includes important languages of India.

We know very little about the parent Indo-European language—Proto-Indo-European, as it is called. Scholars still argue about what it was like, where the people lived, what caused them to break up and spread around the world. We can guess that some 2500 years B.C. they were living together somewhere in Europe or near-Asia. Then, for some reason, the group expanded and threw out migrants. One section found its way to India. Another came into the country we now call Greece. Another moved into the Italian peninsula. Another moved across western Europe and into Britain. Still another went into the Rhineland and Germany and Scandinavia. By the time history begins, the Indo-Europeans (or at least their linguistic descendants) were widely scattered.

It is customary to name eight main branches of the Indo-European family. One branch is called *Indo-Iranian*. One of the groups that split off from the parent group went into the country that used to be called Persia and is now called Iran.

Here the group split again, one part staying in Persia and the other going on over the mountains into India. This last section left the earliest documents of any Indo-European language, some writings called Vedic-Sanskrit. These documents, which are all religious, go back perhaps as far as 1500 B.C., which makes them nearly a thousand years older than any other Indo-European writing. Consequently, they give us our best idea of what Proto-Indo-European was like.

Vedic-Sanskrit, in the course of several hundred years, crystallized into a religious language called Classical Sanskrit. Sanskrit has been to India much what Latin has been to the western world. Like Latin, it survives to the present as a writing system. And just as vernacular languages—Spanish, French, and so on—have evolved from Latin, modern Indian languages have evolved from Sanskrit.

The language of the group that stayed in Iran is called Persian or Iranian. Records of several dialects survive, and the earliest writing is dated about 600 B.C. The *Avesta,* the book of Zoroaster, represents a dialect of Iranian.

A second main branch of Indo-European is *Hellenic.* One offshoot of the original Indo-European community arrived in Greece somewhere around 2000 B.C., conquered the natives, and settled down. There were several dialects of Hellenic, but the one which became most important was Attic Greek—the dialect of the city of Athens. This is the language in which the flowering culture of ancient Greece was expressed; it is the language of Plato, Sophocles, Aristophanes, Pericles.

When Alexander the Great conquered the Near East, Attic Greek went with his armies and became widely spread. It of course changed as a result of being spoken by millions of people for whom it was not the native language. In this development as a trade language for a large area it is called the *koine.* This is the language of the New Testament.

Greek flourished until the coming of the Turks in the Middle Ages. Then it was nearly obliterated, but it was revived in the nineteenth century with the reëstablishment of Greek independence.

A third group of Indo-Europeans migrated into the Italian peninsula. Their variety of Indo-European we call Italic. In ancient times there were several dialects of Italic, but for us the important one is Latin, the language of Rome. The earliest records of Latin go back to about 600 b.c. In the heyday of Rome a great literature was produced in Latin, the writings of Cicero, Virgil, Ovid, Horace, Tacitus. Since then, Latin has had its ups and downs, but it became the medium of Christianity and of western thought, and people have continued to read and write Latin until very recent times. Some people still speak Latin, though presumably the Latin they speak would not be understood by Cicero or Virgil.

Almost as soon as Latin came to be written, the writing crystallized, tended to remain the same, and the speech began to drift away from it. This speech is called Vulgar Latin— that is, the language of the *vulgus,* or people. Vulgar Latin diverged farther and farther from written Latin as the centuries passed, developing differently in the different countries occupied by the Romans. Eventually from Vulgar Latin came Italian, French, Spanish, Portuguese, and Roumanian. These are sometimes called the Romance languages, from the word Roman.

The fourth branch of Indo-European is *Celtic.* The Celts moved west across Europe and settled in what used to be called Gaul and is now called France. Then some of them crossed the English Channel and established themselves in the British Isles. Celtic survived in Gaul until the coming of the Romans; then it was replaced by Vulgar Latin. It survived in Britain until the invasion of the Anglo-Saxons in the fifth century. It then died out in England, but it is still spoken in various forms in Wales, Scotland, and Ireland. With the coming of the Anglo-Saxon invaders in the fifth century, some of the Celts were pushed back across the Channel into Brittany, where the Breton dialect of Celtic is still spoken. Celtic survived in Cornwall until the eighteenth century.

The fifth branch of Indo-European is Balto-Slavic, a group of languages spoken by millions of people in eastern Europe. The Baltic group includes Lettish (the language of Latvia) and Lithuanian. Lithuanian is particularly interesting to philologists because it has been slow in developing and preserves many features of Proto-Indo-European.

Politically more important is the Slavic group. This includes all the Russian dialects, of which the largest are Great Russian, White Russian, and Ukrainian; all of these are fairly similar. Other Slavic languages are Polish, Czechoslovakian, Wend, Bulgarian, Slovenian, and Serbo-Croatian. The latter two are the chief languages of Yugoslavia.

The sixth and seventh branches are Albanian and Armenian. These are important to the philologist and, presumably, to the people who speak them, but otherwise they are of minor interest.

14. Germanic

The last main branch of Indo-European is the one to which English belongs: Germanic. This was the language of the savage tribes who lived mostly along the northern borders of the Roman Empire—the Visigoths and Ostrogoths, the Vandals, the Lombards, the Angles and Saxons. Eventually they overthrew the Roman Empire, established themselves in it and beyond it, became converted to Christianity, and grew somewhat less savage. From Germanic come English and German and several other languages.

Germanic is divided into three main groups—East Germanic, North Germanic, and West Germanic. East Germanic was the language of the Goths, the people who, led by Alaric, sacked Rome in A.D. 410. After settling in Roman territories, the Goths learned Vulgar Latin, and eventually Gothic died out. But before it did, one record of Gothic was made which enables us to know what the language was like. This is a fourth century translation of the Bible, done by a Gothic bishop named Ulfilas.

North Germanic comprises the Scandinavian languages: Danish, Icelandic, Norwegian, Swedish. These languages were of course much more alike a thousand years ago than they are now, and they are sometimes included in the single name Norse or Old Norse. Norse was the speech of the Vikings (Norsemen, Northmen, Normans) who ravaged Europe in the ninth and tenth centuries.

West Germanic is again divided into two groups: High German and Low German. High German is so called because it was spoken in the mountainous region of southern Germany. Low German was the dialect spoken in the lowlands along the northern coast. Modern German, the standard language of present-day Germany, is High German. The Low German languages include Dutch, Frisian, Pennsylvania Dutch, and, finally, English.

So if we trace back the ancestry of English, we find that English is a dialect of Low German, which is a division of West Germanic, which is a division of Germanic, which is a branch of Indo-European. English is then related, nearly or distantly, to such different languages as German, Swedish, French, Spanish, Latin, Greek, Polish, Russian, Welsh, Hindustani, Iranian, and Albanian. It is not related to Hungarian, Finnish, Arabic, Turkish, Chinese.

The closest relative of English is Frisian, spoken in a group of islands off The Netherlands. English and Frisian are so closely related that if you were to visit these islands your

English might be understood if you spoke slowly and simply. English and German are close enough that one can see the relationship with the naked eye: English *pepper,* German *pfeffer;* English *That is good,* German *Das ist gut.* Other relationships are not so apparent. It is not immediately obvious that English *wolf,* Latin *lupus,* Greek *lukos* all come from the same parent word in Proto-Indo-European. They do, though.

SUGGESTIONS

1. One of the most interesting speculations on the birth of language is that advanced by the Danish philologist Otto Jespersen. You will find an account in the article "Language" in the *Encyclopaedia Britannica,* fourteenth edition; this article was written by Jespersen himself. Read the article and write a short explanation of Jespersen's theory, indicating whether or not you find it convincing and why.

2. The relationship of language to thought and culture has been studied and provocatively discussed by a scholar named Benjamin Lee Whorf. Whorf's material has been gathered by the Foreign Service Institute of the Department of State in Washington and published under the title "Four Articles on Metalinguistics." Some of this has been republished by *ETC,* the magazine of general semantics. Whorf's thesis is revolutionary in its implications. If any of this material is available to you, read it, and make a report on Whorf's thesis.

3. Make a chart showing the family relationships of the languages named in Section 13.

4. Make a chart showing the relationships of the Germanic languages as described in Section 14.

5. Look up the following words in the *Oxford English Dictionary* (or its abridgment, the *Shorter Oxford*): *wolf, thin, father, thing, bear* (the verb), *feather, tooth, hound.* The etymology—at the beginning of each entry—will list related forms in other Indo-European languages. Such related forms are called *cognates.* For each word make a list of the cognates given.

3
Something About English

15. Historical Backgrounds

No understanding of the English language can be very satisfactory without a notion of the history of the language. But we shall have to make do with just a notion. The history of English is long and complicated, and we can only hit the high spots.

The history of our language begins a little after A.D. 600. Everything before that is pre-history, which means that we can guess at it but can't prove much. For a thousand years or so before the birth of Christ our linguistic ancestors were savages wandering through the forests of northern Europe. Their language was a part of the Germanic branch of the Indo-European family.

At the time of the Roman Empire—say, from the beginning of the Christian Era to around A.D. 400—the speakers of what was to become English were scattered along the northern coast of Europe. They spoke a dialect of Low German. More exactly, they spoke several different dialects, since they were several different tribes. The names given to the tribes who got to England are *Angles, Saxons,* and *Jutes.* For convenience, we can refer to them all as Anglo-Saxons.

Their first contact with civilization was a rather thin acquaintance with the Roman Empire on whose borders they lived. Probably some of the Anglo-Saxons wandered into the Empire occasionally, and certainly Roman merchants and traders traveled among the tribes. At any rate, this period saw the first of our many borrowings from Latin. Such words as *kettle, wine, cheese, butter, cheap, plum, gem, bishop, church* were borrowed at this time. They show something of the relationship of the Anglo-Saxons with the Romans. The Anglo-Saxons were learning, getting their first taste of civilization.

They still had a long way to go, however, and their first step was to help smash the civilization they were learning from. In the fourth century the Roman power weakened badly. While the Goths were pounding away at the Romans in the Mediterranean countries, their relatives, the Anglo-Saxons, began to attack Britain.

The Romans had been the ruling power in Britain since A.D. 43. They had subjugated the Celts whom they found living there and had succeeded in setting up a Roman administration. The Roman influence did not extend to the outlying parts of the British Isles. In Scotland, Wales, and Ireland the Celts remained free and wild, and they made periodic forays against the Romans in England. Among other defense measures, the Romans built the famous Roman Wall to ward off the tribes in the north.

Even in England the Roman power was thin. Latin did not become the language of the country as it did in Gaul and Spain. The mass of people continued to speak Celtic, with Latin and the Roman civilization it contained in use as a top dressing.

In the fourth century, troubles multiplied for the Romans in Britain. Not only did the untamed tribes of Scotland and Wales grow more and more restive, but the Anglo-Saxons began to make pirate raids on the eastern coast. Furthermore, there was growing difficulty everywhere in the Empire, and the legions in Britain were siphoned off to fight elsewhere. Finally, in A.D. 410, the last Roman ruler in England, bent on becoming emperor, left the islands and took the last of the legions with him. The Celts were left in possession of Britain but almost defenseless against the impending Anglo-Saxon attack.

Not much is surely known about the arrival of the Anglo-Saxons in England. According to the best early source, the eighth-century historian Bede, the Jutes came in 449 in response to a plea from the Celtic king, Vortigern, who wanted their help against the Picts attacking from the north. The Jutes subdued the Picts but then quarreled and fought with Vortigern, and, with reinforcements from the Continent, settled permanently in Kent. Somewhat later the Angles established themselves in eastern England and the Saxons in the south and west. Bede's account is plausible enough, and these were probably the main lines of the invasion.

We do know, however, that the Angles, Saxons, and Jutes were a long time securing themselves in England. Fighting went on for as long as a hundred years before the Celts in England were all killed, driven into Wales, or reduced to slavery. This is the period of King Arthur, who was not entirely mythological. He was a Romanized Celt, a general, though probably not a king. He had some success against the Anglo-Saxons, but it was only temporary. By 550 or so the Anglo-Saxons were firmly established. English was in England.

16. Old English

All this is pre-history, so far as the language is concerned. We have no record of the English language until after 600, when the Anglo-Saxons were converted to Christianity and learned the Latin alphabet. The conversion began, to be precise, in the year 597 and was accomplished within thirty or forty years. The conversion was a great advance for the Anglo-Saxons, not only because of the spiritual benefits but because it reëstablished contact with what remained of Roman civilization. This civilization didn't amount to much in the year 600, but it was certainly superior to anything in England up to that time.

It is customary to divide the history of the English language into three periods: Old English, Middle English, and Modern English. Old English runs from the earliest records —i.e., seventh century—to about 1100; Middle English from 1100 to 1450 or 1500; Modern English from 1500 to the present day. Sometimes Modern English is further divided into Early Modern, 1500–1700, and Late Modern, 1700 to the present.

When England came into history, it was divided into several more or less autonomous kingdoms, some of which at times exercised a certain amount of control over the others. In the century after the conversion the most advanced kingdom was Northumbria, the area between the Humber River and the Scottish border. By A.D. 700 the Northumbrians had developed a respectable civilization, the finest in Europe. It is sometimes called the Northumbrian Renaissance, and it was the first of the several renaissances through which Europe struggled upward out of the ruins of the Roman Empire. It was in this period that the best of the Old English literature was written, including the epic poem *Beowulf*.

In the eighth century, Northumbrian power declined, and the center of influence moved southward to Mercia, the kingdom of the Midlands. A century later the center shifted again, and Wessex, the country of the West Saxons, became the leading power. The most famous king of the West Saxons was Alfred the Great, who reigned in the second half of the ninth century, dying in 901. He was famous not only as a military man and administrator but also as a champion of learning. He founded and supported schools and translated or caused to be translated many books from Latin into English. At this time also much of the Northumbrian literature of two centuries earlier was copied in West Saxon. Indeed, the great bulk of Old English writing which has come down to us is in the West Saxon dialect of 900 or later.

In the military sphere, Alfred's great accomplishment was his successful opposition to the viking invasions. In the ninth and tenth centuries, the Norsemen emerged in their ships from their homelands in Denmark and the Scandinavian peninsula. They traveled far and attacked and plundered at will and almost with impunity. They ravaged Italy and Greece, settled in France, Russia, and Ireland, colonized Iceland and Greenland, and discovered America several centuries before Columbus. Nor did they overlook England.

After many years of hit-and-run raids, the Norsemen landed an army on the east coast of England in the year 866. There was nothing much to oppose them except the Wessex power led by Alfred. The long struggle ended in 877 with a treaty by which a line was drawn roughly from the northwest of England to the southeast. On the eastern side of the line Norse rule was to prevail. This was called the Danelaw. The western side was to be governed by Wessex.

The linguistic result of all this was a considerable injection of Norse into the English language. Norse was at this time not so different from English as Norwegian or Danish is now. Probably speakers of English could understand, more or less, the language of the newcomers who had moved into eastern England. At any rate, there was considerable interchange and word borrowing. Examples of Norse words in the English language are *sky, give, law, egg, outlaw, leg, ugly, scant, sly, crawl, scowl, take, thrust.* There are hundreds more. We have even borrowed some pronouns from Norse—*they, their,* and *them.* These words were borrowed first by the eastern and northern dialects and then in the course of hundreds of years made their way into English generally.

It is supposed also—indeed, it must be true—that the Norsemen influenced the sound structure and the grammar of English. But this is hard to demonstrate in detail.

17. A Specimen of Old English

We may now have an example of Old English. The favorite illustration is the Lord's Prayer, since it needs no translation. This has come to us in several different versions. Here is one:

> Fæder ure þu ðe eart on heofonum si þin nama gehalgod. Tobecume þin rice. Gewurðe þin willa on eorðan swa swa on heofonum. Urne gedæghwamlican hlaf syle us to dæg. And forgyf us ure gyltas swa swa we forgyfaþ urum gyltendum. And ne gelæd þu us on costnunge ac alys us of yfele. Soðlice.

Some of the differences between this and Modern English are merely differences in orthography. For instance, the sign *æ* is what Old English writers used for a vowel sound like that in modern *hat* or *and.* The *th* sounds or modern *thin* or *then* are represented in Old English by þ or ð. But of course there are many differences in sound too. *Ure* is the ancestor of modern *our,* but the first vowel was like that in *too* or *ooze. Hlaf* is modern *loaf;* we have dropped the *h* sound and changed the vowel, which in *hlaf* was pronounced something like the vowel in *father.* Old English had some sounds which we do not have. The sound represented by *y* does not occur in Modern English. If you pronounce the vowel in *bit* with your lips rounded, you may approach it.

In grammar, Old English was much more highly inflected than Modern English is. That is, there were more case endings for nouns, more person and number endings for verbs, a more complicated pronoun system, various endings for adjectives, and so on. Old English nouns had four cases— nominative, genitive, dative, accusative. Adjectives had five —all these and an instrumental case besides. Present-day English has only two cases for nouns—common case and possessive case. Adjectives now have no case system at all. On the other hand, we now use a more rigid word order and more structure words (prepositions, auxiliaries, and the like) to express relationships than Old English did.

Some of this grammar we can see in the Lord's Prayer. *Heofonum,* for instance, is a dative plural; the nominative singular was *heofon. Urne* is an accusative singular; the nominative is *ure.* In *urum gyltendum* both words are dative plural. *Forgyfaþ* is the third person plural form of the verb. Word order is different: "urne gedæghwamlican hlaf syle us" in place of "Give us our daily bread." And so on.

In vocabulary Old English is quite different from Modern English. Most of the Old English words are what we may call native English: that is, words which have not been borrowed from other languages but which have been a part of English ever since English was a part of Indo-European. Old English did certainly contain borrowed words. We have seen that many borrowings were coming in from Norse. Rather large numbers had been borrowed from Latin, too. Some of these were taken while the Anglo-Saxons were still on the Continent (*cheese, butter, bishop, kettle,* etc.); a larger number came into English after the Conversion (*angel, candle, priest, martyr, radish, oyster, purple, school, spend,* etc.). But the great majority of Old English words were native English.

Now, on the contrary, the majority of words in English are borrowed, taken mostly from Latin and French. Of the words in *The American College Dictionary* only about 14 percent are native. Most of these, to be sure, are common, high-frequency words—*the, of, I, and, because, man, mother, road,* etc.; of the thousand most common words in English, some 62 percent are native English. Even so, the modern vocabulary is very much Latinized and Frenchified. The Old English vocabulary was not.

18. Middle English

Sometime between the years 1000 and 1200 various important changes took place in the structure of English, and Old English became Middle English. The political event which facilitated these changes was the Norman Conquest. The Normans, as the name shows, came originally from Scandinavia. In the early tenth century they established themselves in northern France, adopted the French language, and developed a vigorous kingdom and a very passable civilization. In the year 1066, led by Duke William, they crossed the Channel and made themselves masters of England. For the next several hundred years, England was ruled by kings whose first language was French.

One might wonder why, after the Norman Conquest, French did not become the national language, replacing English entirely. The reason is that the Conquest was not a national migration, as the earlier Anglo-Saxon invasion had been. Great numbers of Normans came to England, but they came as rulers and landlords. French became the language of the court, the language of the nobility, the language of polite society, the language of literature. But it did not replace English as the language of the people. There must always have been hundreds of towns and villages in which French was never heard except when visitors of high station passed through.

But English, though it survived as the national language, was profoundly changed after the Norman Conquest. Some of the changes—in sound structure and grammar—would no doubt have taken place whether there had been a Conquest or not. Even before 1066 the case system of English nouns and adjectives was becoming simplified; people came to rely more on word order and prepositions than on inflectional endings to communicate their meanings. The process was speeded up by sound changes which caused many of the endings to sound alike. But no doubt the Conquest facilitated the change. German, which didn't experience a Norman Conquest, is today rather highly inflected compared to its cousin English.

But it is in vocabulary that the effects of the Conquest are most obvious. French ceased, after a hundred years or so, to be the native language of very many people in England, but it continued—and continues still—to be a zealously cultivated second language, the mirror of elegance and civilization. When one spoke English, one introduced not only French ideas and French things but also their French names. This was not only easy but socially useful. To pepper one's conversation with French expressions was to show that one was well-bred, elegant, *au courant*. The last sentence shows that the process is not yet dead. By using *au courant* instead of, say, *abreast of things,* the writer indicates that he is no dull clod who knows only English but an elegant person aware of how things are done in *le haut monde*.

Thus French words came into English, all sorts of them. There were words to do with government: *parliament, majesty, treaty, alliance, tax, government;* church words: *parson, sermon, baptism, incense, crucifix, religion;* words for foods:

veal, beef, mutton, bacon, jelly, peach, lemon, cream, biscuit; colors: *blue, scarlet, vermilion;* household words: *curtain, chair, lamp, towel, blanket, parlor;* play words: *dance, chess, music, leisure, conversation;* literary words: *story, romance, poet, literary;* learned words: *study, logic, grammar, noun, surgeon, anatomy, stomach;* just ordinary words of all sorts: *nice, second, very, age, bucket, gentle, final, fault, flower, cry, count, sure, move, surprise, plain.*

All these and thousands more poured into the English vocabulary between 1100 and 1500, until at the end of that time many people must have had more French words than English at their command. This is not to say that English became French. English remained English in sound structure and in grammar, though these also felt the ripples of French influence. The very heart of the vocabulary, too, remained English. Most of the high-frequency words—the pronouns, the prepositions, the conjunctions, the auxiliaries, as well as a great many ordinary nouns and verbs and adjectives—were not replaced by borrowings.

Middle English, then, was still a Germanic language, but it differed from Old English in many ways. The sound system and the grammar changed a good deal. Speakers made less use of case systems and other inflectional devices and relied more on word order and structure words to express their meanings. This is often said to be a simplification, but it isn't really. Languages don't become simpler; they merely exchange one kind of complexity for another. Modern English is not a simple language, as any foreign speaker who tries to learn it will hasten to tell you.

For us Middle English is simpler than Old English just because it is closer to Modern English. It takes three or four months at least to learn to read Old English prose and more than that for poetry. But a week of good study should put one

in touch with the Middle English poet Chaucer. Indeed, you
may be able to make some sense of Chaucer straight off,
though you would need instruction in pronunciation to make
it sound like poetry. Here is a famous passage from the *General Prologue to the Canterbury Tales,* fourteenth century:

> Ther was also a nonne, a Prioresse,
> That of hir smyling was ful symple and coy,
> Hir gretteste oath was but by Seinte Loy,
> And she was cleped Madame Eglentyne.
> Ful wel she song the service dyvyne,
> Entuned in hir nose ful semely.
> And Frenshe she spak ful faire and fetisly,
> After the scole of Stratford-atte-Bowe,
> For Frenshe of Parys was to hir unknowe.

19. Early Modern English

Sometime between 1400 and 1600 English underwent a
couple of sound changes which made the language of Shakespeare quite different from that of Chaucer. Incidentally,
these changes contributed much to the chaos in which English spelling now finds itself.

One change was the elimination of a vowel sound in certain
unstressed positions at the end of words. For instance, the
words *name, stone, wine, dance* were pronounced as two syllables by Chaucer but as just one by Shakespeare. The *e* in
these words became, as we say, "silent." But it wasn't silent for
Chaucer; it represented a vowel sound. So also the words
laughed, seemed, stored would have been pronounced by
Chaucer as two-syllable words. The change was an important
one because it affected thousands of words and gave a different aspect to the whole language.

The other change is what is called the Great Vowel Shift.
This was a systematic shifting of half a dozen vowels and
diphthongs in stressed syllables. For instance, the word *name*

had in Middle English a vowel something like that in the modern word *father; wine* had the vowel of modern *mean; he* was pronounced something like modern *hey; mouse* sounded like *moose; moon* had the vowel of *moan.* Again the shift was thoroughgoing and affected all the words in which these vowel sounds occurred. Since we still keep the Middle English system of spelling these words, the differences between Modern English and Middle English are often more real than apparent.

The vowel shift has meant also that we have come to use an entirely different set of symbols for representing vowel sounds than is used by writers of such languages as French, Italian, or Spanish, in which no such vowel shift occurred. If you come across a strange word—say, *bine*—in an English book, you will pronounce it according to the English system, with the vowel of *wine* or *dine.* But if you read *bine* in a French, Italian, or Spanish book, you will pronounce it with the vowel of *mean* or *seen.*

These two changes, then, produced the basic differences between Middle English and Modern English. But there were several other developments that had an effect upon the language. One was the invention of printing, an invention introduced into England by William Caxton in the year 1475. Where before books had been rare and costly, they suddenly became cheap and common. More and more people learned to read and write. This was the first of many advances in communication which have worked to unify languages and to arrest the development of dialect differences, though of course printing affects writing principally rather than speech. Among other things it hastened the standardization of spelling.

The period of Early Modern English—that is, the sixteenth and seventeenth centuries—was also the period of the English

Renaissance, when people developed, on the one hand, a keen interest in the past and, on the other, a more daring and imaginative view of the future. New ideas multiplied, and new ideas meant new language. Englishmen had grown accustomed to borrowing words from French as a result of the Norman Conquest; now they borrowed from Latin and Greek. As we have seen, English had been raiding Latin from Old English times and before, but now the floodgates really opened, and thousands of words from the classical languages poured in. *Pedestrian, bonus, anatomy, contradict, climax, dictionary, benefit, multiply, exist, paragraph, initiate, scene, inspire* are random examples. Probably the average educated American today has more words from French in his vocabulary than from native English sources, and more from Latin than from French.

The greatest writer of the Early Modern English period is of course Shakespeare, and the best-known book is the King James Version of the Bible, published in 1611. The Bible (if not Shakespeare) has made many features of Early Modern English perfectly familiar to many people down to present times, even though we do not use these features in present-day speech and writing. For instance, the old pronouns *thou* and *thee* have dropped out of use now, together with their verb forms, but they are still familiar to us in prayer and in Biblical quotation: "Whither thou goest, I will go." Such forms as *hath* and *doth* have been replaced by *has* and *does;* "Goes he hence tonight?" would now be "Is he going away tonight?"; Shakespeare's "Fie on't, sirrah" would be "Nuts to that, Mac." Still, all these expressions linger with us because of the power of the works in which they occur.

It is not always realized, however, that considerable sound changes have taken place between Early Modern English and the English of the present day. Shakespearian actors putting on a play speak the words, properly enough, in their modern pronunciation. But it is very doubtful that this pronunciation would be understood at all by Shakespeare. In Shakespeare's time, the word *reason* was pronounced like modern *raisin;* *face* had the sound of modern *glass;* the *l* in *would, should, palm* was pronounced. In these points and a great many others the English language has moved a long way from what it was in 1600.

20. Recent Developments

The history of English since 1700 is filled with many movements and countermovements, of which we can notice only a couple. One of these is the vigorous attempt made in the eighteenth century, and the rather half-hearted attempts made since, to regulate and control the English language. Many people of the eighteenth century, not understanding very well the forces which govern language, proposed to polish and prune and restrict English, which they felt was proliferating too wildly. There was much talk of an academy which would rule on what people could and could not say and write. The academy never came into being, but the eighteenth century did succeed in establishing certain attitudes which, though they haven't had much effect on the development of the language itself, have certainly changed the native speaker's feeling about the language.

In part a product of the wish to fix and establish the language was the development of the dictionary. The first English dictionary was published in 1603; it was a list of 2500 words briefly defined. Many others were published with gradual improvements until Samuel Johnson published his *English Dictionary* in 1755. This, steadily revised, dominated the field in England for nearly a hundred years. Meanwhile in America, Noah Webster published his dictionary in 1828, and before long dictionary publishing was a big business in this country. The last century has seen the publication of one great dictionary: the twelve-volume *Oxford English Dictionary,* compiled in the course of seventy-five years through the labors of many scholars. We have also, of course, numerous commercial dictionaries which are as good as the public wants them to be if not, indeed, rather better.

Another product of the eighteenth century was the invention of "English grammar." As English came to replace Latin as the language of scholarship it was felt that one should also be able to control and dissect it, parse and analyze it, as one could Latin. What happened in practice was that the grammatical description that applied to Latin was removed and superimposed on English. This was silly, because English is an entirely different kind of language, with its own forms and signals and ways of producing meaning. Nevertheless, English grammars on the Latin model were worked out and taught in the schools. In many schools they are still being taught. This activity is not often popular with school children, but it is sometimes an interesting and instructive exercise in logic. The principal harm in it is that it has tended to keep people from being interested in English and has obscured the real features of English structure.

But probably the most important force on the development of English in the modern period has been the tremendous expansion of English-speaking peoples. In 1500 English was a minor language, spoken by a few people on a small island. Now it is perhaps the greatest language of the world, spoken natively by over a quarter of a billion people and as a second language by many millions more. When we speak of English now, we must specify whether we mean American English, British English, Australian English, Indian English, or what, since the differences are considerable. The American cannot go to England or the Englishman to America confident that he will always understand and be understood. The Alabaman in Iowa or the Iowan in Alabama shows himself a foreigner every time he speaks. It is only because communication has become fast and easy that English in this period of its expansion has not broken into a dozen mutually unintelligible languages.

SUGGESTIONS

1. The influence one people has on another is often mirrored in word borrowings. For instance, English speakers, in developing their interest in music, have borrowed such words as *piano, violin, concert, maestro*. Make a longer list of such musical terms and use it as the basis of a paper on foreign influence on English and American music as shown by word borrowing. Any dictionary will tell you the language or languages from which the words were borrowed. The *Oxford English Dictionary* will give the date of their first occurrence in English writing.

2. Write a similar paper on borrowed words in one of the following fields: drama, architecture, painting, poetry, law, cooking.

3. Consult available histories of the English language and encyclopedia articles and make a report on the relation of one of the following people to the development of English: King Alfred, Orm, William Caxton, Sir Thomas Elyot, Jonathan Swift, Samuel Johnson, Thomas Sheridan.

4. Collect as many older versions of the Lord's Prayer as you can find and trace in them developments of the language.

5. Select a Biblical passage of a couple of hundred words. Compare the version in the King James Bible with that in a modern translation. What differences are to be noted?

6. Take a passage of about two hundred words of modern prose and, using your dictionary, tabulate the words according to source: native English, Latin, French, etc. Discuss the composition of the English vocabulary on the basis of this passage.

4

Something
About Writing

21. Writing and Speech

People who can read and write find it hard to keep speech and writing separate in their minds. It would seem to be easy: speech is obviously one sort of thing and writing another. But we do tend to mix them up, so that when we think we are talking about speech we turn out to be talking about writing, and vice versa. In order to get any useful understanding of either writing or speech, one must avoid confusing them.

If we think about the word *man,* it is usual for us to think of it as a series of letters—*m* and *a* and *n.* That may seem to us the only way we *can* think about it. But clearly it is possible to think about it as a series of sounds without any image of letters coming between. People who can't read and write necessarily think of it that way—small children, for example.

One may ask what difference it makes whether one thinks of a word as a series of letters or as a series of sounds. Not much, perhaps, in the word *man,* in which there happens to be a fairly close connection between letters and sounds. But consider the word *Knight.* Here the image produced by the letters bears very little relation to the pronunciation. No one encountering the word for the first time in speech could guess how it is written; no one seeing it written could guess how it is pronounced.

Or consider a sentence like "English nouns form their plurals by adding *s* or *es*." This is more or less true of English writing, but it has little relevance to English speech. Pronounce *cat/cats, toe/toes, nose/noses, witch/witches,* and listen to what you add to form the plural.

We will best make our way toward an understanding of English writing by remembering that it is not the English language. It is a symbolization (and, as it happens, not a specially good one) of the English language. The letters, the punctuation marks are symbols—"mere" symbols, if you like. They are artificialities. They are invented and man-made, like radios or concertos. But they do have a connection—near or remote—with natural phenomena, and these phenomena are the sounds of the language.

It is not possible to have writing without language. Symbols must be symbols of something. But it is possible to have language without writing. Even today many peoples have no writing systems, and for many tens of thousands of years men lived on this planet and had language but no means of symbolizing it. Language has existed for a hundred thousand years or so, but writing was invented only about six thousand years ago—only yesterday, as these things go.

22. The Beginnings of Writing

The invention of writing was one of the greatest of mankind's achievements, perhaps the very greatest. When writing began, men were able to leave records of their doings, to communicate with one another across space and time. When writing began, history and civilization began. Notice that we have used the word *invention*. We may believe that language grew slowly and, as it were, naturally, that it was evolved gradually by whole peoples scarcely conscious of what they were evolving. But writing was the accomplishment of individual men, geniuses, who had ideas and worked them out. This is not to say that some single person named Ed Jones or Goki Mhotsep sat down and figured out the whole business. The invention of writing has been a slow process with many contributors over thousands of years. For the most part we don't know who the inventors were. Nevertheless it is reasonable to say that writing is an invention, just as painting and law and automobiles are inventions.

We suppose that the first kind of writing consisted simply of pictures. If you wanted to write "man," you drew a picture of a man. If you wanted to write "The man is eating," you drew a picture of a man eating. This kind of writing was used by American Indians among other peoples, and with it they were able to transmit messages like "A war party camped here" or "We have no food." But obviously this purely pictorial writing has its limitations. You can write "My uncle is eating dinner" by drawing a picture of your uncle eating dinner; but it has to be a good picture or the reader may think it means "My father is eating lunch."

The next step forward was the conventionalizing of the pictures so that they referred not to whole ideas but to particular words. Such writing was developed independently by several peoples: the Sumerians and Babylonians (cuneiform), the Egyptians (hieroglyphs), the Mayas and Aztecs, the Hittites, the Chinese. In these scripts the pictures came to stand not only for words but also, in rather complicated ways, for sounds. People began by drawing a picture of, say, a house. At first this picture meant just "house" and no more. Then it came to mean not only "house" but also the sounds of the word for house and was used for these sounds even when they occurred in other words.

We can illustrate the process with modern English. Suppose we begin by drawing a picture of an eye to write "eye."

Then we draw a picture of an ocean to write "ocean" or "sea." Next we have a picture of a man. Put them all together, and they mean "lighthouse keeper" (eye-of-the-ocean man). But— and this is the big step—if we connect the pictures with the *sounds* of the words as well as the meanings, we can put them together to get an entirely different sentence: "I see the man" (eye sea man).

This step was taken in, for example, hieroglyphics. In this script a picture of a mouth means "mouth"; but it also means the sound *r*, a sound which occurred in the ancient Egyptian word for mouth. A picture of a basket with a handle meant a basket with a handle, but it also meant the consonant *k̦*. In other words, hieroglyphic characters are sometimes meaning signs and sometimes sound signs.

The writing grew very complicated. Sometimes the sound signs represented not just one sound but two or three. A basket without a handle, for instance, meant the consonants *n* and *b*. A drawing of a hut meant the consonants *p* and *r*. Vowels were not shown. So a basket without a handle might mean "nib" or "nab" or various other combinations; or it might just mean a basket without a handle. All of this makes hieroglyphics rather hard to read, and presumably it made it rather hard to write too. Messages were sometimes written out with meaning signs and then repeated with sound signs. In addition, use was made of another set of signs called "determiners," whose function was to show which of several meanings was intended. It must have taken quite a long time to learn to be an Egyptian scribe.

23. The Alphabet

The next advance, and the greatest of all, was the invention of the alphabet. This was a matter of cutting out all the meaning signs and all the two-sound and three-sound signs and

	A	B	C	D	E
	Original pictograph	*Pictograph in position of later cuneiform*	*Early Babylonian*	*Assyrian*	*Original or derived meaning*
1					bird
2					fish
3					donkey
4					ox
5					sun day
6					grain
7					orchard
8					to plow to till
9					boomerang to throw to throw down
10					to stand to go

Diagram Showing Pictorial Origin of Ten Cuneiform Signs. (From J. H. Breasted, *Ancient Times, A History of the Early World*, Ginn and Company)

Part of Text of the Hieroglyphic Ritual, Reproduced from the Turin Papyrus. (The American Museum of Natural History)

coming up with a set of characters each of which represented a single sound. (What a "single sound" is can be a serious problem, but we'll just ignore it for the moment.) For an ideal alphabet, two features are necessary: the characters or letters should each stand for one sound and for one sound only; and the letters should be easily distinguishable. It isn't necessary that all the sounds of the language be indicated; that depends on the language. For some languages it is enough to show the consonants. For others both consonants and vowels must be symbolized. For some languages intonation must also be indicated. Whatever is shown, the important thing is that one writing unit stand for just one sound unit.

The shape of the letters doesn't matter at all, provided they are distinguishable one from another. There is nothing in the shape of the letter *b,* a vertical stroke with a loop on the bottom, which has any necessary connection with a sound made by pressing the lips together and permitting the vocal cords to vibrate. We could just as well indicate this sound with *x* or + or [. In fact, given the principle, anyone could invent an entirely new alphabet which would be just as good as the old. Let *x* stand for the first sound in "mother," + for the first sound in "and," [for the first sound in "new." Then an English word for a male human being is spelled *x*+[. If the symbols refer to only one sound, and if their reference is known, then the writing is perfectly easy to read.

In fact, however, the symbols that we use when we write were not arbitrarily selected or created from meaningless marks. The process seems rather to have been an extension of the use of one-sound signs in pictographic writing. For instance, our letter *b* has developed from a drawing of a house. This sound was the first sound in the word for "house" or "tent" in the language of the inventors of the alphabet, so they simply assigned the house picture the function of repre-

SINAITIC	CANAANITE-PHOENICIAN	EARLY GREEK	LATER GREEK	LATIN	ENGLISH
⊬ ⟋	K ⟨	Λ	Λ	A	A
☐ ☐ ☐	⟨ ⟨	⟨B	B	B	B
L Ŀ	⟩	⟩	Γ	C G	C,G
▷ ▷	△ ◺	△	△	D	D
⤲	⟩⟩ ⟩⟩	⟩	E	E	E
─○	Y	Y	Y	F V	F,U,V, W,Y
═ (?)	⌐ ⌐	I	I		Z
⤲ ⦵	⊟ H	⊟	⊟	H	H
	⊗	⊗	⊗		(Th)
⊌ ⤳	⟳	⟩	⟨	I	I,J
+ ⤲	Ⴅ Ⴅⴅ	⤳	K		K
⟩6⟿	⟨⟨	∨⟂⟃	L ∧	L	L
⩘	⟩⟩ ⟩⟩	⟩⟩	⟩⟩	M	M
⟋	⟩ ⟩	∨	N	N	N
⟸ ⟹	⟊ ⟊⟊	⟊	⟊	X	(X)
⬮ ○	○○	○	○	O	O
⬭	⟩⟩)	⟩	Γ	P	P
8 ∞	⟂⟂⟂	M	M		(S)
⦿	φφφ	Φ	φ	Q	Q
⟨⟨⟨	⟨	⟨	P	R	R
⌣	W	⟨	⟨	S	S
+	X	T	T	T	T

Diagram Showing Development of the Alphabet. (From table prepared by Martin Sprengling; courtesy, The Oriental Institute)

senting that sound. Certainly our letter *b* doesn't look much like a house now, but that is simply because hundreds of generations of writers have used it and each generation has changed it a bit, tilting the character, making a stroke a little longer or shorter, opening a loop or closing one, and so on.

Given the fundamental requirements that the letters indicate one sound apiece and be distinguishable from one another, nearly everything about alphabetic writing is a matter of accident and convention. For instance, there is nothing in nature or in language which indicates how writing should be placed on a page. English writing moves from left to right, beginning at the top of the page. But Arabic writing goes from right to left. One is just as easy to read as the other; it is merely a matter of what one is used to. In some early writing, the lines went in alternate directions: first line left to right, second right to left, third left to right, and so on, like a man plowing a field. In some writing the lines are placed vertically. All such features are more or less arbitrary.

24. The Spread of the Alphabet

The alphabet seems to have been invented only once and to have spread from its inventors to the rest of the world. The invention took place some three thousand years ago in the Middle East, the earliest undisputed example being an inscription on what is called the Moabite Stone in a language called North Semitic. Scholars still argue about where the inventors got the idea. Some think they developed their alphabet out of Egyptian hieroglyphs; others that they took a cue from Cretan writing or from some other script. Certainly it is probable that they used letter signs already employed in some kind of writing. What they added was the alphabetic principle of one letter to one sound. No more signs standing for ideas. No more two- or three-consonant signs. No more determiners. Just one letter to one sound.

The North Semitic alphabet consisted of twenty-two characters, and they all stood for consonants, the vowels not being represented. This seems odd to us, because we are used to seeing the vowels, but it is again a matter of what one is used to. No alphabet—certainly not the English alphabet—shows everything that goes on in speech. Much can and must be left out. It would be possible to omit the vowels in English writing and still get the message across more or less: nd stll gt th mssg crss mr r lss.

But it happens to be easier to write some languages without vowel signs than others, because of differences in language structure. In the Semitic languages the consonants are more important than they are in, say, English or Greek, and the vowels are less important. The speakers of Semitic languages make more distinctions with their consonants than we do; we make more distinctions with vowels than they do. Consequently, it has been usual for Semitic languages to be written without vowels, and it still is. In writing Arabic it is possible to put in the vowels, but this is done only for special purposes, as in books for children. In newspapers, vowels are omitted, and the Arabs are perfectly happy about this. Vowels would just clutter up the page, they feel.

North Semitic, the writing of the Moabite Stone, is the parent of all the alphabets now in use in the world. No one looking at Arabic, English, Hebrew, and Russian writing side by side would guess that all these scripts have a common ancestor, but they do. The difference between English and Arabic writing is just the sum of thousands of slight changes accumulating across the centuries.

We need not attempt to trace the descendancy of all modern alphabets from North Semitic; it will suffice to learn something of the ancestry of our own. The transmitter of writing to the western world was Greek. The ancient Greeks, trading in the Mediterranean with Semitic peoples, learned the alphabetic principle and brought it home to Greece. As always, it was necessary to make certain changes to suit the alphabet to the new language, and the most important change made by the Greeks was to symbolize vowel sounds. They did this either by inventing new signs or by assigning unneeded Semitic consonant signs to Greek vowels.

The Greeks borrowed not only the Semitic letters but also their names. The first three were called *aleph, beth, gimel* in Semitic; in Greek they appear as *alpha, beta, gamma*. It is from the names of the first two Greek letters, obviously, that we derive our word *alphabet*. From the first and last letters we get the expression "the alpha and the omega"—i.e., the beginning and the end. From all of them we get the names of college fraternities, this last being the chief employment of Greek letters in America.

The Greek version of the alphabet spread in many directions—into Russia, for example, and the Slavic countries generally. But let us keep to that line of development that leads to Modern English. The Etruscans, a people living in the Italian peninsula, borrowed the alphabet from the Greeks perhaps around 800 B.C. They made the necessary modifications and used the letters to write Etruscan. They bequeathed the alphabet to their conquerors, the Romans, who modified it again and used it to write Latin. Because of the political and military success of the Romans, their version became the most important source for the western world. Some form of it is used now for most of the European languages, and a few decades ago it was adopted by and adapted to Turkish. It is also the base of various special alphabets, such as the international phonetic alphabet.

When the Romans conquered the British Isles, they of course brought Latin and Roman writing with them, but all traces of both were wiped out in the Anglo-Saxon invasions.

The Anglo-Saxons, barbarous though they were, did have an alphabet. It also was a descendant of the Greek alphabet and was called "runic writing." The word *rune* meant "secret," and the name gives us a glimpse of a time when writing was a thing of mystery and high prestige and a man who could write appeared to ordinary people as little less than a magician.

Runic writing did not last very long in England. When, beginning in 597, the Anglo-Saxons were converted to Christianity, Roman writing was reintroduced to the islands, and it has been used ever since for the writing of English. Two runic characters—þ and ð—continued for a time to be used for two sounds that did not occur in Latin—the first sound in *thin* and the first sound in *then*. After the Norman Conquest, scribes began to use the combination *th* to symbolize each of these sounds.

25. The Letters of the Alphabet

In talking about the development of writing, we try to keep two parts of it separate: (1) the relevance or significance of particular characters; (2) the different fashions of writing the characters. The second of these is the province of paleography, a most interesting and very complicated study of which we can say little here. All through the Middle Ages different styles of writing waxed and waned. In some periods writing was good—i.e., clear, easy to read, pleasing to the eye; at other times it was poor—i.e., childish, scrawly, illegible. Every quickening of civilization and intellectual activity, every renaissance, was accompanied by improvement in the writing style.

The invention of printing in the fifteenth century gave writing a new dimension. The early printers, as they cast their types, simply copied such writing styles as pleased them, and

Carolingian Writing. (Bettmann Archive)

the best of these were imitated by other printers and survived. The principal varieties of type now in use—as roman, italic, gothic—go back ultimately to varieties of handwriting popular in different localities during the Middle Ages.

The other feature of writing—the significance of the characters—is of more importance to us. You can take your choice of several ways of making the letter *r*. The crucial thing is to make it in the right places. As we speak of spelling and again of punctuation, we shall be more concerned with the relevance of the marks we make on paper than with the style in which we make them.

One point of interest is the number of letters in the alphabet. This should be controlled by the number of sounds in the language, but languages are often written with fewer characters than are actually needed and occasionally with more. As we have seen, the ancient North Semitic alphabet, in which the consonants alone were represented, had twenty-two letters. Greek, symbolizing vowels also, increased this to twenty-four. In the Latin alphabet there were twenty-three letters. The letter *I* was used for a vowel and also for the first sound in the word *Juno,* which would consequently be written *Iuno.* *V* was also used as both consonant and vowel: *vir* ("man") and *nvl* ("nothing"). There was no *w*, two *v*'s, being used instead. You have probably seen this usage in Latin inscriptions in churches or elsewhere.

In the course of time, the three letters *j, u,* and *w* ("double-u") were added, so that our total is now twenty-six. As we shall see later in more detail, this is not enough for English. Modern English has twenty-four consonant sounds and nine vowel sounds, so if we were to represent just our consonant and vowel sounds accurately, without having to double up and use awkward combinations, we would need thirty-three symbols. If we wanted to write our intonation also, we would need more.

26. Other Features of Writing

The development of writing has been more than the evolution of the letters of the alphabet. Men have had also to invent the distinction between capital letters and small letters, the use of punctuation marks, paragraphing, and all the other features of modern writing. In the beginning there were no such niceties. Very early Greek and also very early Roman writing was just a string of letters of the same size with no space between them and and no punctuation, the writing sometimes going from right to left and sometimes back and forth on the page or stone. It was as if we were to write English like this:

THISMAYGIVEYOUSOMENOTIONOFWHATWRITINGUS
EROTYSAEYREVTONSITIEESUOYSAEKILKOOLOTDE
ADEVENIFYOUREUSEDTOITITTAKESALITTLETIME

The centuries have improved on this. It doesn't make much difference whether we write from left to right or from right to left or up to down or down to up or diagonally. But presumably both writer and reader will get on better if we pick one direction and stick to it, and that is what we've done. It also helps if we break up the line into smaller units, and we've done that too. We write in units that we call "words." Actually it is rather hard to know just what a word is. Why is *streetcar* one and *town car* two? Still, despite the difficulties, we manage somehow, and the page is easier to grasp.

We have also learned to make a distinction between small letter and capital letter, although different epochs and writers of different languages have made different distinctions. Originally small letters were just another style of writing: you wrote in big letters or you wrote in small ones, depending on the occasion. Later, large letters came to be used in certain places in writing which consisted mostly of small letters. In the manuscripts of the Middle Ages it became customary to make the first letter in a book, or in a chapter in a book, very large and beautifully decorated. This letter was called the "capital," from the Latin word *caput,* meaning "head."

In the course of time, writers began making capital letters

(but not elaborate ones) in other places in their books. At first, usage was chaotic, some writers using capitals for some purposes and others for others. At one time it was conventional to capitalize all nouns, as it still is in the writing of German. Gradually the modern customs evolved—capitals for the first word in the sentence, for proper nouns, for the pronoun "I," for pronouns referring to God, and for a few other occasions. The use of capitals isn't altogether logical. Perhaps one could argue that a capital at the beginning of a sentence aids the reader in following the structure, and presumably the use of "He" or "Him" in reference to God shows respect. But it is hard to explain why the pronoun "I" should be capitalized and the pronoun "you" not. Like most features of writing, the use of capitals is partly a matter of accident and convention.

This is true also of punctuation, but to a lesser degree. For the most part, capital letters do not symbolize anything in speech. You do not pronounce "Baker" differently from "baker." But punctuation marks do symbolize something in speech. They reflect what we call *intonation*. You do not pronounce "I've already eaten, George" the same way that you pronounce "I've already eaten George." The difference is in the intonation.

Intonation is such an important part of language that this book devotes a full chapter to it (Chapter 16). Here we shall say only that it consists of three features. One is *stress*—the loudness or softness with which syllables are pronounced; the second is *pitch*—the rate of vibration of the speech sounds as they issue from the vocal cords; the third is *juncture*—the way in which we break our speech into segments.

Intonation symbols—i.e., punctuation marks—have developed only in comparatively modern times, and they still symbolize intonation only in a very rough way. Ancient

Greek and Roman writing was for the most part without punctuation marks—no commas, semicolons, periods, or anything. Punctuation developed in the manuscripts of the Middle Ages. Probably it was first used extensively by preachers as a guide in the delivery of their sermons. By the time printing was invented, writers had developed various dots and squiggles and combinations of dots and squiggles with which they sprinkled their manuscripts. These marks were imitated by the printers when they cast their type, and in the course of centuries various traditions and conventions grew up concerning their employment. These conventions, however, are not altogether whimsical and haphazard. Punctuation does relate, more or less, to the stress, pitch, and juncture of our speech. What the relationship is, we shall see in more detail later on.

27. Progress in Writing

It is easy to find fault with English writing—particularly the spelling—and we shall do so pretty vigorously in other chapters. But we should not lose sight of the fact that over the centuries the history of writing is a story of steady improvement. People have grown more and more skillful, not only in writing but also in reading. We can picture men of ancient Rome standing before an inscription on a stone and laboriously sounding out syllable after syllable. Writing was originally meant to be read aloud, very slowly. It is only in recent times that we have learned to let our eyes skitter across the page, taking in the message in big swoops.

A story told by St. Augustine in the fourth century is illuminating. He tells of going to see Ambrose, Bishop of Milan, and of witnessing a marvel. Ambrose was sitting at his desk reading a book, and he was reading it without moving his lips. Not only was he not sounding the words; he wasn't moving his lips at all! Augustine was one of the best educated men of his times, but it had not struck him that it was possible to read without moving the lips.

Nowadays nearly everyone can read with the mouth closed, everybody can read silently, and most people can read at a pretty good clip—a page a minute or so. This progress is possible because those who are concerned with writing—publishers, authors, editors, printers, typewriter manufacturers—have learned how to make things easier for the reader so that he can develop his reading potentiality. As a reader, you benefit from this efficiency all the time. As a writer, you must learn how to provide it for others.

SUGGESTIONS

1. What is the Rosetta Stone, and what is its connection with the history of writing? Find out by consulting reference books, and write a short report.
2. Look up Champollion, and write a brief account of his accomplishments.
3. The article "Alphabet" in the *Encyclopaedia Britannica* illustrates the letters as they have developed in the last three thousand years. Select one letter and trace its evolution from the Moabite Stone to our present alphabet, copying out the forms given. (This project could be much enlarged by use of other articles in the *Britannica,* other reference works, and the various books and articles on the alphabet. One might also trace a letter through various styles of handwriting.)
4. If your school library possesses books printed before 1700, examine one and compare it with modern practice in spelling, capitalization, and punctuation.
5. Write a paper on some aspect of one of the following topics: handwriting, Morse code, literacy, sign language, military signaling systems, gestures. Remember that you can write well on only a small part of any subject so large as these. A paper on handwriting, for example, might have the title "Why Nobody Can Read My Father's Writing" or "Learning Penmanship in School."

5

How We Learn
to Speak

28. Expert Speakers

We have had a brief look at the nature of language, particularly of the English language, and at the development of writing. We must now turn to language and writing problems as they relate to ourselves, and we may begin by asking ourselves how we learned our language in the first place.

Anyone wishing to understand his native language is inevitably handicapped by the fact that he knows it so well. Actually it is much easier to inspect, dissect, analyze, think about a foreign language than it is one's own. Studying your own language is like studying a lake you're swimming in. You have to crawl out on the shore and look around in order to see what it's like.

No native speaker of English can remember a time when he couldn't speak English. Not only has he been manipulating its complicated structures all his conscious life, but he has been doing so automatically. He never has to stop and think how to make an *n* sound or to recall that the subject comes before the verb and not after it. Indeed, if someone learning English were to ask him about the behavior of English subjects or about the formation of the *n* sound, the native speaker might be hard put to reply.

It may be said that to speak a language perfectly is to speak it automatically, without having to pause for reflection about its sound structure or its grammar. In this sense everyone (except a few people with certain physical or mental defects) is an expert speaker of at least one language. To put it in a slightly different way, any English or American child is a perfect speaker of English. Obviously in saying this, we leave certain features out of account. Clearly some speakers are more clever or persuasive or musical or elegant than others. Some are vulgar, some obscene. Some never say anything worth hearing. Nevertheless, all are perfect speakers of English, all are expert, in the sense that they all have an automatic command of the features of the English language. They can talk English without thinking about it.

Furthermore, we have all been expert speakers of English since about the age of six. By this time the average child has mastered the sound structure of the language. He can make all the vowels and consonants, and he has practically stopped mixing them up. He has absorbed the intonation system of English. He has learned to use practically all the grammatical patterns. By the age of six the native child can speak English better than he will ever learn to speak another language, and he has achieved this mastery with little pain and no conscious effort.

29. First and Second Languages

Learning one's first language is so easy that language teachers have often sought to duplicate the process in teaching foreign languages. This effort has led to what is called the "direct method," in which instruction in French, for example, is given entirely in French. The learner grasps the meaning of nouns by having objects pointed out to him, or he grasps the meaning of sentences by seeing them acted out, or, later on, he learns new words by seeing or hearing them in contexts of familiar words. The theory is that this is what the child does when he learns his native language.

Actually, the analogy is not exact. The great difference is that when we learn our native language there is no other language getting in the way. We have no trouble "thinking in English" because there is no other way we *can* think. The structures of English are precisely what teach us how to think and provide the materials to think with. But when we go to school and study French, we find that it takes a long time and much application to "think in French." No matter what the method of instruction, we find it very hard not to talk French with English sounds and to put French words into English patterns. When we learn our first language, we face the universe directly and learn to clothe it with speech. When we learn a second language, we tend to filter the universe through the language we already know.

People often speak of "easy languages" and "hard languages." You have no doubt heard it remarked that Spanish or German is easy and Russian or Chinese is hard. But this can be true only from a particular point of view. We can say that German is rather similar to English and Chinese quite dissimilar. Presumably it is therefore easier for a speaker of English to learn German than to learn Chinese. But this is not to say that one is absolutely easier or harder than the other. There is no difference. A child born of Chinese parents in Peking will learn Chinese just as readily as an American child in Topeka will learn English, this despite the old joke to the effect that the Chinese must be very bright because they all manage to speak Chinese.

Neither is it true that heredity predisposes one to speak one language more easily than another. Take a baby born in Zanzibar to Swahili-speaking parents. Move him to Indiana and let him hear only English as he grows up, and he will turn out to speak English perfectly with a perfect Indiana accent. There is nothing in the structure of his mouth which makes English sounds particularly hard for him, nothing in the structure of his mind which makes him less able than others to cope with English syntax.

A child, then, a baby, has the potential of speaking any language at all and can learn one as easily as another. He learns, of course, whichever one (or whichever two or three) he hears. Let us suppose him to be an American child in an American home hearing nothing but English. All day long, from the day he gets back from the hospital, he is subjected to a steady bombardment of language, from his parents, his grandparents, his siblings, miscellaneous relatives and friends. He, on his part, produces a good deal of mouth noise too, running the range of what the human mouth is capable of. But in the first couple of years it isn't language, though his mother may think it is. It is just human sound, waiting to be molded into a system.

Along about the second birthday, however, it begins to be language. Certain of the sounds the child makes he hears steadily repeated in the language around him. These he himself repeats. The others, the ones that he can make but that nobody else makes, he tends not to repeat. Slowly they slip out of his repertoire and eventually are beyond his ready power.

30. Learning the Sounds

Language learning goes on all of a piece. The child does not learn first the sounds, then the words, then the sentences. He learns all together. But we can talk about these features only one at a time, and we begin with the sounds. Each language has a certain number of sound units called *phonemes*. This term we shall define in some detail in Chapter 7. Here we will say only that a phoneme is a bundle of similar sounds heard by the speaker of a language as if they were the same sound. The phoneme is the unit by which words are distinguished one from another. If we hear *rib* and *rub* as different words, it is because one contains one vowel phoneme and the other another.

Languages differ considerably in their phonemes. Most dialects of English have twenty-four consonant phonemes and nine vowel phonemes, plus a number of intonation phonemes. Some languages have more, others fewer. Phonemes in one language are not likely to resemble those of another very closely. If we say, for example, that two languages have a phoneme *p,* we are speaking very loosely. They may both have sounds made at the lips, where we make the first sound of *put* or *pain,* but close inspection will usually show that the two phonemes are quite different, made in different ways and containing different varieties of sound.

Futhermore two sounds which are separate phonemes in one language may be parts of the same phoneme in another. For instance, English has two phonemes *s* and *z.* These are what make the difference between *seal* and *zeal* or *gross* and *grows.* Spanish has these two sounds, but they are never used in Spanish to distinguish between words. For this reason, a speaker of Spanish has a hard time hearing any difference between English *seal* and *zeal.*

All this the child copes with as he learns the language. He can make all the sounds, but it takes him a while to learn which ones count in English and to hear the difference between similar ones. This is why he may say *tame* when he means *came.* It isn't that the *t* sound is easier than the *k* sound. It's just that they both sound alike to him. He may also say *came* when he means *tame.*

But all this gets learned, as we have said, by the time the child reaches the age of six or so. By that age he is whizzing along with the English vowels and consonants and the intonation system under good control.

31. Learning the Grammar

He has also learned practically all there is to know about English grammar. This may seem odd in view of the fact that the child of six can often look forward to ten years or so of studying English grammar in school. Nevertheless, there is a sense in which any speaker of English studying English grammar is studying what he already knows. If we think of grammar not as a set of terms or rules or a system of analysis, but as simply the forms of the language and the way in which they occur in speech, then obviously a speaker of English knows English grammar. Knowing that is precisely what makes him a speaker of English.

Consider a simple sentence like "The cats in the corner were eating some fish." This sentence contains a good deal of English grammar. A Russian or Arabic or Japanese child studying English in school would have to sweat like anything to say that sentence and make it come out right. He would have to take care to get the word order right—not to say "The in the corner cats some fish eating were" or any of the other possible permutations. He would have to recall that forms like *cats* pattern with *were,* not *was.* He would puzzle over the verb, wondering if it should be *ate* or *were eaten* or *have eating* or *have eaten* in place of *were eating.* He would have to remember that the word *fish* is peculiar in English—that we say *some cats* but not *some fishes.* And so on. All the features of English, which seem to us to be simply part of the nature of the universe, are actually special facts, peculiar to English, which have to be learned by anyone learning the language.

Here again the child learns painlessly. He has no grammatical habits with which the patterns of English can conflict, so he simply absorbs the patterns that he hears and they become part of his mind. The process goes on rather fast. Observe a three-year-old child, if you happen to have one handy, and notice how much grammar he knows. For example, he can tell the difference between a statement, a question, and a request. Tell him "Close the door," and he'll probably close it. Say "Is the door closed?" and he'll probably answer, yes or no. He responds accurately to the signals which distinguish different kinds of English sentences.

He knows the difference between subjects and objects. He will respond differently to "Mama ate a fish" than he will to "A fish ate Mama." By three or four he has begun to get a good grip on the very complicated English verb system. He practically never says *were eaten* when he means *ate* or *were eating*. Before he goes to school the average child will be casually using participles, infinitives, subordinate clauses, nominative absolutes, objective complements, and all the other things that it will give him such pain to study in the seventh grade. Anything and everything that occurs in the speech around him will become part of his speech.

One proof of the speed with which the child learns English patterns is his early misuse of them. You have no doubt heard children say *mans* for *men* and perhaps *fishes* for *fish*. This happens because the child has such a firm grasp on the regular pattern for forming the plural of English nouns. He has learned *cats, toes, witches* and so many other regular plurals that the pattern has come to have meaning for him as a pattern and he extends it where it doesn't belong. In the same way verb forms like *cried, snowed, petted* may mislead him into *buyed, goed, getted*. But even these mistakes disappear quickly if the words are common ones so that the child hears the usual forms often enough. You seldom hear a child of five say *mans* or *buyed*.

32. Learning Vocabulary

As the child learns sounds and grammar, he of course learns words too, begins building his vocabulary. The difference is that whereas the six-year-old has already practically mastered English sound structure and English grammar, he is only getting started on English vocabulary. Vocabulary learning goes on all our lives, and our vocabularies relate directly to our work, our interests, our favorite pastimes and ways of life. A farmer has a different sort of vocabulary than an airplane mechanic does, a baseball fan a different one than a fisherman. The child of six will command a surprising lot of words—thousands anyway—and they will be simply those that occur regularly in the speech around him. The words that he learns from this point on will be mostly determined by the path he chances to take through the world.

33. Learning "Good English"

One thing more. Remember that a child's language—anybody's language, indeed—is principally a reflection of the language he hears. People sometimes feel that this isn't so—that bright children learn to speak good English and stupid children learn to speak poor English. But there is nothing to this. All children—stupid or bright or indifferent—simply speak whatever is spoken to them. If your parents and cousins and playmates all say "We ain't got no fish," then you say "We ain't got no fish." If they all pronounce "father" with no r, then you pronounce it with no r. You just repeat what you hear.

It is true, of course, that when the child begins to venture into the world the influences on his speech become increasingly complex, and not all the influences are equally influential. As a rule, children learn initially from the previous generation—parents, grandparents, and so on. But they learn also from older brothers and sisters, and when they come to have playmates, they learn from their playmates. When they go to school, they enter into a speech community, the class, and they learn from one another. This last teacher is usually the most powerful by far. Thirty children coming together from different speech backgrounds will quickly rub out differences and produce a new language entity different from the entities contributed by each of the individuals. The language of the class is the language to which the average child will conform —unconsciously, consciously, and at all cost.

Many parents find their first child's first weeks in school a rather harrowing experience so far as language goes. Here is young Alfred whose speech is that of people of education and social prestige. He says "I haven't any" instead of "I ain't got none" and even drops in a *whom* or an *I shall* occasionally. He is sent off to school, and he comes back and Mother asks him how he got along, and he says well, he guesses he done okay. Nothing can be done about this.

SUGGESTIONS

1. If you have had experience in learning a foreign language, describe the experience as it relates to Section 29.
2. If you have the opportunity of observing a preschool child, make a list of the sounds of which he is still uncertain. What sounds does he switch? Are there any that he doesn't make at all? Does he make any that you don't?
3. Enlarge on the statement "Every speaker of English knows English grammar." In what sense is this true? In what sense not?
4. Section 31 gives examples of grammatical mistakes common in the speech of very young children. Find other examples and describe the analogies that cause them.
5. Section 31 discusses the sentence "The cats in the corner were eating some fish," describing the grammatical features that might puzzle foreign learners. Make a similar analysis of the sentence "A friend of mine was trying to get to town."

6

How We Learn
to Write—If We Do

34. Writing and Speaking

Learning to write is an entirely different matter from learning to speak. Just about everything that learning to speak is, learning to write isn't.

In the first place, speaking is universal, or practically so, and writing is not. With the exception only of people with certain handicaps—like being born deaf—everybody on earth can speak at least one language. But considerably less than half the population of the earth can read and write any language. The percentage of literacy will vary from zero, for certain primitive peoples, to something over ninety in very highly civilized countries with universal education. But in no country, certainly not our own, can all the people read and write.

Secondly, the process of learning to speak is a natural one, and the process of learning to write is artificial. Such use of "natural" and "artificial" is no doubt loose and open to philosophic attack. But by natural we mean here simply that speech is an inevitable part of the human environment. The child can't help learning to speak, and he learns with no conscious effort. He doesn't even have to be taught, in any formal sense. He must only be spoken to.

But learning to read and write requires some kind of conscious effort and conscious instruction. Surrounded by the spoken sound, we eventually come to understand it and to be able to reproduce it. But we can be surrounded for decades by the written word without ever becoming able to understand it and reproduce it. Many people live all their lives in the midst of newspapers, books, and billboards without ever learning to read them. Somewhere an effort must be made. You have to sit down, or be sat down, and learn the marks and connect them with the sounds they stand for. Learning to speak is unavoidable. Learning to write is altogether too avoidable. Many children manage to avoid it despite the fact that they are forced to spend years in school in ostensible pursuit of it.

In the third place, the process of learning to speak always goes to some kind of completion, whereas the process of learning to write does not. We saw in the last chapter that we not only master our native language—in the sense of being able to use its forms and patterns automatically in reponse to situations—but master it by the age of six or so. There is nothing really analogous to this in learning to write. Writing never becomes really automatic in the sense that speech does, if only because there is necessarily a longer interval between the situation or idea or stimulus and the achievement of the word or sentence. If it is automatic, it is so as far as our mind only. We still have to cope with questions of spelling and form and the physical problems of marking it down on the paper or stone or sand or whatever our medium is.

Neither can it be said that anybody becomes perfect in writing in the sense in which everybody becomes perfect in speech. For every writer, however skillful and experienced, writing is always to some extent a problem to some extent unsolved. He is always facing new difficulties which he can cope with only by conscious application of his mind or his reference books.

Finally, the ease or difficulty with which one learns to write depends to a considerable extent on the language. This, as we have seen, is not true for speech. It is not noticeably more or less difficult for Chinese, Russian, Finnish, or American children to learn to speak their respective languages. But some writing systems are much harder to learn than others. They are relatively easy if they are relatively phonemic and close to the spoken language. They are relatively hard if the spoken languages have departed from them. Systems based on an alphabet are of course much easier than those based on picture writing. On the scale of difficulty English is middling. There are much more difficult writing systems—like Chinese and Arabic. There are also easier ones—like Spanish and Turkish.

35. Writing and Reading

We begin to learn to write when we begin to understand the significance of letters on paper. All through our lives our ability to write is closely related to our experience, practice, and proficiency in reading.

Most children begin learning to read in the first grade—that is, at about the age of six. You will note that this is the age by which the process of learning to speak has practically reached completion. In recent years, however, it has been pointed out that first-grade children vary considerably in their aptitude for reading, and it is the current opinion of educators that each child has an optimum point for the beginning of instruction in reading. This is called the point of "reading readiness." Thus, the specialists say, though most children may achieve reading readiness by six, others may not reach it until seven or eight. Meanwhile, badgering them with reading lessons is futile.

Conversely, some children are ready to read earlier than six—at five or four or even, in rare cases, at three. If conditions are right, such children will ask for and get explanations about the significance of words and letters and may be reading simple material quite easily by the time they go to school. Children with literate older brothers and sisters are more likely to begin learning to read in the preschool period than others are.

Reading lessons, as such, used to continue for a few years only—say through the third grade. It was then presumed that the child knew how to read and no longer needed special instruction in the activity. From the fourth grade on he read history or geography or literature, but he didn't just read "reading." In recent years, however, educators have become increasingly alarmed over the incompetence in reading of a large part of the school population, and as a result have introduced more and more lessons in reading per se into the later school curriculum. In some schools this will take the form of classes in "remedial reading" for poorer students. In others, reading classes for everybody are continued through the sixth or seventh grade or even into high school. Indeed, some colleges have found it necessary to introduce reading classes, remedial or otherwise.

36. Differences in Proficiency in Reading

Certainly it is true that people with the same education differ widely in reading ability. There is a range to which we find nothing comparable in speaking or in understanding speech. Most obviously, individuals differ in reading speed. One child of ten may read in three hours a book to which another must devote twenty. Much of the effort of remedial reading classes is directed toward the speeding up of slow readers.

Somewhat less obviously, people differ in comprehension of what they read. Deficiency in ability to understand may not always be manifest even to the person who is deficient. You can tell whether it takes you a minute or ten to read a page; but you can't always tell whether you have successfully grasped the author's meaning. You may think you have and be mistaken. It is not uncommon to test college students on the meaning of fairly simple paragraphs and to discover that they have either a very hazy notion of the meaning or a completely wrong one. Sometimes, therefore, the problem is not to speed up the slow reader but to slow down the fast and careless one. Some things should be read fast, others slowly.

37. What Makes a Good Reader

No doubt ability to read is related to several conditions. One is intelligence—or at least a certain kind of intelligence. Writing is a symbolization, and some people are better equipped to deal with symbols than others are. Another is the normal tendency to develop the abilities that are strong and neglect those that are weak. If you're an athletic type and especially good at tennis, you're likely to play a lot and practice a lot and eventually become very much better than you were to begin with. On the other hand, if you're an unathletic and awkward type, you probably don't play tennis if you can avoid it, and so you don't get any better.

So in reading. Of two children, one a pretty fair reader, the other a rather poor one, it is the first who is likely to get better. Most of us like to do what we're reasonably good at. The difficulty is that, whereas we can ordinarily get by fairly well in the world without being able to play tennis, it is harder to survive without some competence in reading and writing.

Home environment, too, has its influence on the development of reading ability. For some children, reading is a school activity only. They live in homes where there are no books, not even a Bible or a dictionary, no magazines, perhaps no newspapers even. Their only literature is the writing on the box of breakfast cereal. Another child may come from a home with a well-stocked library and a strong literary tradition, where Mother or Father reads to the family every night from *The Swiss Family Robinson* or *David Copperfield* and brothers and sisters call one another's attention to good things in *Boy's Life* or the *New Yorker*. Naturally such a child could hardly help becoming a good reader. Home teaches him many times as much as the school does.

38. Reading in the Modern World

Present-day life in some ways favors the development of reading ability, in others it does not. Certainly we are surrounded by much more writing than our ancestors were. A man in Chaucer's London, in the fourteenth century, might well have walked clear through town without ever seeing a single letter of the alphabet. Now almost any block is decorated with thousands of words, from names on mailboxes to notices on telephone poles to neon signs urging the excellence of this coffee or that soap.

It isn't all advertising, either. Look at the millions and millions of magazines that are printed and distributed and presumably read every week. Some magazines have a circulation of three or four million, and presumably most copies are read by more than one person. Hard-cover books have scarcely kept up with other expansions in the economy, but paper books sell by the truck load, and they aren't all trash by any means. For a quarter or thirty-five cents you can get E. M. Forster or Shakespeare or Bertrand Russell or just about anyone you fancy.

Still, there is no denying that many features of our culture work the other way. The literate man of today does not have nearly so many demands made on his literacy as his forefathers did. Most people find it rather easier to curl up with a television set than with a good book, and for those who get bored with television there are a thousand other activities for which ability to read a sign or a ticket stub will suffice. People in general read more today than people used to; but few well-educated people today read as much—or as intensively— as most well-educated people used to.

39. Learning to Write from Reading

Writing ability, as has been said, follows reading ability, though not so closely as speaking follows hearing. As children we more or less automatically reproduce the speech we hear. But reading does not turn into writing so easily—for some people not easily at all.

Individuals appear to differ markedly in their capacity for learning to write from reading. Some children, having been taught the significance of the letters, seem able to go on and pick up the rest by themselves. When they read, they notice what is going on, and when they write, they imitate, consciously or subconsciously. They observe which words are capitalized, and they capitalize them. They notice punctuation marks and how they relate to sentence structures and use them accordingly. As their reading grows more and more mature, their writing develops with it. They pick up phraseology, sentence rhythms, tricks and style, like as not without knowing that they are doing so. Memory no doubt plays a part in it, but it isn't all memory, perhaps not largely so. It is rather an ability to observe and a bent for mimicry. Some students have it so strongly that their writing regularly reflects whatever they have been reading lately. If they have been reading Henry James, they write like Henry James; if Hemingway, Hemingway.

Observation is key to spelling, especially

Probably all really successful authors develop in this way. They are taught by what they read, not by dictionaries and handbooks. A style begins as an imitation of other people's styles and grows into a reflection of the writer's own mind and personality.

For other people, observation and mimicry don't come so easily. Some can read the word *studying* a thousand times and still write it *studing*. They have difficulty transferring what they read to what they write. For such people, repeated instruction in capitalization, punctuation, sentence structure, and such rather dreary matters is unavoidable. These are the ones who must be taught rules and grammar. Actually, all writers have to know the rules and the grammar. But some do it inductively—subconsciously perceiving structure in what they read and making the necessary generalizations. Others need to have it done for them.

Rules and instruction in grammar are therefore useful things, and for some people more useful than for others. But they are no substitute for reading. Memorizing a thousand rules won't make a writer out of you. You must also read as much as you can, and you must train yourself to notice what goes on in what you read. Formal instruction in writing gives you a skeleton which you fill out for yourself. Books on English grammar show you English structure in an abstract way, and make it somewhat easier for you to perceive concrete structure in English writing.

SUGGESTIONS

1. Describe the different kinds of written matter to be found in your room, in your house, or on your block.
2. If you have had any experience with a course in remedial reading, describe the experience.
3. Discuss the kind of reading you do and/or your attitude toward reading.

4. Read several pages from the works of an author with a distinctive and recognizable style—e.g., Ernest Hemingway, Henry James, H. L. Mencken. Then write a piece on another subject, imitating the style of the author you have read.

5. Write an article imitating the style of *Time* magazine.

7
Sounds and Letters

40. How Sounds Are Made

In order to get an understanding of English spelling and its miseries, it is necessary to know a little about English sounds and the letters that symbolize them. This is not a very simple matter. The system of symbolization in English is complicated—not to say chaotic—and the sounds themselves are complicated too.

Let us try first, with as little technicality as possible, to get a notion of how speech sounds are made. The basic material is the stream of air coming from the lungs, passing through the throat, and going out through the mouth or nose. This airstream is modified, interrupted, chopped up in various ways, by different parts of the mouth and throat. For instance, the tongue can move into various positions to stop or channel the airstream. The lips can close or open, and so can the teeth. Parts of the mouth used in speech production are often called "speech organs." However, we might notice that their primary function is not to produce speech. The principal function of the airstream is to take in oxygen and dispel carbon dioxide; teeth are used principally for chewing and biting, lips for pouting and kissing, and so on. The employment of these organs for speech production is accidental, as it were, and came late in human development.

Much of the speech apparatus you are probably not aware of unless you have had special occasion to study it. Behind the teeth is a hard, bony structure called the *alveolar ridge*. Behind and above this is the front part of the roof of the mouth. This is called the *hard palate*. Behind this, where the roof of the mouth becomes soft, is the *velum*. Beyond the ve-

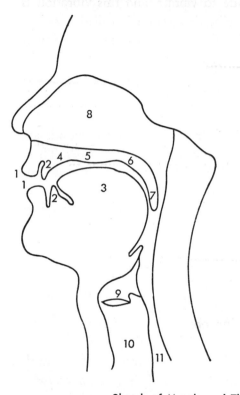

1. lips
2. teeth
3. tongue
4. alveolar ridge
5. hard palate
6. soft palate or velum
7. uvula
8. nasal cavity
9. larynx
10. trachea or windpipe
11. esophagus

Sketch of Mouth and Throat Parts.

lum and hanging down from it is a movable flap called the *uvula*. The tongue in contact with any of these different parts of the mouth will produce different sounds.

Down in the throat is another organ of great importance. This is a pair of elastic bands located in the larynx, just be-hind a man's Adam's apple. These bands are called the *vocal* _cords._ The airstream coming from the lungs must pass through the vocal cords, and these may be either open and relaxed, so that the air passes through unimpeded, or pressed together so that the air forces its way through. In this latter position, the sound is made to vibrate, and this vibration is given the name _voice._ A vibrating sound is called a _voiced sound._ A sound made with the vocal cords open and consequently no vibration is a _voiceless sound._ Say _sip_ and _zip_, lengthening out the first sound in each word: _s-s-s-sip, z-z-z-zip._ The _s_ sound in _sip_ is voiceless; the _z_ sound in _zip_ is voiced.

Besides being either voiced or voiceless, speech sounds are either _stops_ or _fricatives_ or _resonants_ or _flaps_ or _trills._ These terms refer to the way in which the airstream is impeded or shaped after it leaves the vocal cords. If the air is completely closed off at some point, the sound is a stop; such are the first sounds in the words _big, pig, cat, do._ If the air is not completely stopped but made to pass through a narrow opening so as to produce friction, the result is a fricative; the first sounds in _sip, zip, find, this_ are fricatives. Resonants are produced when the air passes from the vocal cords through the mouth or nose without being obstructed. Different resonants are distinguishable because of different shapes given to the mouth by the shifting of the tongue or other parts. Vowels are resonants, and so are the first sounds in _man, new, long,_ and _rise._ Flaps and trills are made by the tongue striking once or several times against some part of the mouth. These are not common in the speech of most Americans.

Besides this, speech sounds are either _oral, nasal,_ or _nasalized._ The uvula, hanging down from the velum, can move back so as to close off the nasal passage or move forward so as to open it. If the nasal passage is closed, the air goes out through the mouth, and the sound is called an oral sound.

Most sounds in English are orals. If the nasal passage is open and the mouth is closed at some point, the air goes out through the nose, and the sound is a nasal. The first and last sounds in *man* and the last sound in *sing* are nasals. If the nasal passage is open and the mouth is open too, the sound is nasalized. Ready examples of nasalized sounds are some of the French vowels.

Finally, sounds are differentiated according to the point at which the airstream is obstructed; if at the lips, the sound is a *labial;* at the teeth, *dental;* at the alveolar ridge, *alveolar;* at the hard palate, *palatal;* at the velum, *velar;* at the uvula, *uvular.* In some languages there are other possibilities.

To describe a sound, one tells whether it is voiced or voiceless, whether it is a stop, fricative, resonant, flap, or trill, where the breath stream is impeded, if it is (labial, dental, etc.), and whether the sound is oral, nasal, or nasalized. The first sound in *this* is a voiced dental oral fricative. Some sounds are somewhat more complicated and require additional vocabulary for their description. Vowels are largely special.

41. The Phoneme

The major points to be stressed are that speech sounds are quite complex and that there are a lot of them. Not all, to be sure, occur in any one language. English, for example, has no velar fricatives—e.g., like the last sound in German *doch.* But even in one language, the number of distinct sounds is considerable. In the words *key, cup,* and *cough* the initial sounds are perceptibly different. In *key* the first sound is a palatal, the tongue stopping the air at the hard palate; in *cup* the stoppage is farther back, and the sound is a velar; in *cough* it is farther back still, nearly uvular.

Again, the *r* sound in *trip* is quite different from the one in *rip.* The first is pronounced with friction and the second isn't. The two *p's* in *papa* are not the same; the first has a puff of air after it and the second hasn't.

This exceeding complexity of speech sounds posed a difficulty for investigators of language structure. As you begin to study a language, you hear, let us say, twenty different consonants. Then as you continue to listen and as your ear grows sharper, you hear more and more distinctions. Presently you can pick out thirty different consonants, then forty. You use laboratory equipment, and the distinctions multiply. Finally you realize that the number of different consonants is infinite —or is limited only by the sensitivity of the laboratory machine. No two speech sounds are exactly the same.

There is nothing very appalling about this. Science has long been aware that no two objects are exactly the same weight, no two pieces of rope the same length. There is always a difference, though it may be infinitesimal. But we are still left with the task of explaining how, if no two speech sounds are alike, speech sounds can still be used to produce understandable language.

The answer has been found in the concept of the *phoneme*, the discovery of which represents the greatest single advance of linguistic science. A phoneme is not a sound; it is rather a bundle of similar sounds. The variations in a phoneme usually sound all alike to a speaker of the language; but to a speaker of another language some of them may sound different. It is the contrast between phonemes which distinguishes between different words.

If, for example, we examine the English words *sip* and *zip,* we find that they are identical except for the first consonant. Call the first consonant in *sip* [s] and the first one in *zip* [z]. Since we can tell the words apart if we hear them and since the only difference between them is that one begins with [s] and the other with [z], it must be that we recognize and react to the difference between [s] and [z], whatever the difference is. This is proof that [s] and [z], in English, contrast significantly and are members of different phonemes. Note the reservation "in English."

42. Allophones

If now we listen carefully to the *r* sounds in *rip* and *trip,* we find that they also are quite different, perhaps just as different as [s] and [z]. The *r* in *trip* is pronounced with friction, and the *r* in *rip* is not. Call the *r* in *rip* [r] and the *r* in *trip* [R]. The question, then, is whether [r] and [R] are members of different phonemes, like [s] and [z]. The answer is no. And the reason is that we can examine all the words in English without ever finding two which are exactly alike except that one contains [r] and the other [R]. *Trip* and *rip* are different because one has [r] and the other [R], but also because one has a *t* and the other doesn't. We have no pairs like *rip* and *Rip.* It is quite possible to pronounce *Rip,* but we don't do it in English. Or, if we do, it doesn't mean anything different from *rip.*

We say then that, in English, [r] and [R] belong to the same phoneme. Or, to use the technical term, we say that they are *allophones* of the same phoneme.

Take one more example. We saw that the words *key, cup,* and *cough* begin with three distinctly different sounds—a palatal in *key,* a velar in *cup,* and a near uvular in *cough.* Call them [k], [ḵ], and [q]. But if we look at the distribution of these sounds in English, we find that [k] occurs only when a front vowel follows; [ḵ] only when a central vowel follows; and [q] only when a back vowel follows. There are therefore (in English) no two words distinguished only because one has [k] and the other [ḵ] or because one has [ḵ] and the other [q]; the vowel will always be different too. Consequently,

[k], [k̟], and [q], in English, are all allophones of the same phoneme.

43. Phonetic and Phonemic Writing

You will see that there are two ways of writing down the sounds of a language. First, you can write the allophones—or all the allophones you can distinguish—using a different symbol for each allophone. This is what is called *phonetic writing*. When we write phonetically, we put the letters between square brackets—e.g., [kiy], [k̟əp], [qɔf], [rip], [tRip]. There is no definite limit to the number of letters you will need to write a language phonetically; it will depend on the fineness of the distinctions one wishes to make or is capable of making.

The other way is to write just the phonemes. We have seen that, in English, [k], [k̟], and [q] are allophones of a single phoneme. We will assign this phoneme a letter, say *k*. It is customary to write phonemes between diagonal lines. We therefore say that [k], [k̟], and [q] are allophones of the phoneme /k/. Now instead of writing [k], [k̟], and [q] where they occur, we just write /k/ for all of them. In the same way, we say that in English [r] and [R] are allophones of the phoneme /r/, and we write /r/ wherever [r] or [R] occurs. If we write our five words phonemically instead of phonetically, they come out /kiy/, /kəp/, /kɔf/, /rip/, and /trip/.

There *is* a limit to the number of symbols needed to write a language phonemically, because each language has a definite and statable number of phonemes. English has twenty-four consonant phonemes and nine vowel phonemes, in addition to twelve intonation phonemes. Analysis of some dialects of English may show a tenth vowel phoneme.

It may be superfluous to remark that we do not say that

phonemic writing is better than phonetic writing. It depends on what one wishes to do. In the analysis of a language, the sounds are first written phonetically and later phonemicized.

44. The Sounds That We Hear

Ordinarily the native speaker of a language does not distinguish between the allophones of a phoneme, does not hear them as different. Ask a speaker of English if *key, cup,* and *cough* begin with the same consonant, and he will say "Sure." (Wouldn't you have?) This is because, as we learn the language, we are trained to hear only those differences which matter, which are used to distinguish between words. It never happens that our understanding of a sentence depends on our being able to tell the difference between [k] and [q], so we never learn how to do so. In some languages, however—Arabic, Hindustani—[k] and [q] are members of different phonemes, are used to distinguish between words, and speakers of these languages learn to hear these sounds as sharply different.

On the other hand, we do use [s] and [z] to distinguish between words—*sip* and *zip, seal* and *zeal.* They are therefore, in English, members of different phonemes—/s/ and /z/— and we have learned to hear them as different. But in Spanish, insofar as both sounds occur, they are members of the same phoneme. A speaker of Spanish learning English will therefore hear *sip* and *zip* as identical words and will have no little trouble learning to tell them apart.

In studying a foreign language we have to pay close attention to allophones. The way in which sounds are grouped into phonemes is sure to be quite different from what it is in English, and the learner has to find out what the system is and practice until he can automatically make the right sounds in the right places. But in studying our own language we can largely ignore the allophones, because our use of them is already automatic, by virtue of our being native speakers of English. We already know when and where to use [k], [ḱ], and [q] and the other allophones of /k/, and so with the allophones of /p/, /l/, /e/, and all the rest.

45. Consonant Phonemes of English

Let us concentrate then on the phonemes of English, beginning with the consonants. English has twenty-four consonant phonemes, sound-bundles which contrast with one another to distinguish between different words. In the following list, key words are given to indicate the sound. Since pronunciation differs in different parts of the country, the key words may occasionally be misleading. But this should give you a general idea. The symbols are those generally used by American linguists.

/p/   The first sound in *poor, pin, prove.*
/t/   The first sound in *take, tin, tree.*
/k/   The first sound in *key, cup, cough.*
/b/   The first sound in *boor, bin, bread.*
/d/   The first sound in *dim, din, dread.*
/g/   The first sound in *give, grim, goose.*
/f/   The first sound in *fine, fin, frame.*
/v/   The first sound in *vine, vim, vale.*
/s/   The first sound in *sip, seal, soul.*
/z/   The first sound in *zip, zeal, zero.*
/š/   The sound spelled *sh* in *shall, smash, shake.*
/ž/   The sound spelled *ge* in *rouge, s* in *treasure, ge* in *garage* (as sometimes pronounced).
/č/   The sound spelled *tch* in *watch* and *ch* in *church.*
/j/   The first sound in *jury, gin, Jack.*
/θ/   The first sound in *theatre, thick, thin.*
/ð/   The first sound in *the, this, then.*
/m/   The first sound in *man, move, mill.*
/n/   The first sound in *new, nudge, near.*

/ŋ/ The last sound in *sing, bang, ring.*
/l/ The first sound in *light, let, laugh.*
/r/ The first sound in *right, reek, roll.*
/y/ The first sound in *you, year, yeast.*
/w/ The first sound in *win, will, witch.*
/h/ The first sound in *hit, him, who.*

46. Vowel Phonemes and Diphthongs

Vowels are a little trickier. English has nine simple vowels plus a number of diphthongs. The key words represent the author's pronunciation. Yours may differ here and there.

/i/ The vowel in *bit, miss, hill.*
/e/ The vowel in *bet, mess, bread.*
/æ/ The vowel in *bat, mass, plaid.*
/ɨ/ A vowel commonly heard in both syllables of *children,* or in the adverb *just* ("He was just here.") This vowel occurs mostly in unstressed syllables.
/ə/ The vowel in *duck, but, flood.* This is also common in unstressed syllables. It occurs in each of the words in "some of the mud."
/a/ The vowel in *not, pot, hot.* (But many people have /ɔ/ in these words.)
/u/ The vowel in *foot, full, put.*
/o/ For some people the vowel in *home* or *whole;* for others this is a diphthong.
/ɔ/ The vowel in *cough, bought, wash.*

English diphthongs are composed of one of the simple vowels followed by a gliding movement of the tongue. Beginning at the position of the vowel the tongue may glide in any of three directions: (1) upward and forward, toward or beyond the position for the vowel /i/; (2) upward and backward, toward or beyond the position for the vowel /u/; (3) toward the position for the central vowel /ə/.

These gliding movements are similar to what happens in the production of some of the consonants. When we pronounce the word *yes*, we begin with the tongue in the position for /i/ and let it glide down to the position for the vowel /e/; it is this gliding motion that produces the *y* sound. Now when we pronounce the word *say*, we produce the vowel /e/ and then let the tongue glide up to the position for /i/. The first sound in *yes* and the last sound in *say* are similar: both are glides and both have to do with the tongue position for /i/. Let us call the first sound in *yes* [y] and the last sound in *say* [ÿ]. [y] and [ÿ] differ in that [y] is a glide away from the /i/ position, and [ÿ] is a glide toward the /i/ position. [y] occurs only before vowels, and [ÿ] occurs only after vowels. The difference between them can therefore never by itself be used to distinguish between different words. We can say consequently that [y] and [ÿ] are allophones of one phoneme, which we write as /y/. For similar reasons, the backward glide is considered an allophone of /w/, and the centering glide is an allophone of /h/, and we use the symbols /y/, /w/, and /h/ after vowels to indicate the English diphthongs.

Since English has nine simple vowels and three different glides, it follows that there are twenty-seven possible diphthongs, thirty-six possible vowel contrasts, taking vowels and diphthongs together. Actually no one speaker of English uses all thirty-six. The average person will use perhaps seven or eight simple vowels and ten or twelve diphthongs. But all thirty-six are not only possible but can be found in regular use in one dialect or another.

We will list here some of the diphthongs that occur widely in America. Again, if your dialect differs from the author's, you may have different phonemes in some of these words.

/iy/   *peel, me, lean, field*
/ey/   *say, hate, train, steak*
/ay/   *smile, I, buy, cry*

/ɔy/   boy, boil, loin, joy
/aw/   house, trout, lout, sound
/uw/   fool, new, tune, you
/ow/   go, groan, blow, rode
/ah/   pa, palm, calm
/ɔh/   saw, flaw, paw

47. Examples of Phonemic Writing

Here are some words written phonemically. This is how they might be pronounced if uttered separately. There would be some differences in connected conversation, and of course they would not be the same in all dialects.

θ = theta
ʒ = this

aim /eym/
write /rayt/
leave /liyv/
leaf /liyf/
blood /bləd/
triumph /trayəmpf/
brought /brɔt/
men /men/
knight /nayt/
jack /jæk/
toes /towz/
wrath /ræθ/
should /šud/
calm /kahm/
length /leŋkθ/

those /ðowz/
thug /θəg/
drip /drip/
fence /fents/
active /æktiv/
church /cɨrc/
rouge /ruwž/
sing /siŋ/
grave /greyv/
banana /bənænə/
walked /wɔkt/
who /huw/
sugar /šɨgər/
cube /kyuwb/
straight /streyt/

Now here is a paragraph as it might be spoken. See if you can read it.

wən mɔrniŋ ðɨs mənθ hwen ay wəz ɔn mə wey tə wərk, ay met ə mæn seliŋ krisməs siylz. ðiyz wərnt ɔrdəneriy krisməs siylz. may, now. ðey wər swimiŋ ərawnd ɨn ə tæŋk ənd dayviŋ fər fiš. ðə mæn səgjestɨd ðət ay bay wən æz ə krisməs prezənt fər may cɨldrɨn, ænd ay mayt əv if ay həd hæd ənəf məniy wiθ miy.

48. Phonemic Spelling and Conventional Spelling

As you see, phonemic writing looks weird and difficult. But the difficulty is more apparent than real, and the strangeness is a commentary on the tremendous gap that has opened between English speech and standard English writing. Phonemic writing is actually quite easy to learn to read, because it is perfectly regular. Each symbol stands for one phoneme and one only. There are no rules, no exceptions, no "i before e" business, or anything of that sort. All one has to remember is the significance of each of the thirty-three letters.

It seems likely that all alphabetic writing begins by being phonemic or nearly so. There is no reason why it should not be. The introducers of the alphabet would not go to the trouble of dreaming up a complicated system when they could just as well do it the easy way and have each letter stand for one sound unit. We can suppose that when the Latin alphabet was first applied to the English language, about A.D. 600, it was used more or less phonemically. Any shortcomings would be a result of the inadequacies of the alphabet rather than of its application. And we assume indeed that the Old English spelling gives a reasonably close idea of the sound of the words.

Since then English spelling has grown steadily worse, as the speech has steadily drifted away from the traditional writing. Our present-day spelling reflects pronunciations of five or six centuries ago rather than those of the present day.

In the past hundred years there have been repeated suggestions that English spelling be reformed, and some very serious efforts have been made to reform it. All of these have come to practically nothing, and we continue to struggle along with the old system. There are certainly serious difficulties in the way of spelling reform. People resist strange things, and you can see yourself how strange phonemic spelling looks when you are used to the old system. Then too, those of us who have already gone through the agony of learning to spell English have a considerable investment in traditional spelling. It would be painful to think that all that effort had been wasted. It has also been pointed out that a spelling reform would cut us off from the literature of the past. You would have to take long and difficult courses to learn to read Shakespeare or even Dickens.

But probably the strongest argument in favor of the old system is that it is standard. Idiotic as it is, it's the same for everybody. There are half a dozen different ways to pronounce the word *card*. You can drop the /r/ or keep it. You can use any of two or three different vowels, with or without glides. All of these pronunciations are respectable and correct somewhere or other. But there is only one respectable and correct way to write the word *card*: c-a-r-d. It is c-a-r-d everywhere in the English-speaking world, no matter how it is pronounced. The result is that, though there is much English speech that you would find difficult or impossible to understand, you can read the English writing of any educated person. We speak English in a thousand different ways, but we all write English in one way.

In time English spelling will probably be reformed. The gap between speech and writing will eventually become too great to be borne, too great for the educational system to cope with. But when it is reformed, it will have to be frozen again. We won't all be able to write as we speak. We shall all have to write the same way, however we speak. If it is decided that *card* should be spelled *ḳard,* it will have to be *ḳard* for those who pronounce it /kærd/ and /kahd/ and /kæhd/ and /kyard/ as well as for those who pronounce it /kard/.

This spelling reform will probably take place about five

hundred years from now. Meanwhile, we have to buckle to and learn the old system.

SUGGESTIONS

1. Read the following:

(1) /pin/	(18) /piŋk/	(35) /rowzɨz/
(2) /græb/	(19) /trɔf/	(36) /əbəv/
(3) /fiš/	(20) /jəj/	(37) /neyšən/
(4) /drap/	(21) /blaws/	(38) /nəkəl/
(5) /riŋ/	(22) /fents/	(39) /kreyvən/
(6) /sayn/	(23) /θruw/	(40) /wɔkt/
(7) /ðen/	(24) /tuwθ/	(41) /skwabəld/
(8) /trayp/	(25) /leŋkθ/	(42) /lɔndriy/
(9) /kliyn/	(26) /muws/	(43) /hwic/
(10) /sneyk/	(27) /maws/	(44) /rəmeynd/
(11) /rak/	(28) /wimɨn/	(45) /rayət/
(12) /rəf/	(29) /məðər/	(46) /əmiybə/
(13) /cəg/	(30) /neybər/	(47) /kreyvd/
(14) /ænt/	(31) /fowniym/	(48) /šɨgər/
(15) /baks/	(32) /pležər/	(49) /məraž/
(16) /bɔyl/	(33) /siŋər/	(50) /šəkɔgow/
(17) /piŋ/	(34) /fiŋgər/	

2. Write the following phonemically, showing your usual pronunciation. Different speakers will differ on some of the words.

(1) man	(13) that	(25) bought
(2) sin	(14) thick	(26) wash
(3) lip	(15) love	(27) seemed
(4) trip	(16) bird	(28) event
(5) fat	(17) write	(29) treasure
(6) pill	(18) right	(30) bear
(7) take	(19) wright	(31) about
(8) gift	(20) tree	(32) physics
(9) might	(21) mope	(33) wriggle
(10) not	(22) blows	(34) chisel
(11) plug	(23) scene	(35) station
(12) tough	(24) knight	(36) matches

(37) blue	(42) glimpse	(47) again
(38) when	(43) garage	(48) chaos
(39) linger	(44) horse	(49) clothes
(40) thistle	(45) hoarse	(50) triumph
(41) hoses	(46) Harvard	

3. The proof that [s] and [z] in English are separate phonemes lies in the fact that we have pairs like [siyl] and [ziyl], words which are exactly alike except that one contains [s] where the other has [z]. [siyl] and [ziyl] are what is called a *minimal pair*. Minimal pairs for [æ] and [e] are *mat/met, laughed/left* ([læft]-[left]), *Hal/hell*. Try to find minimal pairs for the following: [i] and [e], [p] and [b], [d] and [b], [n] and [m], [f] and [v], [l] and [r], [θ] and [ð], [ž] and [š]. (Minimal pairs for the last ones exist, but you will have to be lucky to hit on them.)

4. Try to determine the number of different vowels and diphthongs in your speech by looking for minimal pairs. For example, do you pronounce *bite* and *beat* differently? If so, you have contrasting vowels in these words. How about *bait? But?* How many such contrasts can you find?

5. Speakers of Japanese, learning English, frequently confuse /l/ and and /r/. What does this suggest about the phonemic structure of these sounds in Japanese?

6. If you are studying a foreign language, recount the particular difficulties in pronunciation that you have met. Can you explain these difficulties by contrasts between the sound structure of English and that of your new language?

7. Write a paper making one of the following arguments: (1) English spelling should be reformed; (2) English spelling should not be reformed.

8

How Do You
Spell Ghoti?
fi sh

49. The Unavoidable Problem of Spelling

Anyway you look at it, English spelling is a mess. A system which puts up with pairs like *fine* and *sign, no* and *know, smile* and *aisle, through* and *cough* is a system which falls considerably short of perfection. It has been suggested that a reasonable spelling for the word *fish* would be "ghoti": *gh* as in *rough, o* as in *women, ti* as in *nation.* This example exaggerates the difficulties, but certainly the difficulties are serious.

They are not only serious but unavoidable. The one thing demanded of anyone who pretends to be educated is that he be able to spell. Your arithmetic can be lousy, your knowledge of history and economics can be zero, you can be totally ignorant of the difference between a molecule and an amoeba, and still you can get along. But if you can't spell, you're in trouble every time you pick up a pencil. Of all writing errors, none stand out like mistakes in spelling. Dangle a modifier or split an infinitive, and chances are nobody will notice; but spell *separate* "seperate" and people call you illiterate.

Perhaps the trouble is that English spelling is not quite bad enough. If it were a little worse, nobody could manage it, and we would either reform it or all be bad spellers together. As it is, enough people can learn to spell English to make things hard for those who can't. What makes good spellers good and

poor spellers poor is hard to say. Differences in visual memory
no doubt exist and have a bearing. Experience plays a part;
people who read and write a good deal are apt to be better
spellers than those who don't. Whatever the reasons, the
range of spelling ability in any group of people is likely to be
very wide.

Poor spellers can be divided into two groups: those who try
to improve and those who do not. The latter are exhibiting a
very normal reaction. They are up against a problem that they
see no obvious way of solving, and so they rationalize. They
tell themselves, reasonably enough, that spelling after all isn't
everything. Surely a person can be a poor speller and still be
wise, lovable, and keenly intelligent. Pretty soon they begin
not only to confess their inability to spell but rather to boast
of it, contriving to suggest that any clod can learn to spell but
that only the superior sort, like them, can do the things really
worth doing.

As self-protection this is all very well, and perhaps it is to be
recommended from the medical point of view. But it is no
real solution. You can expatiate all you want on the triviality
of spelling and explain till you're breathless how you demonstrate your excellence on a higher plane. Still if you spell *separate* "seperate," people who spell it "separate" will think
you're a jerk, and don't think they won't.

50. Solving the Problem

The difficulties of English spelling have caused various interesting convulsions in the American education system. A
few decades ago some educators, impressed by the chaotic relationship between sound and symbol, advocated the abandon-
ing of any attempt to show such relationship, and suggested
that children be taught to read words as units, not trying to
sound them out as had formerly been done. (The reformers

ANALYSIS OF SOUNDS

IN THE

ENGLISH LANGUAGE.

Language or Speech is the utterance of articulate sounds or voices, rendered significant by usage, for the expression and communication of thoughts.

Articulate sounds are those which are formed by opening and closing the organs. The closing of the organs is an articulation or jointing, as in *eb, ed, et*. The articulations are represented by the letters called *consonants*. The sounds made with the organs open, are called vowels, as *a, e, o*.

Sounds constitute the *spoken* language, addressed to the *ear*; letters or characters, representing sounds, constitute *written* language, which is presented to the eye.

The letters of a language, arranged in a certain order, compose what is called an *Alphabet*.

The English Alphabet consists of twenty-six letters, or single characters—a, b, c, d, e, f, g, h, i, j, k, l, m, n, o, p, q, r, s, t, u, v, w, x, y, z. The compounds *ch, sh, th*, and *ng* are also used to represent distinct sounds; and another sound is expressed by *si*, or *z*, as in *brasier, azure*, pronounced *brazher, azhur*.

Of the foregoing letters, *a, e, o*, are always vowels; *i* and *u* are vowels or diphthongs; *w* is also a vowel; and *y* is either a vowel, a diphthong, or a consonant.

A, has five sounds, as in late, ask, ball, hat, what.

E, has three sounds, as in mete, met, prey.

I, has three sounds, as in pine, pit, fatigue.

O, has four sounds, as in note, not, move, dove.

U, has three sounds, as in truth, but, bush.

Y, has two sounds, as in chyle, pity.

The sounds of the vowels most generally used, are the *long* and the *short*.

Examples of the first or long sound.	*Examples of the second or short sound.*
a in make, fate, grace.	a in mat, band, grand.
e in me, mete, meter.	e in bet, men, send.
i in pine, bind, strife.	i in bit, pin, wish.
o in note, hold, post.	o in not, boss, bond.
u in true, duty, rude.	u in dun, must, fund.
y in dry, defy, ply.	y in pity, cyst, cylinder.

The long sound of *a* in *late*, when shortened, coincides nearly with that of *e* in *let*.

The long *e*, when shortened, coincides with the short *i* in *pit*, as in *feet, fit*. This short sound of *i* is that of *y* unaccented, at the end of words, as in *glory*.

The short sound of broad *a* in *hall*, is that of short *o* in *holly*, and of *a* in *what*.

Page from Noah Webster, *The Elementary Spelling Book.*

The short sound of *oo* in *pool*, is that of *u* in *pull*, and *oo* in *wool*.

The short sound of *o* in *not*, is somewhat lengthened before *r, s, th,* and *ng,* as in *nor, cross, broth, belong.*

The articulations represented by the consonants are best understood by placing a vowel before them in pronunciation; thus, eb, ed, ef, eg, ek, el, em, en, ep, er, es, et, ev, ez.

Those articulations which wholly interrupt the voice, are called *close,* or *mute,* as eb, ed, eg, ek, ep, et. Those which do not entirely interrupt the voice, are called semi-vowels, as ef, el, em, en, er, es, ev, ez, eth.

Those articulations which are formed by the lips, are called *labials,* as eb, ef, em, ep, ev.

Those which are formed by the tip of the tongue and the teeth, are called *dentals,* as ed, et, eth.

Those which are formed by the tongue and palate, are called *palatals,* as eg, ek, eng.

The letters *s* and *z* are called also sibilants or hissing letters.

B and *p* represent one and the same articulation, or jointing of the lips; but *p* indicates a closer pressure of the lips, which instantly stops all sound.

D and *t* stand for one and the same articulation, which is a pressure of the tongue against the gum at the root of the upper teeth; but *t* stands for a closer articulation than *d,* and stops all sound.

F and *v* stand for one and the same articulation, the upper teeth placed on the under lip; but *f* indicates an aspiration or expulsion of breath without sound; *v,* with sound.

Th in *think* and in *that* represent one and the same articulation; the former with aspiration; the latter with sound.

S and *z* stand for one and the same articulation, attended with hissing; *s* without sound; *z* with sound.

Sh and *zh* have the same distinction as *s* and *z,* aspirated and vocal; but *zh* not occurring in English words, the sound is represented by *si* or other letters; as in *fusion, osier, azure.*

Ng represent the articulation of the body of the tongue with the roof of the mouth. In certain words, as in *sing,* the articulation is moderately close, with a nasal sound; in other words, as in *finger,* the pressure is more close, stopping all sound. A closer pressure is represented by *nk,* as in *bank.* The difference is obvious in *bang, anger, bank,* but the articulation is the same in all cases. See Section 139.

The sounds of *ch* in *church, sh* in *shine,* and *th* in *think* and *thou,* are simple sounds for which the language has no single characters.

B has one sound only, as in *bite;* and after *m* is mute, as in *dumb.*

C has the sound of *k* before *a, o,* and *u,* as in *cat, cot, cup;* and of *s* before *e, i,* and *y,* as in *cell, cit, cycle.* It may be considered as mute before *k,* as in *sick, thick.*

D has one sound only, as in *day, bid.*

F has one sound only, as in *life, fever,* except in *of,* in which it has the sound of *v.*

G before *a, o,* and *u,* is a close palatal articulation, as in *gave, go, gun;* but before *e, i,* and *y,* it is sometimes a close articulation, and sometimes it has a compound sound, like *j,* as in *gem, gin, gyves.*

H is a mark of breathing or aspiration.

Page from Noah Webster, *The Elementary Spelling Book.*

were thinking not only of spelling difficulties but also of the fact that readers *do* read words as units, not as successions of letters.) The new method didn't produce any very good results, and it had some bad ones, so it was gradually modified. In quite recent years it has been violently attacked as the reason American children can't read and write. But actually the attackers were kicking a horse that was nearly dead. Most primary teachers had long since gone back to coping as well as they could with English sounds and their symbolization.

The plain fact is that nobody—certainly not the author of this book—has any very startling suggestions to offer to the poor speller. One must begin by recommending difficult and tiresome virtues: persistence, industry, patience. Spelling may always be a problem for you and sometimes an embarrassment. But surely you can get a lot better than you are if you try.

One can also recommend that you observe that there is *some* relationship between sound and spelling, that you note the relationship, and that you let it help you wherever it can. Obviously it won't help you always. There is nothing in the sound of the word that would clue one to the *g* in *sign* or the *k* in *knowledge* or the first *a* in *separate*. On the other hand, only those who pay no attention at all to sound-symbol relationships can spell *hurrying* "hurring" or *dined* "dinned."

In studying the connections between sounds and symbols, we have one advantage not formerly enjoyed: we know what the sounds are. Only a few years ago no one could have said how many vowels and consonants there are in English speech. Now linguists pretty well agree on twenty-four consonant phonemes and nine vowel phonemes. The system of symbolizing them is as complicated as ever, but at least we can see both sides of the relationship and are thus able to make a description.

We will try here to get an idea of the ways in which English sounds are symbolized. A great and central difficulty is that sounds vary from dialect to dialect. Some people pronounce *hot*/hat/ and some pronounce it /hɔt/. In order to keep the description from becoming staggeringly—instead of merely appallingly—complex, the illustrations are limited to the dialect of the author, a Californian. This dialect is widespread and respectable, but there is certainly no wish to suggest that it is better than other dialects. Some speakers will have to adjust some of the statements to fit the facts of their dialects. Differences will be most common in the vowels.

In reading the following, one must make a constant effort to distinguish sound from symbol. Phonemes and words represented phonemically are written between diagonal lines. Letters of the standard alphabet and words represented in standard spelling are given in italic type.

51. The Symbolization of /p/, /t/, /b/, /d/, /m/, /n/, /l/

Seven of the twenty-four consonant phonemes in English are rather simply represented in standard writing. These are the phonemes /p/, /t/, /b/, /d/, /m/, /n/, and /l/. The standard letters are the same as the phonemic symbols: *p, t, b, d, m, n, l*:

/p/   *pit, mope, people*
/t/   *tame, loot, stuck*
/b/   *be, sob, robin*
/d/   *dirt, raid, sadist*
/m/   *me, Sam, rhyme*
/n/   *nice, loan, land*
/l/   *lad, pale, value*

All seven of these letters are regularly doubled under certain conditions. When suffixes beginning with a vowel—like *able, ed, ing*—are added to words ending in one of these sounds, the letter is doubled if a simple vowel sound immediately precedes. It is not doubled if a diphthong precedes. Thus we have pairs like *hopping* /hapiŋ/ and *hoping* /howpiŋ/. Notice that the *p-pp* contrast indicates a difference in the pronunciation of the *vowel*, not the consonant.

Here are some more pairs. Study them. Awareness of the system may save you from many spelling errors:

copped /kapt/	*coped* /kowpt/
capper /kæpər/	*caper* /keypər/
written /ritɨn/	*writing* /raytɨŋ/
tubby /təbiy/	*Toby* /towbiy/
bedded /bedɨd/	*bided* /baydɨd/
scrammed /skræmd/	*screamed* /skriymd/
planned /plænd/	*planed* /pleynd/
walling /wɔliŋ/	*wailing* /weyliŋ/

52. /g/ and /r/

The sound /g/ is regularly represented by the letter *g*, although this letter is used for other sounds too. Thus we have *get, sag, regal.*

The sound /r/ is generally indicated by *r: roam, roar, cry.* But in a number of words from Old English, /r/ is written *wr: write, wrench, wren.* In some words from Greek the spelling is *rh: rhetoric, rheostat, rhyme.* Another complication for /r/ is that many American speakers do not pronounce it in words like *car, card, fire.*

Like the letters for the seven sounds previously discussed, *g* and *r* are doubled before suffixes to show a preceding simple vowel: *tugged* /təgd/, *scarred* /skard/. Compare the sounds of *scarred* and *scared.*

53. /k/

The sound /k/ has a fairly complicated symbolization. Before the sounds /r/, /l/, and /y/ and before all vowels and diphthongs except /i/, /e/, /ay/, and /iy/, the usual symbol is *c: cry, clam, cute* /kyuwt/, *cat, cot, cut, coot* /kuwt/, *coat* /kowt/. Before /i/, /e/, /ay/, and /iy/ the usual symbol is *k: kit, keg, kite* /kayt/, *keen* /kiyn/. In the middle and at the end of words, the common symbol is *ck* after simple vowels: *back, buck.* After diphthongs the usual spelling is *k* or *ke: poke* /powk/, *pike* /payk/, *peek* /piyk/. Note the pairs *picking* and *peeking, tacking* and *taking.*

In the adjective ending /ik/ the symbol is *c: tragic, dramatic.* In some words borrowed from Greek, /k/ is represented by *ch: Christmas, archaic.*

The combination /ks/ is often spelled *x: sox, Oxford, expel* /ekspel/. The combination /kw/ is regularly spelled *qu: quick, quarrel, question.* This is practically the only use of the letter *q* in English.

54. /f/ and /v/

The sound /f/ is most frequently written *f: fine, after, soften.* At the end of words it is *ff* after simple vowels and *fe* after diphthongs: *scoff* /skɔf/, *life* /layf/. But there are also some peculiar ways of writing /f/. The spelling *gh* stood for a velar sound no longer occurring in English. In some words this sound disappeared. In others it became /f/, and in these words *gh* is still used to spell /f/: *cough, rough, tough.* In a large number of words borrowed from Greek, /f/ is represented by *ph: phone, physics, prophet.*

The sound /v/ is regularly *v: veil, rover, prove. v* is not doubled after simple vowels: *having, lover.*

55. /s/ and /z/

The sound /s/ is another complicated one. The most common symbol is /s/: *sin, sack, wrestle* /resəl/. But before the sounds /e/, /i/, and /iy/ the symbol may be either *s* or *c;*

thus we have pairs like *cellar* and *seller, sent* and *cent, symbol* and *cymbal*. In some words borrowed from Greek, /s/ is represented by *sc: scene, scent, scion* /sayən/. In the middle and at the end of words /s/ is usually represented by *ss* if a simple vowel precedes: *miss, mess*. If a diphthong precedes, /s/ is written *ce* or *se: mice* /mays/, *lease* /liys/. The combination /ks/ is often represented by *x: box*.

The representation of /z/ has got pretty well mixed up with that of /s/. At the beginning of words the regular symbol is *z: zip, zeal, zero*. In the middle of words it is either *s* or *z: miser* /mayzər/, *lazy* /leyziy/. Note pairs like *raise* and *raze*. The plural ending of regular nouns is /z/ after voiced sounds. This is written *s: toes* /towz/, *bags* /bægz/.

56. /š/ and /ž/

The sound /š/ is usually written with the letters *sh: shook, fish, push, crushing*. However, words like *pernicious, nation, mission* illustrate other ways of spelling /š/.

The sound /ž/, not a very common consonant in English, is written either *ge*, as in *rouge* /ruwž/ or *beige* /bež/ or *s* as in *pleasure* /pležər/ or *vision* /vižən/.

57. /č/ and /j/

The sound /č/ is most commonly spelled *ch* at the beginning of words: *chin, child, church*. At the end of words both *ch* and *tch* occur: *watch, match, rich, church*.

The sound /j/ is spelled variously *j, g,* and *dg. j* is used chiefly at the beginning of words: *jug, jail, juice. g* is used for this sound before /i/, /e/, and /ər/: *gem* /jem/, *gin* /jin/, *germ* /jirm/. However, there isn't much regularity; we have both *gist* and *gift, jelly* and *gelid*. In other positions, *dge* is a common spelling for /j/ after simple vowels: *judge, bridge, cadge. ge* is used after diphthongs: *siege, stooge, cage* /keyj/.

58. /θ/ and /ð/

The sounds /θ/ and /ð/ are both represented by the spelling *th*. This foolishness was the contribution of French scribes writing in English after the Norman Conquest. Examples of /θ/ are *thin, both, teeth;* of /ð/, *the, then, this, rather.* At the end of words /θ/ and /ð/ are usually distinguished by writing *th* for /θ/ and *the* for /ð/: *breath* /breθ/, *breathe* /briyð/; *mouth* /mawθ/, *mouthe* /mawð/.

In English writing the letters *th* stand for the sounds /th/ only in compound words, like *fatheaded.*

59. /ŋ/

The sound /ŋ/ is also represented in English by two letters —*ng: sing, hang, long.* In some words, however, *ng* stands for the sounds /ŋg/: *linger* /liŋgər/; compare this with *singer* /siŋər/. Before /k/, /ŋ/ is represented by the letter *n: sink* /siŋk/; probably no one would pronounce this /sink/.

60. /y/, /w/, and /h/

The consonant /y/ is most commonly written *y* at the beginning of words: *you, yet, youth.* But in some words in which the diphthong /uw/ follows, the letter *u* stands for /y/ plus the diphthong: *use* /yuwz/, *union.* The letter *u* may also stand for /yuw/ after /k/, /b/, /p/, /m/, /f/, /h/: *cute* /kyuwt/, *bugle, putrid, mule, fuel, huge.* Then there are special combinations like *beauty* /byuwtiy/, *view* /vyuw/, *feud* /fyuwd/. For many speakers vowel letters will stand for /yuw/ also after /t/, /d/, /n/: *tune* /tyuwn/, *duty* /dyuwtiy/, *new* /nyuw/.

In the middle of words /y/ is often written *i: onion* /ənyən/, *bunion, million.*

The consonant /w/ is generally written *w: wait, will, wife.*

In some words the combination /wə/ is rendered by the letter *o: one* /wən/, *once* /wənts/. The combination /kw/ *is* written *qu: quick, quack, quake.*

The consonant /h/, which in English occurs only at the beginning of syllables, is usually written *h: hit, hope, ham.* In some words it is written *wh: whole* /howl/, *who* /huw/. On the other hand, the letters *wh* very commonly represent the sequence /hw/: *which* /hwic/, *white* /hwayt/.

As we saw in Section 46, /y/, /w/, and /h/ occur not only as consonants but as the second element in diphthongs. Their symbolization as the glide in diphthongs is described in Section 64.

61. Silent Letters

Many of the consonant letters in English don't stand for any sounds at all. Among these "silent letters," as they are called, are the *k* of *knuckle, knee, know;* the *gh* of *brought, through, though;* the *l* of *balm, calm, would;* the *b* of *debt, doubt, crumb;* the *th* of *asthma.*

62. Vowels

Thus we see that the English system of representing consonant sounds is rather complicated. The vowels are worse. We can look only at some of the main variations.

An important feature to notice is the way in which simple vowels in general are distinguished from diphthongs in general. A doubled consonant letter indicates that the preceding vowel letter stands for a simple vowel, not a diphthong. This was illustrated earlier, but here are some more examples:

quitting /kwitiŋ/   *requiting* /riykwaytiŋ/
sloppy /slapiy/   *slopy* /slowpiy/
lopped /lapt/   *loped* /lowpt/

These are words with suffixes. In simple words, the diphthong is shown by a silent *e* after the consonant, the simple vowel by the absence of the *e:*

diphthong

rod /rad/	*rode* /rowd/
hat /hæt/	*hate* /heyt/
sit /sit/	*site* /sayt/
grip /grip/	*gripe* /grayp/

But there are exceptions: we spell /gɔn/ *gone*, not *gon*. And there are many other ways of writing both simple vowels and diphthongs.

63. Simple Vowels

The vowel /i/ is usually written *i: slip, mitt, kiss.* In some words from Greek the letter is *y: abyss, bicycle.* Then we have aberrations like the *ee* in *been* /bin/ and the *ai* in *again* /əgin/ (for those who pronounce it that way).

The letter for the sound /e/ is usually *e: bed, met, debt.* But *ea* is also common: *bread, ready, head.* In the word /sed/ the spelling is *ai: said.* In /eniy/ and /meniy/ it is *a: any, many.* In some words from Greek it is *ae: aesthete* /esθiyt/.

The vowel /æ/ is usually written *a: hat, smack, graft.* But *ai* occurs for this vowel in *plaid* and *au* in *laugh.*

Barred i—/ɨ/—a high central vowel, does not occur very commonly in stressed syllables except before /r/, where it *before "r"* may be represented by various vowel letters: *sir, girl, her, world, curdle.* It also occurs in the stressed syllables of *sugar* and *children.*

/ʌ/

The vowel /ə/, which is called *schwa,* is common in both stressed and unstressed syllables. In stressed syllables the most common letter is *u: but, mud, club.* The letters *oo* are also used: *blood, flood.* In the word /wəz/ the letter is *a: was. ou* renders /ə/ in *trouble.*

The vowel /a/, as it occurs in the author's dialect, is generally written o: hot /hat/, spot /spat/. Sometimes the spelling is a: father, far.

The sound /u/ is commonly spelled either u or oo. We have u for this sound in put, full, puss, oo in foot, look, book. We write ou for /u/ in would and should.

The sound /o/, in those dialects in which it occurs as a simple vowel, is usually spelled o: whole /hol/, home /hom/. Most people, however, would pronounce these words with diphthongs: /howl/, /howm/.

The sound /ɔ/ occurs in the author's dialect in such words as all, wash, lost, cost, cross, and thus is represented by a and o. For a number of words the spelling is au: assault, auto, bauble. In others aw occurs: awkward, bawdy. In still others the spelling is ou: bought.

64. Diphthongs

English diphthongs, as we have seen earlier, are often represented by a single vowel, followed by a single consonant, followed by "silent e." Such are bone /bown/, pine /payn/, pane /peyn/, tune /tuwn/, rode /rowd/. But not all of the diphthongs can be represented in this way, and all diphthongs have various other spellings.

The dipthong /iy/ is occasionally written with e plus silent e: cede, mete, scene. More commonly it is written with a combination of two letters. We have ee in meet, seen, greet, sleep, bee; ea in meat, beach, scream, lean; ie in field, belief, chief, shield; ei in ceiling, seize, weird, inveigle. Sometimes it is rendered by the letter e alone: he, me, be, abstemious. Then there are peculiarities like the ae in anaemic or the oe in amoeba.

The diphthong ey is frequently written with the letter a plus silent e: same, name, lake, ache. The combinations ai and *ay* are also common: *plain, raid, pail* and *way, day, gray.* Less common is *ey,* as in *obey* or *abeyance.*

The diphthong /ay/ may be written with *i* plus silent *e: fine, pile, ride, crime.* In words with silent *g* or silent *gh* there is no silent *e: sign, align, light, bright.* When the syllable begins with /g/, the spelling *ui* occurs: *guide, beguile.* When the diphthong /ay/ is the last sound in the word, it is usually spelled *y* or *uy: sky, cry, guy, buy.*

The diphthong /ɔy/ is regularly spelled *oi* or *oy: boil, adenoids, joint* and *boy, coy, annoy.*

The diphthong /aw/ is spelled *ou* and *ow: house, out, loud* and *town, gown, how, plow.* In some words borrowed from German the spelling is *au: ablaut.*

The diphthong /uw/ is variously rendered. The spelling *u* plus silent *e* occurs in *crude, rude, tune* /tuwn/. (But many speakers pronounce the last word in other ways.) It is spelled *o* plus silent *e* in *move* and *prove.* We have also several combinations of letters: *oo* in *soon, croon, tooth, boo; ue* in *blue, true, hue* /hyuw/; *ew* in *new, stew, few* /fyuw/; *ou* in *amour, acoustics, bivouac, through.*

The writing of the diphthong /ow/ is also complicated. The letter *o* plus silent *e* occurs frequently: *hope, poke, phone.* The letter *o* without the silent *e* renders /ow/ when *ld* follows: *bold, old, scold.* This diphthong is also written with combinations: *oa* in *moan, float, croak; ow* in *blow, snow, crow; ou* in *boulder, shoulder, though.*

One can perhaps see why educators have at times been tempted to give up trying to show the child relationships between sounds and letters. Even if we limit the view to fairly common words and make no attempt to list all the exceptions, the correspondence is very complex. Remember too that the description here is based on one dialect only—the author's. Other speakers may have a different relationship to learn, other diphthongs which the letters stand for, and so on. To be sure, it is wrong to say that there is *no* connection between sound and spelling. You can't write the sound /uw/ with just any letter of the alphabet. You can't write it with *k* or *p* or *a*, for example. But you can write with *u, u-e, oo, ou, ew, o-e,* or *ough.*

65. A Summary of Letter-Sound Relationships

We have been looking at the relationship from sound to letter—taking each sound and seeing how it may be written. By way of summary, let us do it the other way, listing the sounds the letters may stand for. We will take the consonant letters first and then the vowels and the vowel combinations.

b   /b/ in *sob, big; rube*
     silent in *debt, doubt, tomb*

c   /k/ in *cat, tragic, scoot*
     /s/ in *cell, ceiling, cent*
     /š/ in *precious, pernicious, precocious*

d   /d/ in *dumb, radio, sled*
     /t/ in *walked, slapped, missed*

f   /f/ in *fry, often, affable*

g   /g/ in *get, brag, buggy*
     /j/ in *general, gypsy, genial*
     /ž/ in *rouge, beige, mirage*
     silent in *sign, align, benign*

h   /h/ in *he, house, rehearse*
     silent in *honor, honest, hour*

j   /j/ in *jelly, Jim, jug*

k   /k/ in *kiss, kept, shake*
     silent in *know, knee, knuckle*

l /l/ in *leave, well, meddle*
silent in *would, palm, calm*

m /m/ in *mad, scream, timid*

n /n/ in *need, grand, tin*
/ŋ/ in *sink, think, prank*
silent in *autumn, column, hymn*

p /p/ in *sap, pass, rapid*
silent in *psalm, psychology, pseudonym*

q /k/ in *quit, quick, squalid*

r /r/ in *run, eraser, torpid*

s /s/ in *say, rascal, miss*
/z/ in *raise, goes, dreams*
/š/ in *mission, fissure, session*
/ž/ in *treasure, pleasure, measure*

t /t/ in *tin, stuck, last*
/š/ in *patience, ration, caution*

v /v/ in *vase, prove, save*

w /w/ in *was, wish, swoon*

x /ks/ in *ox, exit, lexicon*
/gz/ in *example, exist, exaggerate*

y /y/ in *young, year, beyond*

z /z/ in *crazy, maze, zero*

ch /k/ in *character, archaeology, monarch*
/c/ in *chap, parch, churn*
/š/ in *machine, chic, chivalry*

ck /k/ in *pack, luck, click*

dg /j/ in *sledge, badge, lodge*

gh /f/ in *cough, rough, tough*
silent in *through, bought, bough*

ng /ŋ/ in *cling, bang, ringer*

ph   /f/ in *phobia, philosophy, phoneme*

sc   /sk/ in *scout, scant, scoot*
       /s/ in *scene, scion, coalesce*

sh   /š/ in *shout, smash, rush*

th   /θ/ in *thick, theatre, booth*
       /ð/ in *these, than, smoothe*

wh   /hw/ in *whine, whistle, which*
       /h/ in *who, whose, whom*

a   /æ/ in *back, hat, gamble*
       /a/ in *are, hard, want*
       /ɔ/ in *all, bald, wash*
       /ə/ in *was, above, assist*
       /e/ in *any, many*
       /ey/ in *able, race, late*

e   /e/ in *bed, get, left*
       /ɨ/ in *abbess, goatless, roses*
       /ə/ in *evict, exact, talker*
       /iy/ in *be, he, scene*
       silent in *talked, parked, climbed*
       silent but indicating a preceding diphthong in *race, time,
         blame*

i   /i/ in *pin, miss, quick*
       /ɨ/ in *children, bird, walking*
       /ə/ in *possible, responsible, terrify*
       /ay/ in *side, mile, quite*

o   /ə/ in *abbot, money, some*
       /a/ in *not, plod, dodge*
       /ɔ/ in *horrible, cost, shore*
       /ow/ in *rode, ago, nose*

u   /ə/ in *but, rum, stuck*
       /u/ in *full, put, bull*
       /uw/ in *truth, plume, assume*
       /yuw/ in *use, cube, ambiguity*

y   /i/ in *cymbal, syllable, tyrannical*
    /ay/ in *rhyme, pyre, gyrate*
    /iy/ in *silly, lady, cozy*

ai /ey/ in *plain, trail, raise*
    /e/ in *said, again*

au /ɔ/ in *saunter, taught, gaudy*

aw /ɔ/ in *bawdy, tawdry, awkward*

ay /ey/ in *say, play, tray*

ea /e/ in *ready, dead, bread*
    /iy/ in *leaf, beam, real*
    /ey/ in *steak, break*

ee /iy/ in *flee, agreed, sleep*

ei /iy/ in *seize, inveigle, weird*
    /ey/ in *neighbor, weight, rein*

eu /yuw/ in *euchre, eulogy, feud*

ew /uw/ in *chew, grew, strew*
    /yuw/ in *few, pew, mews*

ey /ey/ in *obey, convey, abeyance*
    /iy/ in *alley, holley, valley*

ie /iy/ in *field, siege, shield*

oa /ow/ in *goat, moan, road*

oi /ɔy/ in *toil, loin, joint*

oo /uw/ in *soon, hoot, poor*
    /ə/ in *flood, blood*
    /u/ in *hoof, foot, look*

ou /aw/ in *house, trout, about*
    /ɔ/ in *thought, bought, trough*
    /u/ in *would, should*

ow /ow/ in *flow, shown, arrow*
    /aw/ in *down, crowd, how*

oy   /ɔy/ in *boy, annoy, coy*

ue   /uw/ in *accrue, blue, avenue*
      /yuw/ in *argue, imbue, barbecue*

66. Advice and Comfort

The question is, what can the poor speller do in the face of this complexity? There are several things. The first is simply to become generally conscious of the relationship of sound to spelling. See what the possibilities are, and don't go beyond them. There is some excuse for spelling *crowd* "croud" or *malign* "maline" or *feud* "fued." But there is none for spelling *marrying* "marring" or *imagine* "imangine."

Secondly, notice that there are various patterns threading through the system. We have noticed the *a-e, o-e, u-e* pattern, where the final *e* indicates a diphthong preceding. Awareness of this will keep you from spelling "plum" when you mean *plume* or "stope" when you mean *stop.* Notice that *ay* and *oy* occur only at the end of root syllables, that in the middle we use *ai* or *oi* or some other combination instead. That is, we would never spell anything like "boyl" or anything like "plai."

Probably the best procedure for most people is *not* to memorize sixty pages of spelling rules. It is not only easier but more efficacious to read casually through such an account as is given in this chapter and then simply to try to notice these things as they occur in written English.

Observe that many of the variations are quite special— really exceptional exceptions. It would be hard to find a word in which *o* stands for /i/ except the word *women.* Learn how to spell *women,* and you have that problem licked. There are not very many words in which *ei* represents the sound /ey/. *k* is silent only before /n/.

Finally, recognize the fact that you're not confronted with

the task of learning to spell all the words in the English language. In the first place, you don't use them all; nobody does. Then, many of the difficult ones you don't use very often— say twice a year or so. It is usually possible to look up such words in a dictionary when the need for them arises, and it is no particular strain to do so.

Of the words that you do use frequently, surely you can spell most correctly already. You are a very bad speller indeed if you misspell more than 5 percent of the different words you write. Probably it is much less than that. So actually your spelling problem will turn out to be centered on a few score of words, at most a few hundred. This is no insuperable difficulty.

The first thing is to find out which words are bothering you. Make a list of the words that are corrected on your English papers. Note the ones that you are always having to look up in a dictionary. Get them out where you can look at them.

Next observe just where you are going wrong. It won't be the whole word that is troubling you usually, but just some point in it. It will be a question of whether to use *e* or *a,* whether to double a consonant, and so on. Some of the words will fit into common patterns. If you have noted the effect of doubled consonants, you should be able to stop writing *pinned* when you mean *pined* and *pined* when you mean *pinned.*

Learn to take words apart to see what they are made of. Learn to notice prefixes and suffixes. If you can spell *appoint,* there is no reason why you can't spell *disappoint.* If you can spell *mission,* you should be able to spell *commission.*

For some few words, learning is simply a matter of brute memory. They fit no pattern; their spelling makes no sense. But even with these there is an easy way and a hard way. The hard way is to write the correct spelling fifty times or to recite it a hundred. This is not only time-consuming but also not very useful. What usually happens is that the word begins to seem grotesque and formless after a dozen or so repetitions. The easy way is to make some association that will help you remember. This is the main trade-trick of memory experts, and there is nothing very occult about it. It is based on the fact that it is much easier to remember something if you can put a handle on it than if you try to recall it all by itself.

The association doesn't have to be complicated. Suppose the word you want to learn is *repetition*. Suppose your doubt is whether to spell it "repetition" or "repitition." Think of *pet*. Think of the word *repetition* and, say, a pet dog at the same time. This is all you have to do, and if you do it, you'll be nine times as likely to remember the correct spelling the next time. Of course, you can make it fancier if you like. You can tell yourself that *repetition* is your pet difficulty or that your pet dog Rover is nothing but a repetition of trouble. But the association doesn't have to be very clever or even meaningful. Just any old association will do.

Take another one: *indispensable*. The question is likely to be whether to write *a* or *i* in the suffix. Think of *able* and say that you are not able to dispense with the *a*. Or take *irresistible,* another *a-i* problem. Say, "i am irresistible."

Many of these association tricks are old-timers, used by many people, and in the repertoire of every primary school teacher. Here are a few well-known ones:

> *separate*   There's a rat in *separate*.
> *cemetery*   There's a lot of ease in the cemetery.
> *villain*   There was a villain living in the villa.
> *grammar*   Misspelling this will mar any English paper.
> *environment*   The trouble is in the iron usually.
> *piece*   Have a piece of pie.

And so on. Find the words that bother you and make your own associations.

SUGGESTIONS

1. Make a list of twenty pairs like *pined/pinned, caned/canned,* showing the significance of the doubled consonant.

2. Make a list of twenty pairs like *claimed/clammed, steamed/stemmed.*

3. Make a list of thirty pairs like *rob/robe, trip/tripe,* showing the significance of the silent *e.*

4. Choose ten words that you have misspelled in the past, and work out for them memory associations like those suggested at the end of Section 66.

5. Find twenty examples of silent letters like the *k* in *knuckle* or the *b* in *doubt.* Don't duplicate examples given in this chapter.

6. From your file of corrected papers, cull all the words that have been misspelled. Write them out first in phonemic and then in standard spelling. Divide them into two groups: one for which the sound gives some clue to the standard spelling; one for which it doesn't.

7. To each set of three examples in Section 65, add one example of your own.

9
Something That Ends with a Period

67. The Sentence

Next to spelling, the most difficult and persistent problem facing anyone learning to write English involves the unit that we call the sentence. From our first writing exercises, back in primary school, we must cope with the fact that English is not written as a continuous mass (as some languages are) but as a succession of segments marked off from one another by the fact that each segment begins with a capital letter and ends with a period. Part of the student's task is to learn how to identify such segments in the stream of English—to learn, in other words, what a sentence is. For many students this is no easy matter.

Neither has it been particularly easy for scholars to say what a sentence is. Many grammarians and philosophers in the past few centuries have turned their thoughts to the problem and have found that it grows more difficult and slippery the more they think about it. There have been more than two hundred definitions of the sentence advanced. Most of these are of little help to the student whose simple and modest wish is to punctuate his English theme satisfactorily, and none of them are without serious logical difficulties.

In quite recent years some light has been thrown on the problem by scholars who have studied not writing but speech.

It can be shown that speech—or at least English speech—is punctuated much as writing is. It is punctuated by a set of pitch patterns—rise and fall of the voice—which coördinate in various ways with the rest of the structure in our utterances. These patterns are complicated. We cannot say, for example, that we have a speech sentence every time the voice falls. Sometimes we do, and sometimes we don't. But however complicated, the patterns are there, and they have a connection with the patterns of writing. Presumably it was the existence of these pitch patterns that moved our ancestors to begin writing in sentences—that is, to mark off segments of the writing with a capital letter at the beginning and a period at the end.

Unfortunately there is nothing in the new studies, any more than in the old, which leads us to a nice short, easily memorized, easily applicable definition of the sentence. All short definitions of the sentence are either untrue or impractical or both. It may be of some interest—and possibly of some use— to look at a few of the definitions of the sentence and to see what their difficulties are.

68. Some Definitions

Perhaps the most familiar definition is this one: "A sentence is a group of words which expresses a complete thought." It will be seen that this depends entirely on the meaning of "complete thought," and the meaning of "complete thought" is not as obvious as it might seem. If we take a group of words like "Flowers bloom in the spring," we might all agree that the thought is complete. The group of words makes a statement sufficient to itself, not depending on any other group of words.

But suppose we have an utterance like "He didn't have any." Is this complete or not? Presumably it is not, for if we were to hear it by itself we could get no sufficient meaning from it. We should have to ask, "Who is he?" and "Any what?" The utterance would be altogether dependent on other utterances preceding or following it. Yet this stretch of words—"He didn't have any"—is undoubtedly a sentence, in the sense that writers of English would have no hesitation in writing it with a capital letter at the beginning and a period at the end.

Thus the words "complete thought" in this definition cannot mean logically complete. For the logically complete thought will often turn out to be not the sentence but the paragraph, the essay, the chapter, the book. In the logical sense we do not complete the thought until we finish writing whatever we are writing.

So if this definition means anything at all, the words "complete thought" must mean something quite special—something like "grammatically complete thought." But of course this begs the question, for we must still ask, "How do we know when a thought is grammatically complete?" What are the forms that make it so?

Another common definition attempts to approach this problem. This is the one which defines a sentence as "a group of words containing a subject and a predicate." This gives us something tangible; the only trouble is that it isn't true.

If we look at the word groups that acceptable writers of English punctuate as sentences, we find that most of them, to be sure, contain subjects and predicates. Not all, but most. Imperative sentences, of course, like "Take your feet off the table," have no subjects, and in dialogue writing, many sentences have neither subject nor predicate. Even in sober and conservative expository writing, like that in most of the articles in *Time* or the *Atlantic Monthly,* the reader will find a considerable number of word groups without subject and predicate punctuated with a capital at the beginning and a period at the end. Still, it is true that most sentences in most expository writing do have subjects and predicates. This is a typical kind of sentence in this kind of writing. By this definition "He didn't have any" is a sentence, for it has a subject —*he*—and a predicate—*didn't have any*. So if the student knows what a subject is and what a predicate is, this definition might be of moderate service to him. He can begin by making sure that all the word groups he punctuates as sentences have subjects and predicates in them.

The trouble is that, whereas most sentences in expository writing have subjects and predicates, most word groups with subjects and predicates aren't sentences. We have seen that "He didn't have any" is a sentence and has a subject and a predicate. But "because he didn't have any" is not a sentence. It has a subject and a predicate—the same ones—but it isn't a sentence, or at least it would not usually be so punctuated by most writers of English. It would ordinarily be attached to some other word group: "I didn't borrow money from him because he didn't have any."

69. Sentence Signals

If you look up the word *sentence* in a modern dictionary, you are likely to find something like this: "A sentence is a language unit which is not, by any grammatical device or signal, shown to be part of some larger language unit." This, of course, begs the question too. We must still ask, "What are the grammatical signals or devices which make language units part of larger language units?" One can only answer by listing or describing these grammatical signals.

For instance, the word *because* is usually such a signal. "He didn't have any" would usually be written alone. "Because he didn't have any" would usually not be, the *because* making it part of some larger unit. Operating in a similar way are such words as *until, if, whether, that, unless, since.* These are members of a word group whose principal function is to subordinate sentence patterns and make them part of larger patterns. We shall look at them in more detail in Chapter 13 and elsewhere.

But this is only one of many possible signals, and some of them are complicated and subtle. "He didn't have any" by itself is a sentence. But in "I suppose he didn't have any" it is part of a sentence, its connection to the larger unit being signaled by its position after the verb *suppose.* The word group "However he tried hard" might well be written as a sentence. We might expect to find a passage like this: "Jim didn't have much chance of making the team. However, he tried hard." But the group "however hard he tried" would seldom be punctuated as a sentence. We would expect to find this attached to something else: "Jim couldn't make the team, however hard he tried." The word order makes a difference. It is the signal.

70. Sentence Signals in Speech

Beneath these conventions of writing lie the facts of speech. We might proceed simply to describe the word patterns that writers of English conventionally punctuate as sentences, but it is illuminating to ask what made them adopt these conventions. We find the answer in the punctuation of speech.

Say this sentence aloud: "He has a brother." Now say it again, as if you intended to finish it, but this time stop at the *a:* "He has a—" Does it sound incomplete? Presumably it does, and the reason is that your voice has not made the pitch drop that signals the end of an English utterance of this type. Try these:

He hasn't any.

He hasn't any—

In the first of these there will be a melodic fall in your voice signaling the finish. This is the way you would say these words if someone had previously said, "Why don't you borrow money from Sam?" In the second your voice will seem to hang suspended. If you say the first, a hearer will receive it as a complete utterance and respond to it. If you say the second, the hearer will wait for you to finish, or perhaps will ask: "Any what? Money? Sisters? Gasoline?"

So with the word groups "however he tried hard" and "however hard he tried." The first would often be spoken with the pitch pattern that indicates completion and would often be punctuated as a sentence in writing. The second would seldom be spoken with such a pitch pattern. The pitch would indicate a connection at one end or the other with other words. It would seldom be punctuated as a sentence in writing.

We shall return to the punctuation of speech in Chapter 16 and describe it in some detail. It bears on several problems of writing besides that of sentence punctuation, and it is well for the student of writing to know something about it. It is of course not true that we punctuate our writing just as we punctuate our speech, any more than we spell words just as we pronounce them. In many features, writers have conventionalized punctuation with little regard to the intonation of speech. Nevertheless, there is considerable connection between intonation and punctuation, just as there is considerable connection between sounds and letters. And it is presumably the things that happen to our voice when we speak that gave writers the idea of using commas, periods, and semicolons in the first place.

71. Sentence Sense

You have probably heard the term "sentence sense" and perhaps have been told that you have it or that you don't have it. If you don't have it, it may seem a rather mysterious thing, as difficult to acquire as a different personality or an ear for music or blue eyes. There *is* such a thing as sentence sense, but there is nothing mystic about it, and it is acquirable, more or less. It is simply an ability to perceive the set of connections between English intonation, the word patterns of English sentences, and the punctuation habits of English writers.

Some students pick this up more or less subconsciously as they begin to read and write. Just as they slowly absorb the complex relationships between English sounds and English letters, so they notice and retain the connections between pitch and word groups and capitals and periods. They see what other writers do, and they do likewise, perhaps without being much aware of the learning process that is going on.

Ask such a student whether "He didn't have any" is a sentence, and he will say, "Of course." He will be equally sure that "if he didn't have any" is not a sentence. Ask him how he knows, and he may be unable to tell you, or he may give question-begging answers, like "The first one is a complete thought and the second one isn't"—which is like saying, "The first one is a sentence because it's a sentence, and the second is not a sentence because it isn't a sentence." Nevertheless, he knows which is which. He has sentence sense, and it derives not from intuition but from an awareness of the tangible facts of the English language.

One may have sentence sense without knowing any of the terminology of English grammar. The word group "my friend having gone to Boston" is not a sentence, and the group

"My friend has gone to Boston" is. One might explain the difference by saying that *having gone* is not a finite verb and *has gone* is one. But one can know the difference between *having gone* and *has gone* and know the bearing which the difference has on English pitch and English punctuation without knowing the term *finite verb.*

Similarly one can explain the difference between "He didn't have any" and "if he didn't have any" by saying that *if* belongs to a class of words, called *subordinators* or *subordinating conjunctions,* the function of which is to signal that a following word group is part of a larger grammatical construction. But the writer with sentence sense can know all of this without being able to state it. He has become aware of the word *if,* has connected it in his mind with words like *because, whether, until,* and recognizes the effect that these words have in English speech and English writing.

But what of the writer who has no sentence sense? Can he acquire it? Yes, he can, with a certain amount of effort. He does it the same way as the writer who gets it without trying, except that he needs to be told what to look for and he needs to train himself to look. Unfortunately he can't get it by memorizing a short definition. English sentences are too complicated to be encapsulated in a definition. What we shall do is not so much define sentences as illustrate them. We shall see the basic patterns that are regularly written as sentences, see what they are composed of, learn how they are expanded and combined, and note their connection with punctuation. As you study the structure of English patterns, you will begin to get a feeling for English sentences—will begin, in other words, to acquire sentence sense.

You may think that you will be unable to understand English intonation because you have no "ear." But this is a groundless worry. Can you distinguish, in speech, between

"Why don't you eat, George?" and "Why don't you eat George?" If so, you can grasp English intonation. Indeed, if you couldn't grasp it, you wouldn't be a speaker of English. Intonation is an important part of our communication process. It is just something of which we are not often consciously aware.

All of these matters, as you will have observed, verge on what we call "grammar," and before we look into them, it will be well to have a few words about grammar in general.

SUGGESTIONS

1. Read a magazine article and copy out all of the word groups that are punctuated as sentences but do not have a subject and a verb.
2. Which of the following word groups would you expect to find punctuated as sentences in English writing?

   (1) they came at the same time   (2) while the guests were saying goodbye   (3) nevertheless we ought to consider it from his point of view   (4) he looked carefully at each   (5) he looked carefully at every   (6) anxious as we were to help   (7) whatever happened to Charlie   (8) the older boys having told him that he couldn't play with them   (9) that has nothing at all to do with it   (10) but think how bad Harry will feel

3. Pronounce the following word groups first as sentences and then as parts of sentences.

   (1) he didn't have any   (2) we ought to take both   (3) however we looked at it   (4) we ought to help the young
4. Have someone read you a longish paragraph from a magazine. Count the sentences that you hear. Compare your count with the number shown by the author's punctuation.

10
Grammarian's Funeral

72. The Meanings of Grammar

The most obvious thing about the word *grammar* is that it gives off a certain odor. To put it somewhat more plainly, it smells. Some students get some kind of mild enjoyment out of studying grammar, but they are assuredly a minority. The teacher's announcement "Now we'll study our grammar" is not likely to make the class burst into little squeals of delight.

Neither does the word *grammar* enjoy any notable prestige among scholars. The present writer, with a rather wide acquaintance among people who study language in one way or another, has never met a single person willing to call himself a grammarian. Ask these people what their vocation is, and they may style themselves philologists or linguists or structuralists or morphophonemicists or various other things, but they will never, never call themselves grammarians, even when grammar is the particular thing they study. A person would just as soon call himself a con man or an alchemist as a grammarian.

A somewhat less obvious point about the word *grammar* is that it has several meanings. To the ordinary citizen it is probably most likely to connote "good or bad English." Thus we remark of someone who says "I ain't got none" or "I never seen him" that his grammar is poor or that he uses bad grammar. Someone who says, "I laid down on the couch" is said to have made a grammatical error.

In the schools—in English classes—the meaning is usually rather different. Here such language difficulties as those cited are likely to come under the head of "usage," and the word *grammar* is reserved for an analytical and terminological study of sentences. Thus the person studying grammar will learn the "parts of speech," their names and their definitions; he will learn such terms as *phrase, clause, interrogative sentence, participle, retained object*. Often he will be called upon to identify these categories in sentences. Sometimes he is made to diagram sentences. In former days he had to "parse" them.

Among professional students of language—linguists or linguistic scientists, as they are called—the word *grammar,* if it is used at all, will mean something different still. It may mean something like "the total set of signals by which a given language expresses its meanings" or "the total structure of a language." It will thus include sound structure as well as inflectional endings, if any, word order, distinctive patterns, and so on. In this sense, grammar is what you learn when you learn a language, and in this sense any native speaker of a language, however uneducated, knows the grammar of his language.

73. The Study of English Grammar

The multiple meanings of *grammar* reflect the rather confused history of the study. We still use the term *grammar school,* and this expression takes us back to a time when grammar was the principal subject learned in the primary grades. But it wasn't English grammar; it was Latin. Throughout the Middle Ages and well into modern times, those children who went to school devoted most of their early years to learning to read and write Latin. Until about two hundred years ago no English or American child studied English in school.

If you could already speak English, what was the purpose of studying it?

But in the middle of the eighteenth century people began to take a conscious interest in English. Along with the other vernacular languages of Europe, English was at this time coming to replace Latin as a medium for serious writing. English dictionaries had been coming out for some time, getting bigger and better every year. Then, about 1760, people began writing English grammars.

It is hard to find anything to praise in these early grammars. One cannot even say that they were good for their time. Compared to contemporary dictionaries—like Samuel Johnson's, which was published in 1755—and to other scholarly works in language, the eighteenth century grammars were mostly amateurish and puerile. Their authors were distinguished neither in their scholarship nor in their insight. To be sure, there were occasional exceptions. One or two grammars of some merit were published. But these were among the least popular and influential. It was the poor grammars that were imitated and that set the pattern for the study of English in the next two centuries.

74. Faults of the Early Grammarians

The defects of these books were numerous and strange, but we need mention only a couple of points here. Their most obvious fault was that they were not English grammars at all; they were Latin grammars disguised. The grammar that the early grammarians knew was Latin grammar, and when they decided to grammarize English, they simply transposed the Latin structure and the Latin terminology and called it English grammar. This was a useless thing to do. English and Latin are strikingly different languages. They not only express their meanings in totally different ways with totally different structural features, but they don't always express the same meanings. Languages are not convertible into one another the way dollars are convertible into francs or pounds, and the first mistake of the eighteenth century grammarians was that they didn't understand this.

This is why, for example, English grammars describe six tenses. English doesn't have six tenses. It has two looked at one way or several dozen looked at another. But it happens that Latin does have six tenses, differentiated by inflectional endings, and the grammarians simply took the English translations of the six Latin tenses and called them the English tense system. In the same way, such features as voice, mood, case, which are important in Latin as in other highly inflected languages, were sought out and emphasized in English. Some grammarians have been so ingenious as to discern five or six cases in the English noun. Meanwhile the essential features of English grammar—the basic signals by which our language transmits its meanings—were largely ignored.

You have probably heard people say that they never really understood English grammar until they studied Latin. This is not surprising. What has passed as English grammar *is* Latin. The only way to understand it is to study Latin.

A second fault of the early grammarians was that they really had no intention of describing the English language. Their intent rather was to regulate and control it, to prune it and make it more neat and elegant.

There is perhaps nothing wrong with this purpose as a purpose, except that it can't be achieved. The grammarian who writes a book to instruct a people in how their language should be employed is stirring the ocean with a coffee spoon. The people may read the book and piously agree with the grammarian, but they will go on using the language pretty much as before. They can't help it. Wiser men understood this. Dr. Johnson, when he began his dictionary, also had some notion of controlling the language, of stabilizing words and their meanings. But before he finished, he had come to realize that the language would roll on in its course despite all the efforts of all the makers of dictionaries.

Furthermore, the grammarians, with their intent to make the language better, had no notion of what better language was. Or rather they had all sorts of notions, many of them foolish. Some grammarians simply assumed that good English was whatever they used; any expressions they didn't use were poor English. This actually was a better criterion than most. It wouldn't have been conspicuously unreasonable to define "good English" as the English of the educated or of the upper classes and to proceed to a description of this English. But in fact nobody did this. There was no systematic attempt to set down the grammatical forms in general use among the educated class or any other class. The grammarian was much more likely to fill his pages with his personal idiosyncracies, cheerfully branding as vulgar any expressions that he happened not to like. Such forms as "ain't" and "he sung a song" were in good use at this time. Their proscription rests on little more than some grammarian's whim.

Still less reasonable was the attempt to use logical or analogical arguments for the banning of this construction or that. Again the fault lay in a misunderstanding of the nature of language. Language isn't logical, or, if it is, its logic is of a different kind entirely from that described by Aristotle.

An easy illustration of this process is the argument used to bury the double negative. Two negatives make a positive, they said, so if you say "I ain't got none" you must mean that you do have some. But this is manifestly untrue. Nobody who says "I ain't got none" ever means or is ever understood to mean that he has some. He always means and is always understood to mean that he hasn't any. Actually in many languages, perhaps in most, the doubling of a negative is simply a way of emphasizing the negative, two no's being felt as twice as negative as one. What the grammarians had done was simply to confuse language with algebra. In algebra two negatives do make a positive. In language they sometimes do and sometimes do not.

Sometimes the grammarian's reasoning was etymological—that is, it was based on the meaning of words or forms at some earlier period in the language. The assumption was that if a word meant something once it should mean that always, and of course the assumption was false, language being subject to change. The complicated rules for the use of *shall* and *will* are based largely on an etymological argument—on what these words meant in Old English, or on what the grammarians thought they meant.

Sometimes the argument was rhetorical, like the one used to banish prepositions from the end of sentences. Here the principle is sound enough: the end of a sentence is an important position, and one can often get the best effect by placing there a word weightier than a preposition. The fault was in trying to make this a universal rule, in saying that one must never end a sentence with a preposition. Obviously one sometimes must, or one's language will be artificial and stilted.

75. English Grammar in the Last Two Centuries

So the first English grammars were made. They were Latin grammars masquerading as English, and they were filled with pontifical pronouncements having very little root in reason. But good or bad they were destined to have an enormous influence and to mold the attitudes of many generations to the English language.

Scores of English grammars were written in the latter half of the eighteenth century. It was good fun and often profitable, and everybody tried his hand at it. There was considerable disagreement among the early books about categories and terminology, but by the end of the century, as the grammarians imitated one another, the grammars began to shake down and the differences to be smoothed out. In 1795 a man named Lindley Murray published a grammar which was a kind of synthesis of the labors of the preceding thirty-five years and which became very popular. It set the style for the next century or more. English grammars changed very little between 1795 and the twentieth century.

In the nineteenth century, courses in English, and particularly in English grammar, became a regular part of the primary school curriculum, not immediately replacing Latin studies but encroaching steadily. Generations of boys and girls were informed, as part of their preparation for life, that there were eight (sometimes nine or ten or six, the number varying somewhat) parts of speech; that a noun was the name of a person, place, or thing; that a verb was a word that expressed action, being, or state of being; that an interrogative sentence was a sentence that asked a question; that the subject of an infinitive is in the accusative case; that the subject of imperative sentences is *you* understood.

They also, usually, learned to diagram sentences. This pleasant and harmless activity, in case you've never been introduced to it, consists in laying out a sentence in such a way as to isolate its parts and indicate the relationships they are presumed to have. Much ingenuity has gone into the devising of diagramming systems. There are ways of showing the relationship of subject and verb, of distinguishing direct objects and indirect objects and object complements, of placing modifiers; there are dotted lines and solid lines and sometimes barred lines, all showing different kinds of relationships; there are straight lines, slanting lines, divided lines; there are special perches for things like expletives and absolute constructions. Diagramming is complicated but not very hard to learn, and, for some people, it is quite a lot of fun, like solving puzzles or algebraic equations. Also it tends to confirm one's grasp of the terminology of Latin grammar.

Students in the nineteenth century also learned to parse sentences. To parse a sentence, you take each word and recite all its grammatical attributes. If, for example, you were parsing the sentence "My brother tortured our cat," you would say that *brother* was a common noun, singular number, masculine gender, third person, nominative case. You would say that *tortured* was a finite verb, past tense, third person, singular number, indicative mood.

76. Is Grammar Useful?

Of course someone was bound eventually to ask what good all this did. Did learning grammatical terminology teach you anything except grammatical terminology? Did learning to parse sentences or diagram sentences cause you to produce better sentences? In the early decades of the twentieth century many educators asked these questions and answered them with a resounding "No." Then they began to gather evidence to prove their conclusions. Many studies were published to show that there was no correlation between grammatical knowledge and skill in writing; that there was, in the popular expression, no "carry-over"; that, in a word, grammar was useless.

In the prevailing mood of those decades, this would seem to settle the matter. Surely school subjects should be useful above all things. If they are not useful, why should they be taught? But of course it could be pointed out that most school subjects are useless to most of the students. Scientific knowledge is mostly useless except to scientists. What does it profit the stockbroker to know that the formula for table salt is NaCl? History is useless to most of those who study it. So are algebra and geometry. And of course nothing could be more useless than poetry, art, and music.

77. Is Grammar True?

But there was still another, and a much more damaging, question to be asked of English grammar. Granted that it's useless, is it true?

This is a question to which there is no simple answer. In one sense the descriptions of language found in English grammars *are* true. They deal—in part at least—with real phenomena actually existing in the language. They name word classes—nouns, verbs, prepositions, and so on—and such classes do occur in English and are observable. So also are such categories as subjects, participles, direct objects, subordinate clauses. Sometimes, to be sure, the grammarians describe categories which do not exist. When they talk about the dative case of nouns, or the optative of verbs, they are chasing ghosts, for these categories do not occur in English, though they do in Latin and Greek. But for the most part English grammars discuss real things.

They do not, however, discuss them truly. The reasoning on which the descriptions rest is a nightmare of confusion, contradiction, circular argument, jumbling of principles, and plain foolishness. The definitions seldom define anything; categories are set up now on one principle, now on another; like things are frequently separated and unlike things thrown together. When we try to find logic in the proceedings, we are forced to conclude that English grammar doesn't have any. Intellectually, it can only be described as a mess.

These shortcomings are easily illustrated. A noun, we are told, is the name of a person, place, or thing. In the sentence "The car is red" *car* is a noun because it names a thing. But *red* must also be a noun, for it names a color. If a color isn't a thing, what is it? But we don't want to call *red* a noun; we want to call it an adjective. So we say that a color isn't really a thing but a quality, and that *red* is an adjective here because it names a quality. Then in "He had a lot of courage" the word *courage* must be an adjective, because it surely names a quality. In truth, the definition has little connection with the thing it purports to define.

A verb, we learn, is a word that expresses action, being, or state of being. Then *departure* must be a verb, because it expresses the action of departing. *Indignation* must be a verb, for it expresses the state of being indignant. Surely the word *action* must be a verb; what expresses action more than *action?* But of course these are not verbs in English and no grammarian would wish to call them so. As with the noun, one is identifying the word class on the basis of features not stated in the definition.

Sometimes the definitions are emptier still. An interrogative sentence is customarily defined as a sentence that asks a question. This is to say simply that a sentence that asks a question is a sentence that asks a question, which is true but not useful. The student learning this definition learns nothing whatsoever about English grammar. He merely learns the term *interrogative sentence.*

Word categories in English grammars are badly confused. What grammarians call *nouns* are essentially a form class; that is, what nouns turn out to have in common is a complicated set of forms not shared by other word classes. The same is true of English verbs. But adjectives, as described in the grammars, are not a form class. They are not even a word class. For adjectives are defined as "words that modify nouns," which means that they are simply a relationship that some words may have with other words.

For this reason English grammars have no way of distinguishing between such expressions as "a dirt farmer" and "a dirty farmer," or "a mess sergeant" and "a messy sergeant." These modifiers are all adjectives according to the definition, for they all modify nouns; but surely there are differences between them, for a dirty farmer is a farmer who is dirty, but a dirt farmer is not a farmer who is dirt. Furthermore, a difference is demonstrated by word order; we say "a dirty dirt farmer" but not "a dirt dirty farmer." We have here a clear contradiction in the system. In "a telephone operator" *telephone* is an adjective by definition, for it modifies a noun. But it is also a noun by definition, for it is indisputably the name of a thing.

The whole description of the English "parts of speech" rests on little more than guess, intuition, and accident. There is no particular reason why we should say that English has eight parts of speech. It just happened that early grammarians sorted out English words in this fashion and later grammarians imitated them.

So it goes. One can go through most English grammars published in the last two hundred years and find on nearly every page sloppy reasoning and slipshod procedure that would never be tolerated in other fields of study. The grammars, as has been said, for the most part deal with real things. They are by no means false in all their details; but they are certainly false as a whole.

The most damaging thing that can be said about English grammars, therefore, is not that they are useless but that they are essentially untrue. Study of them yields no intellectual satisfaction. It is probably this rather than their asserted uselessness which has led to the decline of the study of grammar in modern times. Students and teachers alike have rebelled against having to seek understanding of something which was not ultimately understandable.

78. Reasons for Studying Grammar

Should we conclude, then, that English grammar should no longer be studied? This has indeed been the conclusion of many educators, and an increasing number of students go through the schools studying either no grammar at all or very little. But this solution doesn't seem very satisfactory either, or at least is not so for many students. There are those, as we have seen earlier, who can learn to read and write without very much instruction in reading and writing. They learn through a more or less unconscious imitation of other writers, slowly building up a feeling for sentence structure that doesn't depend much on any ability to analyze sentences. Such students have no obvious need to study English grammar, though they are often the only ones who enjoy it.

But such students are in a minority. Most people, if they are to learn to write passably well, require a good deal of instruction. They need to be told when their sentences need repairing and how to repair them. For this they must have some kind of awareness of the components of sentences and the way they fit together. One doesn't profit much from being told simply that one's writing is poor. One wants also to know what's wrong with it.

Furthermore, many people apparently can acquire a feeling for sentence structure only through some sort of conscious study of sentences. They get a feeling for speech sentences without study, as a result of being native speakers of the language. But a grasp of the somewhat more elaborate, somewhat more conventionalized sentences of writing, an ability to follow them out and get them onto the paper, often requires

some conscious understanding of their forms and structures. One needs to know the basic patterns of English sentences and to perceive how these can be modified and combined to produce normal English prose.

79. The Ideal Grammar

A study of English grammar, then, is for most students not
only useful but necessary—but with certain conditions. One is
that the English grammar really be English grammar and not
Latin grammar. We are interested here in the English structures and the English signals, the English system of transmit-
ting meanings. We are not particularly interested in English
sentences because they translate Latin sentences.

A second condition is that the grammar be rational and
soundly based. It should be logically defensible in the same
way that a chemical analysis is logically defensible. It should
be built on known principles and proceed by rational methods
to tenable conclusions. Such a grammar would be worth
studying. It would not only provide the teacher and student
with efficient tools with which to meet the problems of writing courses; more important, it would yield a true understanding of an important part of the universe. The language
is the medium through which we see the world. To get a
clear view of the language, its structure and its system, is to
achieve the kind of intellectual satisfaction which is the heart
of real education.

80. The Available Grammar

The question is, does such a grammar exist? The answer is,
partly. In this century, and particularly in recent decades,
there has been a growing effort devoted to a scientific study
of language, a study in which speculation, philosophizing,
and impressionistic argument give place to a controlled collection and inspection of data. Linguistic science, as this disci-

pline is called, has not been interested primarily in the field occupied by traditional English grammar. Indeed, it has not been primarily interested in English, but has devoted most of its energies to unraveling problems posed by such remote and exotic languages as Algonquian, Hopi, Swahili, or Mazateco. Furthermore, since linguistic science views speech rather than writing as the fundamental reality of language, it has been chiefly concerned with understanding sound structure rather than sentence structure. Great advances have been made in isolating and describing the basic phenomena of human speech. Problems have one by one given way to continued research until now the sound structure of English and many other languages is pretty well understood and no longer the subject of much argument among scholars.

Linguists have approached the problems of sentence structure, word classification, and the like much more gingerly. The larger the language unit to be studied, the more complicated the description is likely to be. The phoneme is a unit which is now well understood, but such units as word, word class, and sentence are not so well understood as they will some day be.

Still enough progress has been made in recent years to permit us to get a fairly good notion of what English sentence structure is like. The picture is by no means complete, but it is complete enough for the ordinary demands of instruction in writing. It is possible to describe the main lines at least of English sentences and to do so without falling back on circular definition and illogical reasoning.

81. Methods of Grammatical Analysis

To see how the system works, let us observe how linguistic science goes about establishing a word class—a "part of speech," if you like. Let us begin with the words *depart, pretend, assist,* and ask ourselves what these words have in common. We might say, as traditional grammar did, that they all express action. But if we then tried to establish a word class which consisted of all words which express action, we would have to include not only *depart, pretend,* and *assist* but also *departure, pretense,* and *assistance.* These six words could certainly be viewed as a word class. They are a group of words having something in common—viz., a meaning relating in some way to action. But a word class of this sort will turn out to be useless to our purpose. It will not contribute in any way to an understanding of English sentence structure.

We therefore abandon meaning as a possible common characteristic of *depart, pretend,* and *assist* and look for something else. We find that one thing the words have in common is that they occur in a large number of similar or identical positions in English sentences. For example, they all will fill the blank in "Let's _____":

> Let's depart.
> Let's pretend.
> Let's assist.

Or in "They'll _____":

> They'll depart.
> They'll pretend.
> They'll assist.

Or in "He _____ -ed":

> He departed.
> He pretended.
> He assisted.

Depart, assist, and *pretend* therefore have this much in common: they share a number of positions in English sentence patterns. Furthermore, most or all of these positions are not shared by such words as *departure, pretense, assistance.* Nobody who speaks English ever says "Let's departure,"

"They'll pretense" or "He assistanced." We therefore have clear grounds for assuming that *depart, assist,* and *pretend* belong to one class of words and *departure, pretense,* and *assistance* to another class. We can call these word classes by any name we like. For convenience, let's call *depart, assist,* and *pretend* "verbs" and *departure, assistance,* and *pretense* "nouns."

82. Complications

Many difficulties should occur to you at once. Can we, for example, pick any one pattern and define a word class as any word that fits that pattern? No, not usually. If, for example, we defined the English verb as any word that will fill the blank in "Let's _____," we should find that we have excluded a number of words that we shall want to call verbs. For example, the word *describe* does not ordinarily occur in this pattern; we do not usually say "Let's describe." *Describe* does, however, occur in the similar pattern "Let's _____ it."

Now theoretically we have two alternatives. We could say that we have here two word classes, two parts of speech: one, the words that occur in "Let's _____"; the other the words that occur in "Let's _____ it." Or we could say that verbs are words that occur in either of these patterns. The latter will turn out to be the right analysis; that is, it is the analysis which in the long run will yield the simpler description. But the difference between the "Let's _____" words and the "Let's _____ it" words is a real thing, and it could be used to distinguish between two different kinds of verbs. Indeed, it is the basis for the distinction between what traditional grammar has called transitive and intransitive verbs. Transitive verbs are simply those that occur in patterns like "Let's _____ it"; intransitive verbs are those that occur in patterns like "Let's _____."

Another difficulty arises from the fact that some words occur now in one class and now in another. Some words have
three or four possibilities. The word *face,* for example, is
sometimes a verb. It occurs in patterns like "Let's face it" or
"He faced the music," where it is patterning like *describe:*
"Let's describe it" or "He described the music." But it also
occurs in patterns like "That's a nice face," where it is patterning like *description* or *uncle* or *lemon.*

What, then, is an English verb? It is any word occurring
in any of a certain set of positions in English sentences. These
positions are describable or listable, but they are numerous
and complicated. The native speaker of English knows them
all by virtue of being a native speaker. To give him a conscious understanding of the concept "English verb" it is usually necessary only to give a few examples: "An English
verb is a word like *depart, go, eat, face* occurring in such
patterns as "Let's _____," "They want to _____ it," "I'll
_____ later." A foreign speaker would have to learn all the
words and all the patterns in order to get a full understanding
of the English verb. In other words, he would have to learn
English.

Words are verbs only when they occur in verb patterns.
Face is a verb in "Let's face it" but it is not a verb in "His face
is dirty." Many words, of course, occur only in verb patterns
—*depart, assist, pretend,* etc. If this were not so, if all the
words which occur in patterns like "Let's _____ it" also occurred in patterns like "His _____ is dirty," then there
would be no real distinction between nouns and verbs. We
would have one part of speech here, not two. This happens
in some languages. It is the fact that we have some words like
depart and *implore* on one side and others like *departure* and
indignation on the other that marks out the patterns and es-
tablishes the two classes. A part of speech is not just a list of

words and not just a list of patterns; it is the words and the patterns together.

There are further complications. Some positions in English sentences are positions for one word class only; others are shared by two or more word classes. An example of an unshared position is "Let's _____." Any word occurring in the position after *let's* is a verb. Another example is "This is my _____." Any word occurring after *my* in this pattern is a noun. But the blank in "This is _____" is a shared position. For here we may have words of the type *nice, yellow, foolish:*

> This is nice.
> This is yellow.
> This is foolish.

But we also have words of the type *Ed, Angela, foolishness.*

> This is Ed.
> This is Angela.
> This is foolishness.

In other words, the position in "This is _____" is shared by nouns and adjectives.

83. Grammar and Reality

When you hear an English sentence or see one, you always have to be able to recognize the word classes. That is, you must be able to tell whether a word is a noun or an adjective, an adjective or a verb, or whatever. If the word occurs in an unshared position, you can tell what it is by the position. If it occurs in a shared position, it must be marked in some other way—e.g., by one of many possible class endings (like the *-ness* in *foolishness*), by a marker like *a* or *the,* or by the general context. There are many such signals, as we shall see in Chapter 11. If there is no signal at all, then the sentence will always have two possible meanings.

Suppose, for example, someone were to utter the sentence /ðis iz griyn/, just that and no more. Without a clue from the physical context, there would be no way of knowing whether he had said "This is green" or "This is Green." For it happens that the position in "This is _____" is a position for both adjectives and nouns, and it happens further that the word /griyn/ occurs in English both as adjective and noun.

This illustrates an important point: that grammar of this sort is dealing with realities. Its purpose is not to construct a logical apparatus above and apart from the language; it is rather to specify the signals by which speakers of English communicate. A native speaker of English studying this grammar is not learning new facts as he does when he studies history or geography. He is merely becoming consciously aware of a structure which he already grasps thoroughly on the unconscious level and manipulates automatically. If you are a speaker of English, you know English grammar; otherwise you would not be a speaker of English.

Something should be said of the relationship of this grammar to traditional grammar. As you read the following chapters, you will see many similarities between this and grammar you may have studied elsewhere. Traditional grammarians operated on intuition, but often their intuition was right. For the most part, they talked of categories which actually do exist in English. They got balled up not so much on the categories themselves as on the definition and description of them. What we do here partly, therefore, is to indicate the tangible features which inspired these intuitions.

The intuition of traditional grammarians was, however, not always right, and we are therefore compelled to do a good deal of reshuffling. You will find various new categories here. You will find some shifting of old ones. Do not let the use of traditional terms mislead you. *Noun, verb, adjective, conjunc-*

tion, and so on, do not always mean here just what they meant in traditional grammar, and sometimes the differences are large.

Finally, note that the whole intent is different. We are not trying simply to classify words; we are trying to find out what makes the language work. There is no notion of providing a system by which all the words of English can be sorted into eight or ten or twenty pigeonholes. We shall notice four large word classes and a dozen or so small ones. These will not account for all English words in all sentences. A great deal of English will lie outside the description altogether, and we shall simply ignore it. This could of course be described, but it would complicate things unnecessarily. What we aim at here is not a total description of English syntax, but a general view of its main features, its high-frequency patterns. This will prove complicated enough.

SUGGESTIONS

1. Define the term *grammar.*
2. Write a paper describing your studies of grammar in primary and secondary school.
3. The sentence "She's a telephone operator" contains a word which, by the conventional definitions, is both an adjective and a noun. Give further examples.
4. Words can be sorted into word classes by substituting in selected sentence patterns. Fill each of the blanks in the following sentences with ten different words and note the word classes that result.

   (1) We'll _____ a little later. (2) One of the _____s was looking odd. (3) _____ young man went away quietly. (4) A very _____ girl came in. (5) _____ he gets here, we'll have dinner.
5. How many different meanings can you get out of the following: /ðə sənz reyz miyt/? Write out the possibilities in standard spelling, which will distinguish the differences. Note how the ambiguities rest on the fact that the word classes are not signaled.

II
Word Classes
in English

84. The General Picture

Considered on the basis of their patterning—i.e., of the sentence positions in which they occur—English words can be classified in four large groups and a dozen or so small ones. The words in the four large classes are frequently marked by characteristic features of form—endings and the like—and they may therefore be referred to as *form classes.* If we look for traditional names to apply to these form classes, the obvious ones are *noun, verb, adjective, adverb.* The reference of these terms is not always the same as it is in conventional grammar. *Adjective,* for instance, does not mean here "anything that modifies a noun." But there is a good deal of resemblance between the present use of the terms and the traditional one.

In addition to the form classes, English has an indefinite number of small word groups, containing anywhere from one to seventy members each. Their function is to expand and combine English sentence patterns in various ways and in general to indicate the structural relationships between members of the form classes. A convenient general term for these small word groups is *structure groups.* Some of the structure groups have been identified in conventional grammar, and some have not. Those that have been traditionally observed can be given traditional names—*preposition, conjunction, auxiliary*. The others must be given new names.

85. Nouns

We shall look first at the form classes. The largest is the group of words we call *nouns*. A large dictionary will list several hundred thousand words that pattern sometimes or always as nouns. Examples are *grapefruit, lawyer, resentment, hallway, party, thing, person, locality, benzine, lipstick*. What these words have in common is that they occur in similar or identical positions in English sentences. They pattern alike. For example, they will all fill the blank in "I lost my _____":

> I lost my   grapefruit.
>   lawyer.
>   resentment.
>   lipstick.

And so on.

Other typical noun positions are "The _____ was interesting," "Did you see their _____?" "It was full of _____." Any word—any noise—occurring in such positions is a noun, and a great many noises conventionally occur in such positions.

There are some sentence positions in which some nouns occur and others don't. For instance, the blank in "He needed a _____" is a position for *cat, sister-in-law, violin, rest, crocodile, lawyer, valet, Cadillac, nose*, and many other nouns. But it is not a position for *courage, respectability, gasoline, dishonesty, advice*. We say "He needed courage," but not "He needed a courage"; "He needed advice," but not "He needed an advice."

Similarly, "_____ was needed" is a position for the words

courage and *Charlie*. We say "Courage was needed" or "Charlie was needed." But it is not a position for the word *person;* we do not say "Person was needed." On the other hand, *person* will pattern in "_____s were needed," but *courage* and *Charlie* won't. Then there is a difference between *courage* and *Charlie: courage* occurs in "We admired his _____," but *Charlie* doesn't.

On the basis of such slight variations in the patterning, the large noun group can be divided (if one wishes to divide it) into subgroups. This is indeed the real grounds for the distinctions intuitively made between "concrete nouns" and "abstract nouns," "count nouns" and "mass nouns," "common nouns" and "proper nouns."

You will notice that none of this description depends on meaning. It may be true that there is a kind of general meaning common to nouns and other meanings common to other word classes. But this meaning is created precisely by similarity of occurrence in sentence patterns. The structure produces the meaning, not the other way around. We do not, in our use of language, perceive that a word names a person, place, or thing and therefore occurs in a noun pattern. We perceive that it occurs in a noun pattern and therefore names a person, place, or thing.

86. The Plural Form

In addition to the general similarity of patterning, many members of the noun class share various characteristics of form. The most important of these is the plural formation, ways of distinguishing between the concepts "one" and "more than one." Not all nouns form plurals. Nouns of the type *apple, violin, subsidy, finger* do. Proper nouns and also nouns of the type *mush, drivel, courage, honesty* do not.

Of those nouns which do form plurals, the great majority

do so on the same pattern. This is by the addition to the singular form of one of three sounds: /s/, /z/, or /ɨz/. In writing we spell these either *s* or *es*. Singular nouns ending with the phonemes /p/, /t/, /k/, /θ/, or /f/ add /s/ to form the plural: *laps* /læps/, *pets* /pets/, *hicks* /hiks/, *cloths* /klɔθs/, *coughs* /kɔfs/. Those that end with /s/, /z/, /š/, /ž/, /c/, or /j/ add /ɨz/: *kisses* /kisɨz/, *roses* /rowzɨz/, *crashes* /kræšɨz/, *garages* /gəražɨz/ (for those who pronounce *garage* that way), *churches* /cɨrcɨz/, *judges* /jəjɨz/. Those ending in any other phoneme add /z/: *toes* /towz/, *skies* /skayz/, *tubs* /təbz/, *kids* /kidz/, *pigs* /pigz/, *trains* /treynz/, *crumbs* /krəmz/, *pills* /pilz/.

This is the common or regular plural of English nouns. A regular formation is one that speakers of a language learn and apply as a pattern. Speakers of English apply this plural form automatically. We never have to decide consciously whether to add /s/ or /z/ or /ɨz/. We choose the proper form automatically according to the sound with which the singular ends. If it ends in /p/ we add /s/, if in /b/ we add /z/, and so on. Some other combinations would be perfectly possible. For instance, it would be easy enough to pronounce *toes* /tows/ instead of /towz/. But we never do this, because by the age of four or five we have got accustomed to using only the plural /z/ after /ow/ and other vowels.

In addition to the words with the regular plural, English has a hundred or so nouns with special or irregular plurals. Most of these are perfectly familiar to native speakers of English and need not be listed. Examples are *men, mice, teeth, children, oxen, sheep, quail, knives, leaves, phenomena, memoranda, alumni, theses, criteria, minutiae,* and so on. The speaker of English learns these plurals as items, one by one; he does not learn them as patterns. We do not, for example, learn to change a final /f/ preceded by a diphthong to /v/

before adding the plural. There are about a dozen words in which we do this: *leaves, wives, halves, thieves,* etc. But there are many more in which we do not. The plural of *chief* is *chiefs,* not *chieves;* the plural of *goof* is *goofs,* not *gooves.*

There is always a tendency in language for the large regular formations to absorb the small irregular ones. The child learns the regular pattern at a very early age, and then applies it to all new words of the form class. Usually he's right, but sometimes he's wrong. He's right when, having learned *tree,* he says *trees;* he's wrong when, having learned *man,* he says *mans.* In the same way, an adult coming on the word *memorandum* would normally suppose that the plural is *memorandums.* There is no reason why he should guess it to be *memoranda.* The plural of *gum* is not *ga,* the plural of *slum* is not *sla,* so why should the plural of *memorandum* be *memoranda?* So he says *memorandums,* and if enough people do this, *memorandum* goes into the regular class, and the old irregular plural ceases to exist.

Consequently irregular words are mostly common words. The child says *mans,* but he is quickly corrected by the frequent occurrence of *men* in the language he hears. But he doesn't hear *memoranda,* so it doesn't become part of his language.

87. The Possessive Form

In addition to the plural formation, English nouns are characterized by what is called the *possessive* or *genitive* form: *boy's, Edward's, man's, lawyer's.* The possessive is formed on the same pattern as the plural, except that there are no irregular formations. We add /s/, /z/, or /ɨz/ according to what the preceding sound is. Consequently there is no difference in pronunciation between *boys, boy's,* and *boys';* these are all pronounced /bɔyz/. In speech *boys* and *boy's* and *boys'* are differentiated by position only: "I saw the boys," "I saw the boy's nose," "I saw the boys' noses."

In writing, of course, we use the apostrophe sign before the possessive ending but not before the plural ending. This use of the apostrophe became general about the time of Shakespeare, and it was an accident resulting from a mistake. Earlier the apostrophe had been used to indicate a contraction. We still use it so, as in *can't* or *I'll*. A word like *boy's* was regularly spelled *boys* or *boyes*. Then writers got the notion that "the boyes nose" was a contracted form of "the boy his nose," and that they should use an apostrophe to show that "hi-" had been omitted. They were quite wrong. *Boyes* is not a shortened form of *boy his*. But they thought it was, and eventually the practice of using an apostrophe for the possessive became conventional.

88. Noun Suffixes

In addition to the plural and possessive endings, there is a miscellany of suffixes of another kind which mark off nouns from other form classes. For instance, if we add *-ness* to the adjective *good* we get the noun *goodness*. And similarly we have such nouns as *sleepiness, happiness, foolishness, sadness,* and hundreds more all composed of an adjective form plus the noun ending *-ness*.

Other noun suffixes include *-tion,* as in *action, imagination, nation,* with variants of spelling and pronunciation, as in *fusion, tension, electrification, emancipation; -er,* as in *worker, learner, producer; -ity,* as in *electricity, ferocity, simplicity; -ism,* as in *nationalism, feminism, progressivism; -ist,* as in *nationalist, feminist, progressivist; -ship,* as in *courtship, hardship, relationship.* And so on. There are several dozen noun suffixes in use, though some of them, like *-dom* (*wisdom*), occur in only a few words. Every once in a while a new noun suffix comes into being, like *-burger,* which has been extended from *hamburger* to *cheeseburger, nutburger,* and so on.

89. Verbs

Verbs are such words as *eat, go, think, imagine, resist, emancipate, televise, bifurcate.* What these words have in common is possibility of occurrence in a certain set of sentence positions. Such patterns are "Let's _____," "Let's _____ it," "He might _____," "They'll _____ us later," "I can't _____." That is, we say "I can't go," "I can't think," "I can't imagine it," and so on.

This common occurrence in patterns tends to give these words a common meaning, which we might try to sum up as "action" or "being." But again, we cannot use this meaning to define the class, because the patterns produce the meanings, not the meanings the patterns. Furthermore, these meanings are also expressed sometimes by other word classes. For instance, *emancipate* and *emancipation* both express action, but they are not both verbs. *Emancipate* is a verb because we say things like "Lincoln emancipated the slaves." *Emancipation* is not a verb because we do not say things like "Lincoln emancipationed the slaves."

90. Third Person Singular and Present Participle

Like nouns, verbs have a number of formal features. One is the form that occurs after singular noun subjects, like *goes, thinks, imagines, emancipates.* These are usually called "third person singular forms," but this term, besides being rather jargonish, is somewhat misleading. English verbs do not express singular and plural; we do not have one form that means "imagine once" and another which means "imagine several times." We have just a form *imagines* occurring after subjects like *he, Sam, the man* and a form *imagine* occurring after *I, you, they, Sam and Emily, the men.*

Phonemically this form is constructed just like the regular plural of nouns. We add /s/ when the base form ends in /p/, /t/, /k/, /f/: *stops* /staps/, *hates* /heyts/, *kicks* /kiks/, *laughs* /læfs/; we add /ɨz/ after /s/, /z/, /š/, /ž/, /c/, and /j/: *misses* /misɨz/, *supposes* /səpowzɨz/, *smashes* /smæšɨz/, *camouflages* /kæməflažɨz/, *snatches* /snæcɨz/, *fudges* /fəjɨz/; we add /z/ after any other phoneme: *goes* /gowz/, *leans* /liynz/, *smells* /smelz/, *rubs* /rəbz/.

Apart from the verb *be,* which is altogether special, there are only three verbs which make this form irregularly. These are *have-has* /hæv-hæz/, *do-does* /duw-dəz/, and *say-says* /sey-sez/. If these were regular, they would be /hævz/, /duwz/, and /seyz/.

Another verb feature is the *-ing* form, usually called the "present participle." This is thoroughly regular, all verbs simply adding the suffix /ɨŋ/: *going, doing, saying, emancipating,* etc.

91. The Past Tense and Past Participle

A third feature is the past tense. As with the plural of nouns, we have one large regular formation and a number of small irregular ones. Regular verbs form the past tense by adding /t/, /d/, or /ɨd/, according to the final sound of the simple verb. If the simple form ends in /p/, /k/, /f/, /s/, /š/, or /c/ we add /t/: *stopped* /stapt/, *talked* /tɔkt/, *laughed* /læft/, *missed* /mist/, *smashed* /smæšt/, *hatched* /hæct/. If the simple form ends in /t/ or /d/, we add /ɨd/: *hated* /heytɨd/, *ended* /endɨd/, *emancipated* /əmænsəpeytɨd/. If it ends in anything else, we add /d/: *cleaned* /kliynd/, *watered* /wɔtərd/, *bagged* /bægd/, *snubbed* /snəbd/, *snowed* /snowd/, *dried* /drayd/.

This regular class includes all English verbs except about two hundred. These two hundred irregular past tenses are mostly very common verbs, and the forms are familiar to any native speaker of English. Examples are *wrote, ate, fell, told, bent, built, taught, made, put, shot, began.* When such irregular words become uncommon for any reason, they tend to acquire regular forms because children learning the language do not hear the irregular forms often enough. Thus such verbs as *weave, slay, tread* will sometimes be given the regular formations *weaved, slayed, treaded* in place of the older *wove, slew, trod.*

In addition to the past tense, English verbs have a form called the past participle. The difference can be shown by referring to patterns. The past tense is the form that occurs in such patterns as "He _____ last night," where we would find such words as *came, talked, died, ate, fell.* The past participle occurs in such patterns as "He had _____ earlier." Here the forms would be *come, talked, died, eaten, fallen.*

As you see, the past participle is the same as the past tense for some verbs (*talk, die*) and different for others (*come, eat, fall*). All regular verbs and some irregular ones have identical past tense and past participles; the other irregular verbs have different forms, which must be learned specially by the child learning the language.

In addition to endings of the sort described, some English verbs have various suffixes which serve to distinguish them from words of similar meaning in other form classes. Thus the suffix *-ize* occurs in a number of verbs, like *criticize, realize, Americanize, emphasize, canonize.* Other such verb suffixes are *-fy* (*beautify, terrify, simplify*); *-en* (*redden, soften, brighten*); *-ate* (*emancipate, violate, ruminate*). We have also a prefix, *be,* occurring with many verbs: *befriend, bestir, beset, bedevil.*

92. Adjectives

Adjectives are such words as *happy, honest, beautiful, courageous, seedy, indignant, continuous, Byronic, interesting*. It happens that many positions for adjectives are also positions for other word classes and that adjectives are therefore distinguishable more often by form than by position. Thus the position in "He was _____" is a position for adjectives, for we say "He was happy," "He was interesting," etc.; but it is also a position for verbs in *-ing:* "He was smoking," "He was waiting," and for certain kinds of nouns: "He was Charlie," "He was vice-president." The position in "a _____ man" is a position for adjectives: "a happy man," "a seedy man"; but other classes occur here also: "a city man," "a waiting man," etc. In this position, to be sure, pitch patterns will often distinguish the classes in speech.

There are some positions, however, in which only adjectives occur. Such a one is that in "He was very _____," or "It was somewhat _____." Any word occurring in such positions is an adjective, and most adjectives will occur there. Similarly, only adjectives will occur in both blanks of "A _____ person is a person who is _____" or "A _____ thing is a thing that is _____." Thus in the phrase "an oblong car," *oblong* is an adjective, for an oblong car is a car that is oblong. But in "a town car" *town* is not an adjective, for a town car is not a car that is town.

93. Form Characteristics of Adjectives

Form features shared by many adjectives are the endings *-er* and *-est,* as in *smaller/smallest, happier/happiest, nicer/nicest*. Forms like *smaller, happier* are often called comparatives, and forms like *smallest, happiest* are called superlatives. Most one-syllable and many two-syllable adjectives take the endings *-er* and *-est.* Adjectives of more than two syllables usually do not. Adjectives which do not add *-er* and *-est* express similar meanings with *more* and *most: more beautiful, more courageous, most insolent, most solid.*

We have numerous suffixes distinguishing adjectives from related words of other form classes. Examples are *-ful* (*beautiful, fearful, powerful*), *-y* (*seedy, messy, nosey*), *-ic* (*quixotic, carbonic, tragic*), *-ous* (*courageous, nauseous, continuous*), *-al* (*continual, verbal, adjectival*), *-ive* (*productive, vindictive, protective*). There are various others.

94. Adverbs

Adverbs are a rather complicated class. The group contains words like *quickly, decisively, beautifully, sadly, away, on, off, in, often, sometimes, never;* some of these occur in other word classes too. A typical adverb position is that in "He walked _____." Thus we would find sentences like "He walked quickly," "He walked away," "He walked often." Another position is the blank in "He had _____ done it." Here we might find adverbs like *gladly, courageously, never, sometimes.*

Adverbs can be divided into three subgroups distinguished by sometimes subtle differences in patterning. Thus if we take a sentence like "He walked away quickly sometimes" and substitute other words for the three adverbs, we get lists like these:

He walked	away	quickly	sometimes.
	in	angrily	often.
	home	despondently	usually.
	out	happily	later.

We could move the groups around in various ways:

He	sometimes	walked	away	quickly.
	often		in	angrily.
	usually		home	despondently.
	later		out	happily.

If we substituted the most general words we could think of, the words would be *there, thus,* and *then:* "He walked there thus then," or "He then walked there thus." This is the basis of the idea that adverbs express the meanings place (there), manner (thus), and time (then). They do, though these meanings can be expressed by various other grammatical structures also.

The largest of the three groups is that composed of the *thus* adverbs: *quickly, angrily,* etc. It will be seen that nearly all of these consist of an adjective form plus the ending *-ly: quick/ quickly, angry/angrily, beautiful/beautifully.* Most adjectives can be made into adverbs by the addition of *-ly.*

Many of the words in the *there* group occur also, as we shall see in more detail later, in the structure group called prepositions. Such are *in, off, by, under.* We say "He walked in," where *in* is an adverb, and also "He was in the house," where *in* is a preposition. Some words in the *there* group have the endings *-wise, -ways,* or *-ward: sideways, lengthwise, northward.*

The smallest of the three groups is the *then* group: *then, later, earlier, sometimes, often,* etc. These words have no special formal characteristics. They are included among adverbs just because their patterning is very similar to that of *quickly, happily, away,* etc.

95. Determiners *structure grup*

In addition to these four large form classes, English has an indefinite number of small word classes which we will call "structure groups." Some of the structure groups are closely associated with certain of the form classes and others are not. In this chapter we shall notice just those that are.

First we have a group of words which pattern like *the*. We call these words *determiners.* If we take a sentence like "The

young face was interesting" and see what words will substitute for *the,* we find that we can say "His young face was interesting," "Each young face was interesting," "That young
face was interesting." *Each, his,* and *that* therefore all pattern
like *the,* and in these sentences they are all determiners. Other
words that would substitute in this pattern are *my, your, her,
this, its, every, a, an, no, either, neither, one.*

If we change "the young face" to "the young faces," we find
several other words patterning like *the: these, those, our, their,
both, some, many, few, several, all, two, three, four,* etc. If we
substitute for *the* in "The sand was needed," we get also *much,
more,* and *little,* which may be added to the list of determiners.

The most important common feature of determiners is that
they pattern with nouns, serving as a signal that a noun is
going to occur, sooner or later, in the construction that follows. They have a few other functions. For example, they
occasionally pattern with adjectives, as in sentences like "He
gave money to the very poor." But mostly they occur in constructions like "the man," "my old father," "every hungry
little poodle."

Note that the patterning of determiners is quite different
from that of adjectives, words like *hungry, young, handsome.*
They do share a few positions. We can say "the faces" or
"handsome faces." But most of their positions are different.
We say "The man was here," but not "Handsome man was
here," "the handsome man," but not "handsome the man,"
"This man is handsome," but not "This man is the."

96. Pronouns

Rather closely related to nouns is the structure group called
pronouns. Pronouns, indeed, pattern almost exactly like
proper nouns. If we substitute for *Sam* in sentences like "Sam

was here" or "He saw Sam," we would get items like *I, he, himself, this:* "I was here," "He was here," "He saw himself," "He saw this."

The words that occur as pronouns in modern English include *I, me, mine, myself; you, yours, yourself, yourselves; he, him, his, himself; she, her, hers, herself; it, its, itself; we, us, ours, ourselves; they, them, theirs, themselves; this, that, these, those, such; each, either, neither, both, some, few, many, much, none, several, all, any, most; each other, one another; anybody, anyone, anything; somebody, someone, something; everybody, everyone, everything; nobody, no one, nothing; one, two, three, four,* etc.

You will notice that the pronouns arrange themselves in small subgroups. These have been given names in the traditional terminology, like *personal pronoun, demonstrative pronoun, indefinite pronoun,* etc. Such distinctions are real and can be validated on the basis of differences in patterning, but our purposes won't require us to bother with them.

You may notice also that there is considerable overlapping between the determiners and the pronouns, many items occurring on both lists. Just as *face* occurs both as noun and verb ("His face is dirty," "Let's face it") so *each* and *his* occur sometimes as pronouns and sometimes as determiners:

DETERMINERS: *Each* face was dirty.
              He lost *his* dog.
PRONOUNS: *Each* was dirty.
              He lost *his.*

The distinction is simple enough. Such words are determiners when they pattern before nouns; they are pronouns when they replace nouns in the patterns. Or, to make it tangible, they are determiners when they are in positions for *the* but pronouns when they are not.

Notice also that the overlapping is by no means complete.

Many items on the determiner list do not occur as pronouns; e.g., *the, an, my, their, every* never do. Many items on the pronoun list never occur as determiners; e.g., *I, me, mine, myself, someone, everything* never do. If the overlapping *were* complete, we would have just one structure group here; as it is not, we have two.

97. Auxiliaries

Closely associated with verbs is a structure group called *auxiliaries*. An auxiliary is a word patterning like *may* in "may sing" or like *is* in "is singing" or like *has* in "has sung." Substituting in these patterns, we get the following lists:

He	may	sing.	He	is	singing.	He	has	sung.
	can			was			had	
	will		I	am		I	have	
	shall		You	are		It	was	
	might			were		They	were	
	could							
	would							
	should							
	must							
	does							
	did							
	ought to							
	has to							

Some of the items on the auxiliary list occur sometimes as verbs. The notable ones are *do* (*does, did*), *is* (*was, were, are, am*), and *has* (*had, have*). These words are auxiliaries when they pattern before verbs; they are verbs when they do not:

AUXILIARIES: He *does* try.

He *is* trying.

He *has* tried.

VERBS: He *does* his best.

He *is* foolish.

He *has* a car.

98. Intensifiers

We have next a structure group which patterns with adjectives and adverbs. For want of a better term, we shall call them *intensifiers*. These are words like *very* or *pretty* in "He was very good," "It was pretty sad." Some other words in the intensifier group are *rather, somewhat, fairly, really, too, more, most, quite.*

Intensifiers share most of their positions with certain adverbs. That is, we say not only "He was very sick" but also "He was remarkably sick," "He was quietly sick." For this reason, intensifiers have often been lumped in with the adverb class. But there are various significant differences in the patterning; most notably, intensifiers do not pattern with verbs, as adverbs do. We say "He acted remarkably" or "He acted quietly," but we do not say "He acted very" or "He acted rather." There are a few words which occur both as adverbs and as intensifiers. One is *fairly*. It is an adverb in "He acted fairly"; it is an intensifier in "He acted fairly dishonestly." The difference in meaning, which stems from the difference in patterning, is obvious.

99. The Reality of Word Classes

To sum up, English has four very large word classes which we call form classes: *nouns, verbs, adjectives, adverbs*. It has also a number of small word classes which we call *structure groups*. We have so far noted four of these structure groups— *determiners, pronouns, auxiliaries, intensifiers.* We shall encounter others later.

Now these distinctions are not a grammarian's fancy. They are real. It is obviously possible to speak English perfectly well without knowing the terms *noun, verb, determiner*. But it is not possible to speak English without being able to tell the difference between a noun and a verb, a verb and an adjective, a determiner and a pronoun. Actually, as we use the language, we are constantly sorting out these different classes. If it happens, as it sometimes does, that we can't tell whether a word belongs to one class or another, then it will always be true that we cannot understand the sentence.

Consider, for example, the sentence "Swallow drinks slowly." This has two possible meanings. It could be a statement to the effect that a bird is a slow drinker; or it could be a suggestion to someone that he down his liquids slowly. The reason the sentence is ambiguous is that there is no signal to indicate the word classes to which the first two words belong. It happens that *swallow* patterns in the noun class ("That's a swallow") and also in the verb class ("I can't swallow it"). The word *drinks* also patterns as a noun ("He bought the drinks") and as a verb ("He drinks milk"). Here we can't tell which is which.

Or take the sentence "She was charming." *Charming* nowadays usually patterns as an adjective: "Helen's a very charming girl." But it sometimes patterns as a verb: "Helen was charming a snake." *Was* occurs both as a verb before adjectives ("Helen was lovely") and as an auxiliary before verbs ("Helen was working"). In "She was charming" the classes are not signaled. *Charming* is an adjective if the sentence is in answer to "What sort of person was she?" It's a verb in answer to "What was she doing?"

The sentence "He looked hard" is ambiguous because *hard* occurs as an adjective ("He's a hard man") and also as an adverb ("He worked hard"). Further, *looked* is a verb which occurs before adjectives ("He looked cute") and also before adverbs ("He looked carefully").

The sentence "He was potted" is ambiguous because *potted* is sometimes a verb, as in "He potted the plants," but also occurs in slang as an adjective with the meaning "drunk." If someone said, "Sam was potted," and you had no further clue, you couldn't tell whether *potted* was an adjective or a verb. In other words, you couldn't tell whether Sam was drunk or his remains were put into an urn.

In our actual use of language such ambiguous sentences do not often occur, and the reason is that English is full of signals whose function is to keep the word classes sorted out. "Swallow drinks slowly" is ambiguous, but "A swallow drinks slowly" is not. The determiner *a* marks the following word as a noun, and the sentence straightens out. Similarly, in "Swallow your drinks slowly" the determiner *your* marks *drinks* as a noun. "Oriole drinks slowly" is unambiguous because *oriole* does not occur as a verb. "Imbibe drinks slowly" is unambiguous because *imbibe* does not occur as a noun. "Swallow is drinking slowly" is clear because the auxiliary *is* and the suffix *-ing* signal that *drink* is a verb.

"Harold looked hard" is ambiguous, but the following are not:

> Harold seemed hard.
> Harold was hard.
> Harold looked careful.
> Harold looked carefully.

In each of these the word classes are marked, one way or another.

"He was potted" is ambiguous. "He was rather potted" is not. It happens that *rather* patterns with adjectives and not with verbs, and therefore it marks *potted* in this sentence as an adjective. "He was cremated" is not ambiguous, because *cremated* does not pattern as an adjective.

It will be seen that the signals differentiating the word classes of English are various and complex. We shall make no effort to describe them all. The native speaker of English can trace them out for himself. The important thing to notice is that the word classes distinguished are real things. If they were not distinguished and distinguishable, we should not be able to communicate.

SUGGESTIONS

1. It will be seen that words in one form class may have relatives in others. For instance, related to the noun *emancipation* is the verb *emancipate*. Related to the adjective *continuous* are the verb *continue* and the noun *continuation*. The words in the following list ordinarily pattern as noun or verb or adjective. For each word, give the form class to which it usually belongs and the related forms found in other classes.

   continue, courage, bleed, insistent, hard, friendship, devil, conclusion, beautiful, nauseate, sadden, terror, critical, emphatic, gladness, please, electric, rebellious, solve, origin

2. Many words occur in both the noun and the verb classes. E.g., *face* is a noun in "His face is dirty" and a verb in "Let's face it." Decide whether the following words occur as noun only, verb only, or both. Cite sentences to prove your answers.

   face, try, decency, angel, quiet, cloud, speak, book, horse, radio, spend, demand, invite, cook, question, pal, street, neck, come, go, nose, teach, fly, startle, coat, gripe, dog, mink, lack, pitch

3. Give the usual plurals for the following nouns. Answer on the basis of your experience. If you have no experience for some of the words, consult a dictionary. Some words have two possibilities.

   sheep, ox, mouse, ton, deer, calf, bison, roof, thesis, moose, focus, wharf, brother, elf, crisis

4. What generalization can you draw from the fact that *cow, pig, chicken, cat, snake, bird* usually have regular plurals but *deer, quail, buffalo, pheasant, elk, partridge* usually do not? The expressions "three lions" and "three lion" both occur, but in different situations. What are they?

5. Give the usual past tense and past participle for the following verbs. For the past tense see what sounds normal in a pattern like

"He _____ last week" or "He _____ it last week." For the past participle try a pattern like "He had _____ (it) often."

teach, swing, slink, put, sing, fall, freeze, dive, help, broadcast, sweat, shred

6. Determine whether the second word in each of the following phrases is an adjective or not. An adjective will fill both blanks in an expression like "A _____ something is a something that is _____."

(1) an oblong box (2) a shoe box (3) a nosey neighbor (4) a neighborly act (5) a picture gallery (6) an instructive lesson (7) the instructor's opinion (8) a charming smile (9) a bus driver (10) a radio program

7. Use the following words first as determiners and then as pronouns. Consult Section 96 if necessary.

each, her, any, some, three, several, both, few

8. The following sentences, some of which might occur in telegrams or newspaper headlines, are ambiguous. Explain the two meanings. Indicate the word classes that are not clear. Then make additions that will resolve the ambiguity.

(1) She was charming. (2) Grease runs smoothly. (3) Market sinks. (4) Swiss watches strike. (5) Street needs change. (6) Elwood appeared fast. (7) City fathers plan. (8) Radio broadcasts smell.

9. Jabberwocky sentences, in which nonsense words are used as nouns, verbs, adjectives, and adverbs, illustrate the fact that identification of form classes does not depend on meaning. See if you can identify the nouns, verbs, adjectives, and adverbs in the following sentences.

(1) The grivel swoggled a plodge. (2) A rather gooby sebblewidge was borgling its trope. (3) Spinging a repple horboursly, the kallandaff worfled a few cromps. (4) As the grabic sworgmond stroppled down the shaster, a rather spleshy bargdrash nubbed in and spoofered. (5) Never splag a cramish with a morgous gub.

Structure words : as, the . . .

4. As . . . shaster - dependent clause.
adverbial clause.

12

Sentence Patterns

100. Subject-Verb Sentences

The English that we speak and hear and read and write seems to be of utterances infinite in variety. But if we look past word differences into the structure of the language, we find that our expression can be seen as a relatively few structures endlessly repeated.

First of all, English has a unit which we call the _sentence_. We have seen earlier the hazards involved in seeking a philosophical definition of this unit, and we shall try to avoid the quagmire. Like most other language features, sentences are more easily illustrated than defined. All we need say at this point is that in speech we have units which we call sentences and which are marked off from one another by complicated patterns of intonation. In writing, we have comparable units marked off by capital letters at the beginning and periods at the end.

Let us now examine the make-up of these units, the structures that typically compose them. First of all we may ask whether such units always contain a subject and a verb. Well, obviously not always. If you listen to two people chatting back and forth, you will note that many, perhaps most, of their sentences are without subject and verb. A conversation, for example, might plausibly go like this:

"Seen Ed Forash?"
"Not lately. I think he's in Springfield."

"Staying with his brother?"

"Most likely. Or with his father."

"His father live in Springfield? Terre Haute, I thought."

"You're right. Terre Haute."

We see then that the subject-verb sentence is but one kind of sentence and in some types of communication not the most important kind. In other types it predominates. If, for example, you listen to someone giving directions to someone else or describing something or explaining a process, you will find that the great majority of sentences are subject-verb sentences. Similarly in some kinds of writing subject-verb sentences are the rule and subjectless sentences the exception.

In the writing one is called on to do in college work, the great majority of sentences will be of the subject-verb type. We shall therefore limit our study to sentences of this kind. But first we must be a little more precise about what a subject is.

101. Subjects

We have seen that English nouns have singular-plural forms: *tree/trees, boy/boys, man/men,* etc. English verbs also have varying forms—*see/sees, think/thinks, do/does*—the occurrence of which depends on the occurrence of accompanying nouns. Thus if we say, "The boys see the lion," the form *see* occurs because the form *boys* has occurred. If we change *boys* to *boy,* then *see* changes to *sees:* "The boy sees the lion." The word *lion* in this sentence, however, has no effect on the form of the verb, for we say either "The boy sees the lion" or "The boy sees the lions."

When a noun and a verb occur in a sentence in such a way that the form of one is affected by the form of the other, we say that the noun and the verb are *tied*. We say further that a noun tied to a verb is the *subject* of the verb. That is what a subject is: a noun (or equivalent) tied to a verb by a concurrence or agreement of forms.

It will be seen that no other definition of *subject* is very satisfactory. It cannot be defined as the word in front of the verb, because often it isn't, as in "The father of the boys was there" or "Were his brothers here?" Neither can it be defined as the word that names the performer of the action. Many subjects name the performer of the action, but many don't. If we took "performer of the action"as a definition of *subject,* then in the sentence "The boy was eaten by the lion," we should have to say that the subject is *lion,* for *lion* certainly names the performer of this action. But *lion* is not the subject. *Boy* is the subject, for it is tied to *was.* If we change *boy* to *boys,* we change *was* to *were:* "The boys were eaten by the lion."

There are just a few other points to make about subjects. The last example shows that if the verb is accompanied by an auxiliary, the tie is not between noun and verb but between noun and auxiliary:

	SUBJECT	AUXILIARY	VERB
The	boy	was	eaten.
The	boys	were	eaten.
The	man	has	eaten.
The	men	have	eaten.

In English, past tenses of verbs do not have varying forms as present tenses do. Nevertheless, we say that nouns are tied to such verbs, and are their subjects, if they are in positions in which change would occur in the present tense:

	SUBJECT	VERB	
The	boy	drinks	milk.
The	boys	drink	milk.
The	boy	drank	milk.
The	boys	drank	milk.

Similarly, some auxiliaries have invariable forms. But we say that they are tied to nouns, their subjects, when they are in positions where other auxiliaries would show the tie:

Subject		Auxiliary	Verb	
The	boy	is	drinking	milk.
The	boys	are	drinking	milk.
The	boy	does	drink	milk.
The	boys	do	drink	milk.
The	boy	must	drink	milk.
The	boys	must	drink	milk.

Finally, many constructions besides nouns occur as subjects. Such constructions are subjects when they are in subject positions—i.e., positions in which a noun would affect the form of the verb or auxiliary:

Subject		Auxiliary	Verb	
The	boy	was	taming	the lion.
The	boys	were	taming	the lion.
	He	was	taming	the lion.
	They	were	taming	the lion.
	Nobody	was	taming	the lion.
	Milk	is		good for you.
	This	is		good for you.
	Drinking milk	is		good for you.

Using this concept of the subject, we can describe the half a dozen most common sentence patterns of English writing. There are other English sentence patterns besides these. But it will be seen that the great majority of the sentences we write are made up of either one of these patterns, or an expansion of one of them through modification, or a combination of two or more of them.

102. Pattern One

The first pattern is composed basically simply of a noun tied to a verb. If we use the symbol N for *noun* (or *noun equivalent*) and V for *verb* and a double arrow to show the tie, we can write the formula for this pattern as N↔V:

N⟵⟶V	
Lions	roar.
Charlie	roars.
Charlie	roared.
He	left.
That	hurts.

Actually, the pattern occurs rather infrequently in this minimum form. Usually there is some kind of expansion. For instance, the noun may be preceded by a determiner (D) or some other modifier:

D	N⟵⟶V	
The	lion	roared.
My	motor	knocks.

Or the verb may have an auxiliary. In this case, the tie is between the noun and the auxiliary:

D	N⟵⟶Aux.	V
	Charlie	was	roaring.
The	lions	were	roaring.
	He	had	left.
The	car	may	explode.

Or the verb may be modified by an adverb or other modifier:

D	N⟵⟶Aux.	V	Adv.
The	lions	were	roaring	loudly.
	Albert	has	gone	away.
My	brother	may	drop	in.

All of these are variations of pattern one: N↔V. The pattern may be very considerably expanded and still be basically the same. These expansions we shall consider in detail in the next chapter, but here is a preliminary example of pattern one much enlarged:

All the old circus LIONS that my brother is keeping in a shed behind our house ROAR so much every morning about four-thirty
that they wake up the whole neighborhood.

*This is basically still pattern one, N↔V. The rest is just
modification.*

103. Pattern Two

Pattern two is basically a noun tied to a verb with an adjective following. This may be written N↔V Adj. Only a
limited number of verbs occur in this pattern. By far the most
common is the verb *be:*

N◄——————►V		ADJ.
Albert	was	unhappy.
Grass	is	green.
They	were	comfortable.
Alice	looked	foolish.
She	seems	better.

Again, all the usual kinds of expansion can occur without
altering the pattern:

D	N◄——┘—►AUX.		V	ADJ.	ADV.
	Albert		was	unhappy.	
The	boys		were	unhappy.	
The	boys	had	been	unhappy.	
The	boys	had	been	unhappy	often.
The	cake		turned	blue	later.
My	arm		stayed	sore.	
His	story	did	ring	true.	
The	meal		tasted	terrible.	
	This		smells	good.	
	He		sounds	contrite.	
	Alice	was	getting	sick.	
The	cow		ran	dry.	

About a dozen verbs besides *be* occur commonly in this
pattern. Most of them are illustrated in the examples above.

In addition, some fifty other verbs occur here in more or less special contexts, like "run dry," "ring true," "blush pink."

Note that dialect or colloquial sentences like "He done good" or "She dresses very neat" are not examples of pattern two but of pattern one. The correct analysis is that *good* and *neat* are adverbs in such dialects, not adjectives.

104. Pattern Three

The third pattern consists of a noun tied to a verb with a second noun following: N↔V   N. The second noun in this *3,* pattern is what is traditionally called an *object* or a *direct object*. The verb in the pattern is sometimes called a *transitive verb.*

N←	→V	N	*verb carries action to dir. obj.*
Lions	eat	meat.	
Albert	bit	me.	
She	plays	croquet.	

With expansion:

D	N←	→Aux.	V	D	N	Adv.
The	lion		eats		meat.	
The	lion	was	eating	the	meat.	
The	lion	was	eating	the	meat	happily.
My	brother		likes		spaghetti.	
	He	was	washing	the	car.	
	Nobody	had	seen		Florence.	
Some	Egyptians		left	this	package.	

105. Pattern Four

The fourth pattern also consists of a noun tied to a verb *4,* with another noun following. The difference is that in pattern three the two nouns refer to different people or different things, whereas in pattern four they refer to the same person or the same thing:

PATTERN THREE:　That man chased my brother.
PATTERN FOUR:　That man is my brother.

In the first sentence, man and brother are different people:
in the second they are the same person. The signal differentiating the two patterns is of course in the verb. The verb of
pattern four is what is called a *linking verb*. We shall write
this LV, and thus the formula for the pattern will be N↔LV
N. By far the most common linking verb is *be*, though *become*
and *remain* occur in this pattern sometimes. In British English various other verbs occur here.

D	N⟷LV		D	N
That	man	is	my	brother.
	He	is	a	lawyer.
	They	are		lawyers.
	That	's		that.
His	sister	became	my	mother-in-law.
	We	remained		friends.
	Albert	looked	a	fool. (British)
	He	continued	my	friend. (British)

106. Pattern Five

The fifth pattern consists of a noun tied to a verb with two
other nouns (or noun equivalents) following. In traditional
parlance, the first of the following nouns is what is called an
indirect object, the second a *direct object:*

N⟷V		N		N
My	father	gave	my brother	a	beating.
	She	sent	me	her	picture.
	Henry	told	us	a	lie.
	She	brings	us		peaches every day.
Mr.	Goddard	taught	his children		French.
	Stanley	asked	you	a	question.
	I	'll sing	the baby	a	lullaby.

107. Pattern Six

The sixth pattern also has the components noun-verb-noun-noun. The difference between five and six is that in five the second and third nouns refer to different people or different things, whereas in six they refer to the same person or the same thing:

PATTERN FIVE: Albert sent my brother a monkey.

PATTERN SIX: Albert thought my brother a monkey. *obj. complement*

In five, *brother* and *monkey* refer to different individuals; in six, they refer to the same individual.

The signal differentiating patterns five and six—like that distinguishing three and four—is the verb. Some verbs, like *give* and *send,* will ordinarily make the two following nouns refer to different people or things; others, like *think* and *elect,* will make the two nouns refer to the same person or thing. Oddly enough, traditional grammar has no special terms for these verbs, though it does have terms for the nouns involved. The nouns in five, as we have seen, are called, respectively, *indirect object* and *direct object.* Those in six are called *object* and *object complement.* Thus, in "Albert thought my brother a monkey," *brother* is an object, and *monkey* is an object complement.

Just to give it a tag, let's call the verb in pattern six an *object-complement verb* and abbreviate it OV. Then we can distinguish the two patterns like this:

PATTERN FIVE: N↔V   N   N
PATTERN SIX: N↔OV   N   N

Now here are some more examples of pattern six:

N←————→OV		N *object*	N *obj. comp*
Albert	thought	my brother a	fool.
We	elected	Albert	chairman.
Nobody	considered	him a	coward.
I	found	Charlie a big	help.
His teacher	made	him a great	pianist.
I	believed	her an honest	girl.

There are a few verbs which occur in both pattern five and pattern six. Usually there is then some additional signal telling which pattern is meant. If not, the sentence will be ambiguous, since part of understanding English is being able to tell these patterns apart. A verb occurring in both patterns is the verb *call*. It occurs in five in "He called me a taxi," in six in "He called me a fool." It is ambiguous in "The Sultan called me a slave," where it might mean "The Sultan summoned a slave to wait on me" (five) or "The Sultan said I was a slave" (six). This is also the basis of an old joke:

FIRST PERSON: Call me a taxi.
SECOND PERSON: Okay, you're a taxi.

108. Pattern Seven

There are various other patterns occurring now and then in English, but we shall notice only one more. This is a structure introduced by the word *there*. An example is the first sentence in this paragraph. Here is another:

There were some men here.

The word *there* in this pattern is a structure word in a class by itself. If a term is needed for it, it can be called structure-word *there*. This *there* is not an adverb but simply a means of getting this particular pattern started. English does have an adverb *there,* and we can see the difference between the two *there's* in the sentence

There were some men there. *adv.*

The second *there* is an adverb, as we can see from the fact that we can substitute other words of the adverb class for it. We can say "There were some men here," "There were some men outside," etc. But no other word will substitute for the first *there*. We do not say "Here were some men there," or "Outside were some men there." Further, there is a difference in pronunciation between structure-word *there* and adverb *there*, resulting from different stress positions. Adverb *there* is regularly pronounced to rhyme with *wear;* structure-word *there* has various different pronunciations, some people rhyming it with *were.*

Finally, notice that structure-word *there* has lost its meaning. If it still had the adverb meaning, "There were some men there" would be redundant, and "There were some men here" would be a contradiction.

The typical composition of this pattern is THERE V↔N Adv. Notice that we still have a subject tied to the verb, but that it follows the verb instead of preceding it. Instead of an adverb, we may have some equivalent, like a prepositional phrase:

THERE	V←		→N	ADV.
There	were	some	men	here.
There	was	a	man	here.
There	's	a	bucket	outside.
There	are	two	buckets	outside.
There	is	a	snake	under the house.
There	are	many	snakes	under the house.

This is a high-frequency pattern, and it is worth noting because you may get into trouble if, in writing it, you fail to show the tie between subject and verb. For instance, the sentence "There was many snakes under the house" would be considered inelegant and unsuitable to college writing.

There are a few other patterns in which the subject follows the verb. We may note them without numbering them. One is a pattern which is introduced by an adverb of the type *seldom, never, not once:*

> Seldom was the man there.
> Seldom were the men there.
> Never was he on time.
> Never were they on time.
> Not once were they on time.

The adverbs *there* and *here* introduce a verb-subject construction sometimes. The verb is usually *go* or *come* or *be:*

> There goes Charlie.
> There go the boys.
> Here comes Alice.
> Here's Sam.
> Here are the cucumbers.

This *there* is the adverb, not the structure word.

Sometimes verb-subject constructions are introduced by adverbs of the type *up, out, down* or by prepositional phrases:

> Up jumped the tiger.
> Down the street strolled the Robinsons.

But such sentences seldom occur in conversation and not often in writing, except in books for children.

109. Summary of the Sentence Patterns

Let us summarize our seven main sentence patterns:

ONE:	N↔V		Babies cry.
TWO:	N↔V Adj.		Children are noisy.
THREE:	N↔V N		George shoots lions.
FOUR:	N↔LV N		Lions are animals.
FIVE:	N↔V N N		Albert gave Alice a tomato.
SIX:	N↔OV N N		Albert called Alice a tomato.
SEVEN:	THERE V↔N Adv.		There were some men there.

110. Statements, Questions, and Requests

These are all, specifically, *statement* patterns. We have three main sentence divisions in English: *statements, questions,* and *requests.* If definition of these concepts is needed, it can be found in the different effects they have on listeners. A request tends to make the listener do something; a question tends to make him say something—that is, answer; a statement tends to make him go on listening:

> Sit down. (Listener sits down.)
> Is Sam sitting down? (Listener answers "Yes" or "No.")
> Sam is sitting down. (Listener nods head intelligently.)

All seven statement patterns can be converted into questions by procedures familiar to any speaker of English. The first six are made into *yes/no* questions (questions that can be answered by *yes* or *no*) by reversal of subject and verb or subject and auxiliary. Only the verb *be* always reverses simply; other verbs require an auxiliary:

ONE: Do babies cry?
Two: Are children noisy?
THREE: Did George shoot lions?
FOUR: Are lions animals?
FIVE: Did Albert give Alice a tomato?
SIX: Did Albert call Alice a tomato?

Seven signals a question by reversing structure-word *there* and the verb:

SEVEN: Were there some men there?

Questions of another type are signaled by occurrence in the patterns of a structure group called *question words* or *interrogatives.* These are *who, which, what, whom, whose, why, when, where, how.*

Why do babies cry?

Which children were noisy?

The first six patterns occur as requests when the first noun, the subject, is omitted. Request sentences ordinarily have no subjects: *Command :*

ONE: Cry.
TWO: Be noisy.
THREE: Shoot the lions.
FOUR: Be a man.
FIVE: Give Alice a tomato.
SIX: Call Alice a tomato.

The seventh pattern does not occur as a request.

SUGGESTIONS

1. Write minimum sentences from the following formulas.

(1) N↔V   (2) N↔V   Adj.   (3) N↔V   N   (4) N↔LV   N
(5) N↔V   N   N   (6) N↔OV   N   N

2. Expand your minimum sentences, as the "Lions roar" sentence is expanded in Section 102.

3. Change your sentences into *yes/no* questions. Note the alterations in structure.

4. Change your sentences into questions containing interrogatives (*who, which, why,* etc.).

5. Change your sentences into requests.

6. Write a half a dozen sentences on the pattern THERE V↔N   Adv. Note the subject-verb tie.

7. Change these sentences into questions.

13

Expanding
the Patterns

111. Some New Terms

In the last chapter we examined seven high-frequency patterns occurring in English communication. We want now to see how these skeleton patterns are fleshed out by modification.

First we shall need a few new terms. One is *modification structure*. This means simply a word that is modified plus its modifier or modifiers. The word that is modified is called a *headword*. The modifiers of a headword are called *modifiers*. Thus a modification structure consists of a headword plus one or more modifiers of the headword.

In English, the headword of a modification structure is most likely to be a noun or verb. Modification of nouns and verbs in English is extensive and varied. Adjectives and adverbs sometimes stand as headwords of modification structures, but their modification is simpler than that of nouns and verbs. Occasionally some structure words, like prepositions, occur as headwords of modification structures.

All of the form classes and some of the structure words occur as modifiers. Thus a noun headword, as we shall see in detail presently, may be modified by an adjective, by another noun, by a verb, or by an adverb. It may also be modified by a determiner or by certain word groups. A verb may be modified by an adverb, by another verb, by a noun, by an adjective, by an auxiliary or by word groups.

A convenient term for a noun modification structure—that is, a modification structure with a noun as its headword—is *noun cluster*. A modification structure with a verb as its headword is a *verb cluster*. We shall see that noun clusters and verb clusters occupy a very important place in English structure.

Before proceeding to the details of noun clusters and verb clusters, let us have a preliminary example. Take this sentence:

> The young trapeze artist in the center ring was hanging by his thumbs.

This sentence consists of two main parts, a noun cluster and a verb cluster. The noun cluster is *the young trapeze artist in the center ring*. The headword in this cluster is the noun *artist*. This is modified on one side by a determiner (*the*), by an adjective (*young*), by another noun (*trapeze*). On the other side it is modified by a prepositional word group, *in the center ring*. This group contains another noun cluster, *the center ring,* with *ring* as the headword.

The verb cluster is *was hanging by his thumbs*. The headword is the verb *hanging*. This is modified on one side by an auxiliary (*was*), on the other side by a prepositional group, *by his thumbs*.

112. Noun Clusters

The most common noun modifier is a determiner. We have

had the list of determiners earlier (Section 95) and examples
are easy and obvious:

Modifier	Headword
D	N

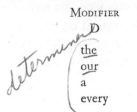

the	ghost
our	friends
a	doorknob
every	church

Nouns are also frequently modified by adjectives:

Modifier	Headword
Adj.	N
yellow	flowers
brave	men
tall	building
sad	story

If a noun headword is modified by a determiner and an
adjective at the same time, as frequently happens, the order
is determiner-adjective-noun:

Modifier	Modifier	Headword
D	Adj.	N
some	yellow	flowers
every	brave	man
that	tall	building
his	sad	story

Nouns may be modified by other nouns:

Modifier	Headword
N	N
trapeze	artist
circus	lion
drugstore	cowboy
ocean	liner

In speech, the stress patterns of most N-N clusters differ markedly from those of an Adj.-N cluster. *Trapeze artist,* for example, would have the primary stress on the second syllable of *trapéze; handsome artist* would have it on the first syllable of *artist.* However some N-N clusters have the same stress pattern as Adj.-N clusters—e.g., *cámpus bus, Student Union, drugstore cowboy.*

If a determiner, an adjective, and a noun all modify a noun headword, the order is determiner-adjective-noun-noun:

MODIFIER	MODIFIER	MODIFIER	HEADWORD
D	Adj.	N	N
a	friendly	trapeze	artist
every	eager	insurance	salesman
her	handsome	drugstore	cowboy
his	lonely	hotel	room

Nouns may also be modified by verbs. There are two types of verbs that commonly modify nouns. One is the type ending in the spelling *-ing: singing, weeping, hesitating.* This is called the *present participle.* We shall write it V-ing. The other is the past participle form, the same form that is used after the auxiliary *have: have invited, have resented, have spoken, have resisted.* Most of these end in the spelling *-ed* (*invited, resented, resisted*): some irregular verbs end otherwise (*spoken, seen, told*). We shall indicate this form with the symbol V-ed.

Here are examples of nouns modified by V-ing verbs:

MODIFIER	HEADWORD
V-ing	N
screaming	child
dripping	faucet
smiling	villain
burning	room

And by V-ed verbs:

Modifier	Headword
V-ed	N
suggested	improvements
pacified	child
written	answer
hidden	gold

113. Meanings of the Modifiers

These different kinds of noun modifiers produce different kinds of meanings with respect to the noun headwords. The different meanings are not easy to sum up in philosophical definitions. For instance, it might be hard to say what meaning the adjectives *green, courageous,* and *perpendicular* have in common in the clusters *green rug, courageous fighter,* and *perpendicular column.* But it is perfectly easy to see the difference between a green rug and a living room rug; for a green rug is a rug that is green, but a living room rug is not a rug that is living room. Similarly, a courageous fighter is a fighter that is courageous, but a New York fighter is not a fighter that is New York; and a perpendicular column is a column that is perpendicular, but a newspaper column is not a column that is newspaper.

Verbs modifying nouns have other class meanings. A screaming child differs from an unhappy child in that a screaming child is a child that screams, whereas an unhappy child is not a child that unhappies. Invited guests are guests that somebody invited; greedy guests are not guests that somebody greedied.

Part of understanding English is being able to sort out the various kinds of modifiers. If it ever happens that you can't tell whether a given modifier is, say, an adjective or a noun, then you won't know the meaning of the cluster. The word *orderly,* for example, occurs as a noun, as in *the General's orderly,* and as an adjective, as in *a very orderly person.* In the cluster *an orderly room,* you can't tell whether *orderly* is a noun or an adjective and consequently can't tell whether it means a room inhabited by orderlies (noun) or a room that is orderly (adjective). Speech, of course, would give a clue in the stress pattern. The cluster *an orderly orderly room,* however, is clear. It means a room for orderlies that is orderly.

There are various layers of complexities below those we have noted. For instance, there are at least two kinds of *-ing* verbs, because *reading room* is not the same sort of structure as *burning room.* A burning room is a room that is burning, but a reading room is not a room that is reading. The cluster *smoking room* is ambiguous in writing because we don't know which modifier is present, whether the room is on fire or is a room where smoking is permitted.

The cluster *moving van* contains an added ambiguity. It usually means a van for moving furniture, where *moving van* is like *reading room.* But it could be like *burning room* and mean a van that is in motion. But *moving,* like some other *-ing* words, occurs sometimes as an adjective—"That's a very moving story." So a moving van might be a van that stirs one's emotions. The cluster *a very moving moving moving van* is, however, not ambiguous. It means a van that is used for moving furniture, that is in motion, and that raises a lump in one's throat, perhaps because it is taking away the ancestral belongings.

Thus the noun cluster contains a considerable variety of meanings depending on the different modifiers that occur. In successful discourse these different modifiers are kept distinct by a set of complex but tangible signals.

114. Modifiers After the Headword

So far we have been concerned with those noun modifiers that occur before the noun headword. There are also noun modifiers occurring after the headword. This, for instance, is the usual position for adverbs modifying nouns. Here are some examples:

Modifier	Headword	Modifier
D	N	Adv.
the	people	there *place*
the	car	outside
the	trees	beyond
the	dinner	afterward *(time)*
our	friends	upstairs

It will be noticed that most adverbs modifying nouns are adverbs of the *there* (place) group, though some time adverbs, like *afterward,* also occur.

Another construction occurring after a noun headword is *prep.* the preposition group. A preposition may be defined as a word patterning like *with* in the construction *the boy with the dog.* Substituting for *with* in this construction, we would get such words as *behind, over, under, by, inside, in front of, near, alongside, ahead of.* Counting such phrases as *in front of* and *ahead of,* there are some seventy words occurring commonly in English as prepositions. A preposition is regularly followed by a noun or noun equivalent, sometimes called the object of the preposition. The preposition and the noun work together as a tight word group and may be referred to as a preposition group, or P-group. Thus in *the boy with the dog,* the P-group is *with the dog,* consisting of the preposition *with* *Prep.* ⎫ P-group and the noun cluster *the dog.* *Noun.* ⎭

Now here are some examples of preposition groups modifying nouns:

MODIFIER	HEADWORD	MODIFIER
D	N	P-group
the	boy	with the dog
a	toy	in the window
the	man	on first
his	place	in the mountains
a	dance	in the moonlight

115. Subordinated Sentences as Noun Modifiers

Nouns may also be modified by sentence patterns, as in the noun cluster *the people who left early*. Here the word group *who left early* is obviously similar to a regular sentence pattern like "He left early," the only difference being that the word *who* stands in place of the subject *he*. *Who* in this sentence is what is called a *subordinator*. It serves to subordinate the sentence pattern to which it belongs, to make it part of a larger construction, the noun cluster. The group of words *who left early* may be called a subordinated sentence, or, for convenience, an S-group.

The subordinators introducing S-groups that modify nouns are *who, whom, whose, which,* and *that*. (The first four of these occur also as interrogatives.) We shall encounter other subordinators when we take up verb clusters. Here are some examples of S-groups as noun modifiers. Notice that the subordinator sometimes takes the place of the subject of the sentence pattern, sometimes of the object, and sometimes of a determiner.

MODIFIER	HEADWORD	subordinator	MODIFIER
D	N	↓	S-group
the	girl	*nom·* who went away
the	house		that had been burglarized
a	gift	*det.* which he gave his mother
a	child		whose parents were in trouble
the	guests	*obj.* whom we had invited

Sometimes the S-group is not introduced by a subordinator, position alone showing its relation to the noun cluster:

MODIFIER	HEADWORD	*no Subordinator* MODIFIER
the	guests	we had invited
the	girl	he left behind
a	pigeon	I had always admired

When a P-group and an S-group modify the same noun headword, the order is rigid: the P-group comes first and the S-group second:

MODIFIER D	HEADWORD N	MODIFIER P-group	MODIFIER S-group
the	men	in the pit	who were working
a	child	of four	that had been crying

In this combination, however, if the signals aren't clear, it is possible to produce ambiguous clusters like *the girl in the car he left behind.*

116. Summary of Modifiers in Noun Clusters

This is not all there is to noun clusters. We shall see later that verb clusters are sometimes a part of noun clusters. But this will do for now. In summary, let us note how a noun headword can be expanded into a large cluster with various kinds of modifiers fore and aft:

tribesmen
the tribesmen (determiner added)
the desert tribesmen (noun added)
the unhappy desert tribesmen (adjective added)

The only modifiers that will stand in front of the determiner are *all* and *both:*

all the unhappy desert tribesmen

Now of course the word *all* can be modified:

> nearly all the unhappy desert tribesmen
> very nearly all the unhappy desert tribesmen

But *nearly* modifies *all,* and *very* modifies *nearly;* they are not modifiers of the noun headword:

> very nearly all the unhappy desert tribesmen in the tent (P-group added)
> very nearly all the unhappy desert tribesmen in the tent who were playing poker (S-group added)

It is still just a noun cluster, not a sentence, and, we might note, it has no punctuation within it.

A noun cluster can occur anywhere that the headword can occur. For instance, *tribesmen* might occur as a subject: "The tribesmen were getting sleepy." So can the cluster:

> Very nearly all the unhappy desert tribesmen in the tent who were playing poker were getting sleepy.

As object in pattern three:

> The police arrested the tribesmen.
> The police arrested very nearly all the unhappy desert tribesmen in the tent who were playing poker.

As indirect object in pattern five:

> I gave the tribesmen some bananas.
> I gave very nearly all the unhappy desert tribesmen in the tent who were playing poker some bananas.

As object in pattern six:

> We considered the tribesmen loafers.
> We considered very nearly all the unhappy desert tribesmen in the tent who were playing poker loafers.

117. Verb Clusters

Verbs may also be modified in a variety of ways. As nouns may be modified by determiners, so verbs may be modified by auxiliaries. The determiner signals that a noun is coming; the auxiliary signals that a verb is coming. The auxiliary adds to the verb such meanings as tense and mood. Note that the form of the verb depends on the particular auxiliary that occurs:

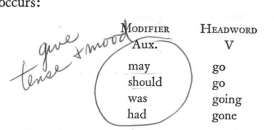

MODIFIER	HEADWORD
Aux.	V
may	go
should	go
was	going
had	gone

Verbs are very commonly modified by other verbs. The verb headword in such clusters has either the form *-ing* or the simple form preceded by the structure word *to*, depending on the particular modifier which occurs:

MODIFIER	HEADWORD
V	V
kept	going
got	going
wanted	to go
started	to go
intended	to go
began	going

You may ask why such verb modifiers are not also called auxiliaries. The difference is that the forms here called auxiliaries pattern with verbs in very special ways, particularly in the asking of questions and in negative sentences. For example, we say, "May he go?" "Should he go?" "Was he going?" "Had he gone?" But we do not say "Kept he going?" "Got he going?" "Wanted he to go?" Similarly we say, "He may not go" but not "He kept not going," "He was going, wasn't he?" But not "He started to go, started not he?"

Verb headwords are also, of course, modified by adverbs.

We have seen that there are three groups of adverbs: place (*there*), manner (*thus*), time (*then*). If all three occur after the same verb headword, the normal order is *there, thus, then:*

HEADWORD V	MODIFIER Adv.	MODIFIER Adv.	MODIFIER Adv.
came	in	noisily	sometimes
looked	up	angrily	then
play	around	mischievously	usually
went	away	unhappily	later

The *then* and *thus* adverbs occur also before the verb headword, the *then* adverbs frequently, the *thus* adverbs sometimes. *There* adverbs do not usually occur before the headword:

MODIFIER Adv.	HEADWORD V	MODIFIER Adv.	MODIFIER Adv.
sometimes	came	in	noisily
often	spoke	up	quietly
never	sang		
always	answered		rudely

MODIFIER Adv.	HEADWORD V	MODIFIER Adv.
noisily	walked	in
angrily	went	away

Verbs may also be modified by nouns. In a sense the noun objects of the basic patterns are modifiers of the verbs in the patterns, but in addition to these we have a number of noun constructions like *this morning, that way, next week,* and these frequently occur as modifiers in verb clusters. Notice that these nouns usually occur with a determiner or with a special time word like *last* or *next:*

HEADWORD	MODIFIER
V	N
came	this morning *noun construction*
worked	last night
leaves	next month
went	that way
returns	every spring

118. P-Groups and S-Groups in Verb Clusters

Preposition groups modify verbs as well as nouns. When they modify verbs, they occur after the verb headword:

HEADWORD	MODIFIER
V	P-group
came	in a hurry
came	in a car
walked	by the river
walked	with his aunt
spoke	to the mayor
left	before dawn

Sometimes a verb headword has more than one P-group modifying it:

HEADWORD	MODIFIER	MODIFIER
V	P-group	P-group
came	in a car	with his aunt
walked	by the river	before dawn

Verb headwords may also be modified by subordinated sentences (S-groups). These S-groups are slightly different from those that occur in noun clusters. In verb clusters the S-group *S-group* is introduced by a subordinator of the type *because, when, if.* These words serve to signal that the sentence pattern that follows is not a separate sentence but is part of another construction. For instance, "George is my friend" is an independent sentence (pattern four). But *since George is my friend,* though it contains the same sentence pattern, is not a separate and independent sentence. The subordinator *since* shows it to be part of some other construction.

Here are examples of verb headwords modified by S-groups:

HEADWORD		MODIFIER
	V	S-group
	comes	when he has time
	left	before the dance was over
	hurried	because she was late
	danced	until we were exhausted
will	speak	if he is asked

If a P-group and an S-group modify the same verb headword, the P-group comes first and the S-group second:

HEADWORD		MODIFIER	MODIFIER
	V	P-group	S-group
	comes	on his bicycle	when he has time
will	speak	to the group	if he is asked

Often a verb cluster will contain a considerable number of the various modifiers:

MODIFIER	MODIFIER	HEADWORD	MODIFIER	MODIFIER
Aux.	Adv.	V	Adv.	P-group
would	usually	go	out	with the boys

MODIFIER
S-group
if he felt well

The order is not quite so rigid as it is in noun clusters, the adverbs in particular having considerable range of movement. However, the position of the modifiers in verb clusters is limited. All of the following, for instance, are easily recognized as un-English:

would go usually out with the boys if he felt well
would out go usually with the boys if he felt well
would go out if he felt well usually with the boys
with the boys would usually go out if he felt well

119. Verb Clusters in the Basic Sentence Patterns

Before we leave verb clusters, we should note that some of the basic sentence patterns also contain verb clusters. For instance, pattern two (N-V-Adj.) always contains not just a verb but a verb cluster. An example of this pattern would be a sentence like "The boys grew tall." This consists of two parts: the noun cluster *the boys*, which is the subject; and the verb cluster *grew tall*. The verb cluster consists of the headword *grew* and the modifier *tall*. Pattern two, in other words, always contains a verb cluster in which an adjective modifies a verb.

This description diverges from that of conventional grammar, which would say that *tall* modifies the subject, *the boys*. But it is impossible to support this notion. The sentence "The boys grew tall" clearly consists of *the boys* as one part and *grew tall* as the other. There is no unit here consisting of *the boys tall*. *The boys* is the subject of *grew tall,* and therefore *tall* patterns with *grew*. We shall return to this point in the next chapter.

Similarly in "Our friends remained loyal," we have a verb cluster *remained loyal* in which the adjective *loyal* modifies the verb headword *remained*. In "He was young" the verb cluster is *was young,* and *young* modifies *was;* it certainly does not modify *he,* for there is no unit here consisting of *he young*.

In sentences like "He locked the door" (pattern three) it is usual to say that *the door* is the object of *locked,* though there would be nothing irrational in calling it also a modifier.

At any rate *locked the door* is a verb cluster with *locked* as the headword. In "She gave the baby a bath" (pattern five) we have a verb cluster *gave the baby a bath* in which the headword is *gave*.

All of these patterns may be expanded by the modifiers we have already noted:

> always locked the door when he went out
> usually gave the baby a bath before lunch in the summertime

120. Adjective and Adverb Clusters

Adjectives and adverbs may also be modified by a variety of other word classes, though in these clusters we do not usually find more than one or two modifiers at a time.

Adjectives are perhaps most commonly modified by intensifiers occurring before the adjective headword:

MODIFIER	HEADWORD
Int.	Adj.
very	unhappy
rather	cool
pretty	silly

We have noted that intensifiers do not modify nouns and verbs; they therefore sometimes serve as a signal that a following word is an adjective, not a noun or a verb. For example, we saw that *an orderly room* is ambiguous, at least in writing, since we don't know whether *orderly* is a noun or an adjective. But *a very orderly room* is unambiguous, for *very* signals the adjective. Similarly *a rather moving van* must mean a van that stirs the emotions; it can't mean a van in motion or a van for moving furniture. "He was rather potted" must mean he was drunk; it can't mean his remains were placed in an urn.

Adjectives are also modified by nouns:

Modifier	Headword
N	Adj.
knee	high
skin	deep
ice	cold
a yard	wide
water	tight

A few adjectives are modified by other adjectives or by verbs:

Modifier	Headword
Adj.	Adj.
icy	cold
bluish	green

Modifier	Headword
V-ing	Adj.
boiling	hot
freezing	cold

Adverbs are rather common modifiers of adjectives:

Modifier	Headword
Adv.	Adj.
quietly	sad
beautifully	true
sadly	beautiful

After the headword adjectives are modified by P-groups and S-groups:

Headword	Modifier
Adj.	
ready	for anything
strong	as a bull — P-group
clever	with his hands P- Group
young	as he was ∽ S-group
silent	when he had nothing to say —S-group

In some constructions such S-groups modify the adjective; in others they don't. For instance, in the sentence "Silent when he had nothing to say, Alfred talked readily enough when he needed to," the S-group modifies the adjective *silent*. But in "He was silent when he had nothing to say," the S-group is part of the verb cluster with *was* as the headword.

Adverbs are most commonly modified by intensifiers:

Modifier Int.	Headword Adv.
very	unhappily
rather	beautifully

They are also modified by other adverbs:

Modifier Adv.	Headword Adv.
remarkably	well
unusually	quickly

The reason *remarkably* is an adverb and *very* is not is that *remarkably* occurs in adverb positions and *very* doesn't. We say "She played remarkably" but not "She played very."

Some adverbs may be modified by S-groups:

	Headword Adv.	Modifier S-group
	quickly	as he could
more	quietly	than one would have imagined

These are the principal—though not the only—modification structures that occur in English. To see just how they fit into the intricacies of English expression, we shall have to take up another subject—immediate constituents.

SUGGESTIONS

1. Illustrate the noun clusters indicated by the following formulas. The symbol for the headword is italicized.

(1) D Adj. *N*   (2) D N *N*   (3) D *N* P-group   (4) D V-ing *N*
(5) D V-ed *N*   (6) D V-ing N *N*   (7) D Adj. *N* S-group   (8) D

Adj. N *N* Adv. (9) D Adj. *N* P-group S-group (10) D V-ing N *N* P-group S-group

2. Construct sentences using the following noun clusters in sentence patterns as indicated in the parentheses.

(1) a young violin player (subject in pattern one) (2) some little children with a big dog (object in pattern three) (3) the bus conductor who was causing trouble (indirect object in pattern five) (4) a car with no wheels that he had bought for six dollars (direct object in pattern five) (5) very nearly all the handsome high school principals in the back of the room who were so pleased with themselves (object in pattern six)

3. Construct verb clusters from the following formulas. The symbol for the headword is italicized.

(1) Aux. *V* (2) Adv. *V* Adv. (3) Aux. Adv. *V* Adv. (4) *V* D N (5) Adv. *V* Adv. Adv. (6) Aux. *V* P-group (7) Adv. *V* P-group S-group (8) Aux. *V* S-group D N (9) V *V* P-group (10) Aux. Adv. *V* Adv. P-group S-group

4. Give further examples of the modification structures illustrated in Section 20.

5. Explain, *in terms of word classes*, the possible ambiguity of the following phrases.

(1) a French teacher (2) a diving champion (3) an unfortunate helper (4) a walking stick (5) a heavy manager

14

Immediate Con-
stituents and
Sentence Modifiers

121. Layers in the Sentence

To grasp the real structure of the English sentence, one must understand not only the words that occur but the principles of their arrangement. An English sentence does not consist simply of a string of words in free relation to one another. It consists of groups of words arranged in a series of levels, each word group being made up of subgroups, until we get down to the single word.

If, for instance, we examine the sentence "The boys of the family usually milked the goats in the morning" we find that it contains twelve words. But these twelve words do not all have the same degree of relationship to one another. The first *the,* for instance, is obviously more closely related to *boys* than it is to *milked; usually* is more closely linked to *milked* than to *family.* As a whole, this sentence consists of two word groups: the noun cluster *the boys of the family* is one; the verb cluster *usually milked the goats in the morning* is the other. The subject of the verb is not just *boys* but the whole cluster, *the boys of the family;* and it is the subject of not just the verb but of the whole verb cluster. *The boys of the family* as a unit works against *usually milked the goats in the morning* as a unit. The whole meaning of the noun cluster applies to the whole meaning of the verb cluster.

Similarly the cluster *the boys of the family* is not just five words in free relation. It consists of two units: *the boys* and *of the family*. The P-group, as a group, modifies *the boys*. *Of the family,* in turn, consists not of three units but two: the preposition *of* is one and the noun cluster *the family* is the other.

The name given by linguists to these different levels of relationship is *immediate constituents.* The immediate constituents of a construction are the two (or, occasionally, more) units of which it is composed. They are constituent because they compose or constitute the structure. They are immediate because they act directly on one another. Since *immediate constituents* is long and hard to pronounce, we usually ab- *I C* breviate it "IC's" (/ay siyz/) and speak of the *IC's* of a construction rather than of its immediate constituents.

A study of immediate constituents is interesting because it is very revealing about the way English works. But it is of more than academic interest. To be easily comprehensible, the IC's of a sentence must be signaled strongly and clearly. That is, the hearer or reader must be able to know instantly what the units are, what goes with what, what modifies what. If the IC's are not so signaled, the sentence will be at best muddy and at worst ambiguous. This is a principal fault of much bad writing.

One way of analyzing a sentence is to cut it into its immediate constituents—that is, to separate out the different levels of meaning. In English this can be done in an almost mechanical manner, according to a fairly simple set of directions. The reason is that the word order in English is comparatively rigid. We shall see that English structure is essentially binary. That is, most constructions consist of just two IC's; each of these consists of two IC's; each of these of two, and so on, until we get down to single words. We shall see also that the units that we separate out are just a few constructions endlessly repeated. The four that predominate are noun clusters, verb clusters, P-groups, and S-groups. It is this constant variation of familiar themes that makes language usable. We are not being confronted constantly with new patterns, but rather with variations of a few old ones.

122. Immediate Constituents of Whole Sentences

If there are no sentence modifiers (something we'll take up in a moment), the IC's of a sentence consist of the subject as one and the verb or verb cluster as the other. We had an example of this in the sentence about milking the goats. Here are some others. The sign "/" marks the division between the IC's.

> My friends / were waiting for me at the station.
> He / hardly knew what he was doing.
> The mountains to the north / were covered with snow.
> The people upstairs / complained.

The subject is most likely to be a noun or noun cluster or a pronoun, but it doesn't have to be:

> Climbing the steps / took a lot out of him.
> What he did / can now be told.
> Now / is the time to make plans for next year.

Sometimes the IC division comes in the middle of a syllable:

> I / 'll see what can be done about it.
> They / 're sure to be home now.

Now look at this sentence:

Usually the boys in the family milked the goats in the morning.

If we divided this sentence between subject and verb, we would get a meaningless unit: *Usually the boys in the family.* Clearly this is wrong, for *usually* does not go just with the noun cluster but with everything that follows. Therefore, this sentence must be divided thus:

Usually / the boys in the family milked the goats in the morning.

That is to say, the IC's of this sentence are the adverb *usually* as one and the whole following sentence pattern as the other. The meaning of *usually* applies to the whole meaning of what follows, not to just the noun cluster or verb cluster alone.

Usually in this sentence is what we call a *sentence modifier* —a construction which modifies a whole sentence pattern. Here are some further examples of sentence modifiers:

Sometimes / we had cheese for breakfast.
Last night / the cat got out.
In the afternoon / Charlie fell in the lake.
When we had finished eating / we washed the dishes.
Sniffing the air / Marjorie predicted rain.

The last example has special complications which we shall consider later.

In all of these examples, the sentence modifiers precede the sentences they modify. This is not the only possible position for them. Sometimes, with special signals operating, they come after the modified sentence or within it. But we shall postpone discussion of such constructions until after we have studied intonation.

In sum, then, the IC divisions of whole sentences may be stated thus: if there is no sentence modifier, the IC's are the subject as one and the verb cluster as the other; if there is a sentence modifier, the IC's are the sentence modifier as one and the sentence pattern as the other. With the sentence modi-

fier cut off, the sentence pattern may then be divided into
subject and verb cluster:

> Usually the boys milked the goats in the morning.
> Usually / the boys milked the goats in the morning.
> the boys / milked the goats in the morning.

123. IC's of Noun Clusters

Noun clusters in English are also arranged in a series of
layers, and again the arrangement is perfectly regular. Let us
begin with this sentence:

> The young trapeze artist on the high wire fell off.

Since there is no sentence modifier, this sentence consists of
a subject and a verb cluster:

> The young trapeze artist on the high wire / fell off.

Now we have a noun cluster on the left. It consists of a headword, *artist,* with three modifiers before it and one after it. In
dividing a noun cluster into its IC's, we first cut off the modifier *after* the headword. If there is more than one, we cut off
the last one first and work back to the headword. Then we
cut off the first modifier before the headword and work in to
the headword. In our example, there is just one modifier after
the headword. We cut that off first: *first modifier*

> the young trapeze artist / on the high wire

That is to say, the IC's of the cluster are *the young trapeze
artist* as one and the P-group *on the high wire* as the other.
The P-group does not modify the headword alone; it modifies
the headword plus the other modifiers.

Now we cut off the first modifier before the headword:

> the / young trapeze artist

The doesn't modify just *artist;* it modifies *young trapeze art-ist.*

> young / trapeze artist

Young modifies *trapeze artist.* And of course *trapeze* modifies *artist:*

> trapeze / artist

So all the cuts go like this:

> The young trapeze artist on the high wire / fell off.
> the young trapeze artist / on the high wire ← *cut after headword first; then cut off first modifier before the headword.*
> the / young trapeze artist
> young / trapeze artist
> trapeze / artist

Now suppose the noun cluster were this: *the young trapeze artist on the high wire who was standing on his hands.* Now we have two modifiers after the headword, a P-group and an S-group. We cut off the last one first:

> the young trapeze artist on the high wire / who was standing on his hands

The last modifier modifies everything that precedes. The rest of the cluster is cut as before.

124. IC's of Verb Clusters

The arrangement of IC's in verb clusters is similar to those in noun clusters except that the direction is reversed. In a noun cluster, we cut off the modifiers *after* the headword first, then those before it. In a verb cluster, we cut off those *before* the headword first, then those after it. Take this sentence:

> The boys / usually answered rudely when they were questioned.

The verb cluster has the headword *answered* with one modifier before it and two after it. We cut off the one "*before*" the headword first:

usually / answered rudely when they were questioned

Usually modifies not just the verb but all the rest of the cluster. What did they do usually? Answered rudely when they were questioned.

Now we cut off the last modifier after the headword:

answered rudely / when they were questioned

The S-group modifies *answered rudely,* not just *answered.* But it doesn't modify *usually;* it is part of the construction modified by *usually. Rudely* modifies *answered:*

answered / rudely

Auxiliaries before the verb are treated just like any other modifiers:

Uncle Andrew / was waiting impatiently at the station.
was / waiting impatiently at the station

The auxiliary *was* modifies all the rest of the cluster, giving *waiting impatiently at the station* a particular meaning of time and connection of number. And similarly:

had been waiting all day
had / been waiting all day
been / waiting all day
waiting / all day

Or:

had often been seen in the office
had / often been seen in the office
often / been seen in the office
been / seen in the office
seen / in the office

Objects, adjectives, etc., in the verb cluster are simply treated as units and are cut off in turn:

    She / cooked the stew in the morning.
    cooked the stew / in the morning
    cooked / the stew

In the morning modifies not just *cooked* but *cooked the stew*. *The stew* patterns against (modifies, if you like) the head-word *cooked*.

The object in the verb cluster may be a noun cluster. It is simply treated as a unit:

    She / cooked a fine Irish stew with dumplings in the morning.
    cooked a fine Irish stew with dumplings / in the morning
    cooked / a fine Irish stew with dumplings

Then of course we could proceed to cut the noun cluster into its IC's:

    a fine Irish stew / with dumplings
    a / fine Irish stew
    fine / Irish stew
    Irish / stew

125. IC's of P-Groups

The arrangement of immediate constituents in P-groups and S-groups is very simple. The IC's of a P-group always consist of the preposition as one and the following noun, noun cluster, or noun equivalent as the other:

    in / the morning
    beside / the lake
    with / a lawnmower

The second constituent of a P-group may be a noun cluster and may be very long; it is still treated as a unit:

    in / the morning of the second day
    beside / the lake near Plattsville
    with / a new lawnmower which he had bought in Colorado for
        forty dollars

In the last example, when we have cut off the preposition we are left with a noun cluster. This would be cut as explained earlier:

> a new lawnmower / which he had bought in Colorado for forty
> dollars   *work into the headword*
> a / new lawnmower
> new / lawnmower ✓

126. IC's of S-Groups

S-groups, it will be remembered, are of two kinds: those which modify nouns and those which modify verbs. The second are simpler, and we'll consider them first. Let's cut a sentence until we reach an S-group:

> He / left town when he heard what had happened.
> left town / when he heard what had happened

The S-group is *when he heard what had happened*. An S-group of this type consists of the subordinator as one IC and the following sentence pattern as the other:

> when / he heard what had happened

He heard what had happened, by itself, is a sentence. The subordinator *when* operates to make this sentence part of a larger construction. Thus the meaning of *when* applies against all that follows.

Similarly:

S-groups

> because / she was crying bitterly
> after / the ball was over
> if / the boys in the family had milked the goats in the morning

Note that in each case we have a sentence pattern remaining on the right. These can be cut into their constituents according to the directions already given:

> the boys in the family / had milked the goats in the morning

Here the subject is divided from the verb cluster. The subject is a noun cluster and would be cut thus:

    the boys / in the family
    the / boys

The P-group in the noun cluster consists of the preposition as one IC and what follows as the other:

    in / the family

The verb cluster remaining is cut like any verb cluster:

    had / milked the goats in the morning
    milked the goats / in the morning
    milked / the goats

And the P-group in the verb cluster:

    in / the morning

S-groups modifying nouns, as well as some occurring as objects in verb clusters, are somewhat different. In these the subordinator is such a word as *who, whose, whom, which,* Subordinator *that, what*. These subordinators do not stand before sentence patterns as subordinators like *because, if, when* do. Rather they are part of the sentence pattern they subordinate, and the cut depends on what part they are. But usually it is just a matter of cutting off the subordinator from the rest.

Let's begin with this noun cluster:

    the people / who usually came early

Here we have an S-group modifying *the people*. In the S-group the subordinator *who* stands in the subject position and is cut off from the following verb cluster like any other subject:

    who / usually came early

And similarly:

some men / that knew what they were doing
that / knew what they were doing

the money / which was found
which / was found

Subordinators replacing the object in such S-groups occur in front of the sentence pattern and are also cut off first:

some people / whom we had seen
whom / we had seen

the money / which Uncle Stanley found
which / Uncle Stanley found

The word *whose,* however, stands in the position of a determiner and makes a unit with the noun it modifies. The IC's are like this:

The people / whose money Uncle Stanley found
whose money / Uncle Stanley found

Such are the principal IC arrangements of English sentences. We have limited the discussion to just a few constructions: sentence patterns, noun clusters, verb clusters, P-groups, and S-groups. These are the important constructions constantly occurring in English sentences. To be sure, there are others, such as adjective clusters. But since an adjective usually has but one modifier, the analysis is no problem: the IC's will be the adjective as one and the modifier as the other: *very/ happy.*

There are some problems in IC analysis which we haven't touched here, such as discontinuous IC's—where one comes inside another. Some of these have no bearing on writing problems and will be omitted here. Those that have will be discussed later. Right now we shall note some ways in which one can go wrong in the constructions already discussed.

127. Complications

Those examples so far given have been straightforward ones. There was no difficulty in dividing them into IC's because there was no doubt about what went with what. But this is not always true. It is only too easy to write sentences in which we can't tell what the IC's are. The meaning of such sentences is always doubtful, and such sentences are therefore always poor.

Take this one:

The people who visited us sometimes drank the milk.

This is a sentence pattern with no sentence modifier, so the IC division should be between subject and verb cluster. The trouble is that we can't tell just what the subject consists of and just what the verb cluster consists of. Is the subject *the people who visited us* or *the people who visited us sometimes?* Is the verb cluster *sometimes drank the milk* or *drank the milk?* There is no signal to tell us. The IC analysis cannot be made, and the sentence is an ambiguous sentence.

No simple rule or set of rules will tell the writer how to avoid or repair such sentences. He must simply be alive to the possibilities and mind what he's doing. If the sentence is ambiguous, he must try some other order. The signals operating in English sentences to keep the IC arrangement clear are tangible but very complicated. We can set them forth in any particular sentence, but we could hardly summarize them for all sentences.

For instance, this sentence is clear:

The people who visited us sometimes always drank the milk.

The cut is between *sometimes* and *always*. How do we know? Because these two time adverbs could not both modify the same verb cluster without contradiction. Therefore the first must modify *visited us* and the second *drank the milk*.

So is this clear:

> The people who visited us|never drank the milk.

The cut is between *us* and *never*. The signal is the fact that the particular adverb *never* regularly patterns before verb clusters, not after them. We say "who never visited us" but not "who visited us never."

The following are clear because *sometimes* is placed where it must modify one part or the other:

> The people who sometimes visited us drank the milk.
> The people who visited us drank the milk sometimes.
> Sometimes the people who visited us drank the milk.

We might note that the original sentence—"The people who visited us sometimes drank the milk"—is ambiguous in writing only, not in speech. In speech there would be a clear intonation signal marking one division or the other. It sometimes happens that writing has developed punctuation to symbolize such intonation signals, but not so here. There is no conventional way of repairing this sentence by punctuation.

128. Ambiguity in Noun Clusters

Noun clusters also present IC problems, particularly in modifiers following the headword. Look at these two clusters; both are clear, but the constructions are quite different:

> the girls in the dining room who wait on us
> the girls in the dining room where we had our meals

In the first sentence, there are two modifiers of the headword *girls;* in cutting the cluster into its IC's, we cut off the last modifier first:

> the girls in the dining room / who wait on us

But in the second sentence the headword has only one modifier following it. For the S-group *where we had our meals* doesn't modify *the girls in the dining room;* it modifies *the dining room,* being part of the P-group *in the dining room where we had our meals.* The cut therefore is like this:

the girls / in the dining room where we had our meals.

The P-group, then, is composed thus:

in / the dining room where we had our meals

And the noun cluster in the P-group:

the dining room / where we had our meals

Such constructions are tricky. If we have a P-group following a noun and an S-group following a P-group, the S-group will have two nouns ahead of it: the first noun and the noun of the P-group. Then there must be some signal showing which noun it goes with. Numerous signals will make the connection. But if none are present, then the IC analysis cannot be made, and the sentence will be ambiguous, like this one:

the girl in the car that was moving

Is the girl in the car moving, or is the car moving? There is no way of knowing, and the cluster is ambiguous.

But note these:

the girl in the car who was moving
the girl in the car which was moving

Here the necessary signals are present. *Who* patterns with nouns for persons only; *which* with nouns for nonpersons only. Therefore *who* connects the S-group with *girl* and *which* connects it with *car*. The IC analysis can be made, and the meaning is clear:

the girl in the car / who was moving
the girl / in the car which was moving

The original sentence was ambiguous because *that* patterns with both persons and nonpersons.

The following sentences are clear also, because in each a number signal is operating:

the girls in the car that were moving
the girls in the car that was moving

Sometimes the conventional patterning of individual words will give a strong enough signal. For instance, the meaning of the following sentences is clear enough:

the girl in the car that was drinking lemonade
the girl in the car that had the top down

We think of girls, not cars, as drinking lemonade, and of cars, not girls, as having the top down, and no one would mistake the meaning of these clusters. But dependence on such signals is a little risky. In all of the following, though one meaning may be more likely, another may tease the readers. These sentences are at least dubious:

the girl in the car that needed water
the girl in the car that needed repairs
the girl in the car that he was thinking of buying
the girl in the car that I got for Christmas
the girl in the car that I loved dearly
the girl in the car that reminded me of Mother

Similar difficulties arise when we have two P-groups following a noun cluster. The second P-group will have two nouns ahead of it, and we must know which it goes with. In the following we don't:

the man by the house with the dogs

Do the dogs go with the house or the man? There is no telling. In these, however, the meaning is clear:

the man by the house with the red roof
the man by the house with a smile on his face

Here signals are working, and the IC analysis can be made:

the man / by the house with the red roof
the man by the house / with a smile on his face

Complications in modifiers before the noun headword are fewer, but there are some. In the first place, it should be noted that words before the headword do not all necessarily modify the noun. Some may modify modifiers of the noun. Look at this for instance:

a very large picture window

Window is the headword, and the determiner is cut off first:

a / very large picture window

But the next cut is not between *very* and *large,* for if we cut it so—*very/large picture window*—the meaning would have to be that the large picture window was very. The meaning is, however, that the picture window was very large, so the IC's are these:

very large / picture window

This presents no writing problem, since the meaning is clear in any case. But the following is ambiguous:

a new car salesman

Is the car salesman new (i.e., newly hired) or does he sell new cars? The difficulty is often resolved in writing by using a hyphen when the adjective modifies the noun immediately following and omitting the hyphen when the adjective modifies the main headword:

new-car salesman (sells new cars)
new car salesman (newly hired)

And similarly:

> old-stamp collector (collects old stamps)
> old stamp collector (collects stamps and is old)
> hot-rod enthusiast (likes hot-rods)
> hot rod enthusiast (likes rods and is hot)
> white-slave dealer (deals in white slaves)
> white slave dealer (deals in slaves and is white)

129. Ambiguity in Verb Clusters

The verb cluster also presents IC problems, since it may be full of noun clusters, P-groups, S-groups, and adverbs, the relationship of which must be clearly shown. In the following example there is no difficulty:

> She / turned to the man with tears in her eyes.
> She / turned to the man with tears in his eyes.

Here the words *her* and *his* are the necessary signals. The P-group *with tears in her eyes* modifies *turned to the man; with tears in his eyes* modifies *the man*. But the following is not clear:

> She / turned to the man in tears.

We can't tell whether the man was in tears or whether that is how she turned to him.

Notice that such small details as the difference between *a* and *the* can provide the necessary signals. The following are clear.

> She / turned to the man with an angry look.
> She / turned to the man with the angry look.

In the first sentence, *with an angry look* modifies the verb cluster; *with the angry look* modifies *the man*. But an addition can change the IC's once again:

> She / turned to the man with the angry look she always wore.

Here is another example of ambiguity:

> She / married the man she met in the Congregational Church.

There are two verbs ahead of the P-group, and we can't tell whether the Church is where she met him or where she married him.

In this one, one meaning is certainly more likely, but the other is possible enough to be bothersome:

> She / married the man she met in the post office.

Adverbs can be a trouble when there are two verbs in the cluster:

> He / waited while she dressed anxiously.

If the intention is to have *anxiously* modify *waited,* it would be better to put it before the S-group:

> He / waited anxiously while she dressed.

Now the IC analysis can be made, and the meaning is clear:

> waited anxiously / while she dressed

130. Avoiding Ambiguity

It is common in books on writing to advise the learner to place modifiers close to the words they are supposed to modify. But this advice can be approved only with considerable qualification. A writer, in constructing noun clusters, verb clusters, and sentences, is bound by certain rather rigid conventions of English word order. He cannot change these conventions without producing unidiomatic sentences. In a verb cluster containing a P-group and an S-group both modifying the same verb headword, the P-group must come first and the S-group second. There is no getting around this. We must write "waited in the living room while she dressed." If we switch the modifiers around we get an entirely different construction—"waited while she dressed in the living room" —in which the P-group no longer modifies the main headword of the cluster.

Such a construction might present an IC difficulty:

> waited in the room he worked in while she dressed

But this cannot be solved by moving the S-group closer to *waited,* for then we should have a different meaning:

> waited while she dressed in the room he worked in

It must be solved by producing some sufficient signal:

> waited in his work room while she dressed
> waited in the room he worked in for her to finish dressing

Or take this earlier example:

> the girl in the car that reminded me of Mother

Suppose the intention is for the S-group to modify *girl.* We cannot accomplish this by moving the S-group closer to *girl,* for then we should have

> the girl that reminded me of Mother in the car

which doesn't mean the same thing.

Or suppose that it's the car that reminds one of Mother. The sentence is still ambiguous, even though the S-group is bang up against the word it is supposed to modify. The reader must still choose between two possible meanings.

The fact is that position is only one of many signals controlling the IC's of a sentence and not necessarily the most important. Other signals may be the difference between a *who* and a *which,* a *was* and a *were,* a *his* and a *her,* an *a* and a *the,* or many others. Sometimes a change of a word can make an ambiguous sentence clear. Sometimes the whole sentence must be radically revised.

The only general advice that can be given is this: to be alive to the possibilities, and then, working within the confines of idiomatic English structure, to see to it that one's sentences can yield one and only one meaning.

SUGGESTIONS

1. Cut the following constructions into their two immediate constituents. *one cut*

(1) An old rug merchant was walking down the hill. (2) Fortunately it was a lovely day. (3) Both the boys live near us. (4) When Gerber gets here, we can start boiling the mushrooms. (5) They're a little young to be thinking of marriage. (6) an old man who had taken part in the attack on Guadalcanal (7) very serious young women (8) a lad on a bicycle who was risking his neck (9) the house near us that was built last year (10) one large tooth hanging by a thread (11) often spoke to us politely (12) was coming home in a basket (13) went to the store on his motorcycle (14) went to the store on the corner (15) goes off in a rage when anyone criticizes him (16) dived into a swimming pool that contained no water (17) answers the phone herself when the maid is out (18) gave an answer that surprised us all (19) with a cat (20) with a cat with green whiskers (21) in an ancient Oldsmobile which he had won in a raffle (22) grabbing the man by the neck (23) grabbing the man who had offered to escort her home (24) who had offered to escort her home (25) because he spoke such beautiful Italian

2. Point out possible ambiguities in the following constructions and explain how they might be made clear.

(1) I saw a boy on a bicycle that had been giving me trouble. (2) The party afterward was a huge success. (3) She found the pin that he had bought her in San Francisco. (4) Henry discovered the mistake I made last night. (5) He smiled at the girl he loved foolishly. (6) I had forgotten the name of the cop on the beat with the bad reputation. (7) Alfonso rebuked the girl who had spoken in quiet indignation. (8) The cannibal genially offered an apple to the guest that was half eaten. (9) The woman who washed his shirts lugubriously wished him a merry Christmas. (10) He gave me a picture of a girl that had stirred his emotions.

15

Combining
the Patterns

131. Three More Structure Groups

We have said that the overwhelming majority of the sentences in ordinary written English consist of either (1) one of a very few basic patterns or (2) one of these patterns expanded through modification or (3) two or more of these patterns combined. In Chapter 12 we considered the basic patterns themselves. In Chapters 13 and 14 we studied the main lines on which they are expanded through modification. In this chapter we shall turn to their combination.

Combination of patterns, or parts of patterns, in English is accomplished chiefly by three groups of structure words. We shall give these structure words the names *conjunctions, subordinators,* and *sentence connectors.* Conjunctions combine either whole patterns or parts of patterns. Subordinators, which we have already encountered in studying modification, make sentence patterns parts of other sentences. Sentence connectors combine whole patterns.

Much of English punctuation revolves around these three structure groups. We shall go into the matter explicitly in Chapter 18, but meanwhile it will do no harm to note the punctuation in the examples given. The punctuation used here is conventional and standard, though, as will be shown later, various other legitimate possibilities exist.

132. Conjunctions

We shall define a conjunction as a word that patterns like *and*. The word *and* has two easily separable positions. It may stand between whole sentence patterns or between parts of patterns. Let us consider the second position first.

And, for instance, may stand between two nouns:

men *and* women

Or between two noun clusters:

some men of great wisdom *and* a few women of surpassing beauty

Or between two verbs:

sulked *and* pouted

Or between two verb clusters:

usually sulked when there was nothing to sulk about *and* always pouted maddeningly

Or between two adverbs or two adjectives:

tall *and* slender
quickly *and* skillfully

Or between two P-groups:

around the track *and* into the showers

Or between two S-groups:

if we have time *and* if nobody stops us
who loved everybody *and* whom everybody loved

In short, *and* can stand between and join practically all the constructions that occur in English sentences. The only limitation is that it ordinarily joins like constructions: nouns and nouns, verbs and verbs, P-groups and P-groups. It does not ordinarily join unlike constructions, like a noun and an adjective or an adjective cluster and an S-group. That is, we would say or write "He was a happy and healthy man," but not "He was a happy and city man." We would write "He was a man happy in his home life and keen about his work," but not usually "He was a man happy in his home life and who was keen about his work."

If we look for other words that pattern like *and* and are therefore, by definition, conjunctions, we find that *or* will substitute for *and* in most positions, as in the following:

> My uncle *and* my aunt came *and* went early *and* late.
> My uncle *or* my aunt came *or* went early *or* late.
>
> Ed *and* Charlie recited poetry *and* played the violin at lunch *and* dinner.
> Ed *or* Charlie recited poetry *or* played the violin at lunch *or* dinner.

Or is therefore also a conjunction. *But* is also a conjunction, though there are more limitations on its occurrence. It stands between adjectives or between adverbs, but it does not usually join other constructions within sentence patterns:

> They were old *and* handsome.
>   old *or* handsome.
>   old *but* handsome.
>
> She played well *and* carefully.
>   well *or* carefully.
>   well *but* carefully.

The simple conjunctions joining parts of sentence patterns are therefore *and, or,* and *but,* with limitations on the occurrence of *but.*

133. Conjunctions Between Sentence Patterns

The second main position for *and* is between two sentence patterns. Note the difference:

The men *and* the boys worked *and* played.
The men worked, *and* the boys played.

In the first sentence, one *and* joins two noun clusters, and the second *and* joins two verbs. In the second sentence, the *and* joins two whole sentence patterns. Note the comma in the second sentence above and in the examples following.

And can join two sentences of the same pattern or two of different patterns:

The men worked, *and* the boys played. (patterns one and one)
The men were handsome, *and* the girls were pretty. (patterns two and two)
He's my friend, *and* I'm his. (patterns four and four)
Ed worked, *and* Charlie played the tuba. (patterns one and three)
He paid me my money, *and* I fainted. (patterns five and one)
He laughed, *and* we thought him a fool. (patterns one and six)
There was a fish in the pool, *and* I caught it. (patterns seven and three)

In this position, between whole sentence patterns, *or* and *but* also occur, and so do several other words, which we may add to the list of conjunctions:

The men worked, and the boys played.
The men worked, or the boys played.
The men worked, but the boys played.
The men worked, for the boys played.
The men worked, yet the boys played.
The men worked, so the boys played.

The word *nor* also stands between two sentence patterns, but with a required rearrangement of the second pattern:

The men worked, nor did the boys play.
The men should work, nor should the boys play.

The seven conjunctions in English are therefore *and, or, but, for, yet, so,* and *nor. And, but,* and *or* combine parts of patterns or whole patterns; *for, yet, so,* and *nor* combine whole patterns only.

Some of these words occur also in other word classes—just as some words occur as either noun or verb, others as either determiner or pronoun. Thus *for* is not a conjunction but a preposition in "He did it for me." *But* is a preposition in "There was no one home but Edna." "*Yet* is an adverb in "He hasn't come yet." *So* is an intensifier in "I'm so sorry" and in a class by itself in "It was raining so hard that we stayed home." Notice that *and* could not be substituted for any of these words in these sentences. They are conjunctions only when they are in a position for *and*.

It may have occurred to you that other words might be substituted for *and* in the examples given. For instance, one might say, "The men worked while the boys played." You may therefore want to ask why *while* is not also a conjunction here. Hold the question until the end of the chapter.

134. Correlatives

Some of the conjunctions—*and, or, nor,* and *but*—pair with the words *both, either, neither,* and *not* to form what are traditionally called correlative conjunctions. Thus:

Both	the men	and	the boys worked.
Either	the men	or	the boys worked.
Neither	the men	nor	the boys worked.
Not	the men	but	the boys worked.

Here the correlatives connect noun clusters. They may connect other constructions within sentence patterns also:

The men were both	handsome	and	wise.
The men were either	handsome	or	wise.
The men were neither	handsome	nor	wise.
The men were not	handsome	but	wise.

Or:

> The men were *not only* handsome *but also* wise.

Either/or may join whole patterns:

> *Either* he goes, *or* I go.

The chief effect of the correlatives is to emphasize the fact that two things or two people are involved. If in place of "Ed and Charlie played the tuba," we write "Both Ed and Charlie played the tuba," we simply bear down a little harder on the fact that both of them did it.

135. Parallel Construction

Apart from punctuation, the writer's main concern in the use of conjunctions—either simple or correlative—is to watch that they connect like constructions. The following would probably be considered blemishes in, for example, magazine writing:

> He was a man of courage and whom we all admired.
> (Better: a courageous man admired by all of us)

> He liked quarreling and to fight with people.
> (Better: He liked to quarrel and to fight with people.)

> He either goes, or I go.
> (Better: Either he goes or I go.)

But there are numerous exceptions to the statement that conjunctions join like constructions. One might easily find in print such a sentence as "She was a nice girl and very easy on the eyes." Study of reputable magazines and books will disclose others, and as a writer matures and deepens his acquaintance with the work of other writers he learns how to break the rules. In general one prefers an idiomatic sentence to a stilted one, and if a sentence comes easy and sounds right, one writes it, whatever the *and* connects. But one tries to be sure that it does sound right.

136. Sentence Connectors *resemble conjunctions*

Sentence connectors go by a bewildering variety of names in traditional grammar. They are called, among other things, *conjunctive adverbs, adverbial conjunctions, coördinating conjunctions, subordinating conjunctions, illative conjunctions.* To this bewilderment, we add still another term: *sentence connector.* We do so to avoid making an illogical connection with conjunctions on the one hand or adverbs on the other. Sentence connectors bear a superficial resemblance to both conjunctions and adverbs, but in their overall patterning they are a group quite apart from other groups, and for purposes of punctuation the writer must learn to keep them apart.

Sentence connectors share one important position with conjunctions: both groups stand between sentence patterns. But in other respects they pattern differently, and the differences have resulted in different punctuation practice.

We shall define a sentence connector as a word patterning like *therefore.* Substituting for *therefore,* we get such a list as the following. Note the punctuation, but don't worry too much about it now. We'll come to it again:

The sky was cloudy; therefore we went for a walk.
The sky was cloudy; however, we went for a walk.
The sky was cloudy; consequently we went for a walk.
The sky was cloudy; nevertheless we went for a walk.
The sky was cloudy; accordingly, we went for a walk.

Or:

The windows were open; therefore the whole place was open.
The windows were open; indeed, the whole place was open.
The windows were open; in fact, the whole place was open.
The windows were open; thus the whole place was open.

The windows were open; that is, the whole place was open.
The windows were open; hence the whole place was open.
The windows were open; furthermore the whole place was open.
The windows were open; moreover, the whole place was open.

Sentence connectors, as we see, stand between sentence patterns. In this they resemble conjunctions. But unlike conjunctions, sentence connectors may also occur at the end of the second pattern:

The sky was cloudy; we went for a walk therefore.
The sky was cloudy; we went for a walk, however.
The sky was cloudy; we went for a walk nevertheless.

The windows were open; the whole place was open therefore.
The windows were open; the whole place was open, indeed.
The windows were open; the whole place was open consequently.

Or sentence connectors may occur inside the second pattern:

The sky was cloudy; we therefore went for a walk.
The sky was cloudy; we nevertheless went for a walk.

The windows were open; the whole place, consequently, was open.
The windows were open; the whole place, that is, was open.

137. Subordinators

We have already encountered subordinators and need only sum them up again for the purpose of distinguishing them from conjunctions and sentence connectors, groups with which they are easily confused.

Subordinators, it will be recalled, are of two types: those which pattern like *who* and those which pattern like *because*. Both types serve to subordinate sentence patterns, making them parts of larger constructions. The two types differ in that the *because* type stands outside the sentence pattern it subordinates, whereas the *who* type is part of the sentence pattern, replacing the subject, object, or determiner.

Subordinators of the *who* type subordinate S-groups which are parts of noun clusters:

> the men *who* were here
> the men *that* were here
> the goat *which* was being milked
> the poodle *whose* hair had been clipped

They may also occur in the object position in verb clusters:

> I know *who* was here.
> I wonder *which* goat was being milked.
> I don't care *what* he did.

Subordinators of the *because* type occur most commonly with S-groups that are verb modifiers or sentence modifiers:

> He did it *because* he wanted to.
> He goes *where* he likes.
> We can't leave *until* the milk curdles.
> I'll see about it *when* I get to Chicago.

> *When* everything was ready, we brought in Uncle Stanley.
> *After* they left, we cleaned up the mess.
> *Because* I was short of money, I wrote to father.

The two groups overlap in that both occur in the object position of verb clusters:

> I knew *who* he was.
> I knew *what* he did.
> I knew *where* he went.
> I knew *when* he was going to skin the cat.

In order to punctuate English conventionally, the writer must distinguish clearly between subordinators, conjunctions, and sentence connectors. There is no difficulty with subordinators of the *who* type. *Who* is not easily confused with words like *and* and *therefore*. Subordinators of the *because* type, however, share some positions with conjunctions and sentence connectors, and the writer may easily mix them up, to the detriment of his writing. In what follows, therefore, we shall concentrate on subordinators of the *because* type and ignore the *who* type.

138. Distinguishing the Three Groups

One way of keeping conjunctions, sentence connectors, and subordinators apart is simply to remember the words that occur in the different groups: *and* and *or* are conjunctions; *therefore* and *nevertheless* are sentence connectors; *because* and *when* are subordinators. However, there is some overlapping, certain words occurring in more than one group. Furthermore, though the conjunction list is short and easily retained, the others are long and hard to manage. It is best to grasp the differences in patterning that make the groups different.

First of all, note the one position the three groups have in common. They all stand between sentence patterns:

SENT. CONNECTOR: The day was cloudy; however we went for a walk.

CONJUNCTION: The day was cloudy, and we went for a walk.

SUBORDINATOR: The day was cloudy until we went for a walk.

It is the fact that they share this position that makes the groups confusable. But each has positions not shared with the others, and these unshared positions cause the groups to be felt as different, often to be pronounced with different intonation, and to be punctuated differently in the shared positions.

Conjunctions are different in that they join not only whole patterns but parts of patterns, or at least some conjunctions do. Thus we say "Ed and Charlie came," but not "Ed therefore Charlie came" or "Ed because Charlie came." Conjunctions differ secondly in that, when they combine whole patterns they must stand between the patterns. Sentence connectors and subordinators may stand between the patterns they join, but they are not confined to this position.

Sentence connectors may stand either between the patterns or at the end of the second pattern or in the middle of the second pattern:

> We asked Sam to join us; *however* he was too tired.
> We asked Sam to join us; he was too tired, *however.*
> We asked Sam to join us; he was, *however,* too tired.
>
> The door was locked; *therefore* we broke a window.
> The door was locked; we broke a window, *therefore.*
> The door was locked; we *therefore* broke a window.

It is only the first position that is shared with conjunctions. We might say, "The door was locked, and we broke a window." But we could not say, "We broke a window and" or "We and broke a window."

Subordinators, like the other groups, may stand between two sentence patterns: "We broke a window because the door was locked." Like conjunctions, but unlike sentence connectors, they cannot move around in the second pattern. That is, we do not say, "We broke a window; the door was locked because" or "We broke a window; the door because was locked."

The peculiarity of subordinators is that, while they always stand at the head of the pattern they subordinate, that whole pattern may occur before the other pattern, thus becoming a sentence modifier. Thus:

> We broke a window because the door was locked.
> Because the door was locked, we broke a window.

The second sentence illustrates the unique position for subordinators. Neither sentence connectors nor conjunctions occur here. We do not say, "Therefore the door was locked, we broke a window," or "Therefore we broke a window, the door was locked," or "And we broke a window, the door was locked."

In sum, the three groups pattern as follows. We use the symbol C for conjunction, S for subordinator, and SC for sentence connector:

CONJUNCTIONS: sentence pattern, C sentence pattern
SUBORDINATORS: sentence pattern S sentence pattern
                   S sentence pattern, sentence pattern
SENT. CONNECTORS: sentence pattern; SC sentence pattern
                   sentence pattern; sentence pattern SC
                   sentence pattern; sentence SC pattern

The first position is the shared position, alike for all three groups except for punctuation and, in speech, intonation.

The second position for subordinators is unique for subordinators. Any word occurring here or capable of occurring here is a subordinator. There are some subordinators which do not occur in this position, but they are not those likely to be confused with conjunctions and sentence connectors.

The second and third positions for sentence connectors are unique for sentence connectors. Any word occurring in these or capable of occurring in them is a sentence connector.

A few words occur sometimes as subordinators and sometimes as sentence connectors. Such a one is *though:*

Though he didn't want to do it, he did it.
He did it; he didn't want to, though.
He did it, though he didn't want to.

In the first sentence *though* is in a position for *because* and is a subordinator. In the second sentence, it is in a position for *therefore* and is a sentence connector. In the third sentence it is in the shared position. Here it is taken as a subordinator. Note that the subordinator *although* would substitute in the first and third sentences but not in the second.

If it happens that one actually can't tell which group a word belongs to, the sentence will be ambiguous. Without a clue from punctuation or intonation, the following sentence would have two meanings:

> He didn't like to do it however he did it.

If *however* is a sentence connector, the sentence means one thing; if it is a subordinator, it means another. The following sentences are clear:

> He didn't like to do it; he did it, however.
> However he did it, he didn't like to do it.

SUGGESTIONS

1. Select a magazine article and check the first thirty occurrences of conjunctions. Tabulate the constructions combined by the conjunctions as noun cluster and noun cluster, P-group and P-group, sentence pattern and sentence pattern. Do you find any conjunctions combining unlike constructions?
2. Write your own illustrations for the six sentence types given in formula form in Section 138 ("sentence pattern, C sentence pattern," etc.).
3. Write sentences from the following formulas. For N use any noun or noun cluster; for V use a verb or verb cluster.

   (1) N↔V, C N↔V   (2) N↔V Adj.; SC N↔V   (3) N↔V S N↔V N   (4) S N↔V Adj., N↔V N N   (5) N↔LV N; N↔V N SC   (6) N↔OV N N, C N↔V N, C V   (7) THERE V↔N Adv.; N↔V N SC

4. Construct sentences using the following words. Identify the structure group to which each belongs and punctuate as illustrated in this chapter.

   yet, if, because, moreover, nor, hence, thus, while, since, nevertheless, accordingly, consequently, whereas, however, so, furthermore.

16

Intonation

supra segmentals
12 in all

139. The Punctuation of Speech

stress
pitch
juncture

In recent years it has become increasingly clear that any discussion of English punctuation that takes no account of the intonation in speech patterns is, if not meaningless, at least highly artificial. Intonation is to punctuation what vowels and consonants are to letters of the alphabet. There is, to be sure, no exact relationship in either case. We do not spell words just as we pronounce them, and our punctuation marks do not come near showing all the intonation that occurs in our sentences. But ultimately we get our letters from the vowels and consonants of speech, and so do we ultimately get our commas and periods and semicolons from the intonation of speech. Therefore, before we go on to examine the punctuation habits of American writers, we need to get a rough idea of the intonation of American speech.

The idea will necessarily be rough because intonation is not an easy thing to study. It is in one sense obvious and plain and in another obscure and difficult. We all of us react accurately to the intonation signals of the language. If we didn't, we would constantly misunderstand and be misunderstood. Gross differences are easy to see. Anyone can perceive a difference between "Was he mad?" and "Was he mad!" and can perceive further that the difference subsists not in vowels and consonants but in something we call "tone of voice." But to understand just what this "tone of voice" consists of, what physical features make one sentence different from the other, is another matter.

The difficulty of studying intonation can be seen in the fact that, although mankind has been studying language for thousands of years, it is only in the last decade or so that linguists have achieved a useful grasp of the features of intonation. Indeed, much still remains obscure, and many details are still being debated. But enough has been done that we can now see the main structure of intonation, or at least of English intonation.

Intonation consists of three features, which are called *stress, pitch,* and *juncture.* Stress is simply the loudness or softness with which sounds are uttered. Pitch is the frequency with which voiced sounds vibrate as they issue from the glottis. If they vibrate relatively fast, we have what we call high pitch; if they vibrate relatively slowly, we have low pitch. Juncture, which is closely related to both pitch and stress, is a way of marking division points in speech by lengthening out the sounds adjacent to the break.

Presumably all languages have intonation. One cannot speak without speaking softly or loudly or without vibration of voiced sounds, and presumably in all languages there is some variation, the discourse being not all on one level of loudness or at one vibration frequency. But languages differ markedly in the use they make of vibration features. Some languages use intonation lexically, to distinguish between different words, much as speakers of English use vowels and consonants. The best known of such languages is Chinese. In Chinese the sounds [ma], for instance, produce any of four different words, depending on the pitch pattern with which they are uttered.

English, like many other languages, uses intonation chiefly for syntactical purposes or for discriminating between differ-

ent emotional states. We have had the examples "Was he
mad?" and "Was he mad!" where one intonation pattern
signals a question and the other an exclamation. Consider
also the many different attitudes or emotions that can be signaled by the intonation used on the word "well" or on the
word "oh."

We shall have various other examples as we examine the
three intonation features one by one.

140. Stress

Stress has been defined as the loudness or softness with
which sounds are uttered. We can see it working in many
pairs of words in which one member is a noun and the other
a verb; the noun in such pairs has a loud stress on the first
syllable and the verb the loud stress on the root syllable. For
instance, if I say, "What's your object?" I pronounce _ob_ more
loudly than _ject_. But if I say, "I object" the _ject_ is louder than
the _ob_. If one were to reverse the stresses in these sentences,
the sentences would sound un-English.

Other such pairs are _súbject_ and _subjéct, cóntrast_ and
contrást, próduce and _prodúce, réwrite_ (_a rewrite man_) and
rewríte, ínvite and the dialectal _invíte_. Stress is thus a signal
distinguishing between members of different form classes,
though sometimes it is only one of the signals. For instance
refúse and _réfuse_ are distinguished by stress and also by contrasting final consonants. _Anticipate_ and _anticipation_ are distinguished by stress and also by the suffix on the noun.

But there are more than two contrasting stresses in English
speech as can be seen by contrasting the pronunciations of
separate in "I'll separate them" and "They are separate." In
both sentences _separate_ has the heaviest stress on the first
syllable. In the adjective, the second and third syllables have

about equal stress. But in the verb the third syllable has a weaker stress than the first but a heavier stress than the second.

Using such and more complicated methods of comparison, linguists have arrived at the conclusion that English speech has four contrasting levels of stress. Since the contrasts are used to distinguish between different meanings, they are phonemic, and the four stress levels are four different phonemes, just as vowels and consonants are phonemes.

The four stress phonemes are named and symbolized as follows:

PRIMARY STRESS (the loudest): /ˊ/   ˊ
SECONDARY STRESS (next to loudest): /ˆ/   ˆ
TERTIARY STRESS (next to softest): /ˋ/   ˋ
WEAK STRESS (the softest): /˘/   ˘

These stress levels are relative, not absolute. That means that primary stresses, for instance, do not all have the same volume. I may generally speak more loudly than you do, so that my typical tertiary stresses are louder than your typical primary stresses. Nevertheless we would each have the four contrasting stress levels in our respective sentences.

Or I may speak more loudly at some times than at others. I can say the sentence "I'll separate them" twice, once very loudly and once very softly. But both times there would be clear stress contrasts between *sep* and *ar* and *ate*.

The four stress contrasts do not appear in every utterance we make. If we speak a two-word sentence, like "Shut up," obviously only two stresses can appear. It is only when we examine longer stretches of speech that the four-stress pattern of English emerges.

The four can be seen in the following sentences. All might be spoken in other ways, but they would frequently be uttered as marked:

John's on the sofa.

Where's the streetcar?

He's a foolish wiseman.

141. Functions of Stress in English

It is not our purpose to learn to analyze accurately the intonation of English sentences. This is a task for the expert. We can content ourselves with noting some of the obvious contrasts that distinguish meanings.

For instance, if the sentence "He is my brother" is pronounced with the primary stress on the first syllable of *brother,* we have a simple statement of fact. You wanted to know who he was, and I told you. But if we shift the primary stress, we get different meanings:

He is my brother. (not the other fellow)

He is my brother. (Why do you deny it?)

He is my brother. (not Sam's)

Or consider these:

That's a nice mess.

That's a nice mess.

That's a nice mess.

Stress is used extensively to signal different kinds of modification. We had the sentence "This is an orderly room," which we called ambiguous. But it is ambiguous in writing only, not in speech:

This is an orderly room. (a room for orderlies)

This is an orderly room. (in good order)

Or:

He's a fine clerk. (a good one)

He's a fine clerk. (collects fines)

Thus we see that, <u>in general, when an adjective modifies</u> <u>a noun, we have primary stress on the noun and secondary on</u> <u>the adjective:</u>

[handwritten: primary on noun / Secondary on adj.]

a handsome man

a strange story

an old streetcar

But when a noun modifies another noun, we generally have <u>primary stress on the modifier and tertiary stress on the head-</u> <u>word:</u>

[handwritten: primary on modifier / tertiary on headword]

a city man

a bottle plant

a used-car dealer

Stress also distinguishes the two kinds of V-ing words that <u>modify nouns. V-ing modifiers like the one in "reading room"</u> <u>take the primary stress on the modifier with tertiary on the</u> <u>headword:</u>

[handwritten: primary on modifier / tertiary on headword]

a reading room

a dancing school

a waiting list

But V-ing modifiers like that in "burning room" have second-ary stress on the modifier and primary on the noun:

[handwritten: primary on noun / Secondary on modifier]

a burning room

a laughing girl

a soaring plane

Consequently, constructions like "a smoking room" can be ambiguous only in writing, never in speech:

a smoking room (a room on fire)

a smoking room (a room for smoking)

Native speakers of English manage these pitch structures so automatically that they seldom think of them. It is only when someone, accidentally or intentionally, does violence to the patterns that the patterns become obvious. It is nothing special to see "a dancing school," but "a dancing school" would be quite a sight. So would "a reading room" or "a laughing girl" (girl who makes her living laughing, like "a dancing girl"?). On the other hand, "calling cards" are fairly common; they're just visiting humorists. And "French teachers" are nearly as plentiful as "French teachers."

142. Pitch

Pitch we have defined as the frequency of vibration of voiced sounds coming from the glottis. The glottis, you may remember, is the opening in the larynx through which the breath passes on its way to the mouth. If the glottis is wide open, there is no vibration, and we get unvoiced sounds, like /s/. If the glottis is partly closed, a tension resulting in vibration is set up, and we get voiced sounds, like /z/. All the vowels and more than half the consonants in English are voiced.

Pitch is of course important to music. In music variation in pitch produces what we call melody. (Notice that you can "sing" the sound z-z-z- but that you can't sing s-s-s-.) But it is important also in ordinary language. We use it in English not only to convey various states of emotion but also as an integral part of our syntax.

English has four pitch phonemes, as it has four stress pho‑
nemes. These are usually given numbers, rather than names.
The number 4 indicates the highest pitch and 1 the lowest,
thus:

HIGH PITCH: /4/
NEXT TO HIGH: /3/
NEXT TO LOW: /2/
LOWEST PITCH: /1/

Like the stress phonemes, these four pitches are relative, not
absolute. They cannot be defined as so many vibrations per
second. They are simply points of contrast set up in the speech
of individuals as they speak particular sentences. In general,
children have higher pitch than adults, and women have
higher pitch than men. Thus a child's low pitch may be
higher than an adult's high pitch. But the child will have the
four pitch contrasts within his register, and the adult will have
them in his.

In scientific work, pitch is usually written with the num‑
bers only, thus:

$$\overset{2}{\text{Where}} \text{ are you } \overset{3}{\text{go}}\overset{1}{\text{ing?}}$$

This would indicate that the sentence begins on the second
pitch level, rises to the third on the first syllable of *going,* and
falls to the first on the second syllable of *going.*

For general purposes, however, it is a little easier to show
pitch with lines rather than numbers. A line just under the
letters indicates pitch 2; a line well under indicates pitch 1; a
line just above the letters indicates pitch 3; and a line well
above indicates pitch 4. Thus:

Then we can show the pitch in "Where are you going?" in this way:

Where are you| go\ing?

143. Functions of Pitch

Let us see, then, some of the uses made of pitch in English. The example already given shows a very common pitch pattern for ordinary statements and for questions introduced by interrogatives. It is a 2–3–1 pattern. We begin on the second pitch, rise to the third on the stressed syllable, and fall to the first at the end. In American English (not so commonly in British) the third pitch level frequently coincides with the primary stress.

But many variations are possible. We can put a bit of panic into the question by rising to the highest (fourth) pitch on the primary stress:

Where are you| go\ing?

Thus a mother might address a child tottering toward the brink of a precipice.

We put in exasperation by rising twice to the third level:

Where |are \you |go\ing?

This suggests that we've had trouble with you before and are getting tired of it.

If we want to insist on the *where,* we get the third level at the beginning:

Where\ are you going?

Don't tell me you're going; I know that; now I want to know *where.*

A double rise will often come after persistent questioning:

Where\are you ⌐go\ing?

I've asked you several times without getting an answer; now I want one.

Thus considerable meaning of one kind and another can be added to the simple question by variation in the pitch.

There is a widely spread notion that we regularly signal questions by a rise in pitch. The voice rises, it is said, at the end of a question, and falls at the end of a statement. This is only partially true. To be sure, most statements in American English end in a fall to the lowest pitch:

He's my ⌐bro\ther.

I'm very fond of ba⌐na\nas.

But, as we have seen, questions may have the same pitch pattern. Indeed, this is the regular pattern for questions beginning with an interrogative—*who, where, whose, what, why,* etc.:

Why did you ⌐k\ill him?

What ⌐h\it me?

However, we have another type of question which does not usually end with a fall in pitch. This is the *yes/no* question— i.e., a question that can be answered by *yes* or *no*. Such questions are signaled not by interrogatives but by a reversal of subject and verb or of subject and auxiliary, as well as by the different pitch pattern: *rise in pitch.*

Did you ⌐kill him?

Are you fond of ba⌐nanas?

Is he ⌐going somewhere?

These sentences can also be uttered with the 2-3-1 pattern, but this will add a note of insistence. Compare these:

Did you ⌐kill him?

Did you ⌐k\ill him?

In the first I am simply making a polite inquiry. In the second, I am attempting to brush aside your evasions and get at the essential fact.

Thus a rising pitch at the end could scarcely be described as *the* question signal in English. A great many questions end in falling pitch, and in the others there are usually more obvious question signals present. Sometimes, however, pitch contrast will be the only signal of a question. Compare these:

He's a good ⌐sal\esman, ⌐isn't he

He's a good ⌐sal\esman, ⌐i\sn't he

The first is a question; it calls for an answer—yes or no. But the second isn't really a question. The person spoken to is not expected to answer but to agree.

We also use rising pitch when we repeat a question, either because we haven't understood it or because we are surprised at its being asked. Thus:

FIRST SPEAKER: Where are you ⌐go\ing?

SECOND SPEAKER: Where am I ⌐going?

This indicates that the second speaker didn't quite catch the question and wants it repeated.

Or consider this colloquy:

Charlie's going to play third ⌐b\ase.

Charlie's going to play third ⌐base?

The repetition of the question without the fall indicates the second speaker's surprise at the assignment. He could show that he is simply stunned by it by saying it this way:

Charlie's going to play third base?

Such words as *who, when, where, how* can signal two entirely different kinds of questions, depending on the pitch:

We need to appoint a secretary.
Okay. W̄\ho?

Let's appoint Ed secretary.
W̲/ho?

The first *who* is an ordinary question. The second *who* indicates either that the speaker didn't catch the name or is surprised at it. And similarly:

I'm going to Europe next summer.
H̄\ow?

I'm going to Europe in a canoe.
H̲/ow?

Thus the variations in English pitch are manifold. But they all carry clear meaning to which we react effortlessly.

144. Juncture

The third feature of English intonation is juncture. This is at once the hardest to understand and, for us, the most important, since it is the part of intonation most directly related to punctuation.

Juncture may be very roughly described as various kinds of breaks or division points in the flow of speech. As there are four stress phonemes and four pitch phonemes, so there are four juncture phonemes, though one of these is quite different from the other three. The juncture phonemes are generally named after the symbols used to indicate them, thus:

PLUS JUNCTURE: /+/   *same pitch*
SINGLE-BAR JUNCTURE: /|/   *do not show punctuation*
DOUBLE-BAR JUNCTURE: /‖/   *comma*
DOUBLE-CROSS JUNCTURE: /⫢/   *period*

145. Plus Juncture

Plus juncture, so called because linguists indicate it with a plus sign when they transcribe speech, is the difference between "gray train" and "great rain." These expressions are uttered with exactly the same vowel and consonant phonemes: /greytreyn/. They are pronounced with the same pitch and stress. There is no pause, in the usual sense, in either. Yet, if one were to read the utterances say fifty times, in mixed up order, to a native speaker of English, he would be able to tell which was which most if not all of the time. The only inference is that he must hear a distinguishing difference. What is it?

What he hears is a different variety in the phonemes. You remember that we said that a phoneme is not a single sound but a bundle of similar sounds called allophones. We have one allophone of /t/ occurring in the final position, as in /set/; another allophone occurs when /t/ is followed by /r/ as in /trip/. Similarly one allophone of /r/ occurs when the sound is initial, as in /rip/; quite a different allophone occurs when /r/ follows /t/, as in /trip/. In "gray train" the hearer hears the allophone of /t/ that precedes /r/ and the allophone of /r/ that follows /t/; in "great rain" he hears the allophone of /t/ that occurs at the end of words and the allophone of /r/ that occurs at the beginning of words. This is indicated in phonemic transcription by writing the sign of plus juncture at one place or the other: /grey+treyn/ or /greyt+reyn/.

Other examples of the operation of plus juncture can be noted in the pronunciation differences between "seem able" and "see Mabel," "another directed person" and "an other-directed person," "fly trap" and "flight wrap," "dough pad" and "dope ad." Often, of course, such similar structures are distinguished by other signals in addition to plus juncture. Thus "neat owl" and "knee towel" would have different allophones of the /t/ phoneme but also a different position for the primary stress.

146. Single-Bar Juncture

Plus juncture is for us of mostly academic interest. Obvious writing problems are not closely bound to the occurrence or nonoccurrence of plus juncture. The other three junctures, however, connect in one way or another with the punctuation marks of writing.

Single-bar juncture is linked to the occurrence of primary stresses in an utterance. Let us take this sentence:

The men of the family milked the goats.

A sentence of this sort is most commonly spoken with just one primary stress; the primary stress falls toward the end of the sentence:

The men of the family milked the góats.

But it could also be uttered with two primary stresses.

The men of the fámily milked the góats.

Now if we say it this way there is a kind of break between *family* and *milked*. This is not so much a pause as a lengthening out of the final syllable of *family*. The pitch stays the same. That is, we go into the word *milked* at about the same pitch that we left off on the last syllable of *family,* like this:

The men of the ⌐fa\mily milked the ⌐g\oats.

Now this break or division in the utterance is called single-bar juncture. It can occur only between primary stresses, and it consists of a lengthening out of the phonemes before the break with a sustension of the pitch level across the break.

The sentence could have three primary stresses. In that case, there would be two single-bar junctures:

The ⌐m\en of the ⌐fa\mily milked the ⌐g\oats.

Or we could write it thus, showing just the junctures:

The men | of the family | milked the goats.

This would be a very slow and emphatic way of speaking the sentence.

A hundred years or so ago it was conventional to mark most single-bar junctures with commas. In recent times, however, the tendency has been toward less punctuation, and modern writers are less likely to use commas where these junctures occur. Learners, who overpunctuate as often as they underpunctuate, often do put commas in such positions. They may write, for example, "The men of the family, milked the goats." If they are challenged by a teacher, they will very likely say, "I put a comma there because there would be a pause there if the sentence were spoken." Presumably what they mean by "pause" is single-bar juncture. As we have seen, there could be such a juncture in this position, a primary stress on family, followed by a lengthening out of the last syllable of the word with the sentence continuing on the same pitch level. But whether there is or not, the experienced writer would not use a comma. Single-bar junctures in such constructions are not ordinarily shown by punctuation.

147. Double-Bar Juncture *associated with punctuation*

Double-bar juncture, however, is usually indicated by punctuation, and it will be useful to understand the difference. Let us compare these two sentences:

> The people who were sick didn't go.
> My friend Al who was sick didn't go.

The first sentence could be spoken with no internal juncture or with one or two single-bar junctures:

> The people who were sick didn't go.
> The people who were sick | didn't go. *one juncture*
> The people | who were sick | didn't go. *two junctures*

These vary principally in emphasis and speed of delivery. None would normally have any punctuation.

But the second sentence is quite different. In the first place, it would normally have three primary stresses, not just one or two:

> My friend Ál who was síck didn't gó.

Secondly, the pitch would go something like this:

> My friend ⌐A\l⌐ who was ⌐s\ick⌐ didn't ⌐g\o.

Note the upturn in the pitch after *Al* and after *sick*. This is double-bar juncture. As in single-bar juncture, there is a lengthening out of the phonemes before the break. But the pitch, instead of continuing level across the break, rises toward, but not to, the next higher pitch.

Many American speakers would use single-bar junctures in this sentence in place of double-bar. But all speakers would use junctures, two of them, in the places indicated. In this sentence type we do not sometimes use the junctures and sometimes not, as in the type, "the people who were sick didn't go."

Double-bar juncture is frequently marked in writing by a comma, though sometimes dashes or other marks are used. Our sentences would of course be punctuated this way:

> The people who were sick didn't go.
> My friend Al, who was sick, didn't go.

This contrast in junctures reflects a contrast in the structure of the sentences. In the first sentence, *who were sick* is part of the noun cluster *the people who were sick*. The S-group modifies the headword *people*. But in the second sentence *who was sick* is not part of a cluster. There is no unit *my friend Al who was sick* in this sentence. *Who was sick* is here really a sentence modifier, another idea applying against the main idea of the sentence. One idea is that Al didn't go, another that Al was sick. But we would not say that the first sentence is separable in this way. In the first sentence *who were sick* is an integral part of the noun cluster. The meaning is not that people were sick and people didn't go but that those particular people who were sick didn't go.

The marking off of sentence modifiers from the sentences they modify is an important function of double-bar juncture. Here are some further examples. If you say them aloud, you may be able to hear the slight upturn of the pitch. Many speakers will normally employ the sustained pitch of single-bar instead. Commas, of course, would replace the juncture signs in conventional writing:

> Ordinarily ‖ we stayed home.
> (Cf. "We ordinarily stayed home" in which *ordinarily* is part of the verb cluster and there is no juncture.)
>
> When he fell on his face ‖ we laughed heartily.
> (Cf. "We laughed heartily when he fell on his face.")
>
> Charlie ‖ having a guilty conscience ‖ consulted the chaplain.
> (Cf. "Anyone having a guilty conscience should consult the chaplain.")

We knew || nevertheless || that there would be trouble.
(Cf. "We nevertheless expected trouble.")

The teacher shook my hand || smiling at me warmly.
(Cf. "The teacher frowned at the girl who was smiling at me warmly.")

Sometimes double-bar juncture will be the only signal distinguishing meanings. Compare these:

Mr. Simkin hired me because I had an honest face.
Mr. Simkin hired me || because I had an honest face.

The first sentence would be a response to the question "Why did Mr. Simkin hire you?" The second would be a response to the question "What did Mr. Simkin do?" In the first sentence, the S-group is a verb modifier. In the second it is a sentence modifier.

We shall have other such examples in the chapter on the punctuation of sentence modifiers.

Double-bar juncture also occurs between units in a series. If we count aloud—*one, two, three, four*—we have double-bar juncture after each unit but the last one: one || two ||three || four. After *one, two,* and *three* there will be a prolongation of the sound accompanied by an upturn in the pitch. If we put a double-bar juncture after *four* in this series, it will signal that we are not done counting, and the hearer will wait for us to say "five."

The same juncture occurs in series of units other than numbers:

We bagged a lion || an antelope || and a giraffe.
He worked all day || danced all night || and died young.
He made his way through the woods || across the stream || and up the mountain.
He was young || courageous || and optimistic.

Commas would indicate these junctures in most American writing.

Double-bar juncture occurs also at the end of certain questions, particularly those of the *yes/no* variety. If we speak the sentence "Is he ready" we will probably rise to the third pitch level on the syllable with primary stress:

Is he⌐ ready

But the sentence will end not on a level third pitch but with the upturn of double-bar juncture, something like this:

Is he⌐ ready⁄

This is normal in questions or other sentences ending on the third pitch.

148. Double-Cross Juncture

The last of the junctures—double-cross juncture—is a falling off into silence, usually from the low pitch. We have seen that the pitch pattern 2–3–1 is most common for statements and some questions in American English:

He's⌐ re\ady.

But the pitch doesn't end with level pitch but falls at the very end:

This fall is double-cross juncture, so called because linguists use a double cross (#) to mark it in transcribing speech. Double-cross juncture is the most important of the features dividing our speech into sentences. It is presumably the feature which gave early writers the idea of using periods.

We shall try in the next few chapters to relate these junctures in some detail to American punctuation practices. We shall see that the relationship is by no means exact, but it is close enough to be worth noting.

SUGGESTIONS

1. Here are some examples contrasting single-bar, double-bar, and double-cross junctures. They are written with the juncture signs rather than with conventional punctuation. Say them aloud and try to hear the difference in the pitch. Remember that all junctures have an elongation of the sounds just before the break, but that single-bar has a level pitch across the break, double-bar a slight rise, and double-cross a slight fall.

   (1) He was the best of the whole group ⧺ (2) He was the best of the whole group ‖ (3) He was the best ‖ it seemed to me ‖ of the whole group ⧺ (4) He was very good ⧺ however he was not the best ⧺ (5) He was very good ⧺ he seemed ‖ however ‖ not the best ⧺ (6) Has anybody seen Charlie ‖ (7) What's happened to Charlie | your roommate ⧺ (8) Why are you reading | Eliot ⧺ (9) Why are you reading Eliot ⧺ (10) The little people | did what they pleased ⧺ (11) I sent my brother ⧺ a troubleshooter ⧺ (12) I sent my brother a troubleshooter ⧺ (13) What did you put in the stew | Stanley ⧺ (14) What did you put in the stew ⧺ Stanley ‖ (15) He bought a jug of wine ‖ a loaf of bread ‖ and a volume of verse ⧺

2. Punctuate the foregoing sentences.

3. Where would the primary stress usually fall in the following constructions?

   (1) a sad story (2) a love story (3) a flying lesson (4) a training school (5) a feeble excuse (6) a swaying streetcar (7) an attractive girl (8) a flower girl

4. Write the following phonemically, showing the plus junctures.

   (1) gray vowel (2) grave owl (3) sly twitch (4) slight witch (5) a niche (6) an itch

5. Take any simple sentence like "He gave his brother the apple" and describe the different meanings, different emphases, different emotive values that it can be made to convey by changes in intonation.

17

Punctuation—Laws
and Lawmakers

149. The Reason Why

Unreflective people confronted by language problems are likely to be pretty meek. You tell them that they mustn't say "ain't" or mustn't split infinitives, and the majority will accept the dictum without argument. It doesn't often occur to the student to ask why not. Is it a government regulation? Is it a matter of logic? Does it have to do with the divine order of the universe? The student does not usually ask such questions, and perhaps the teacher should be thankful he does not. A certain docility undoubtedly makes teaching easier.

But probably the student is better off in the long run if he tries to understand and not just ape and memorize. There are rules of writing and rules of speaking (though "rule" is a somewhat misleading word), and some of these the writer or speaker transgresses at his peril. But these are not of celestial origin. They are produced—by processes of which even the producers may not be much aware—by various users of the language.

Certainly this is true of punctuation practices. We say that in writing we insert a comma before a conjunction which connects two sentence patterns. But it should not be supposed that this direction was given in an appendix to the Ten Commandments received by Moses on Mount Sinai. It is simply a convention that has grown among the many people engaged over centuries in evolving a writing system. How such conventions grow and how they are altered or maintained is the subject of this chapter.

150. Putting Speech on Paper

First of all, we must always bear in mind that writing stems from speech. The marks that we make on paper are, ultimately, symbols for what goes on in our throats and mouths when we talk. We have seen that the symbolization is far from perfect. The writing system may not have been very accurate in the first place, and it is always subject to various kinds of deterioration. Furthermore, writing styles differ from speech styles. When we write, we may use words and phrases that we wouldn't ordinarily speak. Nevertheless, writing is fundamentally a symbolization of speech. If there had been no speech, there would be no writing.

We have already discussed the development of the alphabet, in which our distant forbears, after long experimentation with more unwieldy systems, hit upon the one letter-one phoneme idea. That this was some three thousand years before the term *phoneme* was introduced or the concept defined doesn't matter. The North Semitic peoples knew intuitively what the consonant phonemes in their languages were and learned to use letters to symbolize them. The Greeks added the vowels, and our alphabet was born.

151. The Word Unit

The development of signs to indicate intonation—i.e., punctuation—was much slower, and it has never gone to anything like completion. We saw in Chapter 4 that ancient writers   strungalltheirwordstogetherlikethistheydidntmarkword boundariesorsentenceboundarieseither.   Eventually   they learned to separate words. It may strike us now that words are obviously units and obviously separable. But this is partly because we have grown used to seeing these white spaces between groups of letters. It might not be so obvious if we were just learning to read and write.

How many words are there in "He's opening up"? Four, we answer, because the writing system says so. But if we were inventing the writing system, the answer wouldn't be so easy. The sounds are these: /hiyzowpəniŋəp/. Most people would have two plus junctures: /hiyz+owpəniŋ+əp/. If the inventor of the writing system were sensitive to plus juncture, he might therefore arrive at three units here: *hes* and *opening* and *up*. It would be another step to perceive that /hiyz/ consists of two words, since there is no plus juncture between them. One can see this only by noting the separability of *he* and *s* in different but comparable sentences: "Is he opening up?" "He really is opening up now."

But then, having seen that /hiyz/ consists of two words, the inventor might easily jump to the wrong conclusion that /owpəniŋ/ does too and might write. "He s open ing up." This could be corrected only by the observation that *ing* occurs only after *open* or some other verb and is never, like *up,* separated from the verb. We say "He is opening the place up" but not "He is open the place ing up."

Thus, reacting both to plus juncture and to the distribution of sound groups, writers reached an understanding of the concept of word units. They learned to leave spaces between such units and so to make faster reading possible. Instead of having to sound each letter and sort out the groupings for himself, the experienced reader could pick up and comprehend larger stretches of the message with a single glance.

The process of separating word units has never been perfected. There are some words which are words only because we write them so. There is no reason why *football* should be written as one word and *fountain pen* as two. But by and large the spaces between letters in modern writing represent real divisions, and most such divisions are shown.

152. Periods and Commas

The next step was the marking off of sentence units. The corresponding speech features are junctures correlating with various word arrangements. We have no way of knowing now just what junctures occurred where in the languages of ancient and medieval times. But it is a safe guess that something comparable to the double-cross and double-bar junctures of American speech did occur and gave early writers the concept of the sentence. They began to "point" their writing—that is to put points or dots where the terminal junctures occur in speech.

Along with this grew the habit of using large or "capital" letters at the beginning of such stretches. This was only one of many uses found for capital letters. But their use at the beginning of sentences eventually became standardized, and the sentence was thus marked as such, fore as well as aft.

The use of commas and such other marks as semicolons, colons, dashes, exclamation points, question marks developed later, some just before the invention of printing and some after. The use of these marks also stemmed from the occurrence of pitch and juncture, although the correspondence never was and isn't now very exact. When the marks were invented, nobody had any conscious understanding of intonation. Writers knew only that something happened to their voices at various points in the utterance, and they put in their squiggles to indicate such happenings.

It should be remembered that much early writing was intended to be read aloud. The preacher wrote his sermon and read it to his congregation; the poet wrote an epic and read it to his friends. The punctuation marks were consequently directions to do certain things in the course of the reading— to raise the pitch or drop it, to show that something was ended or not, to indicate a parenthetical insertion after which the main statement would proceed.

153. The Effect of Printing

When printing was invented, in the middle of the fifteenth century, punctuation was abundant and chaotic. Every writer, every scribe had his own system. The early printers had individual systems too, as each printer imitated in type the handwriting that took his fancy. But printing was a big step toward standardization simply because there were fewer printers than there were authors. A printer making the books of dozens of authors would tend to impose similar practices of spelling and punctuation on all of them. Furthermore, whereas a hundred handwritten copies of a book will all be different, a hundred copies printed from the same plates will all be exactly the same. Thus readers saw certain practices repeated regularly while others dropped out of use.

It was the printers of the sixteenth and seventeenth centuries who worked out the main features of modern punctuation. The punctuation marks themselves were shaped in imitation of marks in manuscripts, changed according to the printer's artistic bent or to the exigencies of casting type. Their use was at first diverse. One printer might use a comma or a colon where another would insert a period or a dash or a semicolon. But gradually, as printers imitated one another, punctuation, like spelling, came to be more or less standardized.

154. Recent Trends

Since 1700, changes in punctuation have been much slower and more orderly, but they still go on. In general, the direc-

Thus endeth the seconde book of the recule of the his‐
toryes of Troyes / Whiche bookes were late trans‐
lateor in to frenshe out of latyn / by the labour of the vene
rable persone raoul le feure preest as a fore is said / And
by me Indigne and vnworthy translated in to this rude
englissh / by the comandement of my said redoubtid lady
duches of Bourgone : And for as moche as I suppose
the said two bokes ben not had to fore this tyme in oure
englissh langage, therfore I had the better will to accom
plissh this said werke / whiche werke was begonne in
Brugis / and contynued in gaunt And finysshid in Coleyn
In the tyme of ye troublous world / and of the grete deuy
sions beyng and regnyng as well in the royames of
englond and fraunce as in all other places vnyuersally
thurgh the world that is to wete the yere of our lord a‐
thousand four honderd lxxi . And asfor the thirde book
whiche treteth of the generall and last destruccion of Troye
Hit nedeth not to translate hit in to englissh / ffor as mo‐
che as that worshipfull and religyous man dan John lidgate
monke of Burye dide translate hit but late / after whos
werke I fere to take vpon me that am not worthy to bere
his penner and ynke horne after hym . to medle me in that
werke . But yet for as moche as I am bounde to con‐
templare my saydr ladyes good grace and also that his
werke is in ryme / And as ferre as I knowe hit is not
had in prose in our tonge / And also parauenture / he
translated after some other Auctor than this is / And
yet for as moche as dyuerce men ben of dyuerce desyres .
Some to rede in Ryme and metre. and some in prose
And also be cause that I haue now good leyzer beyng in
Coleyn And haue none other thynge to doo at this tyme

Page from Caxton, *History of Troye*, 1475. (Bettmann Archive)

tion of the last century or so has been toward less punctuation. This reflects an increase of reading speed. When the alphabet was young, readers probably sounded out each letter, one by one. Through the centuries they have learned to pick up groups of letters, words, phrases, whole lines with a single flicker of the eye. Furthermore, the practice of reading aloud has much declined in the last hundred years. Not in many homes nowadays does one find the family grouped in the evening around Father, listening to him read *David Copperfield* in measured phrases. Nowadays, when we shut off the television set and take a book or magazine, we read it to ourselves, and we find that we read it faster if the lines are not too liberally sprinkled with punctuation marks.

Thus in a book printed in the eighteenth century we will often find commas where single-bar juncture might occur:

> The people, that saw the play, liked it very much.

Now such junctures would not be marked; we would write the sentence without commas:

> The people that saw the play liked it very much.

In older books we often find colons or semicolons marking double-bar juncture:

> Though I had not seen Harry in some years; still I recognized him instantly.

In modern books a comma would replace the semicolon. Commas have lost some of their old functions and taken over some of colons and semicolons. Semicolons have come to be used more like periods, usually marking the fall of double-cross juncture.

155. Policing Punctuation

Who regulates punctuation nowadays? Is it the authors of books? The printers? The writers of reference books? All of these play a part, but probably the most important control is in the hands of editors employed by newspapers, magazines, and book publishers.

When a publisher decides to publish a book, he sends the completed manuscript to an editor. The editor goes over it very carefully, line by line and word by word. He (or, more likely, she) writes on the manuscript detailed instructions to the printer about such matters as size of type and kind of type, arrangement of headings and examples, and so on. The editor also checks the writing. If a word is misspelled, it is corrected. If a sentence is unclear, it is rephrased. If punctuation deviates from the habits of the publishing house, it is brought into line. When the change is one about which there can be no argument—as, for instance, when the author has carelessly written "recieve" for "receive"—the correction is made without comment. But if the matter is at all debatable, the editor writes in the margin a query to the author, explaining the reason for the change and asking whether he agrees.

From the editor, the manuscript goes to the printer, whose job is simply to follow exactly the manuscript as annotated and corrected by the editor. The printer is not supposed to tamper with the writing. If a mistake has escaped the notice of both author and editor, the printer will probably print the mistake.

The printer makes first a kind of trial edition of the book called galley proof. These are long sheets not yet divided into pages. The galleys with the manuscript go back to the editor, who checks the proof with the manuscript, correcting any errors the printer may have made as well as those not detected in the first working over of the manuscript.

Galley proof and manuscript are sent next to the author, who now gets a chance to put in his oar. He looks for mistakes so far missed and studies the corrections made by the editor.

If he doesn't approve of the changes, he can change them back again. But he would be expected to explain his reasons for doing so. Proof and manuscript are now returned to the printer, who makes a second trial edition called page proof. Page proof is very like the finished book except that it is not bound. This proof is also read by editor and author, all errors (they hope) are removed, and the proof returns to the printer for the final printing.

Thus every effort is made to assure that the book is conventional so far as the mechanics of writing are concerned. Nobody takes a creative attitude toward spelling or punctuation. The editor is guided by dictionaries, handbooks, perhaps a style manual for the publishing house. The editor does what the dictionaries and handbooks decree. But since dictionaries and handbooks—in theory at least—simply report what is done by publishing houses, a circular check is maintained. Publishers want their books to be daring and different, but not especially in spelling and punctuation. Here everyone wants to do what everyone else does.

In theory the author has control of everything because he has the final say on the proof. But not many authors have strong views on spelling and punctuation. Those that do are likely to be engaged in creative writing of certain kinds, and these will have the coöperation of their editors. Most authors are happy enough to have the editor iron out their difficulties. If an author is both persistent and unconvincing about a comma, the editor may quietly change it anyway before the final printing. The present writer once wished to use the word *sensable:* "sensable distinction" as opposed to "mental distinction." This was written *sensable* in the manuscript, changed to *sensible* by the editor, changed to *sensable* on the galleys by the author, changed again to *sensible* by the editor, changed to *sensable* on page proof by the author, and changed once more to *sensible* by the editor. It appeared as *sensible,* which in the context was not very sensible.

156. Limits on Standardization

Thus the whole tendency in spelling and punctuation is toward stability, toward standardization, toward doing, insofar as possible, what everyone else does. Punctuation, however, is not nearly so susceptible to standardization as spelling is. Confronted by a spelling problem, the editor or author has only to open a dictionary to determine the standard practice. But no dictionary or handbook or style manual can come near covering all punctuation problems that might arise. The punctuation of only the more obvious structures can be reduced to rule, and most of these only in a rather general way.

For instance, a publishing house might have a clear policy on how to punctuate such a series as "the man the boy and the donkey." The house may have a style book which tells whether it should be "the man, the boy, and the donkey" or "the man, the boy and the donkey." (Magazine and book publishers usually put in the second comma; newspapers generally omit it.) But the style book is not very likely to have a rule governing, for example, the first comma in this paragraph or the last comma in the paragraph preceding.

It is because much of punctuation is decided by the judgment of individual authors and editors that change in punctuation habits is possible. Such change does go on, though, as we have seen, it goes slowly.

In the next few chapters we shall study those areas of punctuation about which generalizations—rules, if you like—can be made. It will be seen that even within these areas much variation is possible. Beyond them the writer must be guided by his feeling for sentence structures and for the speech rhythms that accompany them.

SUGGESTIONS

1. Find—in dictionaries or elsewhere—definitions of the word *word*. Analyze the definitions. Do they define a unit of language or a unit of writing? Do they seem logically sound? Are they practical? For instance, would they permit one who did not know the English writing system to determine the number of words in "high school football players" or "Let's drop in on Harry."?

2. If your school library possesses books printed before 1700, examine one and compare it with modern practice in spelling, capitalization, and punctuation.

3. Given the statements made in Sections 155 and 156, what is the proper role of the schools in the regulation of punctuation?

4. If you have had any experience either as author or editor—for example, on a school publication—write a paper describing the experience as it relates to the discussion in this chapter.

5. Write a paper on any aspect of printing or bookmaking. Draw your material from the library or from personal experience. Remember to select a topic narrow enough to permit reasonable development.

18

Punctuating Expanded and Combined Patterns

157. The Base

The child learning to read and write confronts punctuation problems immediately. He must right away grasp the concept of the sentence, with its initial capital and terminal period. He learns that we write, "Dick was cold. He put on his coat" and not "Dick was cold he put on his coat." He also learns what a question mark is, and it is brought home to him that "Dick was cold" and "Was Dick cold" are punctuated differently.

These are very simple matters but also very important. Once the learner has grasped them—and presumably all readers of this book did so many years ago—everything else about English punctuation is graspable.

158. Sentences Without Internal Punctuation

Most of the sentences that we write consist basically of a subject and a verb or verb cluster. (The principal exceptions are request sentences, which contain no subjects.) So long as the sentence contains no sentence modifiers or series (matters to be discussed later), there is usually no internal punctuation. In speech we utter such sentences with double-cross juncture at the end, and this is represented in writing by the period.

But we have neither double-cross nor double-bar juncture within such sentences and hence no commas. There is no comma between the subject and the verb cluster, none within the subject, and none within the verb cluster.

This is obvious when subject and verb are short. Probably no one would wish to insert a comma in "The boys chased the cats." But note how such a sentence can lengthen through modification of noun or verb and still contain no internal punctuation:

> The little boys nearby chased the cats.
> The little boys around the corner chased the cats.
> Some little boys around the corner who delight in cruelty chased the cats.
> Some little boys around the corner who delight in cruelty constantly chased the cats with long whips which they had constructed out of leather straps carelessly discarded by merchants who tend to use the area near where we live as a dumping ground.

Such a sentence as the last may not be admirable for its style. The point is that it can be written without internal punctuation. It consists basically of a noun cluster which is the subject of a verb cluster. If it were spoken, it would probably have a number of primary stresses and hence a number of single-bar junctures, which might strike the ear as pauses. But it would not ordinarily have the rise of double-bar juncture, and in writing it would not need commas.

159. Series

If the sentence contains a series of elements, it will have double-bar juncture after each member of the series but the last. These are represented in writing by commas. Speak the following sentences aloud, and note how your pitch tends to rise where the commas occur.

The boys, the girls, and the old men chased the cats.
The boys around the corner, the girls down the street, and the old
    men chased the cats.
The boys chased the cats, stoned the dogs, and cursed the police.
The boys chased the cats, the dogs, and the donkeys.
I needed four pounds of potatoes, a dozen eggs, a quart of vinegar,
    some rubbing alcohol, and a corkscrew.
He spoke loudly, clearly, and forcefully.
They were young, innocent, and rather foolish.
Some little boys who delighted in cruelty, who were armed with
    whips, and who hated cats were walking down the street.

160. Series of Adjectives

Two or more adjectives occurring before a noun headword
present a special problem. Speak the following, and note the
difference:

> a little old woman
> an old, little woman

The first example would have no juncture; the second would
have some juncture after *old*. There is a difference in the
construction of the cluster. "Little old woman" consists of two
immediate constituents: *little* modifies *old woman*. But "old,
little woman" has three IC's. *Old* and *little* modify *woman*
separately, the meaning being not that the *little woman* is old
but that the woman is *old* and *little*. In cases of doubt, the
student can often recognize such structures by seeing whether
an *and* can be inserted between the modifiers.

Here are some further examples:

> a happy young man
> a happy, talkative man
> a happy, talkative young man
> a young, happy, talkative fellow
> a young, happy, and talkative person
> a little black dog
> a black, dangerous-looking dog

> a vicious, spiteful deed
> a spiteful new supervisor

Note that when all elements of a series are connected by conjunctions there are no junctures in speech and no commas in writing:

> The boys and the girls and the old men chased the cats.
> He was handsome and gay and lovable.
> Cecilia married a handsome and gay young man.

161. Sentence Patterns Joined by Conjunctions

The punctuation of combined patterns has its complications, but it is not a very difficult matter provided that the student can distinguish conjunctions, subordinators, and sentence connectors. The distinction between them was the subject of Chapter 15, which you may wish to review before going on.

Sentence patterns joined by a conjunction (*and, or, but, for, yet, so, nor*) conventionally have a comma, semicolon, or period before the conjunction. The comma is most common:

> He needed more money, but he didn't know how to get it.
> The sun had risen, and it was already uncomfortably warm.
> We had packed only a small amount of food, for we expected to be back by Friday.
> He must have been out of town, or he would have seen the news in the papers.
> The dinner was getting cold, so we didn't wait for Uncle Harry.
> Stanley kept assuring me of his undying loyalty, yet I didn't altogether trust him.
> The soup was watery and the roast beef tough, nor was the dessert very much better.

All of these might also be written with a semicolon or a period in place of the comma:

> He needed more money, but he didn't know how to get it.
> He needed more money; but he didn't know how to get it.
> He needed more money. But he didn't know how to get it.

The difference is one of emphasis. The use of a semicolon or a period tends to bring the reader to a stop at the end of the first pattern and thus to throw a greater weight on the second. Compare also:

> He was asking for trouble, and we gave him some.
> He was asking for trouble. And we gave him some.

There is a widespread notion that one should not begin a sentence with *and* or *but*. This has no basis in fact, as the most cursory inspection of professional writing will demonstrate. The myth seems to stem from a particular difficulty that primary school teachers have with their pupils. Children learning to write tend to produce compositions like this:

> Dick found a little doggie, and it was a nice little doggie, and Dick liked it very much. But Dick's father didn't like the doggie, and he wouldn't let Dick keep it. And this made Dick cry.

Obviously the fault is not so much in the punctuation as in the structure. The composition is just as bad whether the conjunctions are preceded by commas or by periods. But teachers and textbook writers have felt that proscribing conjunctions at the beginning of sentences would help get rid of such *and's* and *but's*. As has been said, this proscription does not reflect professional practice.

Remember that the conjunctions *and, or,* and *but* connect parts of patterns as well as whole patterns. They normally have punctuation before them only when they connect whole patterns, except that there may be a comma before an *and* connecting the last two elements in a series. Compare these:

> He was asking for trouble, and we gave him some.
> He was always sticking his oar in and asking for trouble.
> He was always sticking his oar in, minding other people's business, and asking for trouble.

The people in the back complained, and the man upstairs refused
to pay his rent.

The people in the back and the man upstairs complained and refused to pay their rent.

The people in the back, the man upstairs, and the lady across the
hall complained to the police, wrote letters to the newspapers,
and refused to pay the rent.

162. Sentence Patterns Joined by Sentence Connectors

When two sentence patterns are combined by a sentence
connector (*therefore, however, nevertheless,* etc.), writers
ordinarily use a semicolon or a period between the patterns.
The semicolon is perhaps a little more likely: *Semicolon ;*

He needed more money; however, he didn't know how to get it.

The sun had not yet risen; nevertheless it was already uncom-
fortably warm.

The soup was watery and the roast beef tough; consequently we
refused to pay the bill.

We didn't feel able to drive to the next town; moreover, we were
running low on gas.

The delegates from Laramie angrily stalked out of the meeting,
and they were soon followed by those from Cheyenne; thus the
Conference began to break up.

Such sentence patterns could just as well be separated by
a period:

He needed more money. However, he didn't know how to get it.

The soup was watery and the roast beef tough. Consequently we
refused to pay the bill.

The difference is again a slight one of emphasis. The period
tends to throw a little more weight on the second pattern.

The sentence connector may come within or at the end of
the second pattern. The two patterns are still separated by
period or semicolon:

We were determined to get an early start; we consequently told
the clerk to wake us at two-thirty.
I hadn't seen Lovelace for thirty-five years. I had no trouble recog-
nizing him, however.
The delegates from Terre Haute failed to show up; the meeting
was accordingly postponed.

163. Punctuation After Sentence Connectors

Handbooks sometimes direct us always to put a comma
after a sentence connector as well as a semicolon or period
before it. However, this advice cannot be justified by professional practice. Some sentence connectors usually have a
comma or commas setting them off from the rest of the pattern; others usually do not. Some sentence connectors are set
off in some positions but not in others. The tendency to reduce
punctuation operates here, and these words are not set off as
regularly as they may formerly have been.

The sentence connectors *moreover, indeed, in fact,* and
some others take a comma more often than not.

> Moreover, we were running low on gas.
> Indeed, he looked remarkably well.

Thus, hence, consequently, are more likely not to be punctuated:

> Thus the Conference began to break up.
> Consequently we refused to pay the bill.

Some are punctuated or not according to how the writer feels
about commas:

> However we did what we were told.
> However, we did what we were told.

Position may make a good deal of difference. Read the following aloud:

> We nevertheless tried to help him.
> We tried, nevertheless, to help him.

The first would be spoken without juncture and would not be punctuated. The second would have two junctures, and these should be indicated by commas.

Indeed, the writer's simplest solution here is to become sensitive to double-bar juncture and to put in the comma where he hears it (or wants the reader to hear it) and to omit it otherwise. This is much easier than trying to master a description of conventional practice for all sentence connectors in all positions. Such a description would be very complicated.

The important thing to remember about sentence connectors is that they call for a period or a semicolon between the patterns they join. If you use just a comma or no punctuation at all, you are likely to confuse the reader. Whether you also have a comma after the sentence connector is in comparison a trivial matter.

164. Sentence Patterns Joined by Subordinators

Subordinators also join sentence patterns and also provide punctuation problems, but we shall postpone these until the next chapter. All that needs to be said here is that when a subordinator joins two sentence patterns, the patterns normally have either a comma between them or nothing at all. If you separate them with a semicolon or period, you have what is traditionally called a "fragment" or "fragmentary sentence," like these:

> We stayed home all day. Because we were rather tired.
> He'll have to agree; whether he wants to or not.
> If I had my way; I'd have him arrested.

165. Summary of the Punctuation of Combined Sentence Patterns

The punctuation conventional in American writing of combined sentence patterns can be summed up as follows. (C stands for conjunction, SC for sentence connector, and S for subordinator.)

[handwritten: and, but, so, or, nor]

Sentence pattern, C sentence pattern.
Sentence pattern; C sentence pattern. *[handwritten: only when comma used alway in sentence.]*
Sentence pattern. C sentence pattern.

[handwritten: however]

Sentence pattern; SC sentence pattern. *[handwritten: moreover, thus, nevertheless]*
Sentence pattern. SC sentence pattern.

Sentence pattern S sentence pattern. *[handwritten: because, if, whether]*
Sentence pattern, S sentence pattern.

This is standardized punctuation, and it is standardized on the basis of the three combining structure groups—conjunctions, sentence connectors, and subordinators—rather than on intonation. Nevertheless, there is a fairly close connection between the punctuation marks and the junctures of speech. By and large, commas occur where double-bar junctures occur; by and large, semicolons or periods occur where double-cross junctures occur. The following would be common for speech and writing respectively:

We believed in him com|plet\ely, and we decided to⌐ he\lp him.

We believed in him completely, and we decided to help him.

We believed in him com|plet\ely therefore we decided to⌐ he\lp him.

We believed in him completely; therefore we decided to help him.

The second sentence could, to be sure, be spoken with double-bar juncture instead of double-cross:

We believed in him com|plet\ely/therefore we decided to ⌐he\lp him.

Nevertheless it would regularly be punctuated with semicolon or period.

It should not be supposed that the practices described here are perfectly uniform in professional American writing. Many writers deviate from them in various ways. The continuing tendency to reduce punctuation is reflected in the fact that the comma sometimes disappears before conjunctions connecting short sentence patterns:

> The car broke down again and we were stuck.
> Take it or leave it.

A comma sometimes appears before a sentence connector in place of the semicolon:

> Sam hadn't come, therefore nothing could be done.

Sometimes, particularly in fiction, we find a semicolon before a subordinator:

> Stanley reluctantly agreed to go and milk the cows; because, after all, that was what he was paid for.

But these are all rather special, rather unusual. It is not at all a bad thing for writing to be unusual, but if a writer writes unusually he probably ought to do so intentionally, aware that he is departing from customary practice.

Punctuation, like other conventions of writing, is intended to make things easier for the reader, and reading is easier and faster if the reader encounters the practices that he is used to. But no conventions of writing should serve to strait-jacket the writer, to keep him from making his points with the emphasis he wants. A reader can usually tell when a writer is intentionally diverging from conventions which he understands and when he is just hacking around.

SUGGESTIONS

1. Read the following sentences, listening for double-bar juncture. Punctuate them conventionally.

(1) He carried a saw, a hammer, and a can of nails (2) We all found Gerber sardonic, mordant, and cruel (3) The policeman blew his whistle and waved them on (4) Forash looked up at us, smiled quietly, and went on sharpening the knife (5) The cattle that had strayed during the storm were found in a gulch near Frenchman's Creek (6) The Ambassador was a man who knew the Middle East thoroughly, who spoke Arabic like an Arab, and who had nerves of steel (7) She was a sweet little thing (8) She was a sulky, unhappy, little girl (9) All anybody knew about the new Dean was that he played the banjo and the steel guitar, gave elaborate cocktail parties, and had once spent six months in jail in Little Rock (10) Stewart was a conscientious, hard-working, rather stupid employee (11) Very nearly all the handsome African tribesmen in the tent, who had been playing poker, rose to their feet and walked out in a huff (12) A ragged, filthy child followed us out of the station, across the square, and up the main street, and never let us get more than twenty feet ahead of him

2. What punctuation would be conventional for the following combined patterns?

(1) I had never seen him before, but I had a good idea who he was and what he wanted. (2) Holmes was convinced that at least one murder had been committed; consequently he felt obliged to call the police. (3) Jimson was three hours late for dinner; however, he had a pretty good excuse. (4) The bull had to be killed, so I selected a sword and killed him. (5) Small children will not be admitted, unless they are accompanied by adults. (6) Harry's pigeon wasn't looking very well this morning; indeed, it looked downright ill. (7) I simply had to have Adelaide's coöperation to get the work done; therefore I swallowed my pride and apologized. (8) It pained Arnold deeply to see his old mother beaten by hooligans; however, he was too timid to interfere so he pretended not to notice. (9) It wasn't really what one could call a good play, yet it did have its bright moments. (10) We knew we had to win this one for Coach

Grapefield, we therefore decided to bribe the referee. (11) Bert already knew that Grace had left, he knew, furthermore, that she wasn't coming back. (12) He was desperately tired and he was still a hundred miles from home, he felt that he had to keep going, however. (13) We were all rather fond of Charlie because he had a pleasant smile and a lot of money. (14) Burling felt that the supports were rather weak, he knew, moreover, that a storm had been predicted. (15) James had never got along well with librarians, nor were librarians particularly fond of him.

3. Check the first thirty sentence connectors occurring in a book or magazine and note the punctuation that accompanies them.

4. Write sentences illustrating the formulas given at the beginning of Section 165.

5. The next time you read a magazine article note whether the author ever begins sentences with conjunctions.

19

Punctuating Sentence Modifiers

166. Sentence Modifiers Preceding the Sentence Pattern

In studying immediate constituents (Chapter 14) we encountered such sentences as the following:

Ordinarily, the boys did what they were told.

We saw that the IC's of this sentence are *ordinarily* as one and *the boys did what they were told* as the other. No other division is possible, for *ordinarily the boys* is not a unit and neither is *ordinarily . . . did what they were told. Ordinarily* in this sentence is what is called a sentence modifier. Its meaning applies to the whole of the following sentence pattern, not just to part of the pattern.

Sentence modifiers are usually, though not always, marked off from the sentence they modify by single- or double-bar juncture. They are usually, though not always, set off in writing by commas.

Sentence modifiers may appear in several different positions. They come sometimes in front of the sentence they modify, sometimes after it, and sometimes within it. Punctuation differs somewhat according to the position as well as according to the type of sentence modifier that occurs. We shall consider first the punctuation of sentence modifiers occurring in front of the sentence pattern.

S-groups in this position are regularly separated by a comma from the sentences they modify:

> After they had finished lunch, they proceeded to Rimini.
> When dawn came, we could see the island very plainly.
> Since we had plenty of time, we agreed to play another set.
> If you know what's good for you, you'll mind your own business.
> Whether he likes it or not, the deal is going through.
> Although he was very tired, he kept on going.

Modifiers introduced by subordinators are usually punctuated in this position even when the modifier is not a complete sentence pattern:

> Although very tired, he kept on going.
> If at all possible, try to look up Mr. Oswald.

Adverbs occurring as sentence modifiers are punctuated more often than not, though many writers would omit the comma in the following sentences:

> Ordinarily, the boys did what they were told.
> Fortunately, nobody had told Mary.
> Instantly, the men in the front line dropped their rifles.
> Instinctively, I knew just what she meant.

Here again the tendency to reduce punctuation can be noted. Such adverbs are not set off so regularly as they once were, and time adverbs are not usually punctuated in this position:

> Sometimes he makes me sick and tired.
> Usually we went to bed earlier.

Preposition groups also occur as sentence modifiers in this position. The punctuation of these is extremely varied. Probably most present-day writers and editors prefer to omit the comma, especially when the preposition group is short:

> After lunch we drove on to Rimini.
> In the other room a man was peeling an orange.

With a quiet smile Stanley flicked open his knife.
On a hunch I looked under the table.

Some writers use commas in such sentences, however, and most do when the P-group is long:

> On the pretext of looking for my napkin, I crawled under the table.
>
> In a little secret room which opened off the hall, a man was peeling an orange.

167. Verb Clusters as Sentence Modifiers

Verb clusters also occur commonly as sentence modifiers, especially in writing. Compare these:

> Mary ran into the room.
> Running into the room, Mary announced her engagement.

Ran into the room and *running into the room* are both verb clusters, having the same internal structure. They differ only in relationship to the other parts of the sentence. *Ran into the room* is the main verb cluster of its sentence, having *Mary* as its subject. *Running into the room* is a sentence modifier. Its meaning applies against all that follows. It could not be said that *running into the room* modifies *Mary,* for it could not be shown that *running into the room Mary* is a unit. The immediate constituents of the sentence are clearly *running into the room* as one and *Mary announced her engagement* as the other.

There is, however, a clear difference between verb clusters as sentence modifiers and other constructions as sentence modifiers. When a verb cluster occurs as a sentence modifier, the performer of the action of the verb is expressed by the subject of the main pattern. In our sentence the performer of the action of running is *Mary,* the subject of *announced her engagement.* If the writer does not observe this connection, he may write a sentence that is ambiguous or ludicrous:

Running into the room, the engagement was announced.
Running into the room, Mary's engagement was announced.
Running into the room, Alice was awakened by Mary.

In the first two sentences the structure would suggest that the engagement ran into the room. In the third sentence the subject *Alice* seems to be the runner, which is impossible unless Alice was running in her sleep. These are examples of what are traditionally called "dangling modifiers."

168. Punctuation of Verb Clusters as Sentence Modifiers

Verb clusters occurring as sentence modifiers are always marked by juncture in speech and regularly by a comma in writing. Here are further examples:

Hoping for the best, we pushed on resolutely.
Seeing the ashes in the fireplace, Lovelace knew that someone had been there before him.
Raising the telescope, the Captain took a quick look.
Knowing that the mountain was dangerous, I advised Stanley to take a rope.

The verb in such clusters may be of the V-ed form instead of the V-ing:

Pressed to tell all I knew, I responded promptly.
Awakened by the noise, Virgil looked around him in surprise.

Somewhat similar is a construction in which the verb cluster is part of a preposition group:

In trying to reach the candle, I lost my balance.
By rationing the water carefully, they managed to stay alive.

Such modifiers are also regularly set off by commas. They also show the same connection between the verb in the modifier and the subject of the main pattern. Most writers would avoid sentences like "By rationing the water carefully, many lives were saved."

Adjective clusters also occur as sentence modifiers. They are also regularly punctuated and regularly keep a connection between adjective and following subject:

> Angry at the refusal, Gerber turned and walked away.
> Quick to forgive, Samuel was also quick to take offence.
> Sad at the thought of parting, we tried to talk of other things.

Finally, we have as sentence modifier a construction in which a noun or pronoun is followed by a verb cluster:

> The men having gone out, the ladies discussed them freely.
> The door being open, I cautiously entered the hall.

This is what is traditionally called—for no very good reason— a "nominative absolute" construction. It occurs much more commonly in writing than in speech. It is regularly punctuated as shown.

169. Sentence Modifiers Inside the Sentence Pattern

Sentence modifiers occurring in front of the sentences they modify are marked as sentence modifiers by position as well as by juncture or punctuation. They clearly stand apart from the subject and verb of the main pattern, and they clearly modify the pattern as a whole. Sentence modifiers occurring after the main pattern or within it are more complicated. Here the junctures of speech or the commas of writing may be the only signal that the modifier applies against the whole pattern and not just part of the pattern.

Compare these:

The students coming from out of town protested.
The students, coming from out of town, protested.

The meaning of these sentences is quite different. In the first we are concerned with a student body part of which live in town and part out of it; only those who come from out of town protested. In the second, all the students concerned live out of town and all of them protested.

In traditional terminology, *coming from out of town* would be called a "restrictive modifier" in the first sentence and a "nonrestrictive modifier" in the second. In the first it restricts or limits the meaning of *students;* in the second it does not. But we get closer still to the structure of the sentences if we point out that it is a noun modifier in the first sentence but a sentence modifier in the second. In the first sentence, *the students coming from out of town* is a tight unit, a noun cluster; in the second sentence we have no such unit but instead two separate ideas: the students came from out of town and the students protested. The only connection between *the students* and the modifier is that *the students* names the performer of the action of the verb cluster.

In these sentences there is no distinguishing signal except juncture or punctuation. In speech one could distinguish them only by pronouncing them differently—i.e., by including or omitting two junctures. In writing one distinguishes by inserting or omitting the commas.

Here are some further examples of verb clusters as sentence modifiers in this position. Verb clusters as noun modifiers are given for comparison:

> Angelo, smiling quietly, answered the question.
> The boy smiling quietly was Angelo.

> My father, trying to shave with a bread knife, cut himself badly.
> Any man trying to shave with a bread knife is likely to cut himself.

> The people, not understanding the government's position, were enraged.
> The people not understanding the government's position were enraged.

Some of these sentence modifiers could appear at the end of the sentences they modify:

> The students protested, coming from out of town.
> Angelo answered the question, smiling quietly.
> The people were enraged, not understanding the government's position.

Compare these sentences:

> The policeman chased the boy, waving a big stick.
> The policeman chased the boy waving a big stick.

In the first, *waving a big stick* is a sentence modifier; the policeman waves the stick. In the second it is part of the noun cluster *the boy waving the big stick;* the boy waves it. The only difference is juncture or comma.

170. S-Groups of the Who Type

S-groups also occur as sentence modifiers within or after the sentences they modify. Those occurring within the sentences are most commonly S-groups in which the subordinator is *who (whose, whom)* or *which.* These are similar to the verb clusters we have just considered:

> The students living out of town protested.
> The students, living out of town, protested.

> The students who live out of town protested. — *restrictive*
> The students, who live out of town, protested. — *non-rest.*

In the first of the second pair, the S-group *who live out of town* is a noun modifier and part of the noun cluster. In the second it is a sentence modifier, adding another idea to the sentence: the students (all of them) live out of town, and the students protested.

Similarly:

Angelo, who was smiling quietly, answered the question.
The boy who was smiling quietly was Angelo.

Mr. Quimby, who met us at the airport, is Stanley Quimby's father.
The Mr. Quimby who met us at the airport is Stanley Quimby's father.

The women, who had seen the accident, were called as witnesses.
The women who had seen the accident were called as witnesses.

Notice that the subordinator *that* introduces only noun modifiers, not sentence modifiers. *That* could be substituted for *who* in each of the second sentences of the pairs above but not in the first. *restrictive clause only*

The subordinator *which* sometimes introduces noun modifiers:

The houses which had recently been built on Brompton Road were crumbling rapidly.

But it is perhaps more common in sentence modifiers:

Our house, which had been built in 1689, was beginning to sag.
The goat, which was usually staked behind the house, had been moved to the front lawn.
The next cyclone, which was much worse, struck on the first of the month.

Such modifiers can of course appear at the end of the sentence:

We were met by Mr. Quimby, who is Stanley Quimby's father.
We were worried about our house, which had been built in 1689.

In all of these examples there is a meaning connection between the subordinator and some noun in the main sentence. Thus *which,* in the last example, refers to house; *who* in the preceding one, refers to Mr. Quimby. Such a connection is usual but not universal. Sometimes the reference is more vague:

> Gerber paid me the money, which I thought rather nice of him.
> She has a sweet disposition, which is more than one can say of her mother.

Note the difference between these two:

> Jimson appeared with a dog which startled everybody.
> Jimson appeared with a dog, which startled everybody.

In the first sentence it is the dog that startles everybody; in the second it is Jimson's appearing with it.

171. S-Groups of the Because Type

S-groups introduced by subordinators of the type *because, when, since* are somewhat different. We have seen that when these begin the sentence they are sentence modifiers, regularly separated from the rest of the sentence by a juncture in speech and a comma in writing:

> Because he knew what he was doing, we left him alone.
> When there was nothing else to do, we threw stones at the postman.

At the end of the sentence, however, such S-groups may be either verb modifiers or sentence modifiers. The following sentences differ in pronunciation as they do in punctuation, and they are somewhat different in meaning:

> We left him alone because he knew what he was doing. *answers "why?"*
> We left him alone, because he knew what he was doing. *"What did you do?"*

In the first sentence, the immediate constituents are the subject *we* as one and the following verb cluster as the other. The S-group *because he knew what he was doing* modifies *left him alone*. In the second sentence the IC's are the S-group as one and the sentence pattern *we left him alone* as the other. The S-group modifies the sentence.

The difference in meaning is that the first sentence is a direct answer to such a question as "Why did you leave him alone?" The S-group, which gives the reason, is an integral part of the answer. The second sentence is a reply to such a question as "What did you do?" This is answered by the main pattern "We left him alone." The S-group is just an idea volunteered additionally.

It can be shown that some subordinators in this position usually introduce sentence modifiers, whereas others usually introduce verb modifiers. *Although* and *whereas* are most likely to introduce sentence modifiers:

> I offered to help him, although I didn't know much about automobiles.
>
> Edwin always minded his own business, whereas Edwina was always poking her nose into other people's.

If, when, before most often introduce verb modifiers:

> We'll be glad to help you if we can.
> Mr. Alfonso always visited us when he came to town.
> Put that dynamite away before someone gets hurt.

Since and *while* introduce verb modifiers when they have a time meaning, sentence modifiers when they do not.

> No one had spoken to Alfred since the accident occurred.
> No one would speak to Alfred, since he was blamed for the accident.

> Ted and Lucy cooked dinner while the rest of us were gathering wood for the campfire.
> Some insisted on climbing the peak, while others feared that it was too dangerous.

But a total description of the behavior of the various subordinators would be very complicated. The student's best bet is to become sensitive to juncture, to put in a comma when he wants the reader to hear this juncture, and to omit the comma when he does not. Say the following aloud and note differences in pronunciation:

> I haven't thought much of Beavers since he ran off with my sister. Our family owes a great deal to Beavers, since he married my sister.

> We won't go unless the rain stops.
> We might go to Big Basin, unless you have a better idea.

> He settled in Santa Fe when the West was still wild.
> He settled in Santa Fe in 1872, when the West was still wild.

> They kept trying to repair the dam until the task appeared impossible.
> They kept trying to repair the dam, until suddenly the whole south side gave way.

172. Appositives

Somewhat similar to these sentence modifiers is the construction called the *appositive*. An appositive is a renaming of something that has occurred in a sentence. An appositive is usually marked off from the sentence by juncture in speech and by commas in writing:

> Mr. Alfonso, a friend of my father's, visited us every year.

In this sentence *a friend of my father's* is an appositive. It explains who Mr. Alfonso is and thus adds another idea to the sentence: Mr. Alfonso visited us every year, and Mr. Alfonso was a friend of my father's.

Here are some further examples:

> The rabbit, a small and timid little creature, blinked at us unhappily.

Alice, a girl who knew exactly what she wanted, answered immediately.

The police force of Cedar Rapids, as fine a group of men as ever served a community, resented the accusation.

He buzzed off in his new car, a 1958 Alfa-Romeo.

He invited us into his house, a vermin-infested shack.

Appositives usually follow and clarify a noun, but not always. Sometimes an appositive will be used to sum up the idea of a preceding sentence pattern:

He suggested that we climb the north face, a notion which struck us as idiotic.

Gerber paid me the money, a gesture which I much appreciated.

173. Summary of Comma Punctuation

To recapitulate, the main uses to which commas are put by American writers and editors are these: to separate sentence patterns joined by conjunctions, to separate members of a series, and to set off sentence modifiers from the sentences they modify. We have observed that there is a good deal of variation. Sentence patterns joined by conjunctions may be punctuated in other ways and sometimes are not punctuated at all. The punctuation of sentence modifiers depends to some extent on the kind of modifier and on whether or not it comes before the sentence pattern. Furthermore, writers differ somewhat in their practice. In general one must speak of tendencies rather than of rules or laws.

We have not by any means exhausted the topic of comma punctuation. It would be possible to go much further in linking up the occurrence of commas to various elements of sentence structure. But returns diminish when the description grows too complicated. It is questionable whether any writer learns to punctuate conventionally by absorbing a lengthy list of instructions. Most writers learn best by observing what other writers do.

The student will profit also if he can sharpen his awareness of single-bar and double-bar juncture. These are the features of speech most commonly symbolized by the commas of American writing. Remember that we hear what we read, even when we read silently. Our reception of the symbols on the page is in some sense physical as well as mental. This is shown by our tendency to stumble over words or names that we don't know how to pronounce:

> The next speaker was Mr. Khilaghyzkw, the delegate from Nmomph.

The meaning is perfectly clear however the names are pronounced, and one would think that the silent reader would take in the sentence as readily as if it read "Mr. O'Brien, the delegate from South Dakota." But he does not. His mouth and throat want to come to terms with Khilaghyzkw and Nmomph. They are used to making imperceptible movements as the reading goes on, and here they do not know just what imperceptible movements to make.

So with intonation. "What did you put in the salad, Alice?" and "What did you put in the salad? Alice?" sound different when they are spoken and sound different when they are read, too. If you can become conscious of double-bar and double-cross juncture and distinguish them from the level pitch of single-bar juncture, you will find that many problems of punctuation solve themselves.

Listen for the junctures in these final examples:

> There is, when you stop to think about it, much to be said for his point of view.
> We thought Anita was behaving rather badly.
> Anita, we thought, was behaving rather badly.
> Her behavior, in the opinion of many of us, was inexcusable.
> It was Venezuela, not Brazil, that objected.

Shooting, Henry, would be against the law.
Shooting Henry would be against the law.
Why don't you look inside, Charlie?
Why don't you look inside Charlie?

SUGGESTIONS

1. Identify the sentence modifiers in the following sentences, and decide whether you would mark them off with commas or not. Not all writers would agree on all of the sentences.

(1) If you happen to see Fred, tell him we're looking for him. (2) Unfortunately, the bathtub was already full of orange juice. (3) After the grapes have been harvested, they are trampled by barefooted peasant girls. (4) Noting the look of amusement on Morgan's face, Sally blushed deeply. (5) In a few minutes it was all over. (6) When taken in moderation, snuff is actually beneficial. (7) Under the impression that the woman was his mother, Arnold clapped her cheerfully on the back. (8) When a college girl marries, she can be reasonably sure that the dullest part of her life lies ahead. (9) By taking the Bhooba Pass route, Sluter hoped to reach Lho before the monsoon. (10) Infuriated by the rebuff, Ronaldson tendered his resignation.

2. Describe differences in meaning in the following pairs.

(1) The students coming from out of town protested. The students, coming from out of town, protested. (2) The boys who were not afraid kept on going. The boys, who were not afraid, kept on going. (3) My aunt who lives in South Bend raises mice. My aunt, who lives in South Bend, raises mice. (4) One wintry morning he caught sight of a mountain lion, using very powerful binoculars. One wintry morning he caught sight of a mountain lion using very powerful binoculars. (5) The deans, who are indispensable, will be kept on the payroll. The deans who are indispensable will be kept on the payroll. (6) He rose at three each morning and played the piano, which infuriated the neighbors. He rose at three each morning and played the piano which infuriated the neighbors.

3. Comma punctuation is omitted from the following sentences. Identify the sentences that contain sentence modifiers and indicate what the punctuation should be.

(1) Picking her teeth with a fork, Sally pondered her next move.
(2) Sally, picking her teeth with a fork, pondered her next move.
(3) The little girl pushing the broom is the upstairs maid.
(4) April, which is usually a lovely month in Terre Haute, was cold
and wintry this year. (5) All animals that have been exposed to
the disease should be slaughtered immediately. (6) Miss Driscoll,
frowning slightly, reprimanded the boy who had thrown the ink.
(7) Songs which contain references to patricide cannot be broadcast on the radio. (8) Nodding negligently, Andrew answered in
Italian which he speaks fluently. (9) Grandma who had heard the
whole conversation smiled enigmatically and picked up her cello.
(10) Ralph's greatest ambition was to be a Rotarian, whereas his
brother Henry was perfectly content to be a simple Elk.
(11) Young Montrose has been insufferable since he returned from
Europe. (12) Martha was the logical choice for secretary, since she
knew how to read and write.

4. Identify and punctuate the appositives in the following sentences.

(1) His father, a successful engineer, insisted that he go to college.
(2) He had been living in Brindisi, a city in southern Italy.
(3) Mrs. Pace dropped in with her dog, a rather handsome Airedale.
(4) He was raised by an older sister, a woman with a fierce temper.
(5) He took his B.A. at Cornell, his father's alma mater, and then
did graduate work at Yale. (6) With some reluctance I introduced
Ambrose, our youngest child. (7) He straightened his necktie, a
handsome item depicting tumbling elephants. (8) She had always
wanted to learn Welsh, a language which struck her ear as wonder-
fully musical.

5. Select a magazine or newspaper, and in it identify as many as you
can of the structures discussed in this chapter. Note the punctuation.

20
Dots and Dashes

174. Other Marks

Most of the student's punctuation headaches center around commas, semicolons, and periods. However, there are various other marks—colons, dashes, quotation marks, exclamation marks, parentheses, brackets—with which one has to grapple now and then. Some are important only in some kinds of writing. Thus the author of a technical work needs more complicated symbols for the presentation of his material than does, say, a novelist.

The use of these marks has varied a good deal over the centuries and often differs now from one area to another. British usage, for example, is not always the same as American. We shall note here the practices more or less standard in American writing.

175. Colons

The principal use of the colon is to introduce a list or series:

> Only three books were found in the house: *David Copperfield, Moby Dick,* and *Hamlet.*
>
> We were instructed to make the following purchases: a bar of soap, some matches, a dog collar, and two or three pounds of toothpicks.
>
> Holmes pointed out the clues which led him to suspect murder: first of all, the man was dead; secondly, he had been hated by all who knew him; finally, the handle of a bread knife could be seen protruding from his back.

Colons are also used sometimes to introduce a single example or an explanation of a preceding statement:

> Sluter had only one hope: to try to beat off the crocodiles with a club.   *small letters*
> There is this much to be said for Stanley: he takes good care of his fingernails.

There are a couple of things about colons to notice particularly. One is that a small letter, not a capital, follows it. That is, we do not write ". . . only one hope: To try to. . . ."

The other point is that we usually have a complete sentence pattern before the colon. Students sometimes write sentences like "The only vegetables he could eat were: string beans, peas, and beets." This is unconventional. One would instead do it thus:

> The only vegetables he could eat were string beans, peas, and beets.
> The only vegetables he could eat were these: string beans, peas, and beets.

It may be observed that the present book often transgresses the principle that a complete statement precedes the colon. Here lists of examples, for instance, are often introduced by a colon following such a word as *similarly* or *thus*. The writer would plead the technical exigencies of the work and remark once more that such mechanical devices as punctuation marks exist to help the reader, not to handcuff the writer.

176. Dashes

The functions of dashes overlap those of commas, colons, and parentheses. Their use depends to some extent on the formality or informality of the writing; they occur most commonly in informal writing. To some extent their use depends on the predilections of the writers. Some writers are just fond of dashes.

However, there are some functions peculiar to dashes. One is to mark the breaking off of a statement before it is completed. This would naturally occur most often in the writing of dialogue:

> We might put in a dash of cinnamon and—oh, I'm afraid we don't have any cinnamon.
> He has beautiful long lashes and lots of money and—well, just everything a girl could ask for.

Situations occur sometimes in which dashes will make a sentence clear, where commas would leave it ambiguous. Compare these:

> Two men, Ed and Tommy, went into the mine.
> Two men—Ed and Tommy—went into the mine.

In the first sentence it might not be perfectly clear whether two people or four went into the mine. The dashes of the second sentence mark off Ed and Tommy as an appositive naming the two men.

Similarly, dashes are sometimes used when the writer wants to stress the break marking off the sentence modifier:

> He announced—rather to our horror—that he was going to marry Lucinda.
> Buy the car if you like—if you're quite sure it's the best thing.
> My grandfather—a rather devilish old person with a penchant for practical jokes—added a little kerosene to the salad.

Some writers use dashes in place of colons:

> He demands three things of his employees—responsibility, industry, and common sense.
> Sluter had only one hope—to beat the crocodile to the shore.

Such punctuation is more informal than colon punctuation.

In personal letters some correspondents use dashes almost to the exclusion of other punctuation marks:

I want to tell you about the cabin—it's really a dream in some ways—though not what I expected exactly—the stove is terribly smoky—you know these wood stoves—and it takes hours—simply hours—to make coffee.

This solves punctuation problems all at once, but it may make the reading something of a chore. Obviously it is a strain to which one would subject only a personal friend.

177. Parentheses

Parentheses, which are as formal as dashes are informal, are also used to mark off sentence modifiers when for some reason commas won't serve.

> Two men (probably Thompson and Meyers) will be added to the rescue squad.
> My brother Rudolph (I think you met him when you visited us in Detroit) is going to Mexico with us.
> It is believed (in some circles at least) that Pakistan will offer a compromise plan.

Sometimes a whole sentence will be enclosed in parentheses, to show that it is in some way apart from the run of the text:

> Next add a few drops of lemon juice. (You can use orange juice if you have no lemons.) Cook for twenty minutes on a low fire, stirring constantly.

It would appear that parentheses are not used as much in ordinary writing as they once were, commas or dashes being preferred. In some technical writing—such as scientific papers, bibliographies, textbooks—they are more necessary. In such writing one learns their employment as part of the special trade.

178. Brackets

Brackets are parentheses with the corners squared: [ ]. A writer may easily get through his first five million words or so without ever having to use them, since their functions are special. All the other punctuation marks so far discussed appear as standard equipment on most typewriters, except that the dash is made by striking the hyphen key twice. But if you want square brackets on your typewriter, you have to have them put on specially. You wouldn't do so unless you expected to do a lot of work in a technical field.

Occasionally, however, in term papers or reports required in college work, one comes upon a situation in which brackets are needed. If, for example, one wished to insert a comment or correction into a quoted passage, he would use brackets:

> Sanderwood wrote, "I left Omaha in the early eighties [1879, actually] and went to Denver to seek my fortune."

The use of parentheses here would mean that "1879, actually" was part of the quotation, not the contribution of the quoter.

If a passage gets so involved as to include a parenthesis inside a parenthesis, then one can work it out only with a combination of parentheses and brackets. But almost always there is some happier alternative.

179. Quotation Marks

The obvious use of quotation marks is to enclose quotations, though this is not their only use. The writer should note that quotation marks are used only when the exact words of the speaker are given, not when the message is simply reported. Compare:

> Jimson said, "I'm going to buy a dog."
> Jimson said that he was going to buy a dog.
> Jimson said he was going to buy a dog.
> Jimson said he's going to buy a dog.

Only the first example repeats Jimson's words. The following would mean different things:

> Jimson said, "I'm going to buy a dog."
> Jimson said I'm going to buy a dog.

In the second sentence the "I" would refer not to Jimson but to the writer of the sentence. If you read these examples aloud, you will observe that the direct quotations are marked off by double-bar or double-cross juncture; the others are not.

The student should note the punctuation accompanying the use of quotation marks. A comma ordinarily precedes the quotation, as in the examples above. The "Jimson said" or equivalent can come in the middle of the quotation, in which case it has a comma fore and aft:

> "I intend," Jimson said, "to buy a dog."
> "We believe," he wrote "that Harrison will support us."
> "There is no need," he remarked quietly, "to make a scene."
> "There is no need," he said, with that quiet force that everyone found so impressive, "to make a scene."

But note this:

> "There is no need to make a scene," he said. "We can settle this quietly."

Here the quoted utterance consists of two sentences, and the period after *said* is required.

In American practice the marks closing the quotation come after a period or comma:

> "I believe we'll get along," he said.
> He said, "I believe we'll get along."

They come after a question mark provided that the sentence quoted is a question:

> He said, "Have you been waiting long?"

But if the whole utterance is a question, the marks closing the quotation come before the question mark:

> Did he say, "I hate music"?

180. Special Uses of Quotation Marks

Sometimes writers use quotation marks to disclaim responsibility for a word or phrase:

> The delegate from India insisted that "reciprocity freely reciprocated" was the only reasonable basis for discussion.
> The college production of *Hamlet* was a "real dog."

This practice is, however, easily overdone where slang is concerned. A passage dotted with slang terms carefully enclosed in quotation marks has a mincing appearance, suggesting that the writer is appalled by his own terrible daring. Usually it is best to use slang terms without apology or not at all.

In most of their other uses, quotation marks alternate, in print, with italic type. *This is italic type.* In preparing a manuscript for printing, one indicates the words or phrases to be put in italics by underscoring them once. This has led to the practice of using underscoring for titles and such, even in manuscripts not intended for print.

Editorial policies differ somewhat in when to use quotation marks and when to use italics, but the most common practice seems to be to use italics for titles of books or magazines and quotation marks for titles of parts of books, particularly magazine articles. Thus one would write *Pride and Prejudice,* the *New Yorker,* the New York *Times.* For articles one would write "Pigskin Preview," "The Talk of the Town," "How to Decorate Your Bathtub." We shall return to these matters in discussing bibliographies.

Quotation marks and italics are also used to mark off words that must for some reason be set apart from the rest of the text, for example words that are being discussed as words:

> English words borrowed from Arabic include "algebra," "zero," "alcohol," and "admiral."

English words borrowed from Arabic include *algebra, zero, alcohol,* and *admiral.*

Both methods are common. If you are writing for print, you follow the policy of the publisher. If not, you suit yourself. Notice that when quotation marks are used the commas and periods come inside the quotation marks, as in ordinary quotations.

181. Exclamation Marks

Like most other punctuation marks, exclamation marks may signal real differences in intonation. Speak the following aloud and compare them:

> Does he like candy?
> Does he like candy!

These are no more confusable in speech than in writing, the pitch patterns being entirely different. Sometimes the speech difference is less obvious:

> Our cat is dead.
> Our cat is dead!

These *can* signal a real distinction: the exclamation mark, a high pitch on *dead;* the period, the normal next-to-high pitch on *dead.* But all too often in the work of immature writers, exclamation marks signal only that the writer considers his sentence astounding. The reader may too, but he should ordinarily be allowed to reach the conclusion from the sentence itself, not from an extraneous direction on what he is supposed to feel about it.

Also rather juvenile is the practice of using exclamation marks or question marks as a kind of comment, ironic or otherwise, on words in the text:

Angelo showed up with his four (!) girl friends.
She was wearing her delightful (?) new hat.
They didn't have time (!) to talk to us.

This is like looking over the reader's shoulder and giving him instructions as he reads. Fortunately, we are spared some temptation by the fact that the exclamation mark is not standard equipment on most typewriters.

SUGGESTIONS

1. Look through an issue of a magazine and list the occurrences of the marks described in this chapter. Note the purposes that they serve. See if you find any uses for them that are not discussed here.
2. Examine an article in a scholarly journal in a field of some interest to you—such as natural science, psychology, philology, sociology. Note the special punctuation devised to take care of the needs of the specialized writing.
3. In the following sentences the points marked "x" would normally call for some kind of punctuation. Decide whether, if you were writing the sentence, you would use a comma, a colon, a dash, or a parenthesis where the "x" occurs.

(1) It has been said that there are only three interesting cities in America x New York, San Francisco, and New Orleans. (2) The King listed three names x Willoughby, Carlyle, and Figby-Norton x and said that he would be satisfied with any one of these. (3) There was one other possibility x to abandon football altogether. (4) We might invite Morgan and Alfonso to the x oh, but Alfonso doesn't speak to Morgan, does he? (5) Some languages x for example, Italian and Turkish x have fairly good writing systems. (6) When he went into the world, his father gave him only one piece of advice x never to gamble with strangers. (7) My Uncle Anthony x he is the uncle who raises mushrooms x recently suffered a mild heart attack. (8) It was thought x at least many people thought x that Ceylon would make a counterproposal. (9) We had a number of things to buy x paper napkins, snowshoes, an umbrella, and a small kerosene stove x and we had only half an hour to buy them in. (10) Kirby was looking for a

secretary with certain qualities x an ability to type and take dictation quickly and accurately; fluency in English, French, and Arabic; and, above all, good looks and quiet charm.

4. Add quotation marks and other punctuation as necessary to the following sentences.

(1) Harville said Well, I'll think it over   (2) What do you think Al suggested of broaching the subject to Hopkins   (3) I don't think it was a very funny joke said Amelia quietly   (4) It just happens Dawson remarked with a smile that I know exactly where the body is buried   (5) It's too late now to say you're sorry said Mr. Thustle The damage has been done

21

Speech Communities

182. Directions of Change in Language

Imagine a village of a thousand people all speaking the same language and never hearing any language other than their own. As the decades pass and generation succeeds generation, it will not be very apparent to the speakers of the language that any considerable language change is going on. Oldsters may occasionally be conscious of and annoyed by the speech forms of youngsters. They will notice new words, new expressions, "bad" pronunciations, but will ordinarily put these down to the irresponsibility of youth, and decide piously that the language of the younger generation will revert to decency when the generation grows up.

It doesn't revert, though. The new expressions and the new pronunciations persist, and presently there is another younger generation with its own new expressions and its own pronunciations. And thus the language changes. If members of the village could speak to one another across five hundred years, they would probably find themselves unable to communicate.

Now suppose that the village divides itself and half the people move away. They move across the river or over a mountain and form a new village. Suppose the separation is so complete that the people of New Village have no contact with the people of Old Village. The language of both villages will change, drifting away from the language of their common

305

ancestors. But the drift will not be in the same direction. In both villages there will be new expressions and new pronunciations, but not the same ones. In the course of time the language of Old Village and New Village will be mutually unintelligible with the language they both started with. They will also be mutually unintelligible with one another.

An interesting thing—and one for which there is no perfectly clear explanation—is that the rate of change will not ordinarily be the same for both villages. The language of Old Village changes faster than the language of New Village. One might expect that the opposite would be true—that the emigrants, placed in new surroundings and new conditions, would undergo more rapid language changes. But history reports otherwise. American English, for example, despite the violence and agony and confusion to which the demands of a new continent have subjected it, is probably essentially closer to the language of Shakespeare than London English is.

Suppose one thing more. Suppose Old Village is divided sharply into an upper class and a lower class. The sons and daughters of the upper class go to preparatory school and then to the university; the children of the lower class go to work. The upper-class people learn to read and write and develop a flowering literature; the lower-class people remain illiterate. Dialects develop, and the speech of the two classes steadily diverges. One might suppose that most of the change would go on among the illiterate, that the upper-class people, conscious of their heritage, would tend to preserve the forms and pronunciations of their ancestors. Not so. The opposite is true. In speech, the educated tend to be radical and the uneducated conservative. In England one finds Elizabethan forms and sounds not among Oxford and Cambridge graduates but among the people of backward villages.

A village is a fairly simple kind of speech community—a

group of people steadily in communication with one another, steadily hearing one another's speech. But the village is by no means the basic unit. Within the simplest village there are many smaller units—groupings based on age, class, occupation. All these groups play intricately on one another and against one another, and a language that seems at first a coherent whole will turn out on inspection to be composed of many differing parts. Some forces tend to make these parts diverge; other forces hold them together. Thus the language continues in tension.

183. The Speech Communities of the Child

The child's first speech community is ordinarily his family. The child learns whatever kind of language the family speaks —or, more precisely, whatever kind of language it speaks to him. The child's language learning, now and later, is governed by two obvious motives: the desire to communicate and the desire to be admired. He imitates what he hears. More or less successful imitations usually bring action and reward and tend to be repeated. Unsuccessful ones usually don't bring action and reward and tend to be discarded.

But since language is a complicated business it is sometimes the unsuccessful imitations that bring the reward. The child, making a stab at the word *mother* comes out with *muzzer.* The family decides that this is just too cute for anything and beams and repeats *muzzer,* and the child, feeling that he's scored a bull's eye, goes on saying *muzzer* long after he has mastered *other* and *brother.* Baby talk is not so much invented by the child as sponsored by the parent.

Eventually the child moves out of the family and into another speech community—other children of his neighborhood. He goes to kindergarten and immediately encounters speech habits that conflict with those he has learned. If he goes to school and talks about his *muzzer,* it will be borne in on him by his colleagues that the word is not well chosen. Even *mother* may not pass muster, and he may discover that he gets better results and is altogether happier if he refers to his female parent as his ma or even his old lady.

Children coming together in a kindergarten class bring with them language that is different because it is learned in different homes. It is all to some degree unsuccessfully learned, consisting of not quite perfect imitations of the original. In school all this speech coalesces, differences tend to be ironed out, and the result differs from the original parental speech and differs in pretty much the same way.

The pressures on the child to conform to the speech of his age group, his speech community, are enormous. He may admire his teacher and love his mother; he may even—and even consciously—wish to speak as they do. But he *has* to speak like the rest of the class. If he does not, life becomes intolerable.

The speech changes that go on when the child goes to school are often most distressing to parents. Your little Bertram, at home, has never heard anything but the most elegant English. You send him to school, and what happens? He comes home saying things like "I done real good in school today, Mom." But Bertram really has no choice in the matter. If Clarence and Elbert and the rest of the fellows customarily say "I done real good," then Bertram might as well go around with three noses as say things like "I did very nicely."

Individuals differ of course, and not all children react to the speech community in the same way. Some tend to imitate and others tend to force imitation. But all to some degree have their speech modified by forces over which neither they nor their parents nor their teachers have any real control.

Individuals differ too in their sensitivity to language. For some, language is always a rather embarrassing problem. They steadily make boners, saying the right thing in the wrong place or the wrong way. They have a hard time fitting in. Others tend to change their language slowly, sticking stoutly to their way of saying things, even though their way differs from that of the majority. Still others adopt new language habits almost automatically, responding quickly to whatever speech environment they encounter.

Indeed some children of five or six have been observed to speak two or more different dialects without much awareness that they are doing so. Most commonly, they will speak in one way at home and in another on the playground. At home they say, "I did very nicely" and "I haven't any"; these become, at school, "I done real good" and "I ain't got none."

184. The Class as a Speech Community

Throughout the school years, or at least through the American secondary school, the individual's most important speech community is his age group, his class. Here is where the real power lies. The rule is conformity above all things, and the group uses its power ruthlessly on those who do not conform. Language is one of the chief means by which the school group seeks to establish its entity, and in the high school this is done more or less consciously. The obvious feature is high school slang, picked up from the radio, from other schools, sometimes invented, changing with bewildering speed. Nothing is more satisfactory than to speak today's slang; nothing more futile than to use yesterday's.

There can be few tasks more frustrating than that of the secondary school teacher charged with the responsibility of brushing off and polishing up the speech habits of the younger generation. Efforts to make *real* into *really, ain't* into *am not, I seen him* into *I saw him, he don't* into *he doesn't* meet at best with polite indifference, at worst with mischievous counterattack.

The writer can remember from his own high school days when the class, a crashingly witty bunch, took to pronouncing the word *sure* as *sewer*. "Have you prepared your lesson, Arnold?" Miss Driscoll would ask. "Sewer, Miss Driscoll," Arnold would reply. "I think," said Miss Driscoll, who was pretty quick on her feet too, "that you must mean 'sewerly,' since the construction calls for the adverb not the adjective." We were delighted with the suggestion and went about saying "sewerly" until the very blackboards were nauseated. Miss Driscoll must have wished often that she had left it lay.

185. Confronting the Adult World

When the high school class graduates, the speech community disintegrates as the students fit themselves into new ones. For the first time in the experience of most of the students the speech ways of adult communities begin to exercise real force. For some people the adjustment is a relatively simple one. A boy going to work in a garage may have a good deal of new lingo to pick up, and he may find that the speech that seemed so racy and won such approval in the corridors of Springfield High leaves his more adult associates merely bored. But a normal person will adapt himself without trouble.

For others in other situations settling into new speech communities may be more difficult. The person going into college, into the business world, into scrubbed society may find that he has to think about and work on his speech habits in order not to make a fool of himself too often.

College is a particularly complicated problem. Not only does the freshman confront upperclassmen not particularly disposed to find the speech of Springfield High particularly cute, but the adult world, as represented chiefly by the faculty, becomes increasingly more immediate. The problems of success, of earning a living, of marriage, of attaining a satisfactory adult life loom larger, and they all bring language problems with them. Adaptation is necessary, and the student adapts.

The student adapts, but the adult world adapts too. The thousands of boys and girls coming out of the high schools each spring are affected by the speech of the adult communities into which they move, but they also affect that speech. The new pronunciation habits, developing grammatical features, different vocabulary do by no means all give way before the disapproval of elders. Some of them stay. Elders, sometimes to their dismay, find themselves changing their speech habits under the bombardment of those of their juniors. And then of course the juniors eventually become the elders, and there is no one left to disapprove.

186. The Space Dimension

Speech communities are formed by many features besides that of age. Most obvious is geography. Our country was originally settled by people coming from different parts of England. They spoke different dialects to begin with and as a result regional speech differences existed from the start in the different parts of the country. As speakers of other languages came to America and learned English, they left their mark on the speech of the sections in which they settled. With the westward movement, new pioneers streamed out through the mountain passes and down river valleys, taking the different dialects west and modifying them by new mixtures in new environments.

Today we are all more or less conscious of certain dialect differences in our country. We speak of the "southern accent," "the Brooklyn accent," the "New England accent." Until a few years ago it was often said that American English was divided into three dialects: Southern American (south of the Mason-Dixon line); Eastern American (east of the Connecticut River); and Western American. This description suggests certain gross differences all right, but recent research shows that it is a gross oversimplification.

The starting point of American dialects is the original group of colonies. We had a New England settlement, centering in Massachusetts; a Middle Atlantic settlement, centering in Pennsylvania; a southern settlement, centering in Virginia and the Carolinas. These colonies were different in speech to begin with, since the settlers came from different parts of England. Their differences were increased as the colonies lived for a century and a half or so with only thin communication with either Mother England or each other. By the time of the Revolution the dialects were well established. Within each group there were of course subgroups. Richmond speech differed markedly from that of Savannah. But Savannah and Richmond were more like each other than they were like Philadelphia or Boston.

The Western movement began shortly after the Revolution, and dialects followed geography. The New Englanders moved mostly into upper New York State and the Great Lakes region. The Middle Atlantic colonists went down the Shenandoah Valley and eventually into the heart of the Midwest. The southerners opened up Kentucky and Tennessee, later the lower Mississippi Valley, later still Texas and much of the Southwest. Thus new speech communities were formed, related to the old ones of the seaboard, but each developing new characteristics as lines of settlement crossed.

New complications were added before and after the Revolution by the great waves of immigration of people from countries other than England: Swedes in Delaware, Dutch in

New York, Germans and Scots-Irish in Pennsylvania, Irish in New England, Poles and Greeks and Italians and Portuguese. The bringing in of Negro slaves had an important effect on the speech of the South and later on the whole country. The Spanish in California and the Southwest added their mark. In this century movement of peoples goes on: the trek of southern Negroes to northern and western cities, the migration of people from Arkansas, Oklahoma, and Texas to California. All these have shaped and are shaping American speech.

We speak of America as the melting pot, but the speech communities of this continent are very far from having melted into one. Linguists today can trace very clearly the movements of the early settlers in the still living speech of their descendants. They can follow an eighteenth century speech community West, showing how it crossed this pass and followed that river, threw out an offshoot here, left a pocket there, merged with another group, halted, split, moved on once more. If all other historical evidence were destroyed, the history of the country could still be reconstructed from the speech of modern America.

187. Social Differences

The third great shaper of speech communities is the social class. This has been, and is, more important in England than in America. In England, class differences have often been more prominent than those of age or place. If you were the blacksmith's boy, you might know the son of the local baronet, but you didn't speak his language. You spoke the language of your social group, and he that of his, and over the centuries these social dialects remained widely separated.

England in the twentieth century has been much democratized, but the language differences are far from having disappeared. One can still tell much about a person's family, his school background, his general position in life by the way he speaks. Social lines are hard to cross, and language is perhaps the greatest barrier. You may make a million pounds and own several cars and a place in the country, but your vowels and consonants and nouns and verbs and sentence patterns will still proclaim to the world that you're not a part of the upper crust.

In America, of course, social distinctions have never been so sharp as they are in England. We find it somewhat easier to rise in the world, to move into social environments unknown to our parents. This is possible, partly, because speech differences are slighter; conversely, speech differences are slighter because this is possible. But speech differences do exist. If you've spent all your life driving a cab in Philly and, having inherited a fortune, move to San Francisco's Nob Hill, you will find that your language is different, perhaps embarrassingly so, from that of your new acquaintances.

Language differences on the social plane in America are likely to correlate with education or occupation rather than with birth—simply because education and occupation in America do not depend so much on birth as they do in other countries. A child without family connection can get himself educated at Harvard, Yale, Princeton. In doing so, he acquires the speech habits of the Ivy League and gives up those of his parents.

Exceptions abound. But in general there is a clear difference between the speech habits of the college graduate and those of the high school graduate. The cab driver does not talk like the Standard Oil executive, the college professor like the carnival pitch man, or an Illinois merchant like a sailor shipping out of New Orleans. New York's Madison Avenue and Third Avenue are only a few blocks apart, but they are widely separated in language. And both are different from Broadway.

It should be added that the whole trend of modern life is to reduce rather than to accentuate these differences. In a country where college education becomes increasingly everybody's chance, where executives and refrigerator salesmen and farmers play golf together, where a college professor may drive a cab in the summertime to keep his family alive, it becomes harder and harder to guess a person's education, income, and social status by the way he talks. But it would be absurd to say that language gives no clue at all.

188. Good and Bad

Speech communities, then, are formed by many features: age, geography, education, occupation, social position. Young people speak differently from old people, Kansans differently from Virginians, Yale graduates differently from Dannemora graduates. Now let us pose a delicate question: aren't some of these speech communities better than others? That is, isn't better language heard in some than in others?

Well, yes, of course. One speech community is always better than all the rest. This is the group in which one happens to find oneself. The writer would answer unhesitatingly that the noblest, loveliest, purest English is that heard in the Men's Faculty Club of San Jose State College, San Jose, California. He would admit, of course, that the speech of some of the younger members leaves something to be desired; that certain recent immigrants from Harvard, Michigan, and other foreign parts need to work on the laughable oddities lingering in their speech; and that members of certain departments tend to introduce a lot of queer terms that can only be described as jargon. But in general the English of the Faculty Club is ennobling and sweet.

As a practical matter, good English is whatever English is spoken by the group in which one moves contentedly and at ease. To the bum on Main Street in Los Angeles, good English is the language of other L.A. bums. Should he wander onto the campus of UCLA, he would find the talk there unpleasant, confusing, and comical. He might agree, if pressed, that the college man speaks "correctly" and he doesn't. But in his heart he knows better. He wouldn't talk like them college jerks if you paid him.

If you admire the language of other speech communities more than you do your own, the reasonable hypothesis is that you are dissatisfied with the community itself. It is not precisely other speech that attracts you but the people who use the speech. Conversely, if some language strikes you as unpleasant or foolish or rough, it is presumably because the speakers themselves seem so.

To many people, the sentence "Where is he at?" sounds bad. It is bad, they would say, in and of itself. The sounds are bad. But this is very hard to prove. If "Where is he at?" is bad because it has bad sound combinations, then presumably "Where is the cat?" or "Where is my hat?" are just as bad, yet no one thinks them so. Well, then, "Where is he at?" is bad because it uses too many words. One gets the same meaning from "Where is he?" so why add the *at*? True. Then "He going with us?" is a better sentence than "Is he going with us?" You don't really need the *is,* so why put it in?

Certainly there are some features of language to which we can apply the terms *good* and *bad, better* and *worse.* Clarity is usually better than obscurity; precision is better than vagueness. But these are not often what we have in mind when we speak of good and bad English. If we like the speech of upperclass Englishmen, the presumption is that we admire upperclass Englishmen—their characters, culture, habits of mind. Their sounds and words simply come to connote the people themselves and become admirable therefore. If we knew the same sounds and words from people who were distasteful to us, we would find the speech ugly.

This is not to say that correctness and incorrectness do not exist in speech. They obviously do, but they are relative to the speech community—or communities—in which one operates. As a practical matter, correct speech is that which sounds normal or natural to one's comrades. Incorrect speech is that which evokes in them discomfort or hostility or disdain.

189. Moving Among Speech Communities

For some people correct speech can be a complicated matter indeed. Consider a boy from a small town in Tennessee, educated at the University of Illinois, employed as secretary in a Pittsburgh steel union, and a leading member of the Western Pennsylvania Field and Stream Club. He will need some flexibility in order to appear everywhere as one of the boys, in order not forever to be calling attention to his other connections. If he addresses the union with his college speech, the members may admire his education, but they may not feel that he is really one of them, in tune with their problems. If he uses his Pittsburgh steel dialect at the class reunion, his classmates may feel that his education hasn't really done him much good. Neither Illini nor steel lingo will go over big with the Field and Stream boys, who speak another language entirely. And when he goes home to Tennessee, he must be able to slip into the native dialect, or his aged parents will think him a stranger, with hoity-toity foreign ways, who probably doesn't love them any more.

Not everyone lives such a complicated speech life, and those who do meet the problem in different ways. Some slip from one dialect to another as easily as they would change clothes.

Others stick to their speech everywhere, comfortable in the conviction that it surpasses all others, and often they succeed in persuading the people they encounter that it really does.

SUGGESTIONS

1. Observe and describe speech differences between yourself and older members of your family.
2. Men and women, boys and girls, speak different language. The words and expressions used by one sex would sound grotesque coming from the other. Describe the language of the sex opposite to yours.
3. Write a dialogue in which two men speak to each other in women's language or in which two women speak to each other in men's language.
4. Describe and discuss the language of your high school class. What peculiarities did it have that set it apart from adult speech? How many of these peculiarities do you retain?
5. Select an author some of whose characters speak a marked social or geographical dialect—e.g., Steinbeck, Faulkner, Damon Runyon, P. G. Wodehouse. Define the dialects and describe the forms the author uses to evoke it. Try to estimate the degree to which it represents actual speech.
6. Make a report on the purpose and methods of the *Linguistic Atlas* of the United States. Use the card catalogue and the *Reader's Guide to Periodical Literature* to find material.
7. Compare with other members of the class terms for the following:

   (1) a piece of living room furniture on which several people can sit (2) a piece of bedroom furniture with drawers in which clothes are kept (3) maternal parent (familiar term) (4) paternal parent (familiar term) (5) kitchen utensil in which eggs are fried (6) round breakfast food made of flour and eaten with butter and syrup (7) room in a house used principally for reading, writing, or studying (8) machine for playing records (9) land bordering the ocean (10) 2:45

8. Compare with others pronunciation of the following words.

   apricot, almond, tomato, neither, rodeo, fog, wash, Mary, garage, turpentine

22
Writing Communities

190. The Development of Writing Standards

Just as some kinds of speech go over better some places than others, so different kinds of writing may be appropriate or inappropriate depending on where they are used. But there are important differences. Speech is, essentially, uncontrollable. The schools, by concentrating their fire on a few specific points, such as the double negative, have been able to effect certain developments in the speech of part of the population. But these points are trivial in comparison with the great mass of speech, which education touches hardly at all.

It is true that improved modern communications, particularly the radio, serve to reduce dialects and to standardize speech. Broadcasting companies seek to have their announcers use those speech forms which will seem most normal and inoffensive to the greatest number of listeners. This use gives these forms a further boost and tends to distribute them more widely at the expense of other forms. It is conceivable that a country, a government, a school system could use radio and records and tape recordings to exercise deliberate control over speech. But this has not been seriously proposed, and even this would not keep speech from changing.

But writing can be controlled and has been for several centuries. When western Europe emerged from barbarity, it began increasingly to write in the various vernacular languages as well as in the more respectable Latin. At first there was almost no standardization at all. Kings were weak and barons were strong, and as a result countries were likely to have not one center of court and culture but many. A writer wrote in his native dialect or in the dialect of the court or literary center or abbey in which he found himself. Eventually, however, political power became more concentrated and literary groups followed. Writers flocked to the big cities—London, Paris, Madrid—and they used the dialects of these capitals as the base of their literary work. Eventually the use of these dialects became inescapable for serious work. If you wrote in Devonshire English instead of London English, you proclaimed yourself a country bumpkin, uneducated and untraveled and not worth listening to. Thus London English became "standard English," Parisian French became "standard French," not because of any intrinsic excellence these dialects had but simply because they were the dialects of the capital.

191. Control of the Standard

Thus by the time of Shakespeare the languages of Europe either had or were well on the way to acquiring literary standards. But it was felt that this was not enough, that there ought to be some kind of central agency, governmental or otherwise, which would legislate on correctness in writing. France filled this need with the French Academy, founded in 1635. This organization of scholars undertook to lay down the law on what was good French and what wasn't. It standardized French spelling and sought to bring order in other matters —word usage, grammatical structure, and so on. The Academy is both a result and a cause of the rather superstitious reverence that the French display toward the ideal of correctness in language.

The British, typically, solved the problem more indirectly. In the first half of the eighteenth century there was a good deal of agitation for an English academy on the French model. There were dire warnings, by Jonathan Swift and others, that English was going to pot and had to be controlled. Any nation, it was suggested, in which the citizens were permitted to go about using *rep* in place of *reputation* and *mob* in place of *mobile vulgus,* could not long continue to rule the waves. However, nothing was done, and by 1755, when Samuel Johnson published his dictionary, people had come to feel that England could get along without an academy after all.

Johnson's dictionary was by no means the first English dictionary. The first one came out in 1603, and by the eighteenth century dictionary-making had become a big and profitable business. But Johnson's work was more important and more effective than that of his predecessors. It was advertised as the English counterpart of the dictionary of the French Academy, intended to regulate and stabilize the English language. By the time it was published, Johnson himself had come to realize that neither he nor any other lexicographer was going to regulate the English language, but the dictionary did play an important part in regulating English writing. People felt that all arguments would be settled by reference to "The Dictionary," as it was simply called. If Johnson spelled a word so, that was the correct spelling. If Johnson said that a word ought to be used with a particular meaning, that was how it should be used. If Johnson said a word was "not in good use," a writer wishing to be thought good thought twice about using it.

Since Johnson's day, dictionaries in England and America have continued to be the principal repository of writing standards. English and American dictionaries are commercial, not governmental, enterprises, and the methods by which they are produced have sometimes left something to be desired. Nevertheless, they have acquired unquestioned authority. Most people feel that any question involving not only spelling but also grammar, pronunciation, word usage can be settled once and for all by looking in the dictionary. So far as speech goes, they are wrong; speech obeys other laws. But so far as writing goes, they are not far from right. Dictionaries tend to imitate one another, and therefore they give the writing public pretty much the same answers. And the writing public—authors, editors, teachers—all seek their answers from the dictionary.

192. Variations Within the Standard

Thus English writing, unlike English speech, has been standardized and tends to remain so. But it would be an exaggeration to say that English writing is one homogeneous whole, one community. Writing propriety—correctness—doesn't vary so much with time, place, and circumstance as speech does, but it varies some.

We have first of all the basic separation between England and America. Some differences occur in spelling: *color/colour; center/centre; tire/tyre.* Vastly more occur in vocabulary. There are not only such obvious differences as English *lift* for American *elevator* but many more subtle ones. The English often use the same words but with different meanings or the same words but with much higher or lower frequency. A New York *Herald Tribune* reporter who quit and went to work for the London *Daily Telegraph* would have to make a considerable adjustment in his writing and would no doubt commit many blunders while he was making it.

Nor is there any complete uniformity in the writing on our side of the Atlantic. Magazine writing as a whole differs from newspaper writing as a whole. The difference stems partly from different methods of production. A newspaper is written fast, read fast, and thrown away in an hour; a magazine is composed in relative leisure. Also, a magazine is likely to be read by a relatively selected (though not necessarily select) audience, whereas a newspaper reaches a greater cross section. Writers and editors tailor their work accordingly. Newspapers usually—not always—favor a somewhat more informal style than magazines do, employing words and constructions somewhat more likely to occur in speech. What is correct writing for a magazine may be altogether incorrect for a newspaper, and vice versa.

Since different newspapers are directed to different reading groups, differences among them are sometimes enormous. No one could confuse the New York *Times* with the New York *Daily News*. The *Times* is conservative, leisurely, weighty. Insofar as its writing reflects speech at all, it is the speech of intelligent and articulate people discussing serious subjects in a rather formal way. The *Daily News,* on the other hand, is breezy, slangy, and colloquial. It is talking to a reader who has his coat off, his feet up, and a bottle of beer on the table. Correctness, again, depends on where you stand. A *Daily News* article in the *Times* would be obviously incorrect. But so—obviously—would a *Times* article in the *Daily News*.

Different magazines also have different standards. No reader familiar with all three magazines would need to look at the covers to distinguish articles from the *Saturday Evening Post,* the *Atlantic Monthly,* and the *New Yorker. Post* writing is usually quite clear and simple. The sentences tend to be short, the constructions normal, and the words and phrases running heavily to clichés. *Atlantic* writing is usually much more formal and literary, employing a wider and somewhat more bookish vocabulary. *New Yorker* writing is perhaps the most complicated of the three, with the introductory sentence sometimes winding through half a column or more and replete with parenthetic constructions. But its lucidity is remarkable, and the style is scarcely ever ponderous.

Readers of *Time* magazine will be aware of a particular *Time* style. At different periods in its history, the magazine has given a good deal of attention to making its writing altogether distinctive. One device is the telescoping of compound terms. Thus one writes *cinemagnate* for *cinema magnate,* *GOPolitician,* for *GOP politician, Miamillionaire* for *Miami millionaire.* This practice has fallen off in recent years, perhaps because it is so easily burlesqued: *Timen,* for *Time men.* *Time* has also given attention to grammatical constructions. It likes, or liked, to write "No quitter he" in place of "He was no quitter." It likes to omit the *and* in a compound construction. "The President spent fourteen hours at his desk, saw dozens of visitors."

193. Washington Prose

Not all American writing appears in newspapers, magazines, and commercial books. Tons of it are produced in government offices, and these writing communities have their own little ways. Government writing is regularly criticized and satirized for being roundabout, stuffy, and obscure. It seldom uses one word when it can devise a way of saying the same thing in ten. It seldom uses a simple, plain word when it can think of a longer, more puzzling one. The result has been labeled "gobbledegook" by one of its critics.

One interesting aspect of government writing is the practice of making new verbs from other form classes. All English switches words pretty freely between the noun and verb classes: "The cook cooked the meat," "We dug out a dugout." But government English does it more than most, and particularly with nouns borrowed from Latin and Greek: "The disposition of these documents should not be actualized until they have been thoroughly regulationed in accordance with the advices recently channeled under Directive A387."

domestic engineer (housewife)

No doubt one can go too far in making fun of governmental and military composition. Washington contains major generals and undersecretaries who write very well and who prize clarity in the writing of their subordinates. Efforts are made periodically to clear the jungle. Furthermore, it is undeniable that any operation requires its technical terms—its jargon— and that a complicated operation requires complicated jargon. Still one suspects that much of the muddy writing in the government reflects muddy thinking plus a desire to sound deep and important. Certainly in some government offices, at least, a person gets farther faster if his writing is not too lucid and exact. In this writing community, correctness involves a little pompousness and obscurity.

194. Poetry on Madison Avenue

Another writing community is the business world. Business writing is dominated not only by the commercial necessity of being clear, of making the point, but also by the fear of offending potential customers. Since some customers may be offended if you split an infinitive and others if you don't, business writing isn't often easy.

In general, business writing is more prone to break convention than other writing is. This is particularly true in the most high-powered of business writing—advertising. American advertising is, in a way, very good, because it is able to collect the cream of writing talent. Five hundred years ago a man with a real bent for words moved to London and wrote plays. Today he moves to Madison Avenue and writes advertising copy. Madison Avenue gives some scope to his talents, but it restricts him too, since the final test of his poetry is whether it will sell the article to the largest possible number of customers.

For obvious reasons, advertising tries to keep in close touch with the language predilections of the populace and pretty much ignores literary tradition. Advertising is the only area, for example, in which simplified spelling has made any appreciable progress. Thus we have *Nulaid* (eggs), *Nitey-nite* (pajamas); *E-z-kleen* (cleanser), *Kleenex, U-drive* (car rental) among thousands of others. The spelling is not of course simplified in any consistent way, and the change is not always a simplification: one English shoe brand is called *Easiephit.*

But perhaps the most obvious general characteristic of advertising writing is the cozy and intimate and personal approach to the reader. The copywriter gets together with one on the sofa and pours honeyed words into one's ear: "Goober's Personalized Window Shades have been exquisitely tailored to enhance the alluring loveliness of the inimitable You."

195. Considering the Reader

Writing implies reading, and in whatever writing community one finds oneself, one must consider not only the message one has to convey but also the reader who is going to receive the message. Writing communities are much less complicated and various than speech communities, but the nature of writing makes it possible, and inevitable, to pay more attention to the differences that do exist. In speech situations we must react fast, get on with it, and necessarily we rely chiefly on more or less automatic response. In writing we have the opportunity to choose, to weigh words, to consider consciously the reader's reaction.

Not always do we want to please the reader. If you are writing advertising copy, you obviously want above all things to avoid offense. On the other hand, in a letter of resignation to a tyrannical employer, you may want to be as offensive as all get out. The point is that the writer can control the reader's reaction, whatever he wants it to be, through his knowledge of the reader's language experience, his likes and dislikes and capacities and expectations.

Students often complain of inconsistencies between teachers, particularly English teachers. "Miss Smithfield wanted us to make our compositions breezy and colloquial, and Mr. Osborne said he'd mark us down if we used colloquialisms. What kind of system is that?" It isn't any kind of system; it's just the way it is. You adapt. For Miss Smithfield you breeze dutifully; for Mr. Osborne you wrap yourself in weight and dignity. You may consider Mr. Osborne unduly stuffy or Miss Smithfield frivolous, and you may or may not consider it your bounden duty to oppose your own point of view. Since Mr. O. and Miss S. control the grade book, opposition has obvious difficulties. The student might remember, too, that he gains a good deal through learning to write in two different ways for two different readers.

In writing and speaking as in other matters one always must decide how much to go one's own way and how much to defer to the ways of others. There are no rules. Probably young people must defer more often than not, just because they're young. They want more things: the grade, the job, the promotion, the favor. Above all they need—more than they will as they grow older—the approbation of other people. One of the obvious ways of getting it is to accommodate oneself to other people's linguistic likes and dislikes. Only those who are old and hopeless can afford to say, "I talk as I please and write as I please, and if you don't like it, the hell with you."

SUGGESTIONS

1. Look up and report on Jonathan Swift's remarks on the necessity of controlling the English language. A history of the English language will provide a brief discussion and further references.

2. If your library contains a copy of Johnson's dictionary, read the preface and report on Johnson's views on language control.
3. Compare the writing styles of any two magazines or newspapers familiar to you. How do the differences reflect differences in readership?
4. Make a list of twenty spelling simplifications found in the names of advertised products.
5. Select a piece of government writing that seems to you particularly bad (horrible examples are sometimes printed in the columns of the *New Yorker* magazine) and criticize it in detail. Rewrite it so as to make it more readable.

23

Split Infinitives and Such

196. English Teachers and the Human Race

There is a widespread belief among otherwise intelligent people that a large part of the effort of an English class—say about half—is or should be concentrated on such matters as split infinitives, prepositions at the end of sentences, *who* and *whom, shall* and *will,* and other trivia. We English teachers must be somehow to blame for this popular view of our work, but few of us nowadays would admit that the view is justified. Our responsibilities, we like to think, are larger, and our objectives more important.

Still the attitude persists. It has become a key part of the folklore of American education. The English teacher is looked upon as an arbiter of foolish elegance, a small-time Emily Post, whose duty it is to guard and polish and police a language used only by English teachers or by real people in unwilling contact with English teachers. Many and many a time the writer has been an unhappy participant in such dialogues as this:

OTHER PERSON: What do you do for a living?
ME: I teach English.
OTHER PERSON: Say, I guess I better watch my language.

Or this:

ME: You going to the game?

OTHER PERSON: Yeah, I think I will.

ME: Me too.

OTHER PERSON: Guess I should have said, "I shall," since you're an English teacher, huh?

One thing to do with such people is to slap their ears with a wet salmon. Another thing is to explain that English teachers speak much the same language that everybody else does, that they do not customarily race about correcting the usage of casual acquaintances, and that in their daily labors the distinctions between *shall* and *will* play a very small part or none at all.

But the fact remains that a half a dozen small points of usage are what many people think of when they think of English class. This being so, we shall consider these points here, if only to suggest that they are not worth losing much sleep over.

197. Split Infinitives

A split infinitive is a construction in which something— usually an adverb—comes between the *to* and the verb: *to really know, to quietly expire, to sincerely believe.* Nobody knows just who decided that infinitives should not be split, or on what grounds. Certainly it was not on the grounds of usage. Good writers had always split infinitives when they felt like it, as some good writers still do. It was not on the grounds of clarity of expression. A split infinitive is always as clear as an unsplit one and often clearer, since there is never any doubt about what the adverb modifies.

Possibly it was on the grounds that infinitives are never split in Latin. They never are, for the very good reason that in Latin there is nothing to split. A Latin infinitive has nothing comparable to the English *to,* but consists of a single word

—*comprare, mittere*—and of course the Romans never said *mit-something-tere* or *com-something-prare*.

What ever the reason, the ban on split infinitives got into the early books on English grammar, and in the nineteenth century, as one textbook writer copied another, it became standard equipment. Even today books are to be found in which the student is warned that the splitting of an infinitive is a pretty risky business, not to be undertaken without sober consideration.

The ironic thing is that, today, the warning is not entirely without foundation. Most publishing houses are staffed with people in whom suspicion of split infinitives has been carefully nurtured, and some editors would no sooner let one go by than pass an obscenity. Split infinitives are to be found sometimes in some magazines, in others never. Probably most editors, like most teachers, would prefer a smooth and idiomatic sentence with a split infinitive to a contorted one without.

In speech it is a matter that practically no one worries about. The student is advised that in table conversation he can split all the infinitives he likes with little risk of being thrown out of his boarding house, however elegant a boarding house it may be.

198. Prepositions at the End of the Sentence

We may as well quote Sir Winston Churchill at once and get it over with. Someone having rearranged one of his sentences so as to get the preposition away from the end, Churchill said that this was a kind of pedantic interference up with which he would not put.

The basis of the idea that prepositions should not end sentences is rhetorical rather than grammatical. The end of the sentence is a strong position, and it can be shown that the writer can often get his best effect by letting an important word fall there. The word that reaches the hearer last is the one that lingers. Compare these:

> That's the room he died in.
> That's the room in which he died.
>
> He was a man that everyone had trouble with.
> He was a man with whom everyone had trouble.

The sentences that end in noun or verb—*died, trouble*—are clearly more impressive than those ending in structure words —*in, with*. In speech, *died* and *trouble* would have a primary stress in all of these examples: placing the words at the end avoids a trailing off on words with weak stress. A writer wishing to be impressive or weighty would naturally choose an impressive or weighty structure, but he might with equal reason want his sentences to be light and fluffy.

Sentences in which an important part of the structure is postponed to the end are sometimes called *periodic* sentences. Look at these:

> Henry Morgan galloped onto the field, the message on which all our destinies depended in his hand.
> Onto the field, in his hand the message on which all our destinies depended, galloped Henry Morgan.

The second sentence is periodic. Its central structure does not work out until the very end, and the reader is thus held to the end in a kind of suspense. This kind of writing can be very effective; it can also be ponderous and tiresome.

Two hundred years ago periodic writing was more popular than it is today. You will find splendid examples in Gibbon's *Decline and Fall of the Roman Empire.* It was probably the popularity of such writing that led grammarians contemporary with it to conclude that it was wrong to put prepositions at the end of sentences. As a rule of writing, this is of course nonsense. Our language is so constructed that prepositions and other structure words must frequently fall at the end of sentence patterns. A sustained effort to avoid them would lead to awkward and ponderous writing not likely to be admired by the modern reader.

We can close this discussion with another popular quotation, a sentence with five prepositions (or at least five structure words) at the end. You imagine a boy at bedtime speaking to his father, who is ascending the stairs. The boy says, "What are you bringing that book that I don't want to be read to out of up for?"

199. Who and Whom

Another small problem magnified to appalling proportions is the matter of *who* and *whom*. Traditional grammarians have taken a pretty stern line on this one, feeling that it was a clear question of right and wrong. You use *who* when the word is a subject:

> Who was it?
> He's a man who knows all the answers.
> I wonder who gave it to him.

You use *whom* when it is an object:

> Whom did you see?
> He's a man whom we all trusted.
> I wonder whom he gave it to.

This distinction is clear-cut enough. The trouble is that it doesn't always reflect usage, even the usage of well-educated people. Traditional grammarians, not sufficiently convinced that usage is the supreme lawgiver in language matters, often looked for higher authority in logic or Latin. But if we conclude, as we must, that logic and Latin have really very little

to do with the question, then we must reconsider the behavior
of *who* and *whom.*

It is fairly clear that *whom* is in the process of dying out in
speech. Most educated Americans would say, "Who did you
see?" not "Whom did you see?" and "I wonder who he gave
it to" rather than "I wonder whom he gave it to." In some
structures we have an innocent alternative. Instead of saying,
"a man whom we all trusted," which is likely to sound a little
stilted, we can say "a man that we all trusted" or "a man we
all trusted." *Whom* is inevitable only when a preposition immediately precedes: "With whom are you going?" Practically
no one would say "With who are you going?" But most people in ordinary conversation would put the *with* at the end
and use *who:* "Who are you going with?"

In fact, an assiduous cultivation in speech of the textbook
distinction of *who/whom* is likely to give one's associates the
feeling that one is affected and artificial—perhaps, indeed, an
English teacher in sheep's clothing. There are no doubt some
American speakers for whom something like the textbook
distinction is perfectly natural, bred in the nursery. But they
are a small minority and, like other minorities, have to suffer
for their peculiarities.

Writing is rather a different matter. Writing that gets into
print gets edited, and if the writer fails to straighten out the
who's and *whom's,* the editor probably will. Consequently,
the old distinctions are more or less maintained in serious writing and may continue to be maintained after *whom* has disappeared from speech. Even so, *whom* is likely to sound ponderous in some structures and a writer will sometimes find
means to avoid it—for example, writing "Mr. Jenkins, a man
I knew very well" in place of "Mr. Jenkins, whom I knew
very well."

In either speech or writing it is better to use *who* against the rule than to use *whom* against the rule. If you write, "Mr. Jenkins, who I knew in Paris," the reader may think you ignorant. If you write "Mr. Jenkins, whom I knew was in Paris" the reader may think you not only ignorant but affected as well.

200. Shall and Will

The textbook distinctions separating *shall* and *will* are much more complicated than the *who/whom* distinctions. Actually usage is more complicated too. The result is that, though many people would like to feel that they are using *shall* and *will* in approved places, few can have any real confidence that they are doing so.

The traditional directions go something like this. You use *shall* for the first person, *will* for second or third, if you are simply making an unloaded reference to future time:

I shall go.	We shall go.
You will go.	You will go.
He will go.	They will go.

But if your statement contains some meaning of determination or necessity or insistence or obligation, then you reverse the words:

I will go.	We will go.
You shall go.	You shall go.
He shall go.	They shall go.

In asking a question, you use the form anticipated in the answer. That is, you say, "Will you go?" if you expect the other person to say, "Yes, I will," but "Shall you go?" if you expect him to say "Yes, I shall."

All this is rather fun, but it has little bearing on anything that goes on in American speech. Nearly all American speakers use both *shall* and *will* but in widely varying patterns.

Few, even among the impeccably educated, follow the text-book line exactly.

There is one situation in which the word *shall* is practically obligatory. This is a first person question which calls on the person asked to make a decision. Compare these:

> Shall we find a policeman?
> Will we find a policeman?

The person asked answers the "shall we" question on the basis of whether he wants to find a policeman or not; his volition operates. But he answers the "will we" question on the basis of whether policemen are to be found or not. His will doesn't operate.

This is about the only place in modern American English in which *shall* and *will* signal a clear-cut distinction between a simple future meaning and a future meaning colored by volition, determination, insistence, etc. There was a time when "I will" meant determination and "I shall" did not. But usage has become so mixed up that this signal has weakened to the vanishing point. For most speakers and hearers "I will see Mary tomorrow" is a simple reference to a future occurrence. We can clearly express determination only by giving the sentence a special pitch-stress pattern or by using other words:

> I will too see Mary tomorrow.
> I must see Mary tomorrow.
> I'm determined to see Mary tomorrow.

We might note too that *shall* and *will* are not our only means of referring to future time or even the most important. Compare these:

> He'll go to Kansas City.
> He's going to Kansas City.
> He's going to go to Kansas City.
> He's about to go to Kansas City.

"Be going to" is now for most verbs the most common "pure future" construction: "I'm going to come later," "He's going to help us." Note the shade of difference between "He'll help us" and "He's going to help us." The first suggests willingness on the helper's part, whereas the second is a simple reference to the event.

The words *shall* and *will* do retain a certain amount of connotation, if not much signal of clear meaning. For some speakers "I shall" and "we shall" simply sound a little more elegant, and are used regularly in the first person whether volition is intended or not. For other speakers *shall* in all three persons has a special meaning of determination or urgency; for these people both "I shall" and "you shall" seem more insistent than "I will" or "you will."

For most speakers the contracted negative is "won't." The contraction "shan't" is heard in American speech, but not very frequently.

Probably the best advice that can be given the student on *shall* and *will* is not to worry about them. They give you practically no opportunity to prove yourself uncultured.

201. Subjunctive Mood

Another popular bugaboo is the subjunctive mood. In its earlier stages, English, like the other Indo-European languages, had a special set of verb forms that occurred in special patterns: patterns expressing hopes or wishes, certain subordinated sentences, and so on. These verb forms have been given the ponderous name *subjunctive mood*. The forms occurring in ordinary statements are called *indicative mood*.

At one time subjunctive forms and indicative forms contrasted sharply, and the contrast was a strong and important signal distinguishing different kinds of meaning. As the language developed, however, and as sound changes took place, the differences between subjunctive and indicative were very much reduced. As a result, the signal weakened, and meanings formerly contrasted by these forms are now expressed in other ways.

We still have, however, a few distinctions between subjunctive and indicative. These distinctions no longer carry much meaning load, but they do sometimes have prestige value.

In most present-day verbs subjunctive and indicative contrast only in the third person singular of the present tense:

INDICATIVE: he goes, he thinks, he hopes
SUBJUNCTIVE: he go,   he think   he hope

The subjunctive form of the verb *to be* is the same as the infinitive: *be*. It therefore contrasts with the indicative in all persons:

INDICATIVE: I am, you are, he is, we are, they are
SUBJUNCTIVE: I be, you be, he be, we be, they be

In the past tense, only the verb *to be* preserves any contrast at all:

INDICATIVE: I was, you were, he was, we were, they were
SUBJUNCTIVE: I were, you were, he were, we were, they were

There seems to be only one pattern in present-day English in which the subjunctive occurs regularly among all speakers using the pattern. This is a construction in which an S-group with the subordinator *that* follows a main verb like *insist, urge, recommend*. The verb in the S-group is regularly subjunctive:

> Mallory insisted that Al *come* with us.
> They asked that we *be* barred from the meeting.

Some speakers might not use the pattern at all. Those that do would normally and automatically use the subjunctive (*come, be*), not the indicative (*comes, are*).

In other patterns usage varies. At one time the past subjunctive was regular in what are called "conditions contrary to fact." These are S-groups introduced by *if* in which the thing stated is not true:

> If I *were* you, I'd give myself up.
> If Al *were* my brother, I couldn't be more concerned.

But if the condition is not contrary to fact, the indicative is used:

> If he *was* here, he must have come by plane.

This usage is fairly common among people of education, who may therefore look down their noses at people who say "If I was you," "if Al was my brother."

The present subjunctive occurs—but much less commonly than it used to—in certain S-groups expressing various kinds of possibility:

> If we *be* required to serve, we shall do our best.
> Mortimer will never falter, though he *be* deprived of all his possessions.

Such expressions would be unusual indeed in American speech. They might occur in writing, but even in writing they would have definite archaic flavor.

202. Double Negatives

There is at least one construction which the grammarians have pretty well succeeded in banishing from polite society. This is the double negative:

> We never saw no policemen.
> We don't want no trouble.
> We can't do nothing about it.

The attack on the double negative, as we saw in Chapter 10, is an instructive example of the early grammarians' tendency to confuse language and logic. This construction was respectable enough in Early, Middle, and Shakespearean English, as it is still in languages related to English. Until the eighteenth century no one seems to have worried much about it. If you said "No" once, you meant "No." If you said "No" twice, you meant twice as much "No." If you said "No" fourteen times (as happens in a book translated into English by King Alfred), you meant "No" fourteen times as much.

But the eighteenth century grammarians wouldn't tolerate any such goings-on. Two negatives, as everyone knows, make a positive. Minus one times minus one equals plus one. Ergo, anyone who says, "I don't want no trouble," must mean that he does want trouble. Nobody really thinks, of course, that people who say "I don't want no trouble" mean that they want trouble, but that's the way the argument runs. The lunacy of the argument can be shown if we take it one step farther. Minus one times minus one times minus one equals minus one. Therefore, though "I don't want no trouble" is a positive statement, "I don't never want no trouble" is negative. King Alfred's sentence with its fourteen negatives is positive. If he had used thirteen or fifteen, it would be negative.

But foolish or not, the grammarians' argument has prevailed. So many generations of school children have been taught that the double negative is vulgar that it has indeed become vulgar. If, at a nice dinner party, you remark to your hostess, "I don't want no cake," she will not understand that you want some. But she may very well decide that you should not have been permitted to graduate from the third grade.

203. The Total Effect

It will be seen from the discussion of these points of usage that grammars, grammarians, and teachers of English can sometimes affect a nation's language. Writing is affected more easily than speech, but sometimes, as with the double negative, speech is controlled too, for a part of the population.

But it should also be noted that the matters affected are but the smallest ripples in the language stream. Grammarians have simply picked out, here and there, locutions to work on. The choice has been for the most part accidental and capricious, based often on nothing more than someone's whim. Then slowly all the guns of the education system are trained on these expressions with the result that some people stop using them.

Meanwhile the main body of the language goes its way, developing unnoticed. Its development is controlled, to be sure, but it is not controlled by the education system. The forces that shape the language are in the language itself, expressed by the whole population using the language.

SUGGESTIONS

1. Language and writing can displease sometimes by being too casual and breezy, sometimes by being too formal and stilted. Consider the following sentences according to the effect they would have, if any, (a) in conversation at your dinner table, (b) in conversation with your high school principal, (c) in a letter to a college official.

(1) By whom was the letter written? (2) Who was it sent to? (3) He never said nothing like that. (4) Shall you be here tomorrow? (5) I had to really get in and work. (6) I had really to get in and work. (7) If you was in my position, what would you do? (8) If the situation really be as bad as you say, something should be done at once. (9) It was not Sheila whom we saw but Ernestine. (10) I shan't think any more about it.

2. Collect the *shall's* and *will's* in a magazine article and determine the extent to which they follow the traditional rules mentioned in Section 200.

3. Look into Gibbon's *Decline and Fall of the Roman Empire* and collect a dozen examples of periodic sentences.

24
Slang and Its
Relatives

204. What Slang Is

Slang is one of those things that everybody can recognize and nobody can define. Not only is it hard to wrap slang in a definition; it is also hard to distinguish it from such similar things as colloquialisms, provincialisms, jargon, trade talk. As we shall see, these areas blend into one another, and it is often a waste of time to look for the boundary.

One characteristic of a slang term is that it exists side by side with another, more general term for the same thing. Take for example the word *chick*, which has been used by some speakers in the meaning *girl* or *young woman*. The difference between *chick* and *girl* can be stated only in reference to the people who use the words: some say, "This chick is my sister"; others "This girl is my sister." *Chick* is slang and *girl* is not, because *chick* is used by a limited part of the population, mostly young people, whereas *girl* is used by everybody, including those who use *chick*.

It is often said that a slang term ceases to be slang when it is "accepted by the dictionary." This is not really the test. You will find many slang terms duly registered in dictionaries and still slang terms. The term ceases to be slang when it drives out of use its respectable synonym, or when it acquires a meaning that cannot be expressed otherwise. If, for instance, people ceased to use the word *girl* and all used *chick* instead, then *chick* could no longer be called a slang term.

Such things have happened. The term *hot dog* was once a slang term, but it couldn't be considered so now. No one in America would go up to a counter and order a "sausage sandwich." Similarly *varsity*, originally a slang contraction of *university*, has acquired special meanings which only it expresses and is no longer slang. *Jazz*, when it means a particular kind of music, is scarcely a slang term, since there is no more respectable word meaning that kind of music.

Certainly respectability must enter into any discussion of slang. Slang is essentially not respectable. There is always a more elegant way of saying the thing but one chooses the slang term for reasons. The reason may be a desire to be thought witty or clever or up to date. More often it is a desire to show, by a particular use of language, that one is a member in good standing of a particular group of people.

205. Slang and Crime

Criminals have always been prolific producers of slang because they are so obviously marked off from respectable society. They deliberately widen the gulf by multiplying language differences, and they often use the differences for practical purposes: to recognize one another, to shield their conversation from hostile ears. Criminal groups of the seventeenth and eighteenth centuries in England developed large vocabularies of slang—or *cant,* as it was then called—which rendered their talk almost meaningless to an outsider.

Much of the slang in common use today comes ultimately from characters on the other side of the law. This will be recognizable, for example, in words relating to American money. For "money" in general we have such terms as *dough, lettuce,* the *green* or the *big green, folding stuff,* and various others.

The different denominations all have their slang terms: *singles* or *fish* for one dollar bills; *fin* for a five; *sawbuck* for a ten and *double sawbuck* for a twenty; *C-note* or *century* for a hundred; *grand* for a thousand. All of these are old, well-weathered terms and are familiar to many people who wouldn't dream of holding up a drugstore. But it is clear that they have their highest frequency in those districts where policemen would prefer to go in pairs.

In games slang is common everywhere, but it is most prolific in those games which are more or less disreputable. Bridge and golf have their slang terms, but gambling games have more, and roulette, for which the participants may wear evening clothes, has fewer than craps or poker, for which they usually do not. Poker has a wide variety of slang terms— or at least had when the writer had the game explained to him by an obliging friend. Thus in addition to the general names for the cards—*ace, deuce, king*—another set of slang terms are, or were, in use: *bull* or *bullet* for "ace," *cowboy* for "king," a *pair of ducks* for "a pair of deuces." Two aces and two eights are a *dead man's hand,* three tens are *thirty miles* or *thirty miles of railroad,* a flush of any sort is *all blue.*

Dice, even more disreputable than poker, has a correspondingly higher incidence of slang terms.

The connection between slang and the criminal element is seen again in the dope racket, the terms of which have been made more or less generally familiar by the movies and television. The word *dope* itself is originally slang, but it is now in more general use than *narcotics.* Within the racket, terms abound. The words *marijuana* and *heroin* seem scarcely to occur among users or peddlers of the drugs, as is suggested by the fact that addicts speaking of heroin on a television program pronounced it to rhyme with *groin.* Usually, apparently, they say *H* or *big H* or *horse* or *caballito* (a Spanish word meaning "little horse" or "horsey.") Marijuana is referred to by several slang terms, of which *hay* seems to be most enduring. An injection of a narcotic is a *fix*. To inject it in the vein is to *mainline*. A salesman or peddler is a *pusher*. An addict is a *junkie*. To rid oneself of an addiction is to *kick the habit*. It will be seen that a narcotics addict can discuss his troubles at some length without being understood by anyone outside the circle.

Musicians are another fertile source of slang terms. Again the element of more or less respectability enters: symphony orchestras are less prolific of slang terms than are purveyors of more popular music—jazz, swing, be-bop, rock 'n roll bands. Many of the slang terms in this area, as in others, have only the briefest existence, but others linger. Even the youngest readers will be acquainted with *dig* (understand or appreciate), *cool* (excellent or moving), *crazy* (inspired), *cat* (talented musician or knowledgeable music lover), *real* (exceptionally moving.)

206. School Slang

High school and college slang probably derives as much from music language as from any other source. More than one college professor in the 1950's had to learn that the expression "dig that crazy course," coming from one of his earnest young disciples, was not a criticism but a high tribute. But colleges fill out their slang with terms that apply particularly to college activities. Many of these terms are simple abbreviations: *math, prof, exam, poly sci, econ, phys ed*. Others are names, varying from year to year and from campus to campus, for hard or easy courses, hard or easy teachers, passing and failing, studying, cheating, flattering the teacher (*apple-polishing* is an old term that persists). There are slang terms for those who raise class averages and for those who don't, for campus politicians, for campus reporters, for deans and college presidents, for football players, for serious students, for frivolous students, for fraternity and sorority men and women, for nonfraternity and nonsorority men and women, for pretty girls, for other girls, and for girls in general. Everyone and everything connected with college life can be referred to by a slang term as well as by a more general one.

207. Grammatical Features of Slang

Slang words are mostly nouns and verbs, but the adjective class has its slang too. Any college group at any given time uses one adjective to express general approval. This can be anything at all, even a newly coined noise. It is just something that slips into the pattern "That's very _____," and means that the speaker likes whatever is referred to. When the writer was in college the word was *gruesome*. If, in those days, you said "She's a real gruesome girl," you meant that she attracted you strongly and compelled your admiration.

Since then scores of words have successively taken the place of *gruesome*. The life expectancy of slang in this particular slot is not great. Middle-aged readers will perhaps remember *zorch* and *George,* both illustrations of the truth that all a word has to do to become an adjective is to occur in an adjective pattern. *George,* which until 1952 or so had been an unassuming proper noun, became an adjective as soon as people started saying "That's very George," or, more likely, "That's real George." This started the practice, short-lived, to be sure, of pushing other proper nouns into this position: "That's real Robert" (good), "That's real Tom" (bad), "That's strictly Alexander" (genuine).

Slang connects with grammatical structure at more points than one. For example, it could be stated almost as a law of language that an irregular word which picks up a slang meaning will be regularized. Thus the irregular verb *slay* at one time acquired, in addition to its older meaning of "kill," the slang meaning "interest, amuse": "You really slay me, kid." In this meaning it never occurs with the old past form *slew*. One would say not "He slew me" but always "He slayed me." Similarly *louse* has the plural *lice* when it refers to insects but *louses* when it refers to people.

208. The Life Expectancy of Slang Terms

It is sometimes said that the trouble with slang is that it is constantly changing, that a term becomes old-fashioned almost at birth. It is certainly true that some terms, particularly those that get quick and heavy use, wither faster than the rose. One has only to consider how obsolete terms like *zorch, George, hot* (hot music), *skirt* (girl), *flame* (girl or boy friend), *squire* (escort) sound today.

However, a short but merry life is by no means the rule for slang terms. Some linger on decade after decade, century after century indeed, never becoming quite respectable and never dying out either. The word *dough* for money is just as hardy as it ever was, though no more reputable. Others which seem likely to outlive the century are *cop* (policeman), *nuts* (insane), *plastered* (drunk), *wino* (drunkard), *limey* (Englishman), *jalopy* (automobile), *cram* (study hard). There are thousands of such—well below the salt but also well established at the table.

209. The Effect of Slang

Teachers of English are often libeled to the effect that they are dedicated to a relentless pursuit of slang and are never so happy as when they are stamping out a slang term. This is part of the larger charge that teachers of English aren't people. Everybody uses slang as a natural result of speaking a language, though it is presumably true that the young and effervescent like to play with language more than their elders do. It is also true that what sounds gay and cute and clever to the young may sound merely banal to older ears.

The effect of slang is closely bound with the personality of the user. It is not simply a question of whether the slang is new or not or clever or not or incisive or not. It is a question of the total effect of the speaker. The writer can remember a friend who used a rather small selection of slang, none of it particularly witty, and used it rather constantly with no infusion of new terms; yet his conversation always seemed to have a pleasant sparkle to it, presumably because he himself sparkled pleasantly. On the other hand, there was another character who always—*always*—greeted one with the salutation, "Dig that crazy cat." He usually prefaced this with the expression "Hey, hey!" This grew tiresome.

Slang spreads fast sometimes, but it doesn't transfer very easily. A person who moves into a new group and brings with him an old group's slang *may* find his language admired and imitated. More likely people will consider him boring or affected or unpleasantly foreign. If he persists with his old talk and doesn't adopt that of the new group, he will find that people begin saying, "Here comes that type; let's get out of here."

210. Trade Talk

The language that we call slang merges imperceptibly with other varieties. Every trade or profession, vocation or avocation has a set of terms more or less peculiar to it and often differing little or not at all from what we think of as slang. Trade talk often serves much the same purpose that slang does—to give coherence to the group and to exclude outsiders. If you think of peddling dope as a profession, then such terms

as *fix, mainline, horse, junkie* are not slang but technical terms
of the business.

A familiar example of terms of a trade are those employed
on ships. Since sailors have for centuries led a life apart, a
whole vocabulary has grown up, not only for those activities
peculiar to the sea but also for many that go on under other
names ashore. Thus a sailor speaks of a *ladder,* not a *staircase;*
a *deck,* not a *floor;* a *bulkhead,* not a *wall;* a *head,* not a *toilet;*
a *companionway,* not a *corridor;* a *galley,* not a *kitchen; fore*
and *aft* and *port* and *starboard,* not *front* and *back* and *left*
and *right.*

These terms, as in many other trades, are often jealously
guarded. The landlubber inspecting the ship, the apprentice
making his first trip are likely to evoke the seaman's cheerful
scorn as they use land words for sea things. On the other hand,
the landsman isn't any better off if he comes aboard with the
proper vocabulary. During the Second World War, when
young men were trained ashore in their duties before being assigned to ships, they would often come onto the ships with the
right words and lisp assuredly of going below and going aloft,
of galley and messroom and fo'c'sle. This also would irritate the
oldtimers, who sometimes revenged themselves by talking of
going downstairs instead of below and out on the front porch
instead of to the bow.

Ship talk is but an obvious example of the kind of special
language that any trade or profession or occupation, indeed
any coherent human activity cultivates. In printing, in wres-
tling, in dentistry, in the automobile trade, the participants
tend to develop terms which they use and the outside world
does not. One difference between this trade talk and slang is
that the trade term has a respectability that the slang term
lacks. Thus one can say that *dope addict* is more dignified than
junkie, policeman more dignified than *cop.* But one could

hardly say that ship's *wall* is more dignified than ship's bulk-head.

211. Colloquialisms

Slang and much trade talk too merge imperceptibly with that broad area of language that we call *colloquialism*. "Colloquial" is a rather vague word with different meanings for different people, but it would seem most generally to mean words and constructions that occur more commonly in speech than in writing. As such it would include slang but would not be limited to slang. It would include all the forms that people—educated as well as uneducated—use in conversation but tend to avoid in writing. A further distinction is that *slang* usually denotes words rather than phrases, whereas *colloquialism* can mean a word, a phrase, a sentence—indeed can apply to the whole tone of the utterance.

Compare the sentences "He better take it easy" and "He should proceed carefully." Both might be uttered by people of impeccable breeding and both might occur in writing as well as in speech. The difference is simply one of frequency and likelihood. "He better take it easy" is what you are likely to say if you are chatting casually with someone about the activity of a mutual friend. "He should proceed carefully" is what you are likely to write in a letter to the newspaper.

Colloquialisms are not hard to find, since they make up the bulk of our daily conversation. At random we can compare such colloquial and literary expressions as "do your darndest" (strive), "put something over on someone" (fool), "lend a hand" (assist), "kept his mouth shut" (refused to divulge something), "hit the books pretty hard" (studied diligently), "an awfully cute kid" (a strikingly handsome young man), "who you trying to fool" (whom are you seeking to mislead).

212. Modern Tendencies

At some periods of history people have had the idea that writing is better the farther it is from speech and that colloquialisms should therefore regularly be avoided. But this is scarcely the mood of the present day. Naturally, if you want to sound dignified—and one *does* want to sound dignified sometimes—you choose dignified language and eschew terms that smack of shirtsleeves and ginger ale. If you're seeking a position with a corporation, you might damage your chances by writing, "I sure hope you'll let me take a crack at the job. I got a notion I'd do real well at it. Sure would try anyhow." It would normally be better sense to say, "I am hoping that you will find it possible to try me in the position. I feel that I would be able to do the work successfully. Certainly I would try very hard."

However, it is undeniable that the trend of much modern writing is toward a more colloquial tone. Not only in advertising, which is ever pally, but also in more or less serious books, magazine articles, newspaper accounts, the tendency is to reflect more and more the words and rhythms of ordinary speech. One finds, for example, a greater use than formerly of contracted forms: *don't, shouldn't, he'll,* in place of *do not, should not, he will.* Plain or folksy or even slang words are often preferred to elegant ones, and writers pay less attention than their predecessors did to the niceties of schoolbook grammar.

The explanation of this trend is no doubt to be sought in sociological developments. The educated class, formerly a pretty exclusive group, is now the great mass of the population. Reading and writing, even a hundred years ago, was the accomplishment of relatively few; now everybody does it. Today's writer is talking not to the country club set but to everybody in town, and he tries to talk everybody's language.

But he shouldn't try too hard. Writing should above all be consistent and natural and honest, and the writer who labors the "jus' us plain folks" approach is spotted as a phoney by the plain folks as well as the fancy ones. Here, from a cereal box, is an example of nobody's language:

> Often, when I'm out ridin' the range, I find myself thinkin' about all the dare-devil deeds the Indian Chiefs did in days gone by, and of the unforgettable adventures of the gallant scouts and frontiersmen who met them in battle. I reckon all you young pardners of mine would like to hear all about them, too!

Even the youngest pardners may have an inkling that this cowboy rides the range on his portable typewriter.

213. Clichés

One of the troubles of colorful language, slang or other, is that its color rubs off. The first time you hear and understand an expression like "Dig that crazy cat" you may find it exceptionally expressive, piquant, and moving. The second time you hear it, it isn't quite so exciting. The tenth time it has no effect at all. The fiftieth time it grates a little. The five hundredth time it may make you want to brain the speaker with a trombone.

If language isn't colorful to begin with, it doesn't pale. You can hear the sentence "Listen to that musician" five hundred times with no more pain the last time than the first. Clichés, or trite expressions, are simply dried up metaphors, figures of speech. They are racy ways of saying things but they have slowed down.

The first person who said "It was like walking on eggs" thought up a pretty clever comparison. When you read this for the first time, you get not only the information that the situation was delicate but a picture that reinforces and impresses the message. But this happens the first time only. After that you get only the information that the situation was delicate plus the fact that the writer is not very inventive. So also with "He fought like a tiger," "He behaved like a lamb," "He ran like a deer," "He ate like a pig," "He took a powder," "He pulled the wool over my eyes," "He's all wool and a yard wide," "She's pretty as a picture," "He spelled out the government's policy," "We'd better shake a leg," "An ocean of faces looked up at him," "A forest of masts filled the harbor," "She led him a merry chase," "It slid off him like water off a duck's back," "You can't fly on one wing," "He was as drunk as a lord, but his brother was as sober as a judge." All of these were more or less effective once.

Some groups of people seem to run more to clichés than others. Politicians are notorious, and some of their clichés, like "point with pride" and "view with alarm," have been laughed out of use. Sports writers and announcers also have difficulty avoiding trite phrases. One thinks of such expressions as "the fourth and final quarter" (one knows that the fourth quarter of a football game is the final one, but announcers seldom fail to point it out), "the bags are bulging," "circus catch," "smart little field general." All quarterbacks are smart little field generals, though some of them are also magicians. Line drives, proceeding toward the outfield, always scream, unless they go past something, like first, in which case they whistle. Pitchers are mostly big right-handers or little southpaws. Successful players come through in the clutch.

In fairness we should realize that sports writers and sports announcers deserve sympathy as much as criticism. They have to report, day after day and year after year, activities in which the same features are endlessly repeated. Moreover, they must always report these activities feverishly. The announcer is scarcely at liberty to say that today's football game is a pretty routine affair and the performers of no more than average competence. He must, every Saturday, bubble about how this is the most exciting grid spectacle that he and his colleagues have been privileged to see in a long time and how he wishes all us fans could be out there in the stadium with him to see these two great teams fighting their hearts out.

214. Avoiding Clichés

The cliché is every writer's enemy. Good writers fight clichés all the time, but few, even among the very best, win all the time. The triter the phrase, the more readily it comes to the mind, the more likely it is to slip into the sentence. You want to describe a mob, and you don't want to just say it was a big mob. You want to impress the reader with its size. "Sea of faces," you think, and you write it down. The trouble is that so many other writers have also written it down that it's lost all its blood. It no longer means anything more than "big mob," so you might as well have written "big mob" and been done with it.

The cliché is a difficulty for the young writer particularly, because he may not recognize the cliché when he sees it. "Sea of faces" may strike him as a bright new figure, not only expressive but original. One solution to this problem is experience. As we mature as readers, we become better equipped to recognize the stock phrases of the language as stock phrases. But the principal solution is to learn to distrust the pleasing phrase that comes too readily. It is only reasonable to suppose that the metaphor that jumps at you will have jumped at thousands of others before you.

It is very easy to write, to speak, to think in clichés. That's what most people do. They don't think for themselves but let the popular mind think for them. Their language is not personal but general, composed of public sentences with a few names changed to fit private conditions. There is nothing sinful about talking in clichés, and nobody can avoid it altogether. But those who don't avoid it at all betray laziness and mediocrity.

SUGGESTIONS

1. Give the terms used on your campus for the persons and things listed in Section 206.
2. Compare the slang of your college with that of your high school.
3. Describe the slang of some group of people familiar to you, e.g., musicians, military personnel, golfers, baseball players, gamblers.
4. Describe the trade talk of some trade or profession familiar to you.
5. Make a list of clichés like that given in the third paragraph of Section 213.
6. From the sport pages of your newspaper collect a list of recognizable clichés.

25

A Lot of Latin and Some Greek

215. How to Get Rich

Some years ago a scholar named Johnson O'Connor published an article entitled "Vocabulary and Success." This cited figures to show a rather close correlation between size of vocabulary and earning power. College professors, whose earning power leaves much to be desired, turned out not to be at the top in vocabulary either. The people with the largest vocabularies were the senior executives in business.

The lesson seemed simple and was quickly learned: if you want to make a lot of money, you'd better turn to and beef up your vocabulary. Today the book stores are full of books designed to help you do this, the magazines run vocabulary quizzes to let you check up on how you're getting on, and the colleges are bulging with vocabulary-building classes attended by earnest young people desirous of becoming vice-presidents of Standard Oil.

Of course, that isn't exactly the way it works. You don't build your vocabulary and thus achieve vice-presidential qualities. It is rather that the qualities that tend to make you a vice-president are also those that see to it that your vocabulary gets built. However, it is no doubt true that there is power in vocabulary, that you're better off with a big one than a small one, and that there are some conscious steps you can take to make the one you've got bigger than it is. You don't do it by memorizing the dictionary or even by setting out to learn three new words a day. You do it by reading as much as you can, by developing interests, and by becoming aware of words themselves, how they're built and how they're learned.

216. Vocabulary Size

How big is a big vocabulary? How small is a small one? Vocabulary is an extraordinarily difficult thing to measure. In order to determine how many words a person knows, you must decide (1) what is meant by *word* and (2) what is meant by *know*. Neither of these is easy.

If you're counting words, do you count *happy* and *happily* as one word or two? What about *mouse* and *mice, follow* and *following, king* and *ex-king, seen* and *unseen*? What about *following* in "He's following" and *following* in "He has a large following"? One word or two? Or *grip* in "He gripped my hand," "He has a strong grip," "He bought a grip." Do you count proper names? If the person whose vocabulary is being counted lives on Alhambra Street, is *Alhambra Street* an item in his vocabulary? What about *Sixty-Third Street?*

It is hard to pin down *word* and almost as hard to pin down *know*. Some words we know in the sense that we use them in our speaking and writing; others we know in the sense that we understand them when someone else uses them. The latter, "recognition vocabulary," as it is called, is for most people much larger than the working vocabulary. In both groups there are wide varieties of "knowing." We know some words in the sense that we can give a definition of them, others in the sense that they are vaguely familiar, that we have a feeling of having heard them before. Everyone has a large fringe around the edges of his vocabulary, words not quite known and not quite not known either.

Despite these difficulties, people have been measuring vocabulary for nearly a century, with widely differing results. In general, the estimates have grown steadily larger. The first scholar to delve into the matter did so by listening to the conversation of people picking apples one summer outside his study window. At the end of the summer he reported that the average apple picker had a vocabulary of three hundred words. This figure of course was ridiculously low, and every later investigator raised it. Nowadays it is said that the average college student has a vocabulary of fifty thousand words or more, but of course such estimates are meaningful only in relation to the principles by which the words are counted.

We can get a rough idea of the size of the vocabulary of the language as a whole by looking at its dictionaries. College dictionaries of English list between 100,000 and 150,000 words. Larger dictionaries list up to 600,000. But this would be main entries only. It would not count all the possible derivatives, multiple meanings, or all proper names. It would be possible to count the words in English in such a way that the number would run well into the millions.

If you would like to get a notion of the size of your own vocabulary, there is a way to do it. Take a college dictionary. Note the number of pages and the number of columns to a page, and estimate the number of words to a column. Say there are 1500 pages, two columns to a page, about forty main entries to a column. That would mean that the dictionary contains about 120,000 words: 1500 × 2 × 40. Now go through the dictionary, looking at, say, the top word of the right-hand column of every other page. Make a tally mark for each word you think you know. Say you tally 300 words. You will have looked at 750 words and judged that you know 300 of these, or 40 percent. Forty percent of 120,000, the number of words in the dictionary, is 48,000. So you know 48,000 words. Or, more accurately, you know 48,000 of the words in this dictionary. There may be others, not in the dictionary, which you know also.

217. How Vocabularies Grow

We said in an earlier chapter that a child learns his language by the age of five or six. That is, by that time he has mastered the sound structure and the grammatical structure. He also has acquired a respectable amount of vocabulary, consisting normally of common, high-frequency words: *I, this, other, when, brother, house, tree, dinner,* and so on.

Even at this early age, however, individual vocabularies will differ markedly according to environment. A six-year-old raised on a farm will know a different set of words than a six-year-old raised in a city apartment. And from this age on, one's vocabulary is governed principally by the activities, interests, employment that engage one.

You learn a new set of words, for instance, when you go to school: *teacher, eraser, custodian, chalk, examine, tardy,* etc. These, of course, are in addition to the vocabulary of the subjects you study. You learn to play baseball and acquire another set: *pitcher, catcher, umpire, foul, fan, score, inning.* Later, as you become interested in chess, clothes, fishing, geometry, automobiles, dogs, your vocabulary expands accordingly.

Size of vocabulary in a particular field is closely correlated with proficiency in that field. You're not much of a fisherman if you don't know the names of the different kinds of bait, the articles of tackle, different fish, conditions of the stream, and so on. Presumably you can tell whether a man is a good fisherman or not by giving him the proper vocabulary test. Similarly one might judge the relative competence of two mechanics through vocabulary. The one most familiar with the names of tools, machine parts, and mechanical operations is probably the one most skilled.

No doubt this point can be pushed too far. We are most of us familiar with people who have picked up the jargon of a field, who can prattle about it at great length, but who don't really understand what they are talking about. But it is still true that understanding of a field is achieved principally through words and that as we pick up new interests we automatically pick up more vocabulary.

218. Vocabulary Through Reading

When we speak of someone as having a large vocabulary, we are not usually thinking of specialized vocabularies, like those of mechanics, physicists, or fishermen. We think rather of what might be called literary vocabulary, words more likely to occur in writing than in speech, words of somewhat general application. We think of words like *obtuse, vicarious, autocthonous, insatiable, temporize, platitude.* How do people add such words as these to their vocabulary?

Not, usually, by looking them up in a dictionary. The dictionary, useful article though it is, is easily overvalued as a means of increasing one's vocabulary. We don't usually learn words, either in speech or in writing, by learning their definitions. When you are introduced to baseball, it is unlikely that anyone will provide you with a definition of *pitcher,* saying, "The pitcher is that one of the players who stands on a slightly raised mound of earth and throws the ball in the direction of the slab called 'home plate,' so that another player, called the 'batter,' may try to hit it." What happens is that you hear the word *pitcher,* notice the person to whom it refers, observe his activities, and pretty soon get the general idea.

So it is in reading. Most of the words that we pick up as we read we learn more or less automatically, often without knowing that we are learning them. We learn them from the context. Suppose that, never before having encountered the word *obtuse,* you come across this passage:

> Henrietta found her brother-in-law a little obtuse. He wasn't exactly stupid, just a little slow in catching on.

The writer has of course defined *obtuse* for you, and you would be a little obtuse yourself if you did not get a general notion of what the word means.

219. The Meaning of Meaning

Indeed, the meaning of a word is nothing else but the sum of the contexts in which the word occurs. The verb *plant,* for instance, means "to put in the earth so as to cause to grow." The proof is that it occurs in sentences like "He planted some corn" or "I'm going to plant tulips this fall." It also means "to fix firmly in position." The proof is that we have sentences like "He planted himself in the best chair." It also means "to instill." The proof is sentences like "He planted the notion in my mind."

Words change in meaning when they stop occurring in certain contexts and/or begin occurring in new ones. For instance, the word *pig* used to mean not only a certain kind of animal but also the flesh of that animal. That is, people used to say not only "We killed the pig" and "He keeps pigs" but also "I don't like pig" and "The waiter brought us some pig." Now *pig* has dropped out of the second set of contexts, and *pork* has taken its place. The meaning of *pig* has been restricted.

Dictionaries support this view of meanings when, in addition to giving a synonym or a generalized definition, they cite sentences to show the word in action. This is the only way of getting at the meaning of some words. How would you show the meaning of the word *of* except by showing the variety of phrases in which *of* occurs: *time of day, one of the boys, pound of butter, picture of Louie, picture of Louie's, play of Shakespeare, city of Denver.* Or how could you explain the meaning of *shrug* without mentioning the word *shoulders?* The meaning of *shrug* is determined by the fact that we say "He shrugged his shoulders" and do not say "He shrugged his elbow" or "He shrugged my shoulders."

The lesson to the student is to learn to let the context guide him as much as it will to the meaning of new words. Say that you're reading along and you come on this sentence: "He planted some flimbles in the backyard." You have never seen the word *flimble* before, but consider how much you know about it already: it is a noun, not a verb or adjective; there is more than one of them in the world; it is something that can be planted and therefore, probably, can grow; it is something that can be planted in a backyard. You do not yet know exactly what a flimble is, but certainly you know a good many things that it is not. It is clearly not a kind of fish or tool or person or book. If then, a little further on, you find the sentence, "He gave Ethel a lovely bouquet of flimbles," you know that *flimbles* are not vegetables. The sentence "She liked yellow flimbles better than red ones" gives a clue to the color. Thus each occurrence narrows further the possible meaning of *flimble* until before long you have a very fair notion about flimbles without ever having consulted the dictionary.

This is not to say that you shouldn't look up words in your dictionary. Sometimes the context doesn't reveal enough about the meaning of the word. Sometimes you need a precise understanding of it rather than a general one. Certainly if after it has occurred several times you still don't have much notion what the word means, you should open the dictionary and see what you can find out. But this isn't usually the most efficient way. Usually the context will do it for you. Any time you read a new book you add a number of new words to your vocabulary, dictionary or no dictionary.

The dictionary is often a necessity, however, when a lot of new words come at you all at once. Suppose you read this: "He flugeled some flimbles in the crambon." This also tells you something about *flimble* but not nearly so much. You know that flimbles are things or people or animals and that there are a number of them in existence. You also know that *flimbles* are something that can be flugeled and that they can be flugeled in crambons. But if all you know about flugeling is that it is something that can be done to flimbles, and if you know of crambons only that they are a place (or container?) where flimbles are flugeled, then your understanding of flimble remains imperfect. You might have to look up *flimble* or *flugel* or *crambon,* or possibly all three.

This is one thing that makes hard reading hard: a lot of new words at once. So long as they come at a reasonable rate—one or two a page, say—they are absorbable, and as they are absorbed, they help provide graspable contexts for the next new words. When they come in every other line, there is not enough known context and you have to start thumbing the dictionary.

220. The Composition of the Vocabulary

Because of its peculiar history, the English vocabulary contains a high percentage of borrowed words. All languages have words borrowed from other languages, but English has borrowed more than most. When the Angles and Saxons invaded England in the year 450 or so, most of their words were what we call *native English* or native Teutonic words. That is, they were words which had been in the vocabulary ever since the speakers of the language were members of the Indo-European community. The principal exceptions were a few hundred words that had been borrowed from Roman traders —words like *butter, kettle, wine, cheese.*

Once in England, the English picked up a few words—very few, from the Celts whom they conquered. They took many new words from Latin as a result of the conversion to Christianity. In the ninth century the Danes and Norwegians invaded England, and then and later many Scandinavian words came in.

The real flood started after the Norman Conquest. As the English learned French civilization, they borrowed French words by the thousand. These borrowings were important not only in themselves but also in that they had a profound effect on the English attitude toward word-borrowing. Where before the English had often been content to express a new idea with native word materials—as the Germans still tend to do—now they got in the habit of taking the foreign word along with the foreign idea expressed by it. In the Renaissance, consequently, as people began to explore ancient civilizations as a help toward building a new one, Latin and Greek words came in by the bucketful.

Today, borrowings from French, Latin, and Greek continue as our vocabulary keeps pace with our new activities. Furthermore, as speakers of English have ranged around the globe, they have brought home new words from many other sources. Spanish, Italian, Persian, Chinese, Russian, Hindustani and scores of other languages have contributed to the English vocabulary.

Some figures will help us understand the present composition of our vocabulary. The following estimates are based on *The American College Dictionary,* which contains some 140,000 words. These are distributed as follows:

Latin	36	percent of the total
Native English	14	
Old French (before 1500)	12	
Modern French (after 1500)	9	
Greek	4.5	
Scandinavian	2	
Spanish	2	
Italian	1	
Etymology unknown	6	
Other sources	13.5	

These percentages are very much determined by the size of the dictionary used in the study. If a smaller dictionary were used, the percentage of native English words would be larger, the percentage of Latin and Greek words smaller. If an unabridged dictionary were used, the percentage of Latin and Greek words would be larger, that of native English words smaller. The reason is that common words are likely to be native English; uncommon ones are likely to be borrowed from Latin or Greek or other sources.

The vocabulary may be viewed as a series of concentric rings. At the very heart are the structure words: *the, and, I, to, of,* etc. Everybody knows these, and they occur with very high frequency in our speech. They are nearly all native English words, although *very* comes from French and the pronouns *they, their,* and *them* from Scandinavian. Next come the common nouns, verbs, and adjectives that we learn in early childhood and use frequently all our lives: *man, mother, house, tree, chair, window, go, drink, love, good, nice, old.* Most of these also are native English, but some (*chair, nice*) are from French and others (*window*) are from Scandinavian.

Beyond these we have words of lower frequency, learned for the most part after we start school. The Latin words here appear in increasing numbers: *reply, commit, insist, prediction, dependent.* Farther out still are low-frequency words

that many people never use at all, words of special vocabularies, scientific words, literary words. These are overwhelm-
ingly from Latin and Greek: *magnanimous, syllogism, des-
titution, archaeology, concurrent, obloquy.*

It will be seen that the words likely to be new and strange
to the average reader of college age will lie mostly in the
Latin-Greek area. It is this area, therefore, that repays study.
It turns out that most words from Latin and Greek are composed of a limited number of roots, prefixes, and suffixes, occurring in different combinations. Most of these elements are
more or less familiar to you from other borrowed words already in your vocabulary. If you get used to noticing such
elements, you will often have another clue to add to what the
context tells you.

Take the word *obloquy.* We have the prefix *ob-* in *obstinate*
and *object;* it means something like "against." We have the
root *loq-* in *loquacious* and *soliloquy;* it means something like
"talking." One might therefore guess that *obloquy* would
mean something like "a talking against," and one would be
right.

Let's take a look at some of the other word elements, first
in Latin and then in Greek.

221. Words from Latin

Many of the words that English has borrowed from Latin
are, as one might say, miscellaneous. That is, they do not conform to any obvious pattern and are learned, as native words
are, one by one. Such are *bonus, furious, veto, animal.* But the
majority consist of two or three word elements arranged in
recurring patterns.

Take for example the word *recession.* This is composed of
the Latin prefix *re-,* with the general meaning "back" or
"again"; the Latin verb *cedere, cessus,* with the meaning
"go"; and the Latin suffix *-ion,* an ending indicating that the

word belongs to the noun class. Related to *recession* are the adjective *recessive*, the verb *recede*, and another verb *recess*. We have the prefix of *recession* in *reception, relation, regeneration, renunciation,* and many others. We have the root of *recession* in *concession, procession, secession,* and others. Built along pretty much the same lines as *recession* are *objection, impression, adhesion, dilation, conception,* and so on.

We shall notice here about a dozen Latin prefixes and about fifty Latin roots. These, in various combinations and with various derivatives, account for present-day English words running well into the thousands.

222. Latin Prefixes

The Latin prefixes are most similar in meaning to native English prepositions and adverbs. Thus we say that *re-* means "back" or "again." A verb borrowed from Latin is often translatable by a native English verb-adverb combination: *recede* "go back"; *adhere* "stick to"; *exclude* "shut out." But meanings are slippery, and such synonyms are at best approximate, often not even that. The translations given below are general and merely point toward the meaning. Thus *concur* can be translated "run with" (*con-* "with," *currere* "run"), but *run with* could not sensibly be substituted for *concur* in an English sentence.

There is one other general point to notice. Some of the prefixes in combining with certain roots undergo a sound change called *assimilation,* and this has been reflected in the spelling. Thus the prefix *ad-* appears as *as-* before roots beginning with *s* (*assent*), as *ap* before *p* (*apposition*), as *al-* before *l* (*allude*), as *ar* before *r* (*arrive*), and so on. *Con, ex, ob, in, sub* also undergo assimilation, as will appear in the following examples:

a–, ab– (from or away): *avert* (turn from), *abdicate* (say away), *abduct* (lead away).

ad– (toward or to): *adhere* (stick to), *accede* (go to), *adduce* (lead to), *assent* (feel toward).

con– (with): *consent* (feel with), *conduce* (lead with), *commit* (send with), *confide* (trust with).

di–, dis– (away or apart): *divert* (turn away), *dissent* (feel apart), *dismiss* (send away), *dispel* (drive away).

e–, ex– (out of): *exit* (go out), *elect* (read out), *emit* (send out), *exclude* (shut out).

in– (in or into): *induce* (lead in). *inscribe* (write in), *invert* (turn in), *implication* (something folded in). (Latin gives us another prefix *in* with the meaning "not," as in *invalid, improper, inexact.*)

inter– (between): *intervene* (come between), *intercede* (go between), *interfere* (carry between), *interpose* (put between).

ob– (against): *obloquy* (a speaking against), *object* (throw against), *oppose* (put against), *occur* (run against).

pre– (before): *predict* (say before), *prenatal* (before birth), *prefer* (carry before), *precursor* (a runner before).

pro– (forward): *progress* (go forward), *propel* (drive forward), *proceed* (go forward), *produce* (lead forward).

sub– (under): *subvert* (turn under), *supposition* (something put under), *subscribe* (write under), *submit* (send under).

trans– (across): *transmit* (send across), *transport* (carry across), *transfer* (carry across), *transpose* (put across).

Some of the common roots from Latin will combine with nearly all of these prefixes to produce English words. For example, from the root *mittere, missus* (to send), plus the prefixes we have *admit, commit, dismiss, emit, intermittent, omit, submit,* and *transmit,* as well as others, like *permit,* with prefixes not on the list given here.

223. Latin Roots

Words come into English from Latin nouns and adjectives, as well as verbs, but the common roots are most easily cited in the verb form or forms. Latin verbs had four "principal parts," as they are called. The principal parts of a verb are the basic structures from which all the other forms of the verb may be deduced. The principal parts of a Latin verb are the present tense, the infinitive, the perfect tense, and the past participle. If you know these, you can arrive at all the other forms of the verb, like the present participle, the past tense, the pluperfect tense, and so on.

For example, the principal parts of the verb meaning "send" are *mitto* (I send), *mittere* (to send), *misi* (I have sent), and *missus* (sent). The principal parts of an irregular verb meaning "carry" are *fero* (I carry), *ferre* (to carry), *tuli* (I have carried), and *latus* (carried). Knowing these, the speaker of Latin could produce all the other forms of these verbs.

These roots have come into English mostly from the infinitive form or the past participle form. Thus from the verb meaning "send" we have *submit, remit, commit* from *mittere* and also *submission, remission, comission* from *missus*. From the verb meaning "carry" we have *refer* and *confer* from *ferre* and *relate* and *collate* from *latus*. Sometimes, because of changes resulting from particular sound combinations or because of transmission through French, the root will appear in English in still other forms. For example, from the root *capere, captus,* we have such words as *deceptive* and *deceive*.

We shall give here only the infinitive and part participle of the more important verbs, along with illustrations of the root in English.

agere, actus (do, drive): *act, agent, agitate, agile, transact, agenda, prodigious*

audire, auditus (hear): *audition, audible, audience, auditory, audit, auditorium, auditor*

caedere, cisus (cut, kill): *excision, incision, concise, circumcise, precise, homicide, fratricide*

capere, captus (seize): *capable, receptive, conception, capture, conceive, susceptible, except*

cedere, cessus (go): *proceed, procession, excede, recede, recessive, decease, concede claudere, clausus* (shut): *include, exclude, occlusion, recluse, preclude, seclude, seclusive*

currere, cursus (run): *incur, recur, succor, excursion, cursive, discursive, discourse*

dicere, dictus (say): *dictaphone, predict, interdict, indictment, addict, malediction, benediction*

ducere, ductus (lead): *induce, seduce, conducive, deduction, traduce, reducible, product*

facere, factus (make): *factory, manufacture, confection, perfect, defect, defection, infect*

ferre, latus (carry): *infer, refer, deference, prefer, illative, collation, prelate*

fidere, fisus (be faithful): *confide, confidence, confident, perfidy, infidel, fidelity, Fido*

fundere, fusus (pour): *effusive, infuse, refuse, confuse, profuse, refund, transfusion*

gerere, gestus (carry): *congestion, digestion, gestation, ingestion, belligerent, register, gesture*

gradi, gressus (walk, go): *progress, regression, retrograde, congress, transgress, digress, gradual*

ire, itus (go): *transition, reiterate, itinerary, exit, sedition, ambition*

jacere, jactus (throw): *eject, reject, project, projectile, dejected, subject, interjection*

legere, lectus (choose, read): *elect, select, college, colleague, lectern, collect, legible*

loqui, locutus (speak): *colloquy, obloquy, soliloquy, loquacious, elocution, eloquent, circumlocution*

mittere, missus (send): *transmit, remit, permit, commission, admission, submissive, omit*

pellere, pulsus (drive): *compel, impulsive, repulsive, dispel, impel, propulsion, propellor*

pendere, pensus (hang): *pendant, depend, impending, pendulum, suspenders, dependent, pending*

plicare, plicatus (fold): *implication, supplication, pliable, duplex, comply, multiply, display*

ponere, positus (put): *deponent, component, depose, repose, suppose, transposition, opposition portare, portatus* (carry): *transport, comportment, import, support, portable, purport, deport*

rumpere, ruptus (break): *rupture, disrupt, erupt, corruption, rumpus, abrupt, bankrupt*

scribere, scriptus (write): *transcribe, inscribe, conscription, subscription, superscription, scribble, scribe*

sedere, sessus (sit): *session, obsession, sedentary, assess, residence, supersede, sediment*

sentire, sensus (feel): *sensitive, sensation, sensible, resent, dissent, insensate, assent*

specere, spectus (look): *spectacle, spectacular, inspection, perspicacious, conspicuous, speculate, despicable*

tenere, tentus (hold): *retentive, content, tenable, lieutenant, intent, pretentious, tenure*

tendere, tensus (stretch): *tension, contend, pretend, subtend, tense, tend, tendency*

trahere, tractus (drag): *tractor, traction, intractible, retract, contract, subtract, detract*

vertere, versus (turn): *inversion, subversion, perversion, controvert, divert, versatile, vertigo*

venire, ventus (come): *intervene, supervene, convene, convention, invent, prevent, convent*

videre, visus (see): *provide, visible, television, divide, invidious, provident, evident*

vocare, vocatus (call): *vocal, convocation, revoke, invoke, provoke, vocation, advocation*

224. Greek in English

There have been Greek words in the English vocabulary for thousands of years. Some, like *bishop* and *church*, were borrowed before the Anglo-Saxons ever got to England. But most of these did not come from Greek directly but were transmitted by Latin. Greek was next to unknown in western Europe in the Middle Ages and consequently direct borrowings were few. But in the fifteenth and sixteenth centuries, many speakers of English were learning Greek, and they began quarrying almost immediately. Since then, Greek has remained a prime source for new English words.

Many Greek words in English are quite common: *thermometer, telephone, sympathy, drama, auto, graph*. However, Greek roots have been used principally to build up the vocabularies of such sciences as medicine, physics, psychology, biology, and consequently most of the Greek borrowings are not in every man's vocabulary. Such items as *microcephalic* and *topology* are likely to be new to most readers. They would be new to Plato and Aristotle too, as it happens, as would most of the Greek element in English. We have not, for the most part, borrowed Greek words. Rather, we have taken Greek roots and combined them to express new ideas of our own.

One nice thing about the Greek element in English is that it is visible. The roots are more easily recognized than the Latin roots are. You might stare at the word *prodigious* for a long time without tumbling to the fact that its basic root is the Latin verb *agere, actus*, with the meaning "do." But if you know that *micros* means "small" and *cephalos* means "head," you will quickly perceive that *microcephalic* is a scientific way of saying *pin-headed*. Study of the roots given below will make a great many scientific terms quickly available to you. You can even make up some of your own if you like.

225. Greek Roots

The Greek element in English could also be divided into main roots and prefixes, as the Latin element was. But since it is sometimes hard to decide whether an item is a prefix or a main root, they are here set out together in one alphabetical list. Roots are given as roots, not as words: *path-*, for example, instead of *pathos* (suffering) or *pathein* (to suffer). The translations of the examples—*sympathy* (suffering with)—are mostly literal translations of the roots, not always idiomatic and not always accurate so far as present usage of the words goes.

a–, an– (not, without): *apathy* (without feeling), *asymmetrical* (not symmetrical), *anhydrous* (without water)

anthropo– (man): *anthropoid* (like a man), *philanthropy* (love of man), *anthropomorphic* (having the form of a man)

anti– (against): *antibiotic* (against life), *antipathy* (feeling against), *antistrophe* (turning against)

auto– (self): *autohypnosis* (hypnosis of self), *autobiography* (writing of one's own life), *autointoxication* (self-poisoning)

bio– (life): *biology* (study of life), *biogenesis* (life development), *biolysis* (destruction of life)

cata– (down, back, away): *catastrophe* (turning down), *cataclasm* (a breaking down), *catachresis* (wrong use)

cephalo– (head): *megacephalic* (having a big head), *cephalometry* (measurement of heads), *cephalic* (related to the head)

chron– (time): *chronometer* (measurer of time), *synchronize* (put in time with), *diachronic* (through time)

cracy– (rule): *autocracy* (self-rule), *plutocracy* (rule of the wealthy), *aristocracy* (rule of the best)

demo– (people): *democracy* (rule of the people), *endemic* (in the people), *epidemic* (on the people)

dia– (through, across): *diagram* (writing through), *diagonal* (through an angle), *diameter* (measurement across)

epi– (on): *epitaph* (on a tomb), *epicentric* (on the center), *epilogue* (a speaking on)

eu– (good, well): *eulogy* (a speaking well), *euphony* (good sound), *euphoria* (well-being)

ge– (earth): *geology* (earth study), *geometry* (earth measurement), *George* (worker in the earth)

gen– (birth, born, growing): *genesis* (a being born), *Eugene* (well-born), *acrogen* (something growing on top)

gon– (angle): *trigonometry* (calculation involving three angles), *polygon* (many angles), *pentagon* (five angles)

graph–, gram– (writing): *photograph* (picture writing), *graphic* (written), *cryptogram* (secret writing)

gyn– (woman): *polygyny* (many women), *gynecology* (study of women), *gynarchy* (government by women) *hetero–* (other, different): *heterogenous* (having other forms), *hetero-chromatic* (having more than one color), *heterodox* (of a different opinion)

hexa– (six): *hexachord* (of six tones), *hexagon* (six angles), *hexahedron* (six faces)

homo– (same): *homophone* (same sound), *homosexual* (same sex), *homotaxis* (same arrangement)

hydr– (water): *hydrophobia* (fear of water), *hydromel* (honey and water), *hydrous* (containing water)

hyper– (over, too much): *hypersensitive* (oversensitive), *hyperacidity* (too much acidity), *hyperemia* (too much blood)

hypo– (under): *hypodermic* (under the skin), *hypogeal* (under the earth), *hypoglossal* (under the tongue)

log– (word): *philologist* (lover of words), *prologue* (word before), *logogram* (word symbol)

log– (study): *anthropology* (study of man), *seismology* (study of earthquakes), *orology* (study of mountains)

mega– (big): *megaphone* (big sound), *megalith* (big stone), *megapod* (having big feet)

meter– (measure): *barometer* (measure of weight), *hydrometer* (measure of water), *Nilometer* (measurer of the Nile)

micro– (small): *microcosm* (small world), *microbiology* (study of small life), *microphone* (small sound)

mono– (one): *monopoly* (one seller), *monotone* (one tone), *monograph* (one writing)

morph– (form): *amorphous* (without form), *morphology* (study of forms), *morphogenesis* (growth of a form)

nom– (law): *astronomy* (law of the stars), *agronomy* (law of the fields), *bionomics* (law of life)

nym– (name): *patronymic* (father's name), *pseudonym* (false name), *homonym* (same name)

path– (feeling, suffering): *pathos* (feeling), *empathy* (shared feeling), *pathology* (study of suffering)

penta– (five): *pentagram* (five pointed figure), *pentameter* (verse of five feet), *pentarchy* (rule of five people)

phag– (eat): *autophagous* (self-eating), *geophagous* (dirt-eating), *anthropophagous* (man-eating) *phil–* (love): *dendrophile* (lover of trees), *Anglophile* (lover of the English), *Phillip* (lover of horses)

phob– (hate, fear): *xenophobia* (hatred of foreigners), *Anglophobe* (hater of the English), *acrophobia* (fear of heights)

phon– (sound): *phonology* (study of sounds), *phonic* (pertaining to sound), *phonograph* (sound writer)

poly– (many): *polytechnic* (many crafts), *polymorphous* (many forms), *polydactyl* (many fingers)

pseudo– (false): *pseudoscience* (false science), *pseudoclassic* (false classic), *pseudomorph* (false form)

psyche– (mind, soul): *psychology* (study of the mind), *psychotherapy* (treatment of the mind), *psychopath* (mind sufferer)

scop– (see): *episcopal* (overseeing), *microscope* (seeing small things), *periscope* (seeing around)

soph– (wise): *philosopher* (lover of wisdom), *sophomore* (wise fool), *theosophy* (wisdom about God)

sym– (with, together): *sympathy* (feeling with), *synthesize* (put together), *syndactyl* (having the toes stuck together)

tele– (far): *telephony* (sound sent far), *telemeter* (measurer of distance), *telelectric* (electricity sent far)

tetra– (four): *tetragram* (four-letter word), *tetrameter* (poetic line of four measures), *tetratomic* (having four atoms)

theo– (god): *atheist* (one not believing in God), *theology* (study of God), *theogony* (genealogy of the gods)

therm– (heat): *thermodiffusion* (spread of heat), *thermolysis* (loss of heat), *thermostat* (regulator of heat)

zo– (animal): *zoography* (description of animals), *zoometry* (measurement of animals), *protozoa* (first animals)

These are of course not the only Greek elements floating in present-day English, or even all of the important ones. Others—*tri-, tom-, ped-, pod-, pol-, arch-, hipp-,* etc.—will become familiar to you as you read, provided you learn to observe word roots as you read. Observation of what words are made of is not only interesting but useful. It does speed up vocabulary growth. If your vocabulary grows fast enough, maybe you *will* wind up as vice-president of Standard Oil, though it's perhaps a little early to start pricing yachts.

SUGGESTIONS

1. Estimate the size of your vocabulary, using the procedure outlined in Section 216.

2. Add one example to each set given in Section 222.

3. The list of Latin prefixes given in Section 222 is short. Lengthen it by finding the meanings and an illustration or two of the following:

ante-, bene-, circum-, contra-, intra-, mal-, multi-, per-, post-, retro-, semi-, super-, ultra-.

4. Add one example to each set given in Section 223.

5. Find the meaning of the following Latin forms and give examples of their occurrence in English words.

aqua, ager, amore, animus, ars, bellum, bonus, cadere, caput, citare, civis, clamore, cognoscere, cor, corpus, credere, dare, docere, ego, fallere, finis, genus, gregis, laborare, lex, lux, manus, mare, monere, mori, navis, omnia, opus, pax, petere, placere, putare, quaerere, ridere, rogare, sequi, solvere, stare, surgere, tangere, tempus, terra, verbum, via, vincere.

6. Give the verb with Latin roots that translates literally the verb-adverb combination listed. For example, the answer for *run with* would be *concur: con* "with" and *cur* (from *currere*) "run."

stick to	shut out	hold before
lead on	go with	come between
send across	walk forward	break out
put between	carry across	drive with
turn in	lead back	hang down
drive forward	say between	put between
write under	stick with	see ahead
go forward	send out	write in
turn under	pour out	put against
carry before	put down	pour across

7. Find or devise words with Greek roots that will translate the following. For example, the answer for *many marriages* would be *polygamy*. The answer for *small-headed* would be *microcephalic*.

study of the earth   lover of books
through an angle   seeing big things
good word   fear of water
study of man   without a name
secret name   feeling afar
feeling against   many colors
study of the stars   many women
having six angles

8. Find the meaning of the following Greek forms and illustrate their occurrence in English words:

agogos, apo, archos, aster, ballein, barus, dendron, derma, doxa, dynamis, dys, ergon, gamos, helios, hemi, hodos, kakos, lithos, lysis, meta, neos, orthos, paidos, pan, peri, photos, polis, proto, podos, pyr, toxis, tomos.

9. Use a dictionary to find the derivation of the following proper names: Elizabeth, Irene, Lois, Emily, George, Alphonse, Dorothy, Margaret, Peter, Helen, Barbara, Patricia.

26

How to Find Fault
with a Dictionary

226. Dictionary Worship

It is probably fair to say that most present-day Americans show rather more respect for the dictionary than they do for the Bible. It is significant that we speak of "the dictionary" rather than "a dictionary," as if there were only one. When we say, "The dictionary says so," we feel that we have settled the matter once and for all, that we have carried the appeal to the final authority. The popular feeling seems to be that the dictionary editor visits heaven every few years to receive the material for the next edition.

Well, modern dictionaries are good, but they're not that good. It is true that they are generally more sophisticated linguistically than the people that use them; that they are prepared with great care at considerable expense by squads of experts; that keen competition for a large market keeps them up to date, well presented, and generally sharp. But it is also true that they are prepared by men and women liable, like all men and women, to error. It is further true that the nature of their subject—the word units of a vast, boiling, constantly changing language—makes it impossible, or at least economically unfeasible, for them to be prepared by what could be called scientific methods.

378

It is the intent of this chapter to look at dictionaries in perspective, to trace their growth briefly, and to see what they offer their modern users.

227. The Evolution of the Modern Dictionary

It has been said wisely that nobody ever begins anything. Look behind every bright idea and you find some earlier bright idea that contains its kernel. This is so at least with the English dictionary. It is hard to say which the first one was because we find word lists of one kind or another going deep into the Middle Ages. But these early lists were two-language dictionaries—e.g., Latin words with English translations. The first English-English word list was published in 1603, and this is usually called the first English dictionary.

Interestingly enough, it was not called a dictionary. Its title was *A Table Alphabeticall* and its author a man named Robert Cawdrey. Cawdrey's dictionary contained about 2500 words. They were all "hard words," words that readers, or at least inexperienced readers, might be expected to stumble over. The definitions were fairly primitive—synonyms usually, and not always accurate.

Cawdrey did not pick his 2500 words out of the air. For the most part he got them by copying from an earlier Latin word list. Thus at the very beginning was born that splendid tradition of plagiarism in dictionary-making that has lasted nearly to the present day. Plagiarism in dictionary-making is next to inevitable. Suppose you wanted to produce a dictionary. How could you, how could anyone, arrive at all the words except by looking in dictionaries already in existence? Presumably you would have your own contribution to make, but you would be a plain fool if you didn't check your competitors' books to make sure you hadn't overlooked something important. There is, as it happens, one other way of going about it, but it is fearfully toilsome, and it has been undertaken only once, as we shall see.

Anyway, Cawdrey copied from his predecessors, and his successors copied from him. But each lexicographer produced not only his predecessor's word list but also more words that he had dredged up by himself, and as the seventeenth century wore on, dictionaries, as they had come to be called, grew larger and larger. By the end of the century they were crowding 25,000 words.

They were getting better as well as bigger. Generally they copied not only one another's word lists but one another's definitions as well; nevertheless, there was steady improvement in the definitions. Being much worked over, they grew more accurate, more elaborate, and more refined.

In the second half of the seventeenth century an important addition to the dictionary was made: etymologies. The etymology is that part of the dictionary entry which explains the history of the word. It is now an essential part of dictionaries and is most carefully and accurately done. In the beginning the etymologies were slipshod and primitive. Usually they consisted of a single letter—F or L or G—to indicate whether the word was borrowed from French, Latin, or Greek. Many words were not labeled at all. But once somebody thought of putting in etymologies, all his successors had to include them too or risk losing the market; and, like the definitions, the etymologies, worked over decade after decade, became better and better. Thus free enterprise triumphed again.

The dictionaries of the seventeenth century were all hard-word dictionaries. Nobody made any attempt to include all the words of the language, but only those likely to give a reader trouble. However, shortly after 1700 a man named John Kersey took the step of including common words too. His purpose presumably was to provide a complete spelling list, but he didn't shrink from the difficult task of providing definitions for the common words. These are sufficiently crude. The word *an,* for instance, is given thus "An:as, *an* apron." This may make us smile until we try to define it ourselves. Ultimately the only important thing we can do with words like *an, the, of, with, some* is to show how they are used.

Kersey was a new breed—a man whose main business was making dictionaries, a professional lexicographer. Another was Nathaniel Bailey. Bailey produced several dictionaries, one of which appeared through the eighteenth century in thirty different editions. Presumably most literate homes of that century possessed a Bailey dictionary. So many were printed that they are still readily available on the second-hand book market and can be bought cheap, despite their age, by collectors of old dictionaries.

228. Dr. Johnson

But the great figure of lexicography in the eighteenth century was Dr. Samuel Johnson, the king of literary London in the time of George the Third. Johnson made his reputation with his dictionary, published in 1755 after seven years of labor. It was originally intended, as we have noted earlier, to regulate the English language. It didn't do that, of course, but it did contribute much to the growth of lexicography and indeed exerted considerable influence on English writing.

Students of literature are likely to pass rapidly over the dictionary and concern themselves with Johnson's literary works and with Boswell's great biography of Johnson. They note the dictionary only as the subject of a famous letter to Lord Chesterfield in which Johnson repudiates help offered too late, or as a book containing occasionally waspish definitions:

pension: An allowance made to anyone without an equivalent. In England it is generally understood to mean pay given to a state hireling for treason to his country.

lexicographer: a writer of dictionaries; a harmless drudge.

But Johnson's dictionary, as his contemporaries well knew, was not a collection of amusing definitions but a serious and important work.

Johnson had, first of all, a rare ability for definition, a greater one, possibly, than anyone before or after him. His definitions, sometimes overcomplicated, are mostly strong and clear. He also made a couple of lexicographical innovations. One was the practice of separating and numbering word meanings, thus:

> **man:** 1. Human being. 2. Not a woman. 3. Not a boy. 4. A servant; an attendant; a dependent. 5. A word of familiarity bordering on contempt. 6. It is used in loose signification like the French *on,* one, any one.

This is now of course standard procedure in dictionaries.

Another, even more important innovation, was the citing of contexts to show word meanings or particular usages. As he worked on the dictionary, Johnson read widely in earlier literature and marked passages for secretaries to copy out, and many of these passages found their way into the dictionary. Definition-by-context is not carried through in anything like a complete or systematic way. But in a great many entries, the reader is given not only Johnson's definition but a sentence to show how the word was used by Shakespeare or Milton or Addison or Swift.

Johnson's dictionary went through four editions in his lifetime and more after his death. In the early nineteenth century it was revised by Todd, and in one form or another it continued to be "The Dictionary" in England much as Noah Webster's became "The Dictionary" in America.

Is pride, the *never*-failing vice of fools.   *Pope.*
Thy buſy *never*-meaning face,
Thy ſcrew'd up front, thy ſtate grimace.   *Swift.*

NE'VERTHELESS. *adv.* [*never the leſs.*] Notwithſtanding that.

They plead that even ſuch ceremonies of the church of Rome as contain in them nothing which is not of itſelf agreeable to the word of God, ought *neverthelefs* to be aboliſhed.   *Hooker, b.* iv.

Many of our men were gone to land, and our ſhips ready to depart ; *neverthelefs* the admiral, with ſuch ſhips only as could ſuddenly be put in readineſs, made forth towards them.   *Bacon.*

Creation muſt needs infer providence ; and God's making the world, irrefragably proves that he governs it too; or that a being of a dependent nature remains *neverthelefs* independent upon him in that reſpect.   *South's Sermons.*

NEU'ROLOGY. *n. ſ.* [νεῦρον and λόγος.] A deſcription of the nerves.

NEU'ROTOMY. *n. ſ.* [νεῦρον and τέμνω.] The anatomy of the nerves.

NEU'TER. *adj.* [*neuter,* Latin ; *neutre,* Fr.]

1. Indifferent ; not engaged on either ſide.

The general diviſion of the Britiſh nation is into whigs and tories ; there being very few, if any, who ſtand *neuter* in the diſpute, without ranging themſelves under one of theſe denominations.   *Addiſon's Freeholder,* N°. 54.

2. [In grammar.] A noun that implies no ſex.

The adjectives are *neuter,* and animal muſt be underſtood to make it grammar.   *Dryden.*

A verb *neuter* is that which ſignifies neither action nor paſſion, but ſome ſtate or condition of being ; as, *ſedeo,* I ſit.   *Clarke's Latin Grammar.*

NEU'TER. *n. ſ.* One indifferent and unengaged.

The learned heathens may be looked upon as *neuters* in the matter, when all theſe prophecies were new to them, and their education had left the interpretation of them indifferent.   *Addiſon on the Chriſtian Religion.*

18 D   NEU'TRAL

Part of a Page from Samuel Johnson, *Dictionary.*

Others, however, were making their contributions to lexicography. In the late eighteenth century synonymies were added to entries in dictionaries. These are lists of close synonyms. Thus after *courage* one might find *bravery, boldness, valor, heroism, fortitude,* etc. In the course of time lexicographers undertook to define the shades of meaning between such synonyms. This is not only an integral part of modern dictionaries but has been expanded outside the dictionary proper. We now have "dictionaries of synonyms," such as *Roget's Thesaurus* or *Webster's Dictionary of Synonyms,* devoted entirely to the listing and explication of synonymous words.

Also in the second half of the eighteenth century, dictionaries began to include guides to pronunciation. A pioneer in this department was Thomas Sheridan, the father of the playwright Richard Brinsley Sheridan. The elder Sheridan was also connected with the theatre, as were other people experimenting with pronunciation guides. They of course set down as "correct pronunciation" the pronunciation current in their own theatrical circles. This had a considerable effect on how people thought they ought to pronounce words, if not on how they actually did pronounce them. Probably its effect is still going on.

229. The Oxford English Dictionary

The greatest lexicographical effort in England in the nineteenth century—perhaps the greatest of any century anywhere —was the *Oxford English Dictionary.* This has gone under various names in its long career. It is sometimes called the *Oxford Dictionary,* the *Historical English Dictionary,* and the *New English Dictionary,* and it is variously abbreviated the OED, the OD, the HED, and the NED. It is usually bound in ten or twelve or twenty volumes, and it costs in the neighborhood of 250 dollars.

The idea for the *Oxford English Dictionary* was born and nurtured in the Philological Society in England. In the year 1857 one of its members read a paper criticizing existing dictionaries. He pointed out that the best of them were hit-and-miss affairs, unscientifically produced, impressionistic. He suggested that the Society undertake a new dictionary to be planned along quite different lines. The Society agreed enthusiastically, not knowing that none of them would live long enough to see the project completed.

The idea was that the dictionary would draw its data from English writing and would not only give word meanings but would systematically cite contextual evidence to verify the meanings given. The dictionary would include all words in use between the year 1100 and the date of publication. It was intended to cite the first occurrence of each word in English writing and the last occurrence if the word had dropped out of use, together with other citations across the centuries to show developments in meaning. It was decided that all extant English writing dating from before 1500 should be read and as much of the later writing as possible. In the end, practically all of English literature was covered, together with great quantities of cookbooks, religious tracts, trade manuals, newspapers, and the like.

The reading was done by thousands of volunteers. If you volunteered to read for the dictionary, you would be assigned, say, the works of Jane Austen. You would be told to read the novels carefully, looking for any unusual word, any word unusually used, any word that struck you as new or old or in any way remarkable. When you came on such a word, you wrote it on a slip together with the sentence in which it occurred, noting the page or chapter number and the edition. You were also instructed to excerpt as many ordinary words and their contexts as time permitted. In the end some five million quotations were gathered, of which about a million and a half appeared in the dictionary.

As the slips came in, they were sorted and filed in storehouses and eventually studied by the editors and their assistants. When an editor came to write the entry for the word *buxom,* for example, he began by assembling all the slips on *buxom.* He then deduced its meaning and its changes of meaning from those slips. It didn't matter what he thought it meant or ought to mean or what other dictionaries said about it. He was bound by the slips. They gave him all the variant spellings and different usages and displayed the whole history of the word. Everything he had to say about *buxom* came out of those slips, and in the finished article, he included quotations to demonstrate the meanings given.

In the first quarter of a century, progress on the dictionary was spasmodic. The Philological Society found the undertaking vaster than it had imagined; financial troubles arose; editors died; interest flagged. But in the 1880's a man named James Murray was hired as editor, and the work picked up again. Murray got out the first volume, A to Ant, in 1884. About this time Henry Bradley, a young philologist, was hired as coeditor, and the pace was doubled. After the turn of the century, two more editors, William Craigie and Charles Talbot Onions, were added to the staff. These last were the only ones who saw the work completed in 1928. Murray and Craigie were knighted for their work on the dictionary.

Anyone with any curiosity at all about words should make the acquaintance of the *Oxford English Dictionary*. It is to be found in the reference room of any college library, along with its abridgement, the two-volume *Shorter Oxford*. You may find it rather a maze at first. The entry on the word *set,* the longest entry in the dictionary, runs to some twenty-three small-type, triple-columned pages; there is a good deal to say about *set* if you say everything. But brief acquaintance will quickly make the plan and possibilities clear. You will find there everything known about most English words and, through the words, the key to much in the development of English culture. The *Oxford* has contributed to thousands of scholarly studies that would have been altogether impossible without it. The *Oxford* is itself one of scholarship's greatest triumphs and a monument to the thousands of men and women who contributed their leisure hours for years and decades, for neither money nor fame but only for the satisfaction of extending human knowledge.

230. Dictionaries in America

In America the great pioneer in lexicography was of course Noah Webster, whose name came to be as closely linked with lexicography in this country as Johnson's was in England. Webster was a Connecticut school teacher, a graduate of Yale. He early became a producer of spelling books and an advocate of spelling reform and this interest led him into the making of dictionaries. His *Compendious Dictionary,* published in 1806, included such spellings as *fether* (feather), *hed* (head), *masheen* (machine), *bilt,* (built), *leen* (lean), *thum* (thumb), *magic* (for *magick*), *color* (for *colour*), *center* (for *centre*). Most of these sensible suggestions were rejected by the writing public, and it could not be said that Webster was greatly effective in simplifying English spelling. On the other hand, he was more effective than anyone else has been.

But Webster is famous not as a spelling reformer but as the Webster of Webster's dictionary. Webster brought out his last and greatest effort in lexicography in 1828 under the title *An*

American Dictionary of the English Language. This work is in a sense the American counterpart of Johnson's dictionary. Neither is scientifically controlled in the sense that the *Oxford* was to be. But neither is a mere plagiarism either or a hasty commercial effort. Both Webster and Johnson were intelligent men of strong and independent minds. Both were sufficiently crotchety and opinionated and likely to indulge idiosyncrasies now and then. But they were mostly sane and wise, and they brought more genius to the field of lexicography than it was used to at the time.

Webster's book was revised once in his lifetime. In 1843 the rights were purchased by Charles and George Merriam, and the Merriam firm continued, and continues, to bring out editions of all sizes, all bearing the Webster name. This name quickly acquired enormous commercial value, and one of the problems of the Merriam Company was how to keep it as their very own. Other publishers would, for example, hire somebody named Joseph Webster and publish a "Webster's Dictionary," neglecting to mention that the Webster involved was Joe and not Noah. The consequence was a series of court battles decided now one way and now another. Today one of Merriam's chief competitors in the college field, the World Publishing Company, publishes a dictionary called the *Webster New World Dictionary.* This is done legally and with acquiescence, but not with as much cheerfulness on either side as one would like to see.

The Merriam Company has always enjoyed enough challenge to keep it up to the mark and to maintain a rather heady excitement in American lexicographical circles. One of Noah Webster's early competitors was a man named Joseph Worcester, who followed the Johnson tradition more closely than Webster deigned to. Worcester's dictionary also had its violent partisans, and for some decades it was possible in American literary circles to work up heated argument about whether Webster's or Worcester's was to be accepted as the authority. Even institutions took sides. Yale embraced the work of Webster, its famous son, whereas it was late in the nineteenth century before Harvard men were permitted to peep into anything but Worcester's.

In the late nineteenth and early twentieth centuries Merriam's chief competition came from Funk and Wagnalls, publishers of the *Standard Dictionary*. This competition produced, from edition to edition, added features in both dictionaries: improved synonymies, illustrations, biographical and geographical lists, improved methods in presentation, more research. It also produced more words. It was quickly apparent that the customer eyed with favor that dictionary which contained most words, and the result was that editors bringing out a new edition would make sure that it contained everything the other company's had and then dredge up a few thousand more. Under this stimulus the number of entries in the "unabridged" versions rose to around 600,000. They stopped there, not because the editors ran out of words but because the dictionaries are advertised as portable, and 600,000 words seems to be as many as one can carry from one room to another.

The dictionary popularly called "Webster's Unabridged" has more exactly the title *Webster's New International Dictionary,* second edition. It was published in 1934. It seems to be the intention of the Merriam Company to publish revisions of the big book about every twenty-five years. The *New International* is not comparable to the *Oxford.* Its editors did not enjoy the resources available to the editors of the *Oxford,* and they labored under certain commercial limitations, principally that of space. Even so, the *New International* is (not to search too hard for a metaphor) a great storehouse of information. Its principles are, at least in theory, those of the *Oxford:* the word is defined by the contexts in which it occurs, and the editor is bound by those contexts in writing his article. The Merriam Company keeps a staff of editors and assistants and special experts at work to keep its files up to date and to prepare for the next edition.

231. College Dictionaries

Almost from the beginning of lexicography there has been a market for dictionaries smaller than possible: college dictionaries, high school dictionaries, pocket dictionaries, office dictionaries. The Merriam Company for a long time enjoyed an advantage in the college field as well as in the unabridged class. Until the end of the Second World War, the outstanding dictionary in the college field was the *Webster Collegiate,* fifth edition, published in 1936. A whole generation of college students carried the *Collegiate* from class to class, blissfully unaware that any other dictionaries existed. Few good ones did in America at that time. The John C. Winston Company published a line of small dictionaries, including a college edition. This was in many ways a good book, but it lacked the scope of the *Collegiate,* and it was not a serious challenger.

By 1945, however, the *Collegiate* had come under serious criticism, particularly from linguists. It was argued that the *Collegiate* was not only old but stodgy; that it was authoritarian, laying down the law about correctness, instead of objectively reporting the usage of educated people; that its treatment of pronunciation and other features was unrealistic; that its definitions needed a breath of clarity. Some of this criticism was no doubt justified; some of it stemmed possibly from the tendency of the Merriam Company to give the impression that its dictionaries were produced under the general supervision of the angel Gabriel.

At any rate, shortly after the end of the Second World War, the Merriam monopoly was vigorously challenged. In 1947 Random House and Harper & Brothers jointly brought out *The American College Dictionary* (ACD). In 1949, Merriam answered with a revision of the *Collegiate* under the title *Webster's New Collegiate Dictionary* (WNCD). A few years later the World Publishing Company put *Webster's New World Dictionary* (WNWD) into the ring. The editor of the ACD, Clarence Barnhart, produced the *Thorndike-Barnhart Dictionary* for Scott Foresman. This is similar to the ACD in many features, but of smaller scope.

It should be said first of all that all of these postwar dictionaries are good books. The college student who owns either the WNCD, the ACD, or the WNWD owns a dictionary that is adequate for his normal needs, that is reasonably accurate and up to date, and that is sufficiently easy to use. Whichever one you buy, you buy a lot of scholarship for five or six dollars. Salesmen for the other two dictionaries will take a pretty gloomy view of your chances for success and happiness, but you may not feel especially handicapped. The writer of this book owns all three of these college dictionaries, and he tends to use the one that happens to be closest to hand when he wants to look something up.

However, there are basic differences among the dictionaries. Most obviously, there are differences between the WNCD on the one hand and the ACD and WNWD on the other. In various internal features, which we shall notice in detail in a moment, the ACD and WNWD have adopted new methods which make those of the Merriam book look somewhat antiquated. On the other hand, the Merriam people can argue with some justice that because it publishes the big book, the *New International,* it commands vaster resources for dictionary-making than do its competitors. It is often said that

UNDERSTANDING ENGLISH

the WNCD is the more conservative dictionary, the ACD and the WNWD more liberal, but this would be hard to prove. So far as "liberality" goes, the postwar dictionaries seem pretty much of a piece. Probably they are all more conservative than linguists think they ought to be and much more liberal than the public expects them to be.

The student's problem is not really what dictionary to buy. This is likely to be settled for him by his college bookstore or his instructor. His task is rather to inform himself on what is in whatever dictionary he owns and to learn how to use it.

232. Inside the Dictionary

The big college dictionaries run to around 130,000 or 140,-000 main entries. These are the black-type headings. Obvious derivatives are usually listed within the main entries. Thus, *intelligently* will not rate a paragraph of its own, but will be listed in small type under *intelligent*. But *intelligence* will have an entry of its own. Some prefixes—like *un, non,* and *ex* —attach to thousands of words. The dictionary will not list all the possibilities, but will give a number of examples, usually in smaller type at the bottom of the page.

In addition to ordinary words, dictionaries list a great many names of people and places. The WNCD lists these in two separate sections at the back of the book—a biographical index and a pronouncing gazetteer. The other modern dictionaries throw everything into one alphabetical list. Thus in the ACD you find *Disraeli* between *disquisition* and *disrate.* In the WNCD he's in the back of the book between *Disney* and *Ditmars.*

The college dictionaries contain all the words the student is likely to look up in ordinary work. It is only if your interest is quite special—as when you are working in very specialized science or dialects or old literature—that the college dictionary will fail you. Then you will have to turn to the *Oxford* or the *New International* or a special dictionary for your subject.

233. Grammatical Designations

Right after the word in the alphabetical list, the dictionary will give an abbreviated designation of its "part of speech" —as *n., v., prep.,* for *noun, verb, preposition,* respectively. The grammatical system used is the traditional one, diverging in many respects from that given in this book, though for most words there would be little practical conflict. It should be remembered that in this as in other matters the dictionary can give only ordinary usage, not all possible usage. It may, for example, list *horse* only as a noun, though it obviously occurs also as a verb, as in "Don't horse around."

If the word occurs in two or more grammatical categories, the dictionary will give the definitions for each. For example, the word *face* will be given as *face, n.,* followed by definitions of *face* as a noun. Then, in the main entry, you will find the abbreviation *v.t.,* followed by definitions of *face* as a verb. *T.* here means *transitive,* and that means that the verb occurs in the pattern N-V-N; *v.i.* means *verb intransitive,* which means that the verb occurs in the pattern N-V. *Face* is *v.t.* because we ordinarily say "He faced something" and not just "He faced." You will find these and other abbreviations explained in the front or back of your dictionary, usually on the cover. Abbreviations very frequently used are explained at the bottom of each page.

234. Definitions

Since Johnson's time dictionaries have recognized that words have multiple meanings and have undertaken to separate and number them. A word in a college dictionary may have fifteen or more numbered meanings. The careless student looking up a word is likely to settle for the definition at the top of the list, which may not be what he's after at all. Often you have to search around a bit.

Note also that dictionaries differ in the way in which they arrange the different meanings. The Merriam-Webster dictionaries, like the *Oxford,* list the meanings in historical order. The oldest meaning that the word has had in English is given first, then the one that developed next, and so on. The ACD and the WNWD try to give the meanings in the order of current frequency. Both methods have advantages and disadvantages. The order in the WNCD gives you something of the history of the word; its semantic development unfolds as you read the definitions. On the other hand, the definition your eye first lights on is likely to be obsolete and useless to your present purposes.

235. Etymologies and Synonymies

All modern college dictionaries contain two features which can be of much service to you in strengthening and sharpening your vocabulary. These are the etymologies and the synonymies. The etymology is a very brief explanation of the history of the word, the route by which it has come into English, the elements of which it is made, and so on. The etymology is given in square brackets. In the WNCD and the WNWD it appears at the head of the entry, just after the pronunciation. In the ACD it follows the definitions.

Etymologies are very highly abbreviated in order to conserve space. The abbreviation key is given on the cover of the dictionary, common symbols at the bottom of the page. Thus, in the ACD the etymology of *diminutive* is [ME, t. ML; m.s. *diminutivus,* der. L. *di-, deminutis,* pp., lessened]. Reference to the symbols will allow you to translate this as "This word, which occurs in Middle English, was taken from Medieval

Latin; it is a modification of the stem of *diminutivus,* which derives from Latin *diminutis* or *deminutis,* a past participle meaning 'lessened.' " A very little practice will make the symbols readily familiar to you. The etymologies of all the college

proud (proud), *adj.* **1.** feeling pleasure or satisfaction over something conceived as highly honorable or creditable to oneself (often fol. by *of,* an infinitive, or a clause). **2.** having or cherishing, or proceeding from or showing, a high, esp. an inordinately high, opinion of one's own dignity, importance, or superiority. **3.** having or showing self-respect or self-esteem. **4.** highly gratifying to the feelings or self-esteem. **5.** highly honorable or creditable: *a proud achievement.* **6.** (of things) stately, majestic, or magnificent: *proud cities.* **7.** of lofty dignity or distinction: *a proud name, proud nobles.* **8.** *Poetic.* full of vigor, spirit, or mettle, as an animal. **9.** *Obs.* brave. [ME; late OE *prūd,* c. Icel. *prūdhr* magnificent, stately, gallant, appar. from VL. Cf. OF *prud, prod* gallant, g. L *prōd-* in *prōdesse* be of worth] —**proud′ly,** *adv.*
—**Syn. 2.** PROUD, ARROGANT, HAUGHTY imply a consciousness of, or a belief in, one's superiority in some respect. PROUD implies sensitiveness, lofty self-respect, or jealous preservation of one's dignity, station, and the like. (It may refer to an affectionate admiration or a justifiable pride concerning someone else: *proud of his son.*) ARROGANT applies to insolent or overbearing behavior, arising from an exaggerated belief in one's importance: *arrogant rudeness.* HAUGHTY implies lofty reserve and confident, often disdainful, assumption of superiority over others: *the haughty manner of an ill-bred débutante.* —**Ant. 1.** humble. **2.** modest.

From *The American College Dictionary,* Copyright, 1947–1955, by Random House, Inc.; Text Edition by Harper & Brothers.

dictionaries are quite accurate, the history of words having been thoroughly studied for centuries. Naturally there is no space to give more than an outline of the word's history. The etymologies of the ACD are somewhat more precise than those in the other dictionaries and for that reason apt to be more pleasing to philologists than to the ordinary user, who may sometimes find them harder to penetrate than the etymologies of the WNCD or the WNWD.

Do get in the habit of glancing at the etymology when you look up a word. You will begin to see patterns in wordbuilding that will help you retain words in your vocabulary. You will also make your way into a field most interesting in itself.

The synonymies are also interesting and sometimes helpful.

Lists of synonyms are given mostly for abstract words, like *courage, pride, cleverness*. The synonymy will be given only once for one group of synonyms. For example, if you look up *arrogance,* you may be directed to *pride* for the synonymy.

> **proud** (proud), *adj.*. [AS. *prūt, prūd.*] **1.** Feeling or manifesting pride; as: **a** Possessing or showing too great self-esteem; hence, arrogant; haughty. **b** Exulting (in); being highly pleased; — often with *of;* as, *proud* of one's country. **c** Having a feeling of proper self-respect or self-esteem. **2. a** *Obs.* Valiant. **b** Full of mettle; as, a *proud* steed. **3.** Giving reason or occasion for pride; admirable. **4.** Arising from, or produced by, pride; presumptuous. — **proud'ly,** *adv.*
> **Syn.** (1) **Proud, arrogant, haughty, lordly, insolent, overbearing, supercilious, disdainful** mean exhibiting scorn for inferiors. **Proud,** not always derogatory, may imply imperiousness, conceit, or merely satisfaction; **arrogant** implies a disposition to claim more consideration than is due; **haughty,** consciousness of birth or station; **lordly,** pomposity or a display of power; **insolent,** haughtiness and contemptuousness; **overbearing,** intolerable insolence; **supercilious,** a manner that repels advances; **disdainful,** a more obvious and scornful superciliousness.
> (2) **Proud, vain, vainglorious** mean aware of one's excellence or superiority. **Proud** may imply justified or unjustified self-esteem; **vain,** an excessive desire to win the notice or praise of others; **vainglorious,** excessive vanity leading to boastfulness or an arrogant display of one's power, skill, influence, or the like.
> By permission. From Webster's New Collegiate Dictionary
> Copyright, 1949, 1951, 1953, 1956
> by G. & C. Merriam Co.

There you will find not only the list of synonyms—*pride, arrogance, haughtiness,* etc.—but also an attempt to explain the shades of difference between each word.

236. Status Designations

Words which are in anything less than general respectable use are marked in the dictionary by such designations as *slang, colloquial, provincial, dialectal, vulgar, archaic, obsolete.* These are generally abbreviated, as *obs.* for *obsolete* or *col.* for *colloquial.* Words or meanings pertaining to special fields are so labeled, as *Law, Med.* (medicine), *Teleg.* (telegraphy). Geographical limitations are also given: *U. S.* (United States), *Brit.* (British). Words for which there are no status designations are presumably in current, general, polite use.

It should be said that in applying status designations dictionaries do not walk on very firm ground. We have seen that the lines between slang and colloquial and between colloquial and elegant are not sharp lines, and there is really no controllable procedure by which the lexicographer can decide whether to pin on the label *slang* or *colloquial* or to let the word slip by unreproached. Presumably he often studies all the available evidence and then flips a coin. Here as elsewhere

proud (proud), *adj.* [ME.; AS. *prud, prut;* prob. < OFr. *prud* (cf. Fr. *preux*) < LL. **prodis,* supposedly a back-formation < *prod-esse,* to be of value; cf. PRIDE],   1. having or showing a proper pride in oneself, one's position, etc.   2. having or showing an overweening opinion of oneself, one's position, etc.; arrogant; haughty.   3. feeling or showing great pride or joy.   4. that is an occasion or cause of pride; highly gratifying.   5. arising from or caused by pride; presumptuous.   6. stately; splendid: as, a *proud* fleet.   7. spirited; of high mettle: as, a *proud* stallion.   8. [Obs.], valiant.
   do oneself proud, [Colloq.], to do extremely well.
   proud of, highly pleased with or exulting in.
   SYN.—**proud** is the broadest term in this comparison, ranging in implication from proper self-esteem or pride to an overweening opinion of one's importance (too *proud* to beg, *proud* as a peacock); **arrogant** implies an aggressive, unwarranted assertion of superior importance or privileges (the *arrogant* colonel); **haughty** implies such consciousness of high station, rank, etc. as is displayed in scorn of those one considers beneath one (a *haughty* dowager); **insolent,** in this connection, implies both haughtiness and great contempt, especially as manifested in behavior or speech that insults or affronts others (she has an *insolent* disregard for her servant's feelings); **overbearing** implies extreme, domineering insolence (an *overbearing* supervisor); **supercilious** stresses an aloof, scornful manner towards others (a *supercilious* intellectual snob); **disdainful** implies even stronger and more overt feelings of scorn for that which is regarded as beneath one.—*ANT.* humble.

From *Webster's New World Dictionary* of the American Language, College Edition, Copyright, 1958, by The World Publishing Company.

the student will do well to use his own ears and eyes. They may prove the dictionary wrong. You use the dictionary to improve your language only when better means are not available.

Remember also that a status designation does not necessarily mean that the word should not be used under any circumstances. *Colloquial,* for example, means simply that the word is more likely to occur in conversation than in writing. *Dialectal* means that there are geographical restrictions on it, as, for instance, that it is current only in southern Utah. If you live in southern Utah, you would not conclude from this that you and your neighbors are subnormal because you use the word; you would simply not expect it to be understandable or to sound natural in Buffalo.

237. Pronunciation

All modern dictionaries indicate a pronunciation of each word, usually in parentheses right after the entry. For all dictionaries this remains one of the weakest features, though the lexicographers are not obviously to blame for the shortcomings. If pronunciation is to be clearly indicated, the phonemic principle should be used, and the word spelled with characters of a phonemic alphabet. In practice, dictionaries work out various compromises between a phonemic alphabet and the regular alphabet, include a lot of nonsense about "short vowels" and "long vowels," and often festoon the vowels with various squiggles called "diacritical marks." From all this one can, with application, get a rough notion of how the editor wants the word to be pronounced, but the procedure could scarcely be called efficient.

In defense of the editors, however, one should note that the concept of the phoneme is relatively new. It has perhaps not had time to make its way into the dictionaries. Furthermore, American linguists have not yet settled all the minor points of English phonemics, and the dictionary editor would frequently have to decide which expert to agree with. Finally, the editor has the practical commercial problem of not running too far ahead of the public, of not presenting too quickly a way of showing pronunciation that the buyer would find sudden and shocking. Time will take care of all these difficulties, and one can expect considerable improvement in the pronunciation department in the next few decades.

There has been much improvement in the last one. The editors of the ACD adopted the symbol called *schwa:* ə. This represents the so-called neutral vowel which is very common in syllables that do not have primary or secondary stress. It is for most speakers the first vowel in *event* and *above,* the last two in *sensible.* By adopting *schwa,* the dictionary was able to get rid of a whole host of diacritical marks. The same practice is followed by the WNWD, by the *Thorndike-Barnhart Dictionary,* and by others. The Merriam dictionaries cling to the old system with its confusion of diacritical marks, but they are not likely to do so forever. All dictionaries in future editions can be expected to move closer to the phonemic principle.

The system of representing pronunciation in your dictionary may be overly complicated, but a little practice and reference to the symbol key at the bottom of the page will quickly initiate you. Even the diacritical marks of the WNCD are fathomable with only a little application. Much more important is the whole question of "correct pronunciation."

There is a widespread notion that every word has one and only one correct pronunciation, and that this is inscribed in phonetic symbols on a scroll in heaven or perhaps carved on the wall of Plato's Cave. One feels that there is some principle somewhere, some rule or set of rules, which the dictionary-maker applies to determine which pronunciation is correct. Actually, the only arbiter of pronunciation is usage. There is no other. None whatsoever. If a pronunciation is correct it is so because people, or more likely those particular people whom one admires and wishes to emulate, pronounce the word that way, and for no other reason.

It seems to be very hard to grasp this. The writer recalls a speech teacher who liked to begin his course with a demonstration of the ignorance of the students. He would write a word on the blackboard—say, *illustrate*—and ask each student to pronounce it in turn. Like as not each one would put the stress on the first syllable: *íllustrate.* "You see," the teacher would say triumphantly, "not one of you knows how to pronounce it. The correct pronunciation is *illústrate.*" But observe the flaw. The students were themselves members of the educated class. Many of them were sons and daughters of educated people and moved in circles where the English spoken was good and decent and admired and admirable. If they had not encountered the pronunciation *illústrate,* this was substantial evidence that the pronunciation was not current in educated circles. All the teacher succeeded in proving was that he didn't know how to pronounce the word.

A popular book on pronunciation published some decades ago began with a list of words and the comment that not three educated people out of five hundred could pronounce them correctly. Again, observe the flaw. If 498 educated people pronounced them one way, the inference is that the other two were eccentric. But this seemed not to have occurred to this expert on pronunciation.

Modern dictionaries do much better than this. To be sure, they do not publicize the methods by which they decide what pronunciations to favor. Perhaps they send around questionnaires, or perhaps the editor just asks his secretary what she thinks he should put down. But in general they try to list pronunciations that are current and common and not just traditional. Often they will give two or more pronunciations for a word, listing them in the order of frequency.

Remember also that many words, and particularly many of the words we are likely to look up in the dictionary, do not really have stable pronunciations. These are what are sometimes called "eye words," words that we write and read but do not often speak and hear. If the word is not spoken, it cannot develop a standard pronunciation. Nobody can be altogether sure how to pronounce *schism,* because he so seldom hears it pronounced.

238. You and the Dictionary

It has been said that when an educated American has a word problem he tends to consult the dictionary; when an educated Englishman has a word problem he tends to consult his memory, to recall how the word is used or pronounced by his friends and relatives. The latter is certainly the more reasonable approach, though of course it won't always work. The proper procedure is to solve the problem on the basis of your experience if it lies within your experience; if it does not, you consult the dictionary.

Observe, however, that the dictionary is a more reliable guide in some areas than in others. If the question is one of spelling, you can depend on the dictionary absolutely; all you have to be sure of here is that you are using an American dictionary and not a British one. In etymologies also you can take the dictionary's pronouncements as nearly gospel. Errors in etymology do occur, and occasionally the editor is a little more positive about the history of the word than he ought to be, but such matters will not trouble you until you get pretty well along in the study of philology.

Definitions are a somewhat different matter. As we have seen, the ultimate definer is the context. All the editor can do is make a generalization or a series of generalizations from contexts available to him. It may be that these will not apply exactly to the context you are concerned with. Here you use the dictionary to fill out and clarify what you learn from the passage itself.

In word status and pronunciation you are even more on your own. The only real teacher here is observation of what goes on in the circle you belong to or in the one to which you aspire. The dictionary gives you a more or less informed opinion, but it cannot override the facts that confront you. Don't start correcting your betters if they pronounce a word one way and the dictionary suggests another.

Above all, remember that the dictionary does not make laws. It reports usage, usually accurately, sometimes not. It reports mostly the usage of educated people, therefore of the class to which you belong or into which you are moving. It reports, in some degree, your usage. You may have, quite properly, a low opinion of yourself. You are, after all, an insignificant college freshman, depressingly ignorant, dismally unacquainted with literature. Very likely your lack of culture exhibits itself in everything from bad table manners to poor taste in motion pictures. Nevertheless, you're a member of the educated class or at least hovering on its outskirts. You're going to college, aren't you?

SUGGESTIONS

1. Look up and write out the etymologies of the following words.

   promenade, pajamas, candidate, explode, bowdlerize, bishop, companion, mosquito, assassin, brandy, bride, tawdry, foible, deck, grotto, hazard, hoodoo, ticket, ransack, slogan, buxom, boor, villain, nice

2. Find the status designations given for the following words or for some of their meanings.

   avaunt, aggravate, hefty, dough, hain't, hack, miscreant, tough, grease, topping

3. How many numbered meanings are given in your dictionary for each of the following?

   top, suit, set, interest, go, dip, cut, current, green, labyrinth

4. Find the synonymies in your dictionary that discuss the following words.

   gloom, appropriate, celebrate, intrepid, require, womanly, comical, ignoble, fashion, episode

5. Without using the dictionary, distinguish as well as you can among the following synonyms. Then compare your distinctions with those given in the synonymy in the dictionary.

   arrogant, haughty, proud, insolent, overbearing, disdainful

6. Use the *Oxford English Dictionary* to find the earliest occurrence in English writing of the following words.

camouflage, bonus, raft, admiration, jaunty, agog, gas, violin, embryo, zoo, England, fitful

7. Report on one of the following. Possible references are given in parentheses.

(1) Noah Webster as a Spelling Reformer (Mencken, *The American Language*) (2) Seventeenth Century Dictionaries (Starnes and Noyes, *The English Dictionary from Cawdrey to Johnson*) (3) Difficulties in Making the Oxford Dictionary (Preface to the *Oxford*) (4) Johnson's Views on Lexicography (Preface to Johnson's dictionary) (5) Webster's Dictionary of 1828 (any of numerous books on Noah Webster)

27
How to Say Nothing in Five Hundred Words

239. Nothing About Something

It's Friday afternoon, and you have almost survived another week of classes. You are just looking forward dreamily to the week end when the English instructor says: "For Monday you will turn in a five-hundred word composition on college football."

Well, that puts a good big hole in the week end. You don't have any strong views on college football one way or the other. You get rather excited during the season and go to all the home games and find it rather more fun than not. On the other hand, the class has been reading Robert Hutchins in the anthology and perhaps Shaw's "Eighty-Yard Run," and from the class discussion you have got the idea that the instructor thinks college football is for the birds. You are no fool, you. You can figure out what side to take.

After dinner you get out the portable typewriter that you got for high school graduation. You might as well get it over with and enjoy Saturday and Sunday. Five hundred words is about two double-spaced pages with normal margins. You put in a sheet of paper, think up a title, and you're off:

WHY COLLEGE FOOTBALL SHOULD BE ABOLISHED

College football should be abolished because it's bad for the school and also bad for the players. The players are so busy practicing that they don't have any time for their studies.

This, you feel, is a mighty good start. The only trouble is that it's only thirty-two words. You still have four hundred and sixty-eight to go, and you've pretty well exhausted the subject. It comes to you that you do your best thinking in the morning, so you put away the typewriter and go to the movies. But the next morning you have to do your washing and some math problems, and in the afternoon you go to the game. The English instructor turns up too, and you wonder if you've taken the right side after all. Saturday night you have a date, and Sunday morning you have to go to church. (You shouldn't let English assignments interfere with your religion.) What with one thing and another, it's ten o'clock Sunday night before you get out the typewriter again. You make a pot of coffee and start to fill out your views on college football. Put a little meat on the bones.

WHY COLLEGE FOOTBALL SHOULD BE ABOLISHED

In my opinion, it seems to me that college football should be abolished. The reason why I think this to be true is because I feel that football is bad for the colleges in nearly every respect. As Robert Hutchins says in his article in our anthology in which he discusses college football, it would be better if the colleges had race horses and had races with one another, because then the horses would not have to attend classes. I firmly agree with Mr. Hutchins on this point, and I am sure that many other students would agree too.

One reason why it seems to me that college football is bad is that it has become too commercial. In the olden times when people played football just for the fun of it, maybe college football was all right, but they do not play football just for the fun of it now as they used to in the old days. Nowadays college football is what you might call a big business. Maybe this is not true at all schools, and I don't think it is especially true here at State, but certainly this is the case at most colleges and universities in America nowadays, as Mr. Hutchins points out in his very interesting article. Actually the coaches and alumni go around to the high schools and offer the high school stars large salaries to come to their colleges and play football for them. There was one case where a high school star was offered a convertible if he would play football for a certain college.

Another reason for abolishing college football is that it is bad for the players. They do not have time to get a college education, because they are so busy playing football. A football player has to practice every afternoon from three to six, and then he is so tired that he can't concentrate on his studies. He just feels like dropping off to sleep after dinner, and then the next day he goes to his classes without having studied and maybe he fails the test.

(Good ripe stuff so far, but you're still a hundred and fifty-one words from home. One more push.)

Also I think college football is bad for the colleges and the universities because not very many students get to participate in it. Out of a college of ten thousand students only seventy-five or a hundred play football, if that many. Football is what you might call a spectator sport. That means that most people go to watch it but do not play it themselves.

(Four hundred and fifteen. Well, you still have the conclusion, and when you retype it, you can make the margins a little wider.)

These are the reasons why I agree with Mr. Hutchins that college football should be abolished in American colleges and universities.

On Monday you turn it in, moderately hopeful, and on Friday it comes back marked "weak in content" and sporting a big "D."

This essay is exaggerated a little, not much. The English

instructor will recognize it as reasonably typical of what an assignment on college football will bring in. He knows that nearly half of the class will contrive in five hundred words to say that college football is too commercial and bad for the players. Most of the other half will inform him that college football builds character and prepares one for life and brings prestige to the school. As he reads paper after paper all saying the same thing in almost the same words, all bloodless, five hundred words dripping out of nothing, he wonders how he allowed himself to get trapped into teaching English when he might have had a happy and interesting life as an electrician or a confidence man.

Well, you may ask, what can you do about it? The subject is one on which you have few convictions and little information. Can you be expected to make a dull subject interesting? As a matter of fact, this is precisely what you are expected to do. This is the writer's essential task. All subjects, except sex, are dull until somebody makes them interesting. The writer's job is to find the argument, the approach, the angle, the wording that will take the reader with him. This is seldom easy, and it is particularly hard in subjects that have been much discussed: College Football, Fraternities, Popular Music, Is Chivalry Dead?, and the like. You will feel that there is nothing you can do with such subjects except repeat the old bromides. But there are some things you can do which will make your papers, if not throbbingly alive, at least less insufferably tedious than they might otherwise be.

240. Avoid the Obvious Content

Say the assignment is college football. Say that you've decided to be against it. Begin by putting down the arguments that come to your mind: it is too commercial, it takes the students' minds off their studies, it is hard on the players, it makes the university a kind of circus instead of an intellectual center, for most schools it is financially ruinous. Can you think of any more arguments just off hand? All right. Now when you write your paper, *make sure that you don't use any of the material on this list.* If these are the points that leap to your mind, they will leap to everyone else's too, and whether you get a "C" or a "D" may depend on whether the instructor reads your paper early when he is fresh and tolerant or late, when the sentence "In my opinion, college football has become too commercial," inexorably repeated, has brought him to the brink of lunacy.

Be against college football for some reason or reasons of your own. If they are keen and perceptive ones, that's splendid. But even if they are trivial or foolish or indefensible, you are still ahead so long as they are not everybody else's reasons too. Be against it because the colleges don't spend enough money on it to make it worth while, because it is bad for the characters of the spectators, because the players are forced to attend classes, because the football stars hog all the beautiful women, because it competes with baseball and is therefore un-American and possibly Communist inspired. There are lots of more or less unused reasons for being against college football.

Sometimes it is a good idea to sum up and dispose of the trite and conventional points before going on to your own. This has the advantage of indicating to the reader that you are going to be neither trite nor conventional. Something like this:

> We are often told that college football should be abolished because it has become too commercial or because it is bad for the players. These arguments are no doubt very cogent, but they don't really go to the heart of the matter.

Then you go to the heart of the matter.

241. Take the Less Usual Side

One rather simple way of getting interest into your paper is to take the side of the argument that most of the citizens will want to avoid. If the assignment is an essay on dogs, you can, if you choose, explain that dogs are faithful and lovable companions, intelligent, useful as guardians of the house and protectors of children, indispensable in police work—in short, when all is said and done, man's best friends. Or you can suggest that those big brown eyes conceal, more often than not, a vacuity of mind and an inconstancy of purpose; that the dogs you have known most intimately have been mangy, ill-tempered brutes, incapable of instruction; and that only your nobility of mind and fear of arrest prevent you from kicking the flea-ridden animals when you pass them on the street.

Naturally, personal convictions will sometimes dictate your approach. If the assigned subject is "Is Methodism Rewarding to the Individual?" and you are a pious Methodist, you have really no choice. But few assigned subjects, if any, will fall in this category. Most of them will lie in broad areas of discussion with much to be said on both sides. They are intellectual exercises, and it is legitimate to argue now one way and now another, as debaters do in similar circumstances. Always take the side that looks to you hardest, least defensible. It will almost always turn out to be easier to write interestingly on that side.

This general advice applies where you have a choice of subjects. If you are to choose among "The Value of Fraternities" and "My Favorite High School Teacher" and "What I Think About Beetles," by all means plump for the beetles. By the time the instructor gets to your paper, he will be up to his ears in tedious tales about the French teacher at Bloombury High and assertions about how fraternities build character and prepare one for life. Your views on beetles, whatever they are, are bound to be a refreshing change.

Don't worry too much about figuring out what the instructor thinks about the subject so that you can cuddle up with him. Chances are his views are no stronger than yours. If he does have convictions and you oppose them, his problem is to keep from grading you higher than you deserve in order to show he is not biased. This doesn't mean that you should always cantankerously dissent from what the instructor says; that gets tiresome too. And if the subject assigned is "My Pet Peeve," do not begin, "My pet peeve is the English instructor who assigns papers on 'my pet peeve.'" This was still funny during the War of 1812, but it has sort of lost its edge since then. It is in general good manners to avoid personalities.

242. Slip Out of Abstraction

If you will study the essay on college football in Section 239, you will perceive that one reason for its appalling dullness is that it never gets down to particulars. It is just a series of not very glittering generalities: "football is bad for the colleges," "it has become too commercial," "football is a big business," "it is bad for the players," and so on. Such round phrases thudding against the reader's brain are unlikely to convince him, though they may well render him unconscious.

If you want the reader to believe that college football is bad for the players, you have to do more than say so. You have to display the evil. Take your roommate, Alfred Simkins, the second-string center. Picture poor old Alfy coming home from football practice every evening, bruised and aching, agonizingly tired, scarcely able to shovel the mashed potatoes into his mouth. Let us see him staggering up to the room, getting out his econ textbook, peering desperately at it with his good eye, falling asleep and failing the test in the morning. Let us share his unbearable tension as Saturday draws near. Will he fail, be demoted, lose his monthly allowance, be forced to return to the coal mines? And if he succeeds, what will be his reward? Perhaps a slight ripple of applause when the third-string center replaces him, a moment of elation in the locker room if the team wins, of despair if it loses. What will he look back on when he graduates from college? Toil and torn ligaments. And what will be his future? He is not good enough for pro football, and he is too obscure and weak in econ to succeed in stocks and bonds. College football is tearing the heart from Alfy Simkins and, when it finishes with him, will callously toss aside the shattered hulk.

This is no doubt a weak enough argument for the abolition of college football, but it is a sight better than saying, in three or four variations, that college football (in your opinion) is bad for the players.

Look at the work of any professional writer and notice how constantly he is moving from the generality, the abstract statement, to the concrete example, the facts and figures, the illustration. If he is writing on juvenile delinquency, he does not just tell you that juveniles are (it seems to him) delinquent and that (in his opinion) something should be done about it. He shows you juveniles being delinquent, tearing up movie theatres in Buffalo, stabbing high school principals in Dallas, smoking marijuana in Palo Alto. And more than likely he is moving toward some specific remedy, not just a general wringing of the hands.

It is no doubt possible to be *too* concrete, too illustrative or anecdotal, but few inexperienced writers err this way. For most the soundest advice is to be seeking always for the picture, to be always turning general remarks into seeable examples. Don't say, "Sororities teach girls the social graces." Say, "Sorority life teaches a girl how to carry on a conversation

while pouring tea, without sloshing the tea into the saucer."
Don't say, "I like certain kinds of popular music very much."
Say, "Whenever I hear Gerber Spinklittle play 'Mississippi
Man' on the trombone, my socks creep up my ankles."

243. Get Rid of Obvious Padding

The student toiling away at his weekly English theme is too
often tormented by a figure: five hundred words. How, he
asks himself, is he to achieve this staggering total? Obviously
by never using one word when he can somehow work in ten.

He is therefore seldom content with a plain statement like
"Fast driving is dangerous." This has only four words in it.
He takes thought, and the sentence becomes:

> In my opinion, fast driving is dangerous.

Better, but he can do better still:

> In my opinion, fast driving would seem to be rather dangerous.

If he is really adept, it may come out:

> In my humble opinion, though I do not claim to be an expert on
> this complicated subject, fast driving, in most circumstances,
> would seem to be rather dangerous in many respects, or at least
> so it would seem to me.

Thus four words have been turned into forty, and not an iota
of content has been added.

Now this is a way to go about reaching five hundred words,
and if you are content with a "D" grade, it is as good a way
as any. But if you aim higher, you must work differently. Instead of stuffing your sentences with straw, you must try
steadily to get rid of the padding, to make your sentences lean
and tough. If you are really working at it, your first draft will
greatly exceed the required total, and then you will work it
down, thus:

It is thought in some quarters that fraternities do not contribute
as much as might be expected to campus life.
Some people think that fraternities contribute little to campus
life.

The average doctor who practices in small towns or in the country
must toil night and day to heal the sick.
Most country doctors work long hours.

When I was a little girl, I suffered from shyness and embarrassment in the presence of others.
I was a shy little girl.

It is absolutely necessary for the person employed as a marine
fireman to give the matter of steam pressure his undivided
attention at all times.
The fireman has to keep his eye on the steam gauge.

You may ask how you can arrive at five hundred words at
this rate. Simply. You dig up more real content. Instead of
taking a couple of obvious points off the surface of the topic
and then circling warily around them for six paragraphs, you
work in and explore, figure out the details. You illustrate. You
say that fast driving is dangerous, and then you prove it. How
long does it take to stop a car at forty and at eighty? How
far can you see at night? What happens when a tire blows?
What happens in a head-on collision at fifty miles an hour?
Pretty soon your paper will be full of broken glass and blood
and headless torsos, and reaching five hundred words will not
really be a problem.

244. Call a Fool a Fool

Some of the padding in freshman themes is to be blamed
not on anxiety about the word minimum but on excessive
timidity. The student writes, "In my opinion, the principal of
my high school acted in ways that I believe every unbiased

person would have to call foolish." This isn't exactly what he means. What he means is, "My high school principal was a fool." If he was a fool, call him a fool. Hedging the thing about with "in-my-opinion's" and "it-seems-to-me's" and "as-I-see-it's" and "at-least-from-my-point-of-view's" gains you nothing. Delete these phrases whenever they creep into your paper.

The student's tendency to hedge stems from a modesty that in other circumstances would be commendable. He is, he realizes, young and inexperienced, and he half suspects that he is dopey and fuzzy-minded beyond the average. Probably only too true. But it doesn't help to announce your incompetence six times in every paragraph. Decide what you want to say and say it as vigorously as possible, without apology and in plain words.

Linguistic diffidence can take various forms. One is what we call *euphemism*. This is the tendency to call a spade "a certain garden implement" or women's underwear "unmentionables." It is stronger in some eras than others and in some people than others but it always operates more or less in subjects that are touchy or taboo: death, sex, madness, and so on. Thus we shrink from saying "He died last night" but say instead "passed away," "left us," "joined his Maker," "went to his reward." Or we try to take off the tension with a lighter cliché: "kicked the bucket," "cashed in his chips," "handed in his dinner pail." We have found all sorts of ways to avoid saying *mad:* "mentally ill," "touched," "not quite right upstairs," "feeble-minded," "innocent," "simple," "off his trolley," "not in his right mind." Even such a now plain word as *insane* began as a euphemism with the meaning "not healthy."

Modern science, particularly psychology, contributes many polysyllables in which we can wrap our thoughts and blunt their force. To many writers there is no such thing as a bad schoolboy. Schoolboys are maladjusted or unoriented or misunderstood or in need of guidance or lacking in continued success toward satisfactory integration of the personality as a social unit, but they are never bad. Psychology no doubt makes us better men or women, more sympathetic and tolerant, but it doesn't make writing any easier. Had Shakespeare been confronted with psychology, "To be or not to be" might have come out, "To continue as a social unit or not to do so. That is the personality problem. Whether 'tis a better sign of integration at the conscious level to display a psychic tolerance toward the maladjustments and repressions induced by one's lack of orientation in one's environment or—" But Hamlet would never have finished the soliloquy.

Writing in the modern world, you cannot altogether avoid modern jargon. Nor, in an effort to get away from euphemism, should you salt your paper with four-letter words. But you can do much if you will mount guard against those roundabout phrases, those echoing polysyllables that tend to slip into your writing to rob it of its crispness and force.

245. Beware of the Pat Expression

Other things being equal, avoid phrases like "other things being equal." Those sentences that come to you whole, or in two or three doughy lumps, are sure to be bad sentences. They are no creation of yours but pieces of common thought floating in the community soup.

Pat expressions are hard, often impossible, to avoid, because they come too easily to be noticed and seem too necessary to be dispensed with. No writer avoids them altogether, but good writers avoid them more often than poor writers.

By "pat expressions" we mean such tags as "to all practical intents and purposes," "the pure and simple truth," "from where I sit," "the time of his life," "to the ends of the earth," "in the twinkling of an eye," "as sure as you're born," "over my dead body," "under cover of darkness," "took the easy way out," "when all is said and done," "told him time and time again," "parted the best of friends," "stand up and be counted," "gave him the best years of her life," "worked her fingers to the bone." Like other clichés, these expressions were once forceful. Now we should use them only when we can't possibly think of anything else.

Some pat expressions stand like a wall between the writer and thought. Such a one is "the American way of life." Many student writers feel that when they have said that something accords with the American way of life or does not they have exhausted the subject. Actually, they have stopped at the highest level of abstraction. The American way of life is the complicated set of bonds between a hundred and eighty million ways. All of us know this when we think about it, but the tag phrase too often keeps us from thinking about it.

So with many another phrase dear to the politician: "this great land of ours," "the man in the street," "our national heritage." These may prove our patriotism or give a clue to our political beliefs, but otherwise they add nothing to the paper except words.

246. Colorful Words

The writer builds with words, and no builder uses a raw material more slippery and elusive and treacherous. A writer's work is a constant struggle to get the right word in the right place, to find that particular word that will convey his meaning exactly, that will persuade the reader or soothe him or startle or amuse him. He never succeeds altogether—sometimes he feels that he scarcely succeeds at all—but such successes as he has are what make the thing worth doing.

There is no book of rules for this game. One progresses through everlasting experiment on the basis of ever-widening experience. There are few useful generalizations that one can make about words as words, but there are perhaps a few.

Some words are what we call "colorful." By this we mean that they are calculated to produce a picture or induce an emotion. They are dressy instead of plain, specific instead of general, loud instead of soft. Thus, in place of "Her heart beat," we may write "Her heart *pounded, throbbed, fluttered, danced.*" Instead of "He sat in his chair," we may say, "He *lounged, sprawled, coiled.*" Instead of "It was hot," we may say, "It was *blistering, sultry, muggy, suffocating, steamy, wilting.*"

However, it should not be supposed that the fancy word is always better. Often it is as well to write "Her heart beat" or "It was hot" if that is all it did or all it was. Ages differ in how they like their prose. The nineteenth century liked it rich and smoky. The twentieth has usually preferred it lean and cool. The twentieth century writer, like all writers, is forever seeking the exact word, but he is wary of sounding feverish. He tends to pitch it low, to understate it, to throw it away. He knows that if he gets too colorful, the audience is likely to giggle.

See how this strikes you: "As the rich, golden glow of the sunset died away along the eternal western hills, Angela's limpid blue eyes looked softly and trustingly into Montague's flashing brown ones, and her heart pounded like a drum in time with the joyous song surging in her soul." Some people like that sort of thing, but most modern readers would say, "Good grief," and turn on the television.

247. Colored Words

Some words we would call not so much colorful as colored —that is, loaded with associations, good or bad. All words— except perhaps structure words—have associations of some sort. We have said that the meaning of a word is the sum of the contexts in which it occurs. When we hear a word, we hear with it an echo of all the situations in which we have heard it before.

In some words, these echoes are obvious and discussable. The word *mother,* for example, has, for most people, agreeable associations. When you hear *mother* you probably think of home, safety, love, food, and various other pleasant things. If one writes, "She was like a mother to me," he gets an effect which he would not get in "She was like an aunt to me." The advertiser makes use of the associations of *mother* by working it in when he talks about his product. The politician works it in when he talks about himself.

So also with such words as *home, liberty, fireside, contentment, patriot, tenderness, sacrifice, childlike, manly, bluff, limpid.* All of these words are loaded with favorable associations that would be rather hard to indicate in a straightforward definition. There is more than a literal difference between "They sat around the fireside" and "They sat around the stove." They might have been equally warm and happy around the stove, but *fireside* suggests leisure, grace, quiet tradition, congenial company, and *stove* does not.

Conversely, some words have bad associations. *Mother* suggests pleasant things, but *mother-in-law* does not. Many mothers-in-law are heroically lovable and some mothers drink gin all day and beat their children insensible, but these facts of life are beside the point. The thing is that *mother* sounds good and *mother-in-law* does not.

Or consider the word *intellectual.* This would seem to be a complimentary term, but in point of fact it is not, for it has picked up associations of impracticality and ineffectuality and general dopiness. So also with such words as *liberal, reactionary, Communist, socialist, capitalist, radical, schoolteacher,*

*truck driver, undertaker, operator, salesman, huckster, specu-
lator.* These convey meanings on the literal level, but beyond
that—sometimes, in some places—they convey contempt on
the part of the speaker.

The question of whether to use loaded words or not depends on what is being written. The scientist, the scholar, try
to avoid them; for the poet, the advertising writer, the public
speaker, they are standard equipment. But every writer should
take care that they do not substitute for thought. If you write,
"Anyone who thinks that is nothing but a Socialist (or Communist or capitalist)" you have said nothing except that you
don't like people who think that, and such remarks are effective only with the most naïve readers. It is always a bad mistake to think your readers more naïve than they really are.

248. Colorless Words

But probably most student writers come to grief not with
words that are colorful or those that are colored but with
those that have no color at all. A pet example is *nice,* a word
we would find it hard to dispense with in casual conversation
but which is no longer capable of adding much to a description. Colorless words are those of such general meaning that
in a particular sentence they mean nothing. Slang adjectives,
like *cool* ("That's real cool") tend to explode all over the language. They are applied to everything, lose their original
force, and quickly die.

Beware also of nouns of very general meaning, like *circumstances, cases, instances, aspects, factors, relationships, attitudes, eventualities,* etc. In most circumstances you will find
that those cases of writing which contain too many instances
of words like these will in this and other aspects have factors
leading to unsatisfactory relationships with the reader resulting in unfavorable attitudes on his part and perhaps other

eventualities, like a grade of "D." Notice also what "etc." means. It means "I'd like to make this list longer, but I can't think of any more examples."

SUGGESTIONS

1. The following sentences are wordy. See how much you can shorten them without losing essential meaning.

(1) It is the opinion of many individuals in this land of ours that all young Americans who possess the necessary intelligence and ability should have it in their power to attend some college or university in order to get a higher education. (2) The occupation of being a football coach necessitates a great deal of hard work involving many long hours of toil. (3) My home life during the years of my childhood was not a very happy one owing to numerous disagreements and differences of opinion on the part of my parents. (4) Lorenzo was a world-wide traveler of much renown who had journeyed to many countries and foreign lands and was well known to many people. (5) The modern housewife enjoys the benefits of having and working in an up-to-date kitchen in which numerous labor-saving devices spare her a great deal of the work which housewives of other times used to have to cope with in days gone by.

2. The following topics are somewhat hackneyed. Select one of them and see if you can figure out a new and fresh approach. Organize and write the paper.

(1) The Value of Fraternities (2) Campus Politics (3) Christmas (4) Faults of the Opposite Sex (5) An Ideal Holiday

3. Write a paper on one of the following unpopular subjects.

(1) Dogs Are Not Man's Best Friends (2) Too Many People Go to College (3) Why All College Students Should Study Greek (4) Cars Are Useless Luxuries (5) Why People Shouldn't Have Hobbies

4. The following statements are general and abstract. Frame sentences which will convey the ideas concretely, as illustrated in Section 242.

(1) Sororities teach girls the social graces. (2) Most American boys are interested in cars. (3) My grandmother was a rather irritable old lady. (4) Mountain air is very refreshing. (5) Po-

licemen are usually courteous and pleasant. (6) My last high school English class lacked discipline. (7) Religion can be very comforting to people. (8) Door-to-door selling builds character.

5. For the italicized word in each of the following phrases substitute another word which has a harsher or less favorable connotation. For example, for *firm* in "a firm refusal" one could substitute *obstinate:* "an obstinate refusal." For *childlike* in "a childlike smile" one could substitute *childish*.

(1) a *strict* teacher (2) an *affectionate* mother (3) a *courageous* driver (4) filled with *pride* (5) a *naughty* boy (6) acted *unwisely* (7) a *careful* worker (8) a *plain* dress (9) a large *dog* (10) a little *cottage*

6. Make a detailed criticism of the essay on college football in Section 239.

28
Paragraphs and Logic

249. Between Indentations

It is conventional for books on college composition to contain a chapter on paragraph writing. Lest this book be thought unconventional, we shall put one in here, with the warning, however, that the subject is slippery. We shall see that it is possible to analyze paragraphs and to categorize them; that many have what is called a "topic sentence"; that some are deductive in organization, others inductive, others based on a contrast or a comparison or an illustration. Such analysis has its uses. It trains the inexperienced writer in orderliness and suggests to him possibilities for developing his ideas. But it is not of course the way the professional goes about paragraphing.

The experienced writer does not—or at least, does not usually—think, "Now let's see, what would be a suitable topic sentence for this one." He doesn't think about topic sentences at all. Neither does he stop to reflect whether to develop his next paragraph inductively or to have a shot at a comparison or contrast. He pretty much lets his material control his paragraph-building, automatically avoiding structural monotony and developing his thoughts in an orderly way. The beginner can learn something about paragraphs by conscious study. But, as in other matters, he learns most by intelligent observation and much practice.

One reason why paragraph study is difficult is that no one

can say just what a paragraph is. Paragraphs are much harder to define than sentences, which are hard enough. Of course we can define a paragraph as that stretch of writing between indentations, but to say what sort of unit lies between those indentations or to give instruction on where the indentations should come is another matter. In a short and simple paper, the paragraphing may be obvious. If the writer is making three main points about something and making them briefly, we might advise him to express them in three paragraphs, one paragraph per main point. But in most writing the structure does not stick out so obviously, and the writer is confronted with various legitimate possibilities.

Paragraphing does not depend altogether on logical organization. It rests to some extent on fashion and convention. Paragraphs nowadays are generally shorter than they were fifty or a hundred years ago. In books of the last century, a paragraph often ran through several pages, but the modern reader wants to come up for air oftener. He is alarmed by a solid mass of writing and comforted when it is broken up into chunks. This may or may not indicate that we are more frivolous and flutter-brained than our ancestors were.

At any rate, the present-day writer, when he sees his paragraph lengthening out, will throw in a transition phrase like "at any rate" and treat the reader to a new indentation. This may not represent a major structural break but be simply (as here) a further development of the point of the preceding paragraph. Similarly, the first two paragraphs of this chapter might easily have been one and probably would have been a few decades ago.

One usually tries, however, to avoid a succession of very short paragraphs. Several paragraphs consisting of a line or two or three suggest superficiality, a flitting from one point to another with no bother about development. This hummingbird paragraphing has been used consciously and sometimes with good effect by some professional writers, but mostly it is indicative of immaturity or laziness or both. It is common in the literary efforts of small children.

250. Outlining

An important device for securing logical development and reasonable paragraphing for a composition is the outline. This again is something that the professional writer can and usually does dispense with just because he is a professional. He certainly organizes his paper, but he may do it in his head or with the aid of a few rough notes. But the inexperienced writer is well advised to proceed on the basis of a careful plan, especially for a long piece of writing. Many teachers requires that the outline be turned in along with the finished paper.

So far as form goes, there are two kinds of outlines: sentence outlines and topic outlines. Some instructors like one and some the other. In a sentence outline, each point is made in a complete subject-verb sentence, like this:

> THOUGHTS ON SPIDERS
> I. I have never been able to understand why so many people dislike spiders.
> II. Personally, I am rather fond of spiders.
>   A. Their working habits are interesting and instructive.
>   B. They are clean and unobtrusive.
>   C. Their lethal qualities have been much exaggerated.
> III. If people were better informed about spiders, the common feeling against them would surely change.

In a topic outline, each point is expressed in a word or phrase:

> THOUGHTS ON SPIDERS
> I. The common prejudice against spiders.
> II. The good points of spiders.
>   A. Their interesting habits.

  B. Their good manners.
  C. Their relative innocuousness.
 III. A reasonable evaluation.

These outlines suggest a very simple organization—beginning, body, conclusion, with the body divided into three points. Sometimes you will have four or five main headings and perhaps more subdivisions. But avoid making your outline too complicated; a very detailed blueprint is likely to cramp you in the production of the paper. Also if the outline is very long and detailed and the paper follows it closely, the instructor may guess that you wrote the paper first and the outline afterwards. The outline should be a brief sketch of intention, no more.

A long paper, however, may have a correspondingly long outline. In a term paper running over two thousand words, you may need not only more main headings but subdivisions of the subdivisions of the subdivisions. The usual practice is to use roman numerals for the main headings, capital letters for the first subdivisions, Arabic numerals for the next rank, and small letters for the next, like this:

  II. The good points of spiders.
  A. Their interesting habits.
      1. The making of the web.
         a. The materials of the web.
         b. The starting of the web.
         c. The finished product.
      2. The food problem.
         a. How the web catches the prey.
         b. The advance of the spider.
         c. Delicacies and plain fare.
         d. Some practical difficulties.
      3. The spider at play.
      4. The sex life of the spider.
         a. Mating.
         b. Birth and care of the young.

B. Their good manners.
  1. The spider's willingness to mind his own business.
  2. His quietness and self-control.
  3. His cleanliness.
C. Their relative innocuousness.
  1. The poisonous species.
    a. Their rarity.
    b. Improbability of death from a spider's bite.
  2. The nonpoisonous species.
III. A reasonable evaluation.

There are a couple of matters of form to notice. The usual punctuation is that shown here: in a topic outline, a capital for the first word and a period at the end, no interior capitalization; in a sentence outline, conventional sentence punctuation; for both types, a period after the number or letter introducing each item.

Notice also that there are at least two items in each subdivision. If you have an *A,* you must have a *B;* if you have a 1, you must have a 2; if you have an *a,* you must have a *b.* It is considered illogical to subdivide into one, like this:

  1. The poisonous species.
    a. Their rarity.
  2. The nonpoisonous species.

If you can't think of anything to say about poisonous species except that they are rare, and if you want to get that idea into the outline, then you bring it into the first item:

  1. The rarity of poisonous species.
  2. The nonpoisonous species.

251. The Outline and the Paragraph

You will find that a good outline—or even a mediocre one —will solve many paragraphing problems. The outline tends to mark off the major thought units, just as the paragraphs do in the finished paper. Not that each item in the outline must turn up as a paragraph in the paper. Usually you do not have *more* than one outline item to a paragraph. If item II A 4 a is "Mating" and item II A 4 b is "Birth and care of the young," you will probably give at least a paragraph to each; if not, your outline was too detailed to begin with. But you might well give more than a paragraph to an outline item. You might find that you have more to say about the mating of spiders than a paragraph will conveniently hold, and run on for two or three or four.

The only danger likely to result from following an outline is that the organization will stick out too obviously. A paper should be well organized but not obviously so. It is not necessary, when you come to a new point on the outline, to say, "I have now concluded point number three and am about to proceed to point number four." What is wanted is a smooth and graceful transition. We shall consider ways of effecting such transitions presently.

252. Topic Sentences

A topic sentence is a sentence which states in a general way a point which the rest of the paragraph develops or illustrates. Consider, for example, the following paragraphs:

> It is true that big-time college football works a certain amount of hardship on the players involved. Certainly they have to put in a great many hours of work under the most exacting discipline. Furthermore, this football work—in theory at least—is laid on top of a normal college study load; consequently, the football man cannot be expected to do as well in classwork as the student whose every afternoon and weekend is free. Nor can we deny that football is at best dangerous, at worst lethal. Too many broken bones and torn muscles, plaster casts and crutches testify to the contrary.

Here the topic sentence is the first sentence: "It is true that big-time college football works a certain amount of hardship on the players involved." The rest of the paragraph is a detailing of that general idea, examples of the various hardships. The topic sentence is most likely, as here, to be the first sentence, but not necessarily. The paper might go on:

> But this is only part of the story. It is also true that football players take many benefits from football. Even the third stringer. . . .

Here the first sentence is a transition sentence, and the topic sentence is the second: "It is also true that football players take many benefits from football." The paragraph would then go on to detail the benefits.

Less commonly, topic sentences appear at the end of the paragraph. Here is an example:

> Alfred was learning that his troubles were not nearly so important to other people as they were to him. He was learning what it was like to have problems that no one was willing or able to solve for him. He was learning to smile in public and to cry alone, to keep the important things within him and to let only the trivial ones come out. He was learning, in other words, to be an adult.

Here it is the last sentence that generalizes the point and summarizes the paragraph.

It may strike you, if you make the experiment, that topic sentences are a good deal easier to find in paragraphs written to illustrate them than they are in random paragraphs from, say, a magazine article. This is true, and the reason is that the professional writer is at some pains to cover the structure, to flesh out the skeleton. His control is sure enough so that he doesn't have to put up neon signs to make sure that the reader doesn't lose his way. He sees to it that there is only one road, and he quietly takes the reader along it. He doesn't have always to say, "This, in general, is what I'm going to talk about in this paragraph" or "What I have just said amounts to the following." He often does that—often writes topic sentences—but he doesn't have to. Sometimes it will suffice to leave the general point of the paragraph implied and unstated.

The writer of less experience, however, often does lose his way and mislead his reader. Often he isn't too sure himself what his general point is or whether he is making one point or three or none. It is therefore good training to pay some attention to topic sentences, to make sure that you know what the paragraph is about by saying what it is about. One advantage of making a sentence outline is that you thereby write your topic sentences, or most of them, in advance. They peel off the outline as you go, you develop them, and there you are. A paper written so may be somewhat stiff, too obtrusively organized, but as writing faults go, this is not a bad one.

253. Varieties of Paragraph Development

The particular ways in which paragraphs are organized are likely to be evoked by the nature of the subject. Furthermore, one does not ordinarily, in the agony of creation, pause to decide whether the next paragraph shall be type H or type D. Still, most people can profit from studying specimen paragraphs, analyzing them, and noting various ways by which general ideas can be developed.

Probably the most common kind of organization is the deductive order, in which one states a general proposition and then cites detailed data supporting it. We have already had examples. The paragraph about college football in Section 252 is organized deductively. It begins with the general statement that football is hard on the players and then proceeds to specific hardships.

The opposite of *deductive* is *inductive*. In a paragraph organized inductively, the writer begins with specific facts or particular data and pulls them into a generalization at the end of the paragraph. The paragraph about Alfred in Section 252 is organized inductively. We have first a series of statements about particular things that Alfred is learning and at the end a general statement about what this learning amounts to. The inductive paragraph has a suspenseful quality which may make it very effective.

A paragraph may have as its basis a comparison. This is just a simile worked out elaborately to paragraph length. Instead of saying "Melanie was like a dog," you say,

> Any of Melanie's friends would have been deeply offended to hear her likened to a dog, but the likeness was undeniable. She had the same blind trust in and fidelity to those who fed and petted her. She frolicked when her masters were cheerful and sat quietly in her corner when they were grave. Like a dog, she was generally suspicious of strangers and would sniff and bristle until someone she trusted vouched for them. When circumstances put her on her own, her judgment was no better than that of many a pup: she was only too likely to fawn at the door-to-door salesman and growl at the man who came to read the meter.

Logically opposite to the comparison but similar in construction is the contrast. Differences between two things are explained and developed through the paragraph. There are two obvious ways to go about it. One can describe one thing and then the thing contrasting:

> While we were living on the farm, I kept ducks and my brother Elwood kept pigeons. I thought then, and think now, that he made a poor choice. Surely there is no bird or beast less interesting

than the pigeon. It has neither dignity nor charm. One cannot call it foolish, because it has no affairs to be foolish about or sensible either. Its only activity is a dismal fluttering about the yard in search of crumbs. The duck, on the other hand, is a creature of nobility and worth. Who could fail to be engaged at the sight of the mother duck out for a stroll, with her offspring trooping along behind? They head for the horse trough, and she boosts them in, and off they float like miniature lake steamers, graceful and debonair. The duck, one feels, has purpose and polish and a place in the scheme of things.

Or one can make the contrast point by point:

> While we were living on the farm, I kept ducks and my brother Elwood kept pigeons. I thought then, and think now, that he made a poor choice. Surely there is no bird or beast less interesting than the pigeon, whereas the duck is a constant source of amusement and delight. While the pigeon is fluttering dismally about the yard in search of crumbs, the duck is out for a morning stroll or having its bath or arranging its feathers or reprimanding its young. The pigeon is clearly a superfluity whose presence can only be tolerated, but the duck is a solid citizen with a secure place in the scheme of things. I could never understand how Elwood could prefer his stupid and stolid pigeons to my graceful, noble ducks.

Many paragraphs in expository writing are essentially definitions, and these have their own organization. One may begin with an explanation of the need for defining the word or concept and then proceed to the details. Such paragraphs often involve some kind of contrast—between the meaning sometimes given to the word and the meaning the writer intends it to have:

> Before going further, we should be clear on what is meant by "the professional class." The word *profession* is nowadays very widely applied, so that one speaks sometimes of the advertising profession, the engineering profession, the safe-cracking profession, indeed. I use the word here, however, in an older and more

restricted sense. By "professional class" I shall mean those callings attained usually by special postgraduate study. I include the doctor, the dentist, the lawyer, the minister, the teacher but exclude the advertiser, the engineer, the writer, the artist, the businessman.

These are a few obvious ways in which paragraphs may be developed. You will perceive that logical classification of paragraphs is a difficult and very slippery business. Paragraphs in professional writing are not likely to be simply one thing or another but complicated blends. Thus a paragraph may be deductive in order and at the same time imply a definition, suggest a contrast, and be strewn with illustrations. To go through a magazine article trying to categorize the paragraphs according to a logical scheme would certainly be a maddening exercise and probably not a very fruitful one.

What the student wishing to improve his paragraphs should seek for is first of all some kind of order, whether it is simple or complicated. Too many student paragraphs are merely aimless. They should have some logical direction, be moving to or from a general point, be growing out of or into a definition or contrast or comparison or whatever the content directs. Secondly, they should be meaty. Follow the point you are making to its conclusions, work it out. Don't just say that spiders are interesting and that you like them a lot. Take the reader into the spider's home life and let him see just what it is that engages your interest.

Above all, illustrate and illustrate and illustrate. Your general statements hold the paper together and make it understandable. Your specific statements make it readable.

254. Beginnings and Endings

The writer has not only to see to it that his paper has a tight and logical organization, proceeding point by point to a conclusion. He has also to conceal this organization from the reader. The paragraphs should not thud against the reader successively like massive blocks but should flow into one another with smoothness and grace.

Such smoothness is ordinarily achieved by the use of sentence connectors (*however, therefore, consequently, nevertheless,* etc.), by conjunctions (*and, but, nor, yet,* etc.), by certain pronouns or determiners (*such, this, these*), by various transitional phrases (*on the other hand, in addition to, on the contrary, for example, as a matter of fact*). Look at a book or magazine and notice how often some such device occurs in the first sentences of paragraphs.

If you make no transition at all, the reader may be confused. Suppose you are writing on spiders. One paragraph discusses how interesting they are, the next their commendable cleanliness. Suppose you write this:

> . . . and in many other ways. I could sit all day long watching spiders, and indeed I often do.
> They are very clean. Nobody could ever say that spiders are careless about personal hygiene. Most spiders. . . .

You have been talking about their interesting ways. Is their cleanliness another interesting way, or is it another point? It is another point, but the reader may not realize it unless you help him. There are innumerable ways to make the transition. You can do it obviously:

> My second point about spiders is that they are very clean.
> My second reason for liking spiders is their cleanliness.

But it is better to be a little more subtle:

> Spiders are not only interesting but also very clean.
> Spiders are among the cleanest of God's creatures as well as the most interesting.
> We should note in addition the spider's remarkable cleanliness.

Or simply:

> Spiders are also very clean.

Transitions are particularly important when the direction of the paper takes a sharp turn. Suppose you have been discussing the hardships endured by the football player and wish now to point out his rewards, and suppose you write:

> . . . bruises and broken legs. One sometimes wonders how men are persuaded to go out for football.
> The football player receives many rewards. He. . . .

The reader would have a hard time figuring out what you are about. You have to show the change in direction. This may be done with a transition word or two or may be accomplished more elaborately:

> But the football player receives many rewards.
> But in truth the football player is amply rewarded for his broken bones.
> This, however, is only one side of the picture. Actually the football player is amply rewarded.

Take some care with the end of the paragraph as well as the beginning. Don't let it vapor off like this one:

> Most of the borrowed words in the English vocabulary come from Latin, French, or Greek. The French borrowings are the result of the Norman Conquest and the consequent English interest in and admiration for French things and ideas. Words from Latin and Greek have come into English in all periods but most importantly during and since the Renaissance with its renewal of enthusiasm for ancient culture. Of course many other languages, like Italian, Spanish, and Arabic, have also contributed to the English vocabulary.

Left at this, the paragraph is weak. The last sentence wanders off from the main point, and the reader is left uncertain about what the writer is getting at. Something like this is needed:

. . . Of course many other languages, like Italian, Spanish, and Arabic, have also contributed to the English vocabulary. But this contribution is really trivial compared to that of Latin, French, and Greek.

Finally, we might say something about beginning and ending the theme as a whole. Writers go to some pains to engage the reader in the first sentence, knowing that if they don't they may not have a chance in the second. It is sometimes pleasant to begin startlingly, with what fiction writers call a "narrative hook":

Have you ever swallowed a scorpion?

Though he probably doesn't know it, the average homeowner has on his kitchen shelf a can of poison sufficient to wipe out a town of five thousand people.

I have decided never to enter another supermarket as long as I live.

But one can begin more quietly and soberly with results just as good. The thing to avoid is the prosy and tedious beginning that circles around the subject before coming to grips with it:

I am going to write on the advantages and disadvantages of college football. I do not know very much about this complicated and interesting subject, but I believe that college football has more disadvantages than advantages. I am therefore going to discuss the advantages.

The first advantage to college football that I wish to stress is. . . .

The only reader who would read farther is the instructor getting paid for it, and he would feel that he was not getting paid enough.

Avoid also the use of the title in the first sentence of the paper. If, for example, the title is "My Relations with Spiders," the first sentence should not be, "On the whole, my relations with spiders have been very pleasant ones." Either the sentence or the title should be changed.

The last paragraph is just as important as the first. It is what leaves the reader moved or unmoved. In classwork, it may make the instructor decide to drop the grade to a "D" or boost it to a "B." It is often a good idea, particularly in a serious paper, to summarize the argument or restate the thesis in the last paragraph. Again, one tries to be reasonably subtle and to avoid conclusions like:

> *avoid* In conclusion, I wish to state that I think football should be abolished in our colleges. I hope that the reasons I have given will have convinced the reader.

One might say instead:

> It is too much to hope that the colleges will soon abolish football. As we have seen, it is supported by too many interests, too intricately enmeshed in the college machinery. But this cannot keep us from saying that the colleges *should* abolish it, and the sooner the better. Ripping it out of college life will be painful and shattering, but leaving it in will be ruinous.

Try to save your strongest punch for the end. Leave your reader laughing if you can, or leave him breathless or angry or weeping, but don't just wander off and leave him.

SUGGESTIONS

1. Develop a paragraph from each of the following topic sentences.

(1) The coeducational college has certain obvious advantages. (2) To be sure, some television programs are worthless. (3) In some ways the oldest child in the family is better off than the youngest. (4) The life of the modern housewife is not altogether a happy one. (5) Let us try to be clear on what we mean by politics. (6) Women are usually more sensitive than men.

2. Examine the first twenty paragraphs of a magazine article and describe the transitional devices used to link them.

3. Illustrate four different kinds of paragraph development by writing four paragraphs in imitation of those illustrated in Sections 252 and 253.

4. Make both a sentence and a topic outline for a five-hundred word paper on one of the following subjects. The subject you choose may have to be narrowed and focused to make it containable in five hundred words.

(1) Gardens   (2) The Parking Problem   (3) Traveling with One's Family   (4) Boarding Houses   (5) The Best Job I Ever Had (6) Commuting

5. Write a paper from your outline.

29
Facts and Fancy

255. The Term Paper

In most freshman English courses the students are required at some time to write what is called a "term paper" or "research paper." This is a longish paper—anywhere from two thousand to ten thousand words—based on research and involving footnotes, outline, and bibliography. It is a headache for all concerned.

It is debatable—and frequently debated—how much one actually learns from writing the term paper, and, further, how much value there is to what is learned. Certainly, the mechanical matters—footnotes and width of margins and section headings and the like—are not of earth-shaking importance. The topics investigated ("The Dangers of Antibiotics," "Early New Orleans Jazz," "The Dred Scott Decision") seldom produce lifelong interests. Of more value is the training received from having to grapple with a large subject, to prune and organize it and get it down on paper.

But clearly the chief worth of the term paper lies in what it teaches about how to deal with facts, how to distinguish between facts and opinion, about what is evidence and what is not. An ability to look at the data and on the basis of the data to form a cool and objective judgment is one of the marks of a mature and sophisticated person. It is also one of the marks of civilization; a chief reason why the western world has been able to make its spectacular advances is that enough of its citizens have been able to brush through the fog of superstition and hearsay knowledge and look the facts in the eye.

In the succeeding chapters we shall discuss how to gather information and, having gathered it, what to do with it. In this chapter we shall be concerned with information itself and the task, often difficult but always important, of distinguishing between fact and fancy.

256. Deductive and Inductive Reasoning

We employed the terms *deductive* and *inductive* in discussing paragraph development, saying that the deductive order is that which proceeds from the general statement to the particulars presented in illustration or proof, whereas the inductive order is that which proceeds from the particulars to the general statement. The terms are also, and more significantly, applied to the process of reasoning. In deductive reasoning, we begin with a general truth or proposition and figure out what the facts must be; in inductive reasoning we begin with the facts and let them lead us to the general truth.

Deductive reasoning was the prime tool of premodern thought. To be sure, it was not the only tool. There have always been people, not content to sit in their studies and think, who conducted practical experiments and learned much about the practical world. There were many such in the ancient world; the ancient Greeks not only knew that the earth was round but knew how far it was around it, and some were aware that it was not the center of the universe. But most thinkers did simply sit in their studies and think, and they thought deductively. They supposed that some truths were unchallengeable and that beginning with these one could understand anything worth understanding.

Deductive reasoning did sometimes produce knowledge

and lead to truth, but more often it produced learned non-sense. We have only to consider such ancient sciences as astrology, alchemy, and medicine. You begin with the assumption that the position of the stars influences people's lives, and you arrive presently at a most elaborate scheme involving ascendants, planetary positions, and phases of the moon. Or you begin with the notion that the functioning of the body is regulated by the proportions in it of four fluids or "humours," and pretty soon you have not only a totally erroneous description of human physiology, but a myriad of ingenious treatments through which doctors could push their patients into the grave rather more quickly than they would have arrived there by normal processes. Medical science has only recently recovered from the errors into which deductive reasoning led it—perhaps, indeed, has not altogether recovered yet.

Toward the end of the Middle Ages, more and more people began to go about it in the other way: instead of imagining facts to fit conclusions, they formed conclusions to fit facts. Galileo dropping objects of different weights off his tower is a famous example. They dropped at the same speed and thereby blasted many a venerable conclusion about the physical universe into oblivion. Copernicus, Kepler, da Vinci, Francis Bacon, Harvey, Newton, Lavoisier and many others looked at other facts and drew other conclusions and as a result utterly changed the world and our notions about it.

Inductive reasoning is the basis not only of the modern physical sciences but of all modern scholarship. The scholar, whether he is investigating the antecedents of the Mayan civilization or the relationship of divorce to juvenile delinquency or the table manners of George the Second, must begin by assembling all the pertinent data. He may very well have his notions about what conclusions the data will lead him to, but he must be careful not to arrive at the conclusions ahead of the facts. If the facts turn out to contradict his notions, then he revises his notions; he doesn't revise the facts. That, at least, is what he is supposed to do. Sometimes it is difficult.

257. Proving a Thesis

Let us consider Galileo climbing up the Tower of Pisa with a one-pound ball and a ten-pound ball. The learned doctors of philosophy would have told him that the ten-pound ball would drop ten times as fast as the one-pound ball, being ten times the weight, and would have cited numerous treatises to prove it. Now Galileo wasn't toiling up the tower to prove that the learned doctors were right. What fun would there be in that? He had a hunch (*hypothesis* would be a more dignified term) that they were wrong, and he was out to prove them wrong.

Well, he dropped the balls, and sure enough, they fell at the same speed, and Galileo was able to climb down the tower and write a paper that would knock out another piece of the wall of medieval thought. But suppose it had turned out otherwise. Suppose the big ball *had* fallen ten times as fast as the other. Then scholarly integrity would have left him only one course—to go down and report that he had proved conclusively that the authorities had been right all the time and he, Galileo, altogether wrong. Nothing could be more joyless, but he would have had no decent alternative.

The decisions that scholars have to make are not usually so clear-cut, and for that reason are likely to be more difficult and painful. You begin by toying with the notion that what are called the plays of Shakespeare were actually written by Thomas Middleton. What a spectacular thing this would be if it could be proved. You see a bit of evidence here and there supporting the hypothesis, and you seize these bits and look for more. Not really meaning to, you tend to ignore evidence pointing the other way. Pretty soon you're half blind. You can see the Middleton evidence and can't see the other, or, if the other is forced on you, you become adept at twisting it and reinterpreting it to fit your purpose. You have intended to proceed inductively, going from facts to conclusion, but because of your psychological investment in Middleton as the author of Shakespeare, you have ended by reasoning deductively: accepting the conclusion and arranging the facts to fit it.

Such pressure bears not only on professional scholars but on all scholars, including those preparing research papers for the freshman English course. You decide to write a paper on "The Common Cold." Your instructor tells you, as he surely will, that this is too big a subject and that you must cut it down, so you decide to write on "The Connection Between Colds and Wet Feet." Something you read suggests that there may not be any connection, and you think how nice it would be if it should turn out so. You would have a good strong paper attacking what you would show to be only a popular superstition. So you read the literature on the subject, hoping for the best. If you are really of a scientific turn, you persuade all your relatives to sit around in wet socks and see if they get more colds than usual. If all the evidence supports your hypothesis, well and good. You have your ammunition.

But maybe it won't turn out that way. Maybe the evidence will show that Grandma was on the right track when she said, "Elbert, take off those wet clothes before you catch your death of cold." Worse still, maybe the evidence will be inconclusive, some of it pointing one way and some the other. No matter. Whatever the evidence is, that is what you're stuck with. You do your very best to look at the data with a clear and disinterested eye, especially when it conflicts with your pet notions, and you never, never, never deliberately ignore a piece of evidence just because it is convenient to ignore it.

258. Authorities

In Geoffrey Chaucer's *Prologue to the Canterbury Tales* there is a portrait of a fourteenth century physician. Chaucer, wishing to impress his reader with what a splendid doctor this doctor was, tells us that he was intimately familiar with all the old medical authorities. He knew the works of Hippocrates and Galen and Averroes and many another eminent medical man of a hundred or five hundred or fifteen hundred years back. He was careful to carry out the treatments recommended by these scholars.

Nothing could so clearly illustrate the difference between modern and ancient science. Suppose you asked someone to recommend a doctor, and he said, "Why don't you try Dr. Whooziz? Whooziz is very well versed in the works of the great medical men of 1850 or even earlier. He will give you exactly the same treatment that Galen gave his patients in the second century." Whatever doctor you chose, it wouldn't be Whooziz.

The modern world—or at least the modern scientific world —has an entirely different attitude toward authoritative pronouncements than the world of the Middle Ages had. In earlier days, the more ancient and musty an idea was, the better it was, the more venerable and unchallengeable. An idea became enshrined when it was written down by an eminent man, and to say "Galen says so" or "Aquinas rules" or "We learn from Anselm" was to settle the matter beyond appeal.

Nowadays we feel that knowledge is cumulative and progressive. Every scholar is better than the last because, presumably, he begins where the last one left off. Any green physicist in the University of Minnesota is a better physicist than Isaac Newton, because he knows what Newton knew and also what has been learned since. He is probably not as great an intellect, but he is certainly a better physicist. In any scientific or scholarly investigation we begin with what is already known and go on from there. This is not to say that we scorn or necessarily reject the statements of our predecessors; it is to say simply that we are not limited by them.

The modern physical scientists have been able to emancipate themselves from authority, because they are able to put everything to the test of controlled laboratory experiment. If Smithers says that water boils at 212 degrees and Judkins says, no, he thinks it boils at 206, you don't have to take the word of either one of them. You can get some water and a bunsen burner and a thermometer and find out for yourself. But in historical studies, and most term papers are in some sense historical studies, we do have to depend to some extent on authorities, and we therefore have to develop some skill in measuring their dependability.

259. Evaluating Sources

First of all, we make a fundamental distinction between *primary sources* and *secondary sources,* and when we have a choice we prefer to work from primary sources. Suppose you are writing a paper on the early history of Santa Fe, New Mexico. The primary sources would be documents contemporary with the early settlement: contemporary newspapers, diaries of early settlers, letters, records of births and deaths, records of property transactions, contemporary accounts of all kinds. Secondary sources would be histories, articles, encyclopedia accounts relating to the settlement of the town. In the nature of things, students writing term papers have to depend mostly or altogether on secondary sources; the primary sources will usually be too widely scattered or otherwise inaccessible to be utilized. But occasionally a student will have a chance to check a historian's statement against the primary material on which it rests, and he should of course do so. Very occasionally a student will have access to primary material which no other writer has seen. This is interesting indeed.

In using either primary or secondary sources, but particularly secondary, the student must ponder the question of reliability. He must rid himself of the notion that any statement automatically becomes true when it is printed in a book. Any fool can write a book and many fools have, and they have written a vast quantity of nonsense and downright lies in them too. The student who aspires to scholarship must learn how to tell the lies from the truth and the sense from the nonsense. This is not easy when the field is one which one doesn't know very well.

One thing to do is, in evaluating secondary sources, to pay attention to the date of your authority. Usually, in scientific or scholarly pursuits, later works are to be preferred to earlier ones because the later writer has the benefit of all intervening research. If you are writing on the prospects of curing cancer, you will obviously be better informed by an article written in 1958 than by one written in 1938. If you are writing on the Anglo-Saxon invasion of England in the fifth century, a twentieth century history is more reliable than a nineteenth century one because it can take account of recent archaeological finds and is also likely to employ a somewhat more rigorous scientific method.

Sometimes an early historical work will for special reasons have special value. The earliest full-scale account of the history of the unhappy Donner party, snowbound in the Sierras in 1846, was written by one C. F. McGlashan in 1880. Unlike later historians, McGlashan was able to interview many of the survivors, and his work therefore rests on primary material unavailable to his successors. One therefore has to give a McGlashan statement about actions and motives of the Donner people a little special weight; he may have had evidence for it that we know nothing about. One doesn't have to believe it necessarily, but one does have to give it special weight. At any rate, always pay attention to the date of your authorities. If you don't, you may be betrayed into idiocies. The student discussing the liquor problem writes, "W. E. Gorgenshed argues that the saloon is on the way out because it cannot resist the progressive forces in modern America." This seems rather puzzling until you look in the bibliography and discover that Mr. Gorgenshed wrote his book in 1906.

260. Popular Writing and Scholarly Writing

Consider also the audience for whom your authority is writing. If he is addressing scholars, other experts in the field, his remarks are more likely to be trustworthy than if he is addressing the general public. An article on cancer in the *American Medical Journal* is more likely to be reliable than an article on cancer in the *Reader's Digest*. An article on Russia in the *American Slavic and East European Review* is more likely to be reliable than an article on Russia in the *Saturday Evening Post*. To get into a scholarly journal, an article has to be pretty sound. It has to satisfy the critical eye of editors who are probably experts in the matter themselves. The editor of a scholarly magazine is jealously guarding the reputation of the magazine and the integrity of the field. But the editor of the popular magazine has no particular competence in the various fields of scholarship and no stake in their integrity. He is interested primarily in circulation. He would like the material in his articles to be true, of course, but his primary concern is not that it be true but that it be interesting.

Beware also of books that are popularizations of such fields as physics, mathematics, anthropology, linguistics, medicine.

Some popularizations are very good indeed, but most of them are poor. It is a very hard thing to take an intricate and complicated field of study and make it understandable to the layman (let alone interesting) without violently distorting the facts. A popularization by an expert in the field is likely to be true but not interesting. A popularization by a nonexpert is likely to be interesting but not true.

The freshman student given a choice between a scholarly book or article and a popularization will almost always plump for the popularization, and for most understandable reasons. Often he will be able to understand the scholarly work only with great difficulty, perhaps not at all. But if you do use popularizations, be careful. Look up the author in *Who's Who* and see what else he has written, what positions he has held, what standing he has among scholars. Don't go by what his publisher or editor says about him. If he has written an article on cancer, you can bet that he will be billed as "a renowned physician." Maybe he is; and maybe he's a quack with no standing among medical men. If he has written a piece on Russia, the magazine will surely introduce him as "an outstanding expert on foreign affairs." Maybe so; and maybe he's a hack that the editor called in to whomp up an article on Russia.

Try to make allowance for whatever bias your authorities may have. Most scholars try to be objective in what they write, but they don't all succeed by any means. Many writers who are not scholars do not even try. If you are trying to assign the blame for the Second World War, you will of course read the works of Adolph Hitler and also those of Sir Winston Churchill, but you will not expect to find in either a cool and objective report. If you are writing a paper on the liquor problem, you cannot expect to get an unbiased analysis from the president of the WCTU or from the president of a distillery. You might get useful data from both, but you would have to make your own evaluation of it.

261. Common Sense

Common sense has been defined as that quality which persuades us that the earth is flat. More charitably, it is the faculty which permits us to move reasonably and adequately in our social milieu, to manage our affairs satisfactorily, to avoid disastrous mistakes.

But in scholarship, whose aim is to get at the truth, common sense will often prove a rather serious handicap. The practical man's common sense will often turn out on inspection to be a mélange of prejudice, hearsay knowledge, and superstition. The reason it works so well in practical matters is that other practical people have the same prejudices and superstition. Common sense changes from one place and time to another. To people of the Middle Ages it was only common sense that the configuration of the stars and planets at one's birth influenced the events of one's life. This was a reasonable and practical thing to believe in the twelfth century, when most other people believed the same thing.

Similarly one may suppose that to a Russian Communist it is only common sense that the people should have no say in the management of a "people's democracy." To give the people a free vote, common sense tells him, would leave them prey to subtle and dangerous forces of reaction which, common sense hammers home, are lurking behind every Russian hedge. This Russian common sense no doubt works very well as long as the Russian Communist is in the company of other Russian Communists, people with the same education, the same fears and prejudices as he. When he gets out into the

United Nations and finds that people there oppose his views, he no doubt concludes that they are either simply wicked or are lacking in common sense.

In our daily pursuits we all have to rely on common sense most of the time. That is, we have to proceed according to general, untested views that we have received unquestioningly from the world around us. We cannot analyze each glass of water to determine whether or not it is free from harmful bacteria. We must let common sense tell us that it is safe to drink or that it is not. But when we become scientists and scholars, when we write term papers for our English classes, then we must be moderately skeptical about what common sense tells us.

Suppose you are writing a paper on the evils of smoking. You have proceeded through such points as the financial disadvantages, the messiness of the habit, the inconvenience to nonsmokers, and have come to the effects on health. Common sense tells you that to take that smoke into the lungs hour after hour, year after year, will have most deleterious effects on lungs, heart, and liver, and very likely common sense tells you true. But consider how very difficult it has been for scientists to prove it true. Hundreds of scientists have made thousands of experiments at a cost of millions of dollars and have achieved results that are still somewhat tentative and very complicated. For a term-paper writer, on the basis of what common sense tells him, to make simple and positive statements about what cigarette smoking does to the inner organs would be presumptuous indeed.

Beware, then, when you find you have written an expression like "Common sense tells us" or "As everybody knows" or "It is common knowledge that" or "Nobody believes." These, you will find, can frequently be translated: "My father says,"

"Most of the fellows in my fraternity agree," "The football coach at my high school told us," "Very few Republican protestants that I have met believe" and so on.

It is common knowledge that little boys who smoke cigarettes get their growth stunted. The present writer knows this to be common knowledge, because his grandmother, who imparted the information to him, said it was common knowledge. He therefore did not smoke cigarettes when he was a little boy, and he grew to be nearly six feet tall. This, he feels, pretty well proves that his grandmother was right. Consequently he does not permit *his* little boys to smoke cigarettes and stunt their growth. Besides, common sense tells him who would have to pay for the cigarettes.

SUGGESTIONS

1. Read an encyclopedia account of the life of one of the following: Galileo, Francis Bacon, Copernicus, William of Ockham, Joseph Priestly, Kepler, Lavoisier, Newton, Harvey. Report on the man's contribution to scientific thought.

2. Typical primary and secondary sources for a paper on the settlement of Santa Fe are described in Section 259. What would be likely primary sources for the following: Abraham Lincoln's education; the conquest of Mexico by the Spaniards; the fate of the Donner party?

3. *Time* magazine makes no bones about the fact that it prints not only what happens but also what its editors think about what happens. Select a *Time* article on politics or national or foreign affairs. Analyze it carefully with a view to distinguishing fact from editorial opinion.

4. Make a list of ten books or articles on a subject on which you might write a research paper. Discuss their relative reliability, considering dates, reputation of the authors, reputation of the publishers.

30
Finding the Facts

262. The Library

The scholar's principal fact receptacle is the library or libraries available to him. The prestige of a university depends not only on the fortunes of its football team but also, very much, on the size and quality of its library. A university with a fine library can attract great scholars, can produce work of lasting significance, and can make of itself a fertile intellectual center. If you want to found a university, you have to begin by assembling a library.

Libraries vary tremendously in size and importance. The largest in this country is the Library of Congress, with many millions of volumes. Other great libraries include those of Yale and Harvard, the New York Public Library, and the libraries of many state universities, like Michigan and California. In England there are such famous libraries as the Bodleian in Oxford and the British Museum in London. The importance of a library does not depend entirely on its size. Many scholars travel to Los Angeles to study in the Huntington Library, which has one of the world's most important collections of rare books and manuscripts.

Libraries are not built by money alone. It is not a question of collecting fifty million dollars and sending in an order to the book publishers. Time and patience and skill are also required, especially time. Many books necessary to a good collection are long out of print and can be had, if at all, only through second-hand book dealers or through purchase of other libraries. This is why it is those schools that have been collecting for centuries, like Harvard, that have the great libraries.

Many college libraries are of course very much smaller than those we have named. It may be that the library of your school contains only fifty or a hundred thousand volumes. If these have been well selected, it will be found that they suffice for general work in general fields, though as you dig deeper into a subject, you may feel the need for works unavailable to you. In that case, you will have to travel or do without. Libraries can borrow books from other libraries, but they do not often do so for the benefit of undergraduates.

Even a small library is a complicated organism. If you use the library at all, it will pay you to understand quite clearly just how it works. Nothing is more futile than to wander aimlessly about the place in the hope of stumbling on the book you want. Nothing is more high-schoolish than to expect the librarians to select your books for you. With a little application you can learn to find what you want quickly and efficiently. Then you will have more time to sit around in the Student Union drinking coffee.

263. The Card Catalogue and the Stacks

The card catalogue is the directory to the contents of the library. It is the set or sets of file drawers located, usually, somewhere near the circulation desk. Here, on three-by-five cards, are listed all the books, reference works, magazines that the library contains. For most books there are at least three cards in the catalogue, sometimes more. A book will be listed once under the name of the author, again by title, and again by subject. Thus a book entitled *The Assassination of Lincoln* by W. H. Snowbird will be found under S (for Snowbird), under A (for Assassination), under L (for Lincoln), and under U (for United States history).

Author and title cards present no particular problem. If you know the book you want by author or by title, you can quickly locate it in the card catalogue. Frequently, however, one uses the card catalogue to find out just what books the library has on a given subject, and here a little thought is required. Large subjects, like the *United States, France, Agriculture,* may fill several drawers in the card catalogue. Such subjects are subdivided. The general subject *France,* for example, will have such subdivisions as *bibliography, biography, description and travel, foreign relations, history, industry,* the fineness of the subdivision depending on the number of books on this subject in the library. Some of these subjects will be further subdivided, *history* by periods, *foreign relations* according to other countries concerned. The point is that in looking up material on a small part of a large subject, you may have to do a certain amount of poking around in the card catalogue.

Whether it is filed under author, title, or subject, a card in the catalogue contains pretty much the same information. A typical card looks like this:

720.973
    Ravenel, Beatrice St. Julien.
    Architects of Charleston by Beatrice St. Julien Ravenel
    Introduction by William Watts Ball. Photographs by Carl
    Julien. Charleston, Carolina art association 1945
        xvi, 329p. illus 25½ cm
        "Reference notes": p. 265–304. Bibliography: p. 305–314

      1. Architects—Charleston, S.C. 2. Architecture—Charleston, S.C. 1. Julien,
    Carl 11. Carolina art association, Charleston, S.C.
    Library of Congress   NA 735.C35R3

The number at the top, 720.973, is what is called the "call number." This indicates where the book is to be found in the stacks. There are two chief systems for arranging books in libraries: the Dewey Decimal and the Library of Congress. Of these the most common by far is the Dewey Decimal, in which subjects are distributed among ten large categories. The first will have the numbers 001 to 099, the second 100 to 199, and so on. For example, books on philosophy are in the 100 series, books on language in the 400 series, books on history in the 900 series. Within each series, books are assigned numbers according to subdivisions of the subject; history will be divided into English history, French history, Mexican history, and so on, and numbered accordingly. Numbers after the period allow identification of different books on the same subject.

After the call number on the card, we have the author's name and the title of the book. Then come the names of collaborators (Ball, Julien). After this is given the place of publication, followed by the publisher and the date of publication. The numeral xvi indicates that there are sixteen pages of "front matter" numbered in Roman numerals, and the 329 is the number of pages of main text in Arabic numerals. *Illus.* means that the book contains illustrations, the 25½ is the height in centimeters.

Additional information about the content of the book is often given. For this one we are told that it has something called "reference notes" and a bibliography. The next two lines give other headings under which the book is catalogued: *Architects—Charleston, S.C.* and *Architecture—Charleston, S.C.,* in addition to an entry under the photographer's name and one for the art association. These references to other headings can be very valuable. If, for instance, you don't know the subject heading for your particular topic but do know the author or title of one book on that topic, you can look up that book and find the subject heading or headings under which it is catalogued. This will bring you to other books in this field.

Finally, at the bottom, we have the information that the book is in the Library of Congress and are given the Library of Congress call number.

N5300
.R56
1953   Robb, David Metheny, 1903–
            Art in the western world, by David M. Robb and J. J.
        Garrison. 3d ed. New York, Harper ₍1953₎
            xxi, 1050 p. illus., col. map (on lining paper) 24 cm.
        Bibliography : p. 980–1008.

            1. Art—Hist. 2. Architecture—Hist. 3. Sculpture—Hist. 4. Paint-
        ing—Hist.   i. Garrison, Jesse Janes, 1901–   joint author.
        ii. Title.

            N5300.R56 1953   709   52–10831

            Library of Congress   ₍10₎

A Library of Congress Card.

Some libraries have, in addition to the main stacks, special collections housed elsewhere. If the book in question is in a special collection, its location will be indicated along with the call number. An *R* before the call number means that the book is shelved in the reference room.

264. The Stacks

Near the card catalogue is the circulation desk, with a passage leading into the stacks, where the books are kept. Stacks are either open or closed. Small libraries, or the libraries of small schools, are usually open. That means that the students are permitted to go in themselves, get the books, bring them back to the circulation desk, and check them out. If the stacks in your college are open, you are fortunate, because you can save time in getting your books and can also have the pleasure of wandering among the library's goodies and finding new things. The stacks will be posted with cards telling you where the various series are shelved, and you simply follow the numbers until you get what you want. The thing to remember is to write down the call number before you go in; otherwise, by the time you get to the 800's you won't be just sure whether the book you want is 823.645s or 832.456s.

Large libraries, or the libraries of schools with large student bodies, have closed stacks. Graduate students and faculty are usually permitted to enter these, but the much-persecuted undergraduate is not. Here you must fill out a slip giving the call number, title, and so on, and you present this slip at the circulation desk. Someone takes the slip and disappears into the stacks. Forty-five minutes later he returns with the information that the book you want is not in. This is one of the frustrations that make scholarship difficult. The thing is to persevere.

265. Periodicals

Libraries contain not only books but magazines. Even a smallish library may subscribe to hundreds of different magazines, ranging from popular ones like *Time* or the *Reader's Digest* to more scholarly journals, like the *Publications of the Modern Language Association* or the *Journal of Modern History*. Large libraries may receive thousands of different periodical publications.

When a current issue of a magazine is received by a library, it is immediately made available to the users. Some libraries have a periodical room, in which current issues of magazines are shelved, usually in alphabetical order. You go and get your magazine and sit down and read it; you can't ordinarily check out magazines for home use. In some libraries magazines are scattered according to the type of magazine. Thus magazines of general interest will be found in one room, magazines on education in another, those on science in another, and so on.

Recent back issues of a magazine are usually kept at the desk of the periodical room or the room in which they are received and may be had on request. When a number of issues have been thus collected, they will be sent to the bindery to be bound. The bound volume is then placed in the stacks. Some magazines are shelved under the Dewey Decimal system or the Library of Congress system, but it is more usual for periodicals to be put on their own floor or floors in the stacks and there arranged alphabetically, as from the *Agricultural Digest* to the *Yale Review*.

Thus if you want a current issue of a magazine, you look on the shelf in the reading room. If you want an issue of a few months back, you ask at the desk. If you want an older issue, you look in the stacks. Issues of a year or so back may be at the bindery and thus out of circulation for what sometimes seems an unconscionably long period.

Many libraries contain a useful gadget called a Kardex. This is an arrangement of cards on a revolving stand, one card for each periodical received by the library. The card will tell in what room the periodical is to be found, whether it is a weekly, monthly, or quarterly, and what back issues the library contains.

266. Indexes to Periodical Literature

Periodicals are a most important source of information. Many studies of the first significance are published in magazines rather than in books. But the output of periodical literature is so overwhelming that the scholar would have little hope of finding what he needs without some kind of guide. Fortunately guides exist. The two most important are the *Reader's Guide to Periodical Literature* and the *International Index to Periodicals*. Both of these index and classify the contents of certain magazines, the chief difference between them being in the magazines indexed. Generally speaking, the *Reader's Guide* indexes popular and semipopular magazines, the *International Index* the more scholarly journals. Then there are numerous other more specialized indexes, like the *Agricultural Index,* the *Education Index, Poole's Index to Periodical Literature* (covering American magazines from 1802 to 1906), and so on.

Like the card catalogue, the periodical guides list articles by author, title, and subject, all in one alphabetical list. The subject entries are subdivided, elaborately for subjects much written about, and there are numerous cross references. If, for example, you look under *Germany,* you will find, first of all, a notice suggesting that you see also *Berlin, Adenauer,* and various other entries. Then there will be subheadings like *army, civilization, economic conditions, foreign relations, history,* and so on. Some of these will be subdivided further— *History,* for example, into groups of articles on particular historical periods. Then there will be separate listings for West Germany and East Germany, both subdivided. The moral is that it may take some poking around in the general subject to make sure that you haven't missed what you are looking for.

Here are a couple of typical entries from the *Reader's Guide.* The first is an author entry, the second a subject entry.

FOGARTY, Michael Patrick
   Birth of a problem in race relations. Commonweal 63: 254–5 D 9 '55

FOLKLORE
   Ireland
   Jack o' the lantern. J. M. Collins. Am Mercury 81:8–10 Jl '55

The first one could be translated thus: "Michael Patrick Fogarty has an article entitled "Birth of a Problem in Race Relations" on pages 254–255 of volume 63 of the magazine *Commonweal.* The date of this issue is December 9, 1955."

The second one means: "There is an article on folklore with particular reference to Ireland entitled "Jack O' the Lantern" and written by J. M. Collins. This appears on pages 8–10 of volume 81 of the *American Mercury*. The date of this issue is July, 1955." In the front pages of each index will be found an explanation of abbreviations, plus a list and description of the magazines indexed.

The guides to periodicals are kept right up to date, and your library will receive indexes of the contents of latest magazines regularly. These are cumulated into lists embracing longer periods, usually two or three years, and bound accordingly. Most of the guides were begun about the beginning of this century. Consequently, if you wished to find all the articles published on a given topic in the years covered by the guides, you would have to consult numerous volumes for each guide.

267. Encyclopedias

Not too many centuries ago it was possible for one man, if he was diligent and clever enough and if he lived long enough, to learn just about everything that the scholarly world had to teach him. Some men, at least, came pretty close to it. This point was passed in the later Middle Ages, and soon the world's knowledge was far beyond the grasp of any single man. A scholar could not hope to know everything. The best he could hope for was to be able to put his finger on the facts he needed when he needed them. An important aid to this end was the encyclopedia, a development of the eighteenth century. The idea of the encyclopedia was that numerous scholars should contribute articles on their particular fields and thus provide a survey of the world's knowledge for everyone.

Encyclopedias continue to be an important aid to scholarship. Your instructor is not likely to be too well pleased if you *confine* your researches to what you find in encyclopedias, but the encyclopedia is an excellent place to begin if you know nothing about your subject to start with. And sometimes there is information in encyclopedias that is not available anywhere else.

The best known of these books is the *Encyclopaedia Britannica*. This was begun in the eighteenth century in Scotland, but it is now in American control, having passed through the hands of the Sears Roebuck Company into the keeping of the University of Chicago. It continues, however, to present knowledge from the British point of view. The article on "Education," for example, will discuss first of all the history and present status of education in Great Britain; this will then be followed by a somewhat shorter discussion of education in the United States.

The *Britannica* has gone through a number of revisions to keep pace with the growth of knowledge and has now reached the fourteenth edition. The present intention is that the book will not again be revised as a whole but that part of it will be inspected each year and brought up to date if necessary, the book continuing to be published as the fourteenth edition. It is therefore necessary, particularly in fast-moving subjects, to notice not only the number of the edition but also the date of issue.

Britannica articles are written by specialists, sometimes by very famous men. Some of England's greatest authors have contributed articles to the *Britannica*. The articles are signed by initials only, but the full names and credentials of the authors are given in the front of the first volume. Articles on important subjects are followed by bibliographies which are useful in taking one further into the subject.

Another important encyclopedia is the *Encyclopedia Americana*. This covers the same general ground as the

Britannica, but covers it from the American point of view. It may be therefore more useful on purely American subjects. Both the *Britannica* and the *Americana* present very detailed analyses of the subjects they deal with. Sometimes what one wants is a shorter, more general account. Such are to be found in various smaller books, like the *Columbia Encyclopedia.*

In addition to these general works, there are numerous encyclopedias that are specialized in one way or another. We might mention, for instance, the *Catholic Encyclopedia* (particularly good for subjects having to do with the Middle Ages) and the *Jewish Encyclopedia.* The *Encyclopedia of the Social Sciences* is an excellent source book for economics, sociology, political science, and so on. There are encyclopedias (or cyclopedias) for agriculture, education, sports, and numerous other fields.

Encyclopedias are regularly shelved not in the stacks but in the reference room, where they can be easily consulted. They cannot ordinarily be withdrawn from the library.

268. Biographical Works

Many investigations call for knowledge of the facts of people's lives. There are numerous publications in which such facts are gathered. A pioneer work is the *Dictionary of National Biography,* or DNB. This contains the biographies of dead Englishmen. (*National* means here British, and the British cannot get into the DNB until they have joined their ancestors.) The DNB is a very large work, bound in dozens of volumes. The articles maintain a high order of scholarship, are often quite detailed, and sometimes contain information not to be found elsewhere. The American counterpart of the DNB is the *Dictionary of American Biography,* or DAB.

For living people one consults *Who's Who* (British) or the American counterpart, *Who's Who in America.* The articles in these works are normally brief, giving birth dates of the individuals, place of residence, publications, and the salient career facts. The articles are written by the individuals themselves and so are not always entirely trustworthy, particularly in such matters as birth dates.

In recent times there has been a veritable spate of specialized *Who's Who's,* giving biographical data on persons of prominence in particular places or particular fields. There are such works as *Who's Who in Central Europe, Who's Who in Education, Who's Who Among Italian-Americans,* and many others.

269. Other Reference Works

The modern scholarly world produces new material in almost frightening volume. In every field from microbiology to basketball so much is written, so much published, that just keeping track of what is being done is a staggering task. For any subject on which much is published there will be people working to catalogue the publications. Bibliographies of special fields are printed by the hundreds. As you deepen your penetration of a field, you will want to ascertain what bibliographies of it are available. Even in such an inquiry, you will find books to guide you. There are several bibliographies of bibliographies, of which we might mention *Guide to Reference Books* by Constance M. Winchell and *Basic Reference Sources* by Louis Shores.

Another reference work of much value is the *Book Review Digest,* which is usually shelved in the reference room or the periodical room. The BRD is a periodical report of the reviews printed in various magazines of new books. If, for example, you want to know the critical opinion of *The FBI Story* by Don Whitehead, you can look under the author's name in the volume of the BRD for the period in which the book was published. This will tell you where reviews are to be found, give a brief selection from each review, and indicate for each review whether it was favorable, unfavorable, or neither.

Frequently it is desired to check a quotation, either to find out who said something or precisely what it was that was said. Who was it, for example, who remarked that power corrupts and absolute power corrupts absolutely? And is that an accurate quotation? You can find out by looking in one of the collections of quotations, of which Bartlett's is the most famous. Quotations are indexed according to the key word in the quotations. In this example, one would look in the index under *power,* and there be referred to the page that contains the full quotation. Sometimes you have to try two or three words.

For more or less miscellaneous information there are many more or less miscellaneous reference books. If, for example, you wanted to know the population of Juneau, Alaska, you could look in the index of the *World Almanac* under "Alaska" and there be directed to the page containing the figures. In the same book you could find birth and death statistics for Colorado, the boiling point of alcohol, an account of recent riots in Cyprus, records of the attendance at Rose Bowl football games, and so on. Other much used almanacs are the *Information Please Almanac* and *Whitaker's Almanac,* the latter with a British slant. Somewhat similar but more restricted in scope are the yearbooks like the *American Yearbook* and the *Statesman's Year-Book.* These report events of the last year in such fields as social science, politics, science, international organizations, humanities.

A kind of reference work of mammoth importance in some investigations is the concordance. A concordance is an alphabetical listing of all the words in the works of a particular author, showing the place or places in the author's works in which the word occurs. Concordances exist for the Bible, for Shakespeare, Chaucer, Milton, Emerson, Wordsworth, and various other writers. If, for example, you want to study Shakespeare's use of the word *pleasure,* the Shakespeare concordance will direct you to all the passages in which that word occurs.

We have by no means exhausted the reference works available to the scholar. Many specialized guides of one kind or another exist and are indispensable for work in certain fields. It is the scholar's business to seek out those pertinent to his particular needs. An hour spent in moving along the shelves of your reference room will give you a general notion of what your library has to offer and may save you a great deal of time later on.

270. Choosing a Subject and Building a Bibliography

The student in a composition or communications course does not always have a great deal to say about the choice of the subject for his research paper. Some instructors permit a completely free choice, but many restrict the choice in some way. It is not unusual, for the whole class to be asked to write in the same field—United States history, perhaps, or international relations, or educational practices. Such restrictions may arise from the fact that the class, in previous work, has evolved a particular common interest. Or they may be dictated by the resources of the library. Or it may be that the instructor will feel he can give better bibliographical or organizational guidance in some fields than in others. Since the research paper is commonly taught in an English course, it is not uncommon for an English subject to be required: a thorough analysis of a novel or a poem, for example.

Whatever subject your instructor requires or permits you to choose, there is one thing that he is nearly certain to ask: that it be severely restricted in scope. The inexperienced student almost always wants to write his paper on some subject impossibly immense. He will suggest titles like "The History of Russia" or "The Prospects of Curing Cancer" or "Abraham Lincoln." These are not feasible. The only person qualified to write a short *book* on the general subject "Abraham Lincoln" is someone who has lived long enough to have read the important materials on the subject—say thirty or forty years. Nobody is competent to write a three-thousand-word paper on such a subject.

The ideal subject for the research paper is one that is broad enough so that sufficient library materials can be found and narrow enough so that the student can read *all* the materials. If you want to write about Lincoln, you have to think of ways to narrow the subject. You might begin by cutting it to Lincoln's childhood. This is still much too large. You cut it again to Lincoln's schooling. Still too large. You cut again and perhaps wind up with a title like "Illinois Schoolhouses in Lincoln's Time" or "How Lincoln Got to School" or "The Curriculum in Lincoln's School." This might or might not be suitable; it would depend on the resources of your library. It is frequently necessary, after starting on the research paper, to broaden or narrow it somewhat in response to the available materials. It is always better to narrow it if that is possible.

Once you have selected (or been assigned) a topic, the next chore is to build your bibliography. If you know little or nothing about the field, it is often well to begin by reading the pertinent articles in the *Britannica* and the *Americana.* These will ordinarily extend far beyond your particular topic, but they will enable you to see your topic in its general context. At the end of the encyclopedia articles, you will usually find references to books and other articles on the same subject. Copy these down carefully, and your bibliography is begun.

Next take your list to the card catalogue to ascertain which of the books your library has available. Look them up on author or title cards, but note also the subject headings (bottom of the card) under which they are listed. Go to the drawers for these headings and find out what other books on the same subject the library has. Add these to your list. Now withdraw some or all of the books from the stacks and look them over rapidly. Note the material in them that is pertinent to your particular subject. Look also for further bibliographical references. In some books you will find bibliography at the back of the book; in others it will be given after each chapter; in still others, references will be given in footnotes. Add to your list any titles that seem pertinent.

Your bibliography will probably contain references to journals and magazines as well as to books. Find out (e.g., through the Kardex) which of these magazines your library receives. Look in the *Reader's Guide* and the *International Index* for further titles. By now you should know what subject headings to consult; under these headings, you will find some of the titles you have already listed, and, probably, new ones.

If you proceed in some such way as this, you will find that a bibliography snowballs. Once you crack into the subject, you will discover all sorts of new leads. One book leads you to another, one article refers you to three more. Soon you may find the available material overwhelming. In that case, you simply restrict your topic still further and congratulate yourself. You are heading in the right direction.

SUGGESTIONS

1. Locate the following in your college library: the *Britannica,* the *Americana,* the DNB, the BRD, the *Reader's Guide, Bartlett.*
2. Find and list the special encyclopedias and cyclopedias owned by your library.
3. Answer the following questions.

(1) What is the birth date of Henry Clay? (2) In what magazines can reviews of the novel *The Caine Mutiny* be found? (3) What are the chief publications of the American author Samuel Eliot Morrison? (4) What is the origin of the saying "Tell it to the Marines"? (5) Did Shakespeare use the word *henchman* and if so where? (6) Did the present Prime Minister of England go to Cambridge? (7) Is there a bibliography of research in chemistry? (8) How many football games did Purdue win in 1955?

4. The following subjects are obviously too large to be contained in a term paper. For each one suggest a more precise topic which you think *could* be managed in three thousand words.

(1) opera in America (2) the British in Egypt (3) Theodore Roosevelt (4) sailing ships (5) automobile racing (6) American architecture (7) raising mink (8) Nathaniel Hawthorne (9) Guadalcanal (10) space travel

5. Select one of your titles in number 4, and begin a bibliography on it. Find at least ten relevant articles or books.

31

The Difference
Between Plagiarism
and Research

271. Simple Honesty

The research paper assignment often strikes the student as a task of altogether unmanageable proportions. Three thousand words, the instructor says, and the student's imagination boggles. The instructor goes on to speak of original investigation, smooth and clear writing, footnotes, bibliography, outlines, and before long the student is altogether on the ropes. Nobody told him that college was going to be like this. Isn't there any way around it?

Well, of course. There are ways around anything. For example, you can borrow an old paper from one of your fraternity brothers or sorority sisters, put your name on it, and turn it in. Or you can hire some impecunious English major to write your paper for you. Or you can copy an article out of an out-of-the-way magazine and hand it in as your own work. There are lots of such ways around the research paper.

But there is a drawback to using such methods quite apart from the fact that you'll probably get caught. The drawback is that it ain't honest. To steal someone else's ideas and try to palm them off as one's own is rather worse than stealing money. It will seem, in this cynical age, an altogether quixotic notion that a "D" grade well earned will do you more good than an unearned "A," but it is nevertheless true, and anyone who doesn't see it misses the point of education.

You will find that the research paper is never as bad as you think it is going to be. After you have received the assignment and gone home and had an aspirin and a little nap, the shock will wear off. You pull yourself together and go to the library and poke around, and presently the possibilities will look increasingly possible. As the work progresses, you may find great satisfaction in what you learn and in what you build. It doesn't matter whether your product is excellent or not. An amateur can derive much pleasure from building a little house or putting together an automobile, even though he knows perfectly well that any professional could do the job better and quicker. The thing is that he does it himself.

272. Complicated Honesty

But even when one's intentions are pure and one's purposes noble, keeping the research paper honest can become a rather thorny problem. Probably few students in decent colleges would wish to break the rules deliberately by handing in a fake paper, yet many will go astray through a misunderstanding of what is wanted and what is permitted. Any research paper assignment is likely to bring in a number of offerings that are nothing but grand larceny, and this with no felonious intent at all on the part of the offenders.

The difficulty lies in the nature of research. In creative writing there is no such problem: one either creates his material out of his own mind or copies someone else's. But in research one necessarily works with other people's material, other people's ideas and words and phrases. On the basis of what others have done, one tries to proceed to something new of one's own. But sometimes it is difficult to keep quite clear the distinction between one's own contribution and that of one's sources. This is particularly true when the sources are secondary rather than primary.

There is an old gag that plagiarism is copying from one book and research is copying from two. It isn't that simple. It may be that in secondary school you were permitted—perhaps even encouraged—to copy a few paragraphs from one encyclopedia, add a few more from another, paste in a couple of pictures, and call the result a term paper. This won't go in college. It is not of course expected that the term paper in a freshman class be an important and original contribution to knowledge. But it is expected, ordinarily, that the synthesis, at least, be original, that the writing—except for quotations moderately used—be the student's own, and that the use of sources be clearly indicated. Achieving this calls for some study of technique.

273. Quoting and Crediting

The rule is that whenever you use the exact words of some other writer, you put quotation marks around those words and indicate whom they belong to. If you take an idea or a fact or an argument or opinion from someone else, but phrase it in your own words, then you do not use quotation marks, but you do indicate—in a footnote or otherwise—the source from whom you have borrowed.

The question, however, of just what constitutes borrowing is a complicated one, and crediting therefore requires a little judgment. Everything we know we have learned from some source, but much of what we know is common knowledge, and of course facts available to everyone need not be credited. If, for example, you are writing a paper on Abraham Lincoln, and you note that he was born in 1809, it would not be necessary to give the source of your information. This is an undisputed fact available in any biography of Lincoln, and it need not be attributed to any particular source. But if you were to say that Geoffrey Chaucer was born in 1343, then it would be necessary to indicate your source. This is a date about which there is some doubt, and you would have to say "according to so-and-so," or perhaps, simply, "according to some authorities."

274. Fact and Opinion

If you say that Lincoln's mother's name was Nancy Hanks, you don't have to give your source. Lincoln's mother's name is not disputed. But if you say that Lincoln's mother was an irritable woman, your basis for having this opinion should be indicated. Obviously, you cannot know from personal experience that she was irritable, and it is scarcely an undisputed fact. You would have to direct the reader to the foundation of your statement, the manner of doing so depending on the use you were making of the statement. If Mrs. Lincoln's personality was of only casual importance to the point of your paper, it might suffice to say, "Most of Lincoln's biographers agree that Mrs. Lincoln was irritable." But if her irritability was of central importance, then you would have to go into the matter carefully, indicating which biographers thought her irritable and which did not and indicating also the facts on which these writers base their opinions.

A rule of thumb on when to credit and when not to might go like this: whenever you think a reader might ask, "How does he know that?" put in a footnote telling him. When in doubt it is probably better to credit too much than too little.

Quotations are regularly credited to their owners, together with an indication of the exact place in which the passage quoted occurs. The only exceptions would be very familiar quotations, known to everyone. If you toss off a line like

"There is a divinity doth hedge a king," you would insult your reader by informing him that it occurs in *Hamlet,* a play by William Shakespeare.

275. Excessive Quotation

Papers which consist of long quotations tied together by brief transitions do not achieve the purposes of the assignment. The paper should be in the main an original expression, a new synthesis achieved by the student after study of available materials. In those parts where you lean heavily on a particular source it is ordinarily better to paraphrase or summarize (giving credit to the source, to be sure) than to quote directly. Limit quotations to those passages where you feel that you cannot say the thing otherwise than the author did, or to those where the exact words of the author are of importance to the point you are making. In some papers—discussions of literary works, for example—fairly lengthy quotation is of course unavoidable.

When you do quote, quote carefully and exactly. When you use someone else's words, you have a responsibility to convey them accurately and not change his meaning either through carelessness or intent. It is possible to omit part of a passage through the use of what are called suspension points—three dots. For example, suppose the passage to be quoted runs: "Mrs. Lincoln, it must be admitted, was a very irritable woman." You could quote it thus: "Mrs. Lincoln . . . was a very irritable woman." But you must be careful not to modify the statement by omission. If the passage were "Mrs. Lincoln, in the opinion of some who knew her, was a very irritable woman," then it would be wrong to quote, "Mrs. Lincoln . . . was a very irritable woman." For this would be making your author state as a bald fact what he had given cautiously as an opinion.

And of course it is the worst of sins deliberately to alter the author's meaning. This has been done occasionally by people quoting critical opinions. For instance, suppose a critic of a play has written: "This is one of the finest examples of total incompetence in playwriting that I have ever seen." An unscrupulous producer might quote this in his advertising thus: "This is one of the finest examples of . . . playwriting that I have ever seen." But no nice producer would do so.

276. Paraphrasing

One of the trickiest bits in the research paper is to paraphrase or summarize accurately without plagiarism. The difference between a paraphrase and a summary is one of length in respect to the original passage. A paraphrase is about as long as the original, but expressed in different words. A summary is shorter than the original and expressed in different words. In both, the tricky part is the "different words." If you paraphrase or summarize another writer, it will be true that you are both using the same language to discuss the same subject. If he is writing about swallows and you are paraphrasing him, you will both necessarily have to use the word swallows.

What you must learn to do is distinguish between language which is shared by everyone and that which is the creation and therefore in some sense the personal property of a particular writer. If P. V. Pettiquale writes, "Swallows build nests in trees," you, in paraphrasing P. V. Pettiquale, might also write, "Swallows build nests in trees." But if P. V. Pettiquale writes, "The swallow sings his heart-warming little song as he darts among the treetops," and you, without quotation marks, write, "The swallow sings a heart-warming little song" or "The swallow darts among the treetops," then you are plagiarizing. These phrases, wretched though they are, are the property of P. V. Pettiquale and may not be lifted from him without acknowledgment.

In such a matter as this, one learns most easily from examples. We shall give here a couple of original passages, each followed first by a plagiarized version and then by a legitimate paraphrase.

ORIGINAL PASSAGE:

> Paul Forash was reasonably typical of the scouts and trappers who opened up the Far West. Born in Kentucky of poor parents, he never went to school, never learned to read and write. But in other matters his education was ruthless and complete. In an environment where man's best friend was his rifle, Forash became an expert marksman. Survival depended on understanding the myriad mysteries of the forest, and he quickly learned the ways of its denizens. He learned self-reliance in as hard a way as imaginable: he was orphaned at the age of eleven, when his parents were killed in an Indian raid.

PLAGIARIZED VERSION:

> Paul Forash was rather typical of the people who opened up the West. He was born in Kentucky of poor parents, and he never went to school or learned to read and write. His education was ruthless and complete in other matters, however. Because he lived where man's best friend was his rifle, he quickly became an expert shot. In those days one had to understand the myriad mysteries of the forest in order to survive, and Forash quickly learned the ways of its denizens. He learned self-reliance in a very hard way: his parents were killed in an Indian raid when he was eleven, and he was left an orphan.

Here most of the intended paraphrase is lifted from the original; it is, in fact, almost direct quotation. The first sentence has the same structure as the original, the only differences being that *rather* is substituted for *reasonably* and *people* for *scouts and trappers,* and *Far* is omitted. The three parts of the second sentence are taken over and only put together in slightly different ways. Such expressions as "education was ruthless and complete," "man's best friend was his rifle," "myriad mysteries of the forest," "ways of its denizens" are all creations of the original writer and could not properly be taken over without quotation marks.

LEGITIMATE PARAPHRASE:

> In his personality and background, Paul Forash is a good example of the scouts and trappers of the early West. His parents, Kentuckians, were poor, and he did not have much ordinary education; indeed, he remained illiterate all his life. He did, however, become expert in forest lore and such matters as trapping and shooting. His parents were killed by Indians when he was only eleven years old, and as a result he was forced at a tender age to get along on his own.

Note that the paraphrase is much more prosaic than the original. Its intent is merely to get down all the facts of the original passage, not necessarily to convey its emotional tone. If such a paraphrase were used in a research paper, it would still be necessary to credit the material to the author of the original. But the absence of quotation marks would indicate that just the data, not the wording, was derived.

Here is another example:

ORIGINAL PASSAGE:

> Traffic in Rome during the rush hour makes one wonder whether the internal combustion engine was such a good idea after all. Rome, which was not laid out with the automobile in mind, is so constructed that to get from one part of town to another, one almost always has to drive through the center. The result is that the center is a seething mess all day long and a genuine nightmare in the four peak periods when the citizens are going to and from work. The cars and buses boil up Via Tritone, meet an opposing stream coming down from Piazza Barberini, and are joined by a third pouring out of the Tunnel. Then the converging masses try to funnel into the impossibly narrow Via Due Macelli,

and one wonders why it does not occur to the good people to put the automobile, which has clearly had its day, in a museum, and go on foot. They would not only live longer but would save an appreciable amount of time.

PLAGIARIZED VERSION:

> During the rush hour the traffic in Rome is so heavy that it some-times seems it would have been better if the internal combustion engine had not been invented. Rome is built in such a way that to get from one part of the city to another one must pass through the center. The result of this is that the center of town is a seething mess all day long; during the four rush periods it is a nightmare. Cars and buses boil up Via Tritone and meet an op-posing stream coming down from Piazza Barberini. There they are met by a third stream emerging from the Tunnel. Then all three groups try to get into the Via Due Macelli. It does not seem to occur to the good people to put their cars in museums and go on foot. They do not realize that the automobile has had its day, and that if they were to go on foot they would not only live longer but save an appreciable amount of time.

The plagiarism here is not so obvious as in the first example, but there is plagiarism nonetheless. What is retained is pre-cisely that which is the property of the original author—bits of irony, out-of-the-ordinary turns of expression, and so on. Examples are "internal combustion engine," "seething mess," "nightmare," "boil up," "good people." It would be necessary either to find other expressions for these or to put them in quotes.

LEGITIMATE PARAPHRASE:

> Rush-hour traffic in Rome is enough to make one doubt the use-fulness of the automobile. The streets of Rome are laid out in such a way that it is usually necessary, in going from one part of town to another, to drive through the center. This crowds the down-town area badly all day long but particularly in the four daily periods when people are going to or from work. An example of the resulting traffic jam is to be seen in Via Due Macelli. Three

large streams of traffic converge here and try to make their way into this very narrow street. Progress is so slow and difficult that one expects the drivers to give up, put away their cars and go on foot. They would escape a good deal of nervous strain and would save time too.

277. Summarizing

In practice, one is rather more likely to summarize than to paraphrase—that is, to make a brief digest of the material needed rather than a lengthy translation of it. The summary presents the difficulties of the paraphrase plus a few of its own. One has still the problem of avoiding plagiarism. In addition, one must condense the material without losing the original intent and emphasis. One must leave out a good deal and yet be careful not to leave out anything of central importance. And of course one must be careful not to miss the point. Summary writing—or précis writing, as it is sometimes called—is an exacting exercise. It is often taught, quite apart from its relevance to research work, for the training in writing and thinking that it provides.

We shall take a passage and follow it with several summaries, some bad and some better. The passage is from the London *Times,* December 1, 1956. It is part of a review of a play, *The Diary of Anne Frank*.

> The purely theatrical effect of this piece is touchingly to communicate the sensation of hiding for a period of years from the Gestapo without once ceasing to dread discovery. If we did not share the feelings of the Jewish fugitives in the overcrowded loft of an Amsterdam office building we should soon tire of what is after all only another picture of life in a tenement. But the authors have done their work so well that there is no evading the special tension inherent in the situation; though some of the less strong nerved in the audience may find the sensation thus communicated far from agreeable.
>
> The piece also seeks effects which are not purely theatrical. It

is a skillful dramatization of an authentic diary kept by a young Jewish girl and found after she had met her death in Belsen. The actuality of the events that the diary records sets up an emotional response of its own and no doubt plays its part in the contrived stage atmosphere of jumpiness. But those who are to get the most out of the evening would do well to treat the whole thing as a well invented story for the stage.

The diary gives a vivid picture of the stresses and strains on the temper and character of the two families huddled into the same cramped refuge. And when the good and bad qualities of the refugees have been sufficiently exposed the developing characters of the young diarist and her shy lover emerge to give the play shape and force.

FIRST SUMMARY:

The play explains what it is like to hide from the Gestapo. However, we soon get tired of it, because it is just a picture of slum life. People who do not have strong nerves will find the play disagreeable. One good thing about the play is that it is based on real events. This makes it more exciting. It tells what it is like for two families to live in a small hiding place. The love story at the end improves the story.

The worst feature of this rather poor summary is that it rests on essential misreading of the original. The review is a most favorable one, but the summary suggests that it is not. There is a plain mistake in the second sentence, where "we *would* soon grow tired of it" has become " we *do* soon grow tired of it." The rest of the summary misrepresents the author's intent chiefly by including the subordinate comments and passing over the main ones.

SECOND SUMMARY:

This piece touchingly communicates the sensation of hiding from the Gestapo. We share the feelings of the Jewish fugitives in the overcrowded loft; if we did not we should tire of another picture of life in a tenement. But there is no evading the special tension in the situation. There are some effects which are not purely theatrical. It is based on a real diary of a Jewish girl found after she died in Belsen. The actuality contributes to the atmosphere of jumpiness. The diary gives a vivid picture of the two families huddled into the same cramped refuge. The developing characters of the young diarist and her shy lover emerge to give the play shape and force.

This is merely a pasting together of scraps of sentences taken from the original. Not only is it rampant plagiarism, but it fails to present a clear statement of the review.

THIRD SUMMARY:

From this play we come to understand what it is like to be in constant fear of arrest by the Gestapo. The play would be dull if we didn't share the feelings of the Jewish refugees. However, the authors have communicated the tension of the situation very clearly, and theatre-goers who do not have good nerves will find the play very unpleasant. The play is based on actual facts—on a diary of a Jewish girl which was found after her execution. This makes the story more exciting than it would otherwise have been. The characters of the family are well shown, and the love affair gives a point to the narrative.

This is a much better summary than the first two, but it is not without flaws. There is more relative emphasis than in the original on the necessity of having strong nerves. The suggestion that it is best to consider the play as if it were *not* based on actual facts is missed. The last sentence is not quite an accurate representation of what was said.

FOURTH SUMMARY:

This play communicates forcibly the strains and tensions of two Jewish families hiding in a loft under constant fear of discovery by the Gestapo. The authors have succeeded in creating an emotional sensation calling for strong nerves on the part of the audience. Part of the power of the play rests on the fact that the events related are real, being based on the diary of a Jewish girl later executed at Belsen. But this is not really relevant to the

the theatrical value of the play. The difficulties of the two families are shown vividly, and the characters of the girl and her lover give form to the whole.

This is the best of the four summaries. It retains the main tenor of the original review and reports the details reasonably well. As is usual in a summary of a good piece of writing, there is some loss. The second sentence from the end, for example, is an oversimplification of what the critic wrote.

278. Taking Notes

When you write your research paper, you will probably not be able to pile up on your desk all the materials on which the paper is to be based. Some of them cannot be taken from the reference room or the periodical room. Others must be returned early to the stacks. As you go through your sources, you must therefore collect your data in the form of notes and write your paper from these. Good note-taking is not only a matter of knowledge and intelligence. It depends also—perhaps more so—on such qualities as patience and carefulness. Hasty and careless note-taking may result in many hours of chasing back after volumes and references that you thought you had finished with.

One may take notes either in a notebook or on cards, but most scholars find cards—three-by-five or four-by-six—more satisfactory. The thing about cards is that they can be arranged and rearranged as desired. When you have gathered all your data and made the outline of your paper, then you simply arrange the cards according to where the material falls on your outline. Writing the paper is then largely a matter of flipping over the cards and pushing along.

It is often advisable to keep two sets of cards—note cards and bibliography cards. On the bibliography cards you set down the bibliographical facts of all the sources pertinent to the subject that you encounter. These include, for a book, the author's name, the title, the date of publication, the publisher's name, and the number of pages. We shall discuss forms in the next chapter. For a magazine, you note on the bibliography card the author and title of the article, the name of the magazine, the volume, the pages on which the article is printed, and the date of the issue. Start a bibliography card whenever you find a new reference. You can fill out the bibliographical facts from the card catalogue or from the book or magazine itself.

On the note cards, you put, at the top, an indication of the work from which the note is taken. All you need here is enough to identify the book or magazine, since you will have all the bibliographical data on the bibliography card. Also you must remember to put down the particular page number of the passage quoted or summarized; this you must have for your footnote.

Note cards will contain sometimes quotations, sometimes summaries or paraphrases. Often one will quote a passage when taking notes and then summarize or merely refer to it when writing the paper. When you copy directly from a book or article, be sure to use quotation marks on your note card: otherwise you may be unsure whose words are involved when you come to write your paper. Much plagiarism is probably mere carelessness, but it may be penalized just as severely as intentional plagiarism by the instructor or the college cheating committee.

The important thing is to take care to get all you will need while you have the book in front of you. There is nothing so disheartening as to go sprinting back to the library a few hours before the paper is due, intent on finding a page number or checking a quotation, only to find that the book has been lent to another borrower or the magazine sent to the bindery.

SUGGESTIONS

1. Write a paraphrase of the following passage.

Neither training nor heritage has equipped 55-year-old King Saud for the test history has set him—to bring Arabia's medieval society into workable relationship to the 20th century, which is flooding in on it. His father Ibn Saud was a desert warrior, whose domains were oases deep in Arabia's barren heartland. The Saudis were fanatic disciples of Mohammed Wahab, Islam's 18th century Martin Luther, who cried that Islam had fallen on evil ways. Ibn Saud became the scourging sword of Wahabism, a zealot whose savagery in the name of Allah struck terror throughout the length and breadth of Arabia's inner desert. The aristocratic Hashemites, who ruled in the holy land of the west coast and sent their sons to Harrow for education and Paris for experience, laughed at the Saudis as narrow and ignorant yokels. Faced with a choice in World War I, the British backed the Hashemites. But in 1924, Ibn Saud and his Wahabis stormed down from the remote desert and swept the soft-living Hashemites into the sea. Like avenging angels, they drove the prostitutes from the holy cities of Medina and Mecca, smashed the tombs not hallowed by the Koran. Wahabi vigilantes roved the streets, wrecking shops that failed to close at prayer time, beating those caught smoking, ruling the land in an austere discipline that Arabia had not known in centuries. (*Time,* January 28, 1957)

2. Here is a quotation followed by four summaries of varying worth. Criticize and evaluate the summaries, considering how accurately they reflect the meaning of the original, how well they keep the proportions and emphases of the original, and how successful they are in avoiding plagiarism. None of the summaries are flawless.

The English language uses many words of foreign origin. Before the eleventh century, English made new words out of native roots and stems, largely by combining materials already in use in the language, because the English-speaking people were relatively isolated on their islands. The Norman conquest which brought

French rule to the English began a contact with other cultures which has never ceased. When two speech communities meet in any kind of regular contact—in trade, in war, in day-to-day interchange of any kind—they trade words. When one society has prestige of any kind over another, the greater flow is from the respected group to the other. When any language is considered worth learning by another people—for its elegance, for the knowledge expressed in it, or for favors to be earned through knowing it —it forms a kind of mine of words to be exploited by the people who see its value. Thus the English-speaking people have borrowed freely from the French, Latin, and Greek, and at particular times for special reasons from German, Italian, Spanish, and most of the languages of the world. Borrowing is the respect that our people have paid to the accomplishments, the prestige, or the power of other nations. (Lloyd and Warfel, *American English in Its Cultural Setting,* Knopf, 1956, pp. 434–435)

(1) English uses many foreign words. The Norman Conquest brought French rule to England and a contact with other cultures. Two speech communities tend to trade words. When one society has more prestige than another, the greater flow is from that society to the other. When a language is learned by another people, it forms a kind of mine of words to be exploited. For this reason English has borrowed from the French, Latin, and Greek, and at particular times for special reasons from other languages.

(2) English has borrowed many words from other languages, particularly since the Norman Conquest. Two speech communities in communication tend to borrow from one another, the greater borrowing being done by the language with less prestige. When people learn foreign languages, they gain a store of words, some of which they may take into the native language. English has borrowed from most of the languages of the world, but particularly from French, Latin, and Greek. Word-borrowing is a sign that the lending language is thought in some sense superior.

(3) English contains many borrowed words. Speakers of English used to make new words out of native roots. This was chiefly because they were not in touch with other languages. After the Norman Conquest, word-borrowing went on much more rapidly. The

new languages that were learned were thoroughly exploited by the English-speaking peoples. English has borrowed from all the languages of the world but particularly from French, Latin, and Greek.

(4) English has many borrowed words. Before the Norman Conquest, English made new words out of native materials. This was difficult. Later they discovered that they could get new words more easily by trading with other people. They generally traded with people that had more prestige than they did. Sometimes they learned foreign languages, like French, Latin, and Greek, and took words from them. This shows that they had a high regard for these languages.

3. Write summaries of the following selections.

(1) The drawbacks of life on the farm had, of course, been felt by earlier generations, but never before with such compelling force. At least since the adoption of a national land policy in 1785, isolation and loneliness had been the almost inescapable conditions of country existence, for by the ordinance of that year the government rejected the New England system of farmer communities and provided for large, scattered, individual holdings. These tendencies were confirmed and strengthened by the homestead law of 1862. Thus in the less developed parts of the Middle West such as Minnesota and Wisconsin, or in the near-by territory of Dakota, country neighbors dwelt too far apart for friendly intercourse, being but four to the square mile when land was held in quarter sections and even farther away if the homesteads were larger or tracts remained unoccupied. Even in the older farming districts families generally lived out of sight of other habitations; they had no mail deliveries; and the balm of a telephone was denied to all but a tiny minority.

As urban communities increased in number and importance, the farmer's feeling of isolation was deepened by a knowledge of the pleasant town life not many miles away. The craving for solitudes is not as natural as the craving for multitudes; and the companionable sense of rubbing elbows, even if anonymously, with one's fellows compensates for many of life's repulses and frustrations. If the chief historian of the Scandinavian Americans is correct, the cheerlessness and hardships of farm life accounted for the uncommonly high proportion of insanity among the Norwegians and Swedes in the Middle West. Certainly where families of different nationalities occupied the same neighborhood social intercourse was at a minimum, though a homogeneous immigrant community sometimes succeeded for a time in keeping alive the friendly social customs of the home land. (Arthur M. Schlesinger, *The Rise of the City,* Macmillan, 1933, pp. 58–59)

(2) When a man goes calling at a house that is equipped with both doorbell and knocker, which does he use? Usually, we may guess, the bell, if it is a modern sort, because pressing a button is such a supremely simple operation and because you never know whether a knocker will be stiff or no. He keeps the knocker in reserve, and falls back upon it when the bell turns out to be broken, or when its ring fails to rise above the whine of the vacuum cleaner, or the chatter and chink of the cocktail party, or the murmuration of the wireless. The knocker, in fact, has suffered a decline in the past few decades. After holding the field almost unchallenged in humble homes for generations, and sharing it with bells of all kinds at the portals of the great, it has gradually found its importance diminished. It survives, massive and proud, on the doors of older houses, but all the new little places are equipped with bells, and though often these houses have a knocker as well it is a poor sort of imitation of the genuine article—so small and light that no one can get a proper grip of the thing, or raise more than a faint tin-tin out of it. Which is perhaps just as well, for if some new doors were provided with a really substantial piece of hardware, and a visitor were to wield it with old-fashioned gusto, there is no telling what damage he might do to the whole delicate structure. (*The London Times,* December 4, 1956)

(3) The advantages the President holds within his party are based on two main facts which touch on our disinclination to change. (1) Through the use of his patronage, he will have created a dependency that has a material stake in his survival. If he is overthrown, all who live on his bounty risk his fate. They have every reason of self-interest, therefore to stick by him. They will desert only if the seditionists within the party show themselves strong enough to deny the President a further nomination; or only when the President announces that he has no interest in another term. In

the latter event in particular, when the President's power to coerce and reward is lifted, small armies form around ducal figures who either promise to be a new source of rewards, or will reaffirm the existing pattern of rewards if they win the party's scepter and then the nation's throne. (2) The second advantage the President holds is that the party cannot deny him a renomination without inviting the charge that it fooled the people four years before when it backed a man it now admits to be unqualified. To avoid any such self-condemnation, the party may be forced to conceal its errors by repeating them for a second time. (Sidney Hyman, *The American President*, Harper, 1954, pp. 91–92)

32
Ibid. and Op. Cit.

279. Matters of Form

Writing a research paper is hard work, heaven knows, but it has its compensations. One is the formal aspect of the paper, the footnotes and bibliography. The forms of the research paper have their purposes: to communicate clearly, in a standardized way, the relationship of the author to his material; to verify and support the statements made; and to direct the earnest reader to other works in the field. But they also exude an aroma of ceremony which many students find pleasurable. When you chuck in an *ibid.* or a *vide supra,* you feel that you have indeed joined the ranks of scholars.

The forms are the easiest part of the term paper. All in the world you have to do is follow exactly the specific directions given here—or (more likely) these directions as emended by your instructor. There is really no excuse for going wrong on formal matters. Either you follow directions or you don't. One teacher was in the habit of giving three grades on the research paper—one for the research, one for the writing, and one for the forms—and the last grade was either "A" or "F." He reasoned that the student either used the forms correctly or did not.

It should be said that professional practice in the use of footnotes and bibliographical items is not so standardized as may appear from what follows. There is some tendency toward standardization at present, but different scholarly journals have somewhat different rules, and the scholar conforms to the habits of the journal for which he is writing. The forms given here are usual for college writing, but your instructor may very well suggest various changes.

280. The Outward Shape of the Paper

A term paper usually has a title page. This contains, first, the title of the paper, followed by the student's name. Below this appears the name of the course, the section number, the instructor's name, and the date. All should be arranged pleasingly on the page. It is common for the title to be written a quarter or a third of the way down the page, centered, with the author's name three spaces below. The other information may be written toward the lower left-hand corner.

A paper, as distinguished from a book, does not ordinarily have a table of contents. However, most instructors require an outline, and this follows the title page. Neither the title page nor the page or pages of the outline is numbered. No number appears on the first page of the paper proper either, but this page counts as number one in the numbering.

The title and author's name appear again on the first page of the text. Center the title about a quarter of the way down the page, double-space (skip a line if you are writing in longhand) and then write your name, thus:

Illinois Schoolhouses in the Time of Lincoln
by George V. Sooner

Remember that important words in a title are capitalized. Now triple-space (or skip two lines) and begin your paper. The text of the paper should be double-spaced throughout.

Leave ample margins. Since you will probably be putting the paper in a cover, the left-hand margin should be an inch and a half, to allow for the binding. Other margins should be about an inch. One difficulty in a research paper is the foot-notes. Some instructors want them at the end of the paper, where they present no difficulty, but it is more usual to put them at the bottom of each page, and for this you have to calculate and count lines. There is a form you can buy which, slipped into the typewriter behind the page, will show you where you are.

Figure the number of lines you get on a page, leaving the proper top and bottom margin. Say it is twenty-six. Now suppose as you come down the page you have inserted references for three footnotes of one line each. End the text at line twenty-two. Double-space and underscore, either clear across the page or part way. Double-space again and write your first footnote. Double-space again for the second and again for the third. This will bring you out on line twenty-six with the bottom margin intact, and the page will look like this:

> the part of Illinois where Lincoln lived many schools had no floors at all.[6] There was a further difficulty which is often forgotten by
>
> ———————————
>
> [4] Purvis Belcher, *The Days of Lincoln*, p. 63.
> [5] *Ibid.*, p. 201.
> [6] S. V. Alhambra, *The Little Red Schoolhouse*, p. 98.

It is customary to double-space between footnotes but to single-space *within* them when they run to more than one line. If you have a long footnote, you have further calculating to do.

Pages should be numbered consecutively, with the page number at the top of each page except the first one. Footnotes are also numbered consecutively, from 1 to 33, or however many footnotes there are. It is not usual to begin a new set of footnote numbers with each new page, and present-day schol-ars don't use asterisks, daggers, and double-daggers. Note, in the example above, that the footnote number is raised slightly above the line, both in the footnote itself and in the reference to it in the text.

281. The Form of Footnotes

The most usual function of a footnote is simply to identify the source of a quotation or of facts presented in the text. It is a bare reference, enabling the reader to identify the source. It is not usually necessary to give the full bibliographical data for the source, because this will be contained in the bibliography at the end of the paper.

When a book is referred to for the first time, one gives the author's name (first name first), the title, and the page or pages from which the quotation or information is taken, thus:

[12] Garvis D. Whinlocker, *The Beetle World,* p. 113.
[13] V. S. Tuft, *My Life Among the Insects,* pp. 47–48.

Note that titles of books and magazines are italicized, not enclosed in quotation marks. (In manuscript or typescript, you indicate italics by underlining.) Note the commas. Note the abbreviation *p.* for *page* and *pp.* for *pages.* Note the period at the end.

If a book has two authors, give them both, as they appear on the title page of the book:

[7] V. S. Tuft and Andrew Peebles, *Criminals and Crime,* p. 80.

Sometimes the title page will give the author's name followed by the abbreviation *et al.* (Latin *et alia:* "and others") or the words "and others." Show this in the footnote:

[41] Gerber Pinkus *et al., The Revolt of the Doctors,* p. 322.

Note that Latin abbreviations are italicized.

References to magazine articles are somewhat different. A signed article—i.e., one for which an author's name is given— is footnoted thus:

[17] Arleigh Clemson, "Does the U.S. Have a Foreign Policy?" *The Atlantic Monthly*, 62:87.

The title of the article is enclosed in quotation marks; the title of the magazine is italicized. The number before the colon indicates the volume number, the one after it the page number; this reference therefore means "on page 87 of volume 62."

Many magazine articles are unsigned—i.e., have no author's name attached. References to such articles look like this:

[6] "Revolt in the Pentagon," *Newsweek*, 15:225.

One does *not* use the term "anonymous" for such articles. This is not an anonymous article but an unsigned one.

Some instructors prefer the date rather than the volume number:

[6] "Revolt in the Pentagon," *Newsweek*, April 17, 1954, p. 33.

References to newspapers usually give the date, often with no article title:

[18] The New York *Times*, Oct. 16, 1917, p. 5.

Note that the name of the city is not italicized, only *Times*.

A reference to any multivolume work must give the volume number:

[23] A. B. Geffry *et al.*, *The Ways of Mankind*, VI, 97.

But if the reference is to an encyclopedia or a dictionary or any work alphabetically arranged, it is simpler to refer to the entry:

[27] *Encyclopaedia Britannica*, *s.v.* "Calligraphy."

The abbreviation *s.v.* stands for *sub verbo*, Latin for "under the word." If the reader wants to check the reference, he looks under the word *calligraphy*. One might also give the edition of the encyclopedia used, but this is not necessary provided that this information appears in the bibliography.

It will sometimes happen that part of the reference is given in the text of the paper. It is not necessary to repeat this in the footnote. For example, if you have written "As Purvis Belcher says," and then gone on to quote Belcher, the footnote may be given thus:

    [4] *The Days of Lincoln*, p. 63.

If you say in the text, "As Purvis Belcher says in *The Days of Lincoln*," you need give only the page number in the footnote:

    [4] p. 63.

282. Fancy Work

The conventions of footnoting include an impressive array of abbreviations of Latin terms. Most of these one can get along without perfectly well, and indeed most present-day scholars avoid them. However, one should at least know what they mean in case one meets them elsewhere.

One convention that does save time is the familiar *ibid.* This stands for *ibidem,* which means "in the same place." It is used when the reference is the same as that of the footnote immediately preceding. For example:

    [6] S. V. Alhambra, *The Little Red Schoolhouse*, p. 98.
    [7] *Ibid.*, p. 201.
    [8] *Ibid.*, p. 45.

This would show that references 7 and 8 are also to Alhambra's *The Little Red Schoolhouse,* though on different pages. It would not be necessary, in this example, that references 6, 7, and 8 be on the same page of your text. You can use *ibid.* as long as necessary, provided that there are no intervening references to other books. Note that *ibid.* is italicized (because it's Latin) and that it has a period after it (because it is an abbreviation).

If there *are* intervening footnotes, then you cannot use *ibid.* in reference to the previously cited work. This is where you use *op. cit.*, if you wish. *Op. cit.* stands for *opere citato,* "in the work cited." It might go like this:

[6] S. V. Alhambra, *The Little Red Schoolhouse,* p. 98.
[7] *Ibid.,* p. 45.
[8] Donald Churchmouse, *Frontier Days,* p. 305.
[9] Alhambra, *op. cit.,* p. 222.
[10] Churchmouse, *op. cit.,* p. 165.
[11] *Ibid.,* p. 23.

Here footnote 9 refers to *The Little Red Schoolhouse;* 10 and 11 refer to *Frontier Days.*

Actually most scholars and an increasing number of scholarly journals avoid *op. cit.* and in a second reference simply give the name of the author and the page number:

[9] Alhambra, p. 222.
[10] Churchmouse, p. 165.

When one has referred previously to two or more books by the same author, then one must give also the title:

[9] Alhambra, *The Little Red Schoolhouse,* p. 222.

In this case, *op. cit.* couldn't be used since it wouldn't mean anything.

The term *loc. cit.* stands for *loco citato,* "in the place cited." This would mean not only in the same book but on the same page:

[9] Alhambra, *loc. cit.*

The page number is therefore not given. This is seldom used in modern articles.

The term *passim,* not an abbreviation, means "everywhere." It is used when it is impossible to direct the reader to any particular page as the source of the information, and it directs him to look all through the book to check the reference:

> [16] Angela Dormant, *The Good Old Days, passim.*

But one should never use *passim* when it is possible to specify a particular page or pages.

When the reference is to poetry, one should give the line numbers whenever possible. For many works it is necessary to give further information, like act or scene or book:

> [25] *Hamlet,* Act V, Scene 2, 18–23.
> [26] *Paradise Lost,* Book II, 189.
> [27] Wordsworth, *Tintern Abbey,* 83–101.

The abbreviation *v.s.* stands for *vide supra,* and it is simply a fancy way of saying "see above." It is just as easy to say "see above." The abbreviation *cf.* stands for *confer,* "bring together." We might translate it "compare." You use it when you want to direct the reader to some similar or comparable passage elsewhere:

> [8] Donald Churchmouse, *Frontier Days,* p. 304. *Cf.* also the similar arguments of S. V. Alhambra, *The Little Red School-house,* p. 98.

The abbreviation *ff* means "and the pages following." Thus "Churchmouse, *Frontier Days,* p. 301 ff" means on page 301 and the pages following."

Numerous other abbreviations can be found in standard reference works, but most of them are dispensable in the ordinary paper. If one has a complicated direction to give, he can give it in English. This is likely to be clearer, though perhaps not so much fun. In all of these matters of form it is important to be consistent, to stick to the forms you choose or are directed to by your instructor.

283. Other Use of Footnotes

Footnotes can be made to serve other purposes than that of giving references. They can be used, for example, to define terms. A definition footnote might run like this:

> [21] I am using the word *language* in this paper to refer to speech only, not to writing. Thus we avoid such expressions as "written language" and "spoken language," and speak of *language* on the one hand and *writing* on the other.

This would be inserted immediately after the first occurrence of the word *language* in the text.

You may use footnotes also to take care of material which would seem digressive in the text, material that is relevant to the point you are making but that is not really part of the argument. Sometimes one has something which he feels should be said but which will break the flow of the paper. Put it in a footnote. Sometimes one has turned up a bit of information which he can't resist imparting, but which he knows isn't pertinent. Put it in a footnote. Sometimes one has a good joke but doesn't know just how to work it in. Put it in a footnote.

But exercise some moderation in footnotes as in all things else. It is possible to get footnote happy and wind up with half your material in the text and the other half below the line. This makes the reader swing his head up and down like a spectator at a vertical tennis match.

284. The Bibliography

At the end of the paper comes the bibliography, a list of pertinent books and magazine articles, together with certain facts intended to enable the reader to find the books and articles himself if he wishes to consult them. Bibliographies can differ considerably in scope. At one extreme, you might include all the works on the subject that you know about, whether you have seen them or used them yourself or not. At the other extreme, you would list only those works to which you have referred in the footnotes. The latter is the more common practice for term papers.

Bibliography items are arranged in alphabetical order, according to the last name of the author, if there is one, and according to the first word of the title (excluding *the, a,* or *an*), where there is no author. Encyclopedias and other reference works are alphabetized according to the title of the book. Thus *Encyclopaedia Britannica* would come between a book by R. V. Eastman and an unsigned article entitled "Everyday Manners" in the magazine *Commonweal.*

A typical bibliography entry for a book looks like this:

> Eastman, R. V., *The Decline of the Whaling Industry.* New York: Harper & Brothers, 1957. 603 pp.

Note the details. The last name of the author is given first, followed by a comma, then first name and initials, then another comma, then the title, underlined, and a period. Then you give the place of publication, a colon, the publisher's name, a comma, and the date of publication. Finally you indicate the number of pages: some instructors prefer to dispense with the number of pages, and it is certainly dispensable, though it does give some clue to the scope of the work involved. This data, which is to be found on the title page of the book or in the card catalogue, will enable the reader to put his hands on the book if he wants to.

Here are other bibliography forms. A book with two authors:

Plumbline, Albert F., and Arthur Cole, *Trapping on Moose Bay.*
New York: Harcourt, Brace, 1934. 225 pp.

A translated book:

Tornusciolo, Sebastiano, *Flowers of Fear.* Tr. by George Scanlon.
New York: Dutton, 1958. 684 pp.

A book which is part of a series:

Harkins, Jackson, *The Eskimos.* The World Around Us, vol. 17.
New York: Dutton, 1949. 461 pp.

A book which consists of several volumes:

Untergang, Thomas, *Germanic Philology.* London: Allan and
Unwin, 1932–36. 6 vols.

An encyclopedia:

The Encyclopaedia Britannica, fourteenth edition. Chicago: The
University of Chicago, 1952. 24 vols.

A signed magazine article:

Sturgeon, Wallace, "Wordsworth Revisited," *The Publications of
the Modern Language Association,* 62:181–214.

An unsigned magazine article:

"The Life of the Party," *Western Motoring,* 11:55–57.

A newspaper:

The San Jose *Mercury Herald,* October 19, 1955.

If you have kept up your bibliography cards as you went
along, making the bibliography will be a simple matter of
alphabetizing the cards and copying the information. Make
one alphabetical list, unless your instructor directs you to list
books and magazines separately. Single-space within items
and double-space between them. Use reverse indentation, so
that the alphabetized part will stick out. The bibliography
page should be headed simply *Bibliography.*

When your paper is finished, buy a folder at the bookstore, and attach it to the paper. Don't put the pages in loose. If the paper does not have binder holes, cut them with one of the gadgets that perform that service. Don't pretty up the cover with fancy printing or pictures. This is amateurish. Just put your name on the outside cover for easy identification, hand in the paper, and hope for the best.

SUGGESTIONS

1. Put the following into conventional footnote form.

(1) A reference to page 16 of a book entitled *Essays on Easter* by Merrill F. Wehr. (2) A reference to an article entitled "One Way Out" by Raymond Byroade on page 18, volume 45, of *Harper's Magazine*. (3) A reference to an article entitled "American Gestapo" in *Time,* November 16, 1957. (4) A reference to page 382 and the pages following of a book entitled *Egypt at the Crossroads* by Paul Wente and Edward G. Forand. (5) A reference to lines 65–77 of Book Two of Wordsworth's poem *The Excursion.* (6) A reference to the article on the word *rheumatism* in *The American College Dictionary.* (7) A reference to an article on page 3 of the Chicago *Tribune,* August 10, 1950. (8) A reference to page 95, volume 3, of a book called *Marine Engineering* by Casey Clark and others.

2. Arrange the following data as a bibliography, punctuating conventionally.

(1) Vincent Bosco—Italian Opera—Macmillan—New York—1956 —368 pages. (2) Old Hit at the Met—Time—April 16, 1956. (3) Scott Hopkins—The Last Time I Saw Verdi—Dent—London —1952—562 pages. (4) The Encyclopaedia Britannica—University of Chicago—Chicago—1951—24 volumes. (5) Alfredo Cecco— Young Verdi—translator, Maria Tillona—Little, Brown—Boston— 1939—429 pages. (6) Ruth Shaheen and Bette Afifi—Verdi's Librettists—Harcourt, Brace—New York—1948—321 pages. (7) David Bothmer—Notes on Simon Boccanegra—Etude—Volume 16

—pages 25–27. (8) Warren Clubb—Verdi and Piave—Harper—New York—1932—280 pages. (9) Divismo at La Scala—the London Times—August 3, 1953. (10) George Habeeb—The Language of Music—Knopf—New York—1945–48—3 volumes.

Index